FREE MARKETS
WITH SOLIDARITY &
SUSTAINABILITY

FREE MARKETS

WITH SOLIDARITY &
SUSTAINABILITY

Facing the Challenge

EDITED BY MARTIN SCHLAG &
JUAN A. MERCADO

The Catholic University of America Press
Washington, D.C.

Library of Congress Cataloging-in-Publication Data
Names: Schlag, Martin, editor. | Mercado, Juan Andrés, 1967– editor.
Title: Free markets with solidarity and sustainability : facing the challenge
/ edited by Martin Schlag and Juan Andrés Mercado.
Description: Washington, D.C. : The Catholic University of America Press, 2016. |
Includes bibliographical references and index.
Identifiers: LCCN 2015039958 | ISBN 9780813228433 (cloth)
Subjects: LCSH: Free enterprise—Religious aspects—Catholic Church. |
Free enterprise—Moral and ethical aspects. | Solidarity. |
Social responsibility of business.
Classification: LCC HB95 .F737 2016 | DDC 261.8/5—dc23 LC record
available at http://lccn.loc.gov/2015039958

To Professor Domènec Melé,
for all he has done to renew business ethics

Contents

Part II. Assessing the Encyclical Tradition

Part III. Offering Practical Models and Education

Tables and Figures

FREE MARKETS
WITH SOLIDARITY &
SUSTAINABILITY

Freedom, Solidarity, and Sustainability

Philosophical and Theological Roots

Martin Schlag & Juan Andrés Mercado

The motivation behind the interdisciplinary approach that characterizes the present volume was succinctly and sagaciously described by Plato when he wrote that there is nothing more beautiful than friends coming together to talk of things human and divine.[1] This, we hold, can truly be said of the ideals of which we treat in this book: freedom, solidarity, and sustainability. They are divine and human: sustainability means using resources in such a way that future generations will be able to use them. Solidarity is the virtue of pursuing not only personal happiness but also the common good.

The central concept, however, is freedom: "free" is the first word in the title of this book, in which we have brought together American and European authors. Freedom in this context means political and, more generally, social liberty. The American experience of ordered liberty has shown that social freedom requires a combination of institutions and virtues. Such a combination means that America, and the liberty

---

1. Plato makes this assertion in his dialogue *Phaedrus* in connection with the "Myth of the Cicada." According to this myth, when the Muses and their music came into being, there were some humans who were so absorbed by the beauty and its pleasure that they forgot to eat and drink, and, without noticing it, they died. The Muses changed them into cicadas and granted them the special gift of being able to sing all day without eating or drinking. The cicadas observe us, and if we fall asleep at noon instead of discussing, they despise us. If, however, we speak of philosophical topics, they report our names to the highest Muses, Calliope and Urania. The reward is a beautiful voice. Plato, "Phaedrus," in *The Collected Dialogues of Plato, including the Letters*, ed. Edith Hamilton and Huntington Cairns (Princeton, N.J.: Princeton University Press, 1994), 258D–59D.

symbolized thereby, is an idea. "America is not geography; it is a form of government, a way of life.... The heart of the American idea is to transform self-interest into a personal interest in the public good."[2]

This ordered liberty is the distinctive Anglo-American definition of freedom: liberty *under* law, liberty to do what citizens ought to do, law as enablement for freedom. This is different from the continental European tradition, which tends to understand liberty as liberty *from* law, seeing law as a limitation of liberty (i.e., whatever is not forbidden is allowed).[3]

The Anglo-American conception is the result of a pragmatic approach to social ethics. In this context, traditional Catholic social teaching has been criticized for applying a conception of deductive natural law to society.[4] Until Pius XII, Catholic social teaching conceived of societal order as something preestablished by God, by means of the order of the universe and the social nature of man. Man, therefore, had to respect this order of natural law and submit his liberty to the common good that was prior to his individual self. This entailed a vision of society as an organism from whose nature norms could be deduced.[5]

The liberal political tradition, on the other hand, has deliberately been more a matter of practice than of theory. It has set before the world an original conception of the common good, in which the protection of the individual rights is central to, as well as prior to, the common good. With a pragmatic attitude of letting things happen, trying things out in practice, keeping what proves to be advantageous, and discarding what is not, countries with an Anglo-American tradition have achieved polities with a high level of public spiritedness, civic consciousness, and responsibility.

For the framers of the American Constitution (and this is their ex-

---

2. Michael Novak, *Free Persons and the Common Good* (Lanham, Md.: Madison Books, 1989), 64.

3. Cf. the classic formulation in Article 4 of the French *Déclaration des Droits de l'Homme et du Citoyen of 1789*. For more details, see Friedrich August von Hayek, *The Constitution of Liberty. The Definitive Edition*, ed. Ronald Hamowy (Chicago: University of Chicago Press, 2011 [1960]), 232ff; Michael Novak, *The Catholic Ethic and the Spirit of Capitalism* (New York: Free Press, 1993), 93ff.

4. Joseph Ratzinger, "Naturrecht, Evangelium und Ideologie in der katholischen Soziallehre. Katholische Erwägungen zum Thema," in *Christlicher Glaube und Ideologie*, ed. Klaus von Bismarck, Walter Dirks, and Hans Götz Oxenius (Stuttgart/Berlin/Mainz: Kreuz-Verlag, 1964), 24–39.

5. Thomas Ebert, *Soziale Gerechtigkeit: Ideen—Geschichte—Kontroversen* (Bonn: Bundeszentrale für politische Bildung, 2010), 204; Rudolf Uertz, *Vom Gottesrecht zum Menschenrecht: Das katholische Staatsdenken in Deutschland von der Französischen Revolution bis zum II. Vatikanischen Konzil (1789–1965)* (Paderborn: Schöningh, 2005).

traordinary insight), it was clear that virtues alone were not sufficient for the real world, a society composed of men with a fallen nature. Institutions are necessary as well. They have to counterbalance the "structural diseases" inherent in the democratic political system. Factions, abuse of power, and individualism are among these diseases. The social and political genius of the founders concerned the practical ordering of institutions.[6] One of these institutions is the separation of the social system into three independent and rival systems that monitor each other: the political, the economic, and the moral-cultural subsystem. These three subsystems combine to form "democratic capitalism," as Michael Novak calls it, thus intentionally overcoming the Marxist reduction of capitalism (i.e., a solely economic system based on private property, free markets, and the accumulation of wealth).[7] Each of these three subsystems is in itself a combination of institutions and virtues. They are integral parts of the whole, in a relationship of mutual balance and control. This balance is an essential demand of democratic capitalism; neither of the three systems must be made to be subordinate to another. Novak's criticism of socialism is that it constitutes the submission of the economic to the political system. Socialists do not accept the institutional separation of the political system from the economic system: "In the name of the moral-cultural values of socialism, they desire to subordinate the economic system to the political system, thus collapsing the triune order of democratic capitalism into the unitary order of socialism."[8]

Despite these and other thinkers' warnings, our polities and economies in Europe, as well as in the United States, have turned socialist in response to the perception of the potential immorality of capitalism by both the people and governments. The weakest link of "democratic capitalism" is the moral-cultural system because capitalism destroys the very moral foundations on which it depends. Capitalism creates wealth and prosperity for the whole population; material well-being fosters consumption and laziness and reduces the spirit of sacrifice and thrift. Advertising instills the desire for goods we do not need, and we become

6. Novak, *Free Persons*, 46.

7. In Europe, the common understanding of the word "capitalism" is negative. Europeans, as well as the Magisterium, prefer expressions like "free market economy," "social market economy," and "ordoliberalism."

8. Michael Novak, *The Spirit of Democratic Capitalism* (New York: Touchstone, 1982), 112.

caught in the "treadmills of desire and dissatisfaction," brought about
by the law of the decreasing marginal benefits of an increasing number
of material goods.

Furthermore, as Michael Sandel has put it, "markets crowd out morals."[9] Markets have limits: we do not sell our children, or our votes, or
buy the Nobel prize, or friendship, pardon, and gifts. In the last decades,
however, argues Sandel, we have drifted from *having* a market economy to *being* a market society. Sandel calls for a public debate on what
should be for sale, and this, he correctly says, is a debate over values, or
over what we hold sacred. Applying market logic (exchange for money)
where it does not fit transforms the realities being sold: a Nobel prize
for sale is no longer a Nobel prize. Markets are not ethically neutral but
tend to corrupt, dissolve, or displace moral nonmarket norms. Sandel
echoes Novak's view on the importance of morality when he writes,
"Altruism, generosity, solidarity, and civic spirit are not like commodities that are depleted with use. They are more like muscles that develop
and grow stronger with exercise. One of the defects of a market-driven
society is that it lets these virtues languish. To renew our public life we
need to exercise them more strenuously."[10]

That is why we think it is not enough to make the moral case for
free enterprise, and there are two reasons for this: (1) as Alexis de Tocqueville already pointed out in the nineteenth century, businesspeople
in free enterprise tend to be individualistic. Individualism, while not
egoism, is the attitude of concerning oneself only with the accumulation of personal wealth and leaving the common good to others. Going
into politics, which is concerned specifically with the common good,
can be a large economic and personal risk. (2) As Adam Smith already
observed, economic power tends to usurp political power through monopolies, trusts, cartels, and lobbies. The American dream is not only
endangered by big government. It is also being destroyed by the 1 percent of people who have the money to buy political decisions, thereby
undermining the institutional independence of the political subsystem
based on the democratic representation of the people.

Making the moral case for free enterprise is important, but it is not

9. Michael J. Sandel, *What Money Can't Buy: The Moral Limits of Markets* (New York: Farrar,
Straus and Giroux, 2012), 113ff.
10. Ibid., 130.

enough. We need to make the moral case for morals. Freedom is an ethical issue and an important value. In reality, true freedom is simultaneously a precondition and an outcome of the ethical life: without freedom, there is no morality. Therefore, free markets are the only ethical form of economy. However, being free is not enough for being moral. To be moral persons, one has to pursue what really makes one happy, that is, the true human good. The moral perspective of life is what brings about the flourishing of the human person *as* a person, what fulfills him or her to the utmost possible degree. In this sense, *logos* goes before *ethos*. To be good, human actions must be conducive to what is truly good for man: they must be based on truth.

We think this is what the church means with its call to the "new evangelization." This expression was coined by Saint John Paul II in a rather offhanded manner during his visit to Poland in 1979. Since then, it has become an emblematic phrase blazoned on the banners of new spiritual movements and of the World Youth Days, which attract millions of young people to Christ. In 2010 Pope Benedict XVI established the Pontifical Council for "Promoting New Evangelization," and the bishops' synod in October 2012 was dedicated specifically to this endeavor. *New evangelization* means "fresh vigor," to "announce again the eternal message of Jesus Christ, the wellspring of life and hope."[11] Pope Francis as well has brought "fresh vigor" into the way evangelization is understood. His call to spread the Gospel with joy and enthusiasm requires discerning the different situations in which people live, of which the economy is also a part.

What does the "new evangelization" of the economy mean? Where does the church want to take us, or how does it intend to be involved in the process? For the social teaching of the church, it is important to understand the economy and to use a language that is positive and encouraging rather than negative and accusatory. Unfortunately, Novak's complaint from the 1990s sometimes still rings true: theologians know too little (or speak too much) about economics: "Their professional vocabulary, for the most part, so misses the point that it is painful to listen to them."[12]

11. *Lineamenta for the Bishops' Synod on the New Evangelization* (Rome: Libreria Editrice Vaticana, 2011), 13 and 2. http://www.vatican.va/roman_curia/synod/documents/rc_synod_doc_20110202_lineamenta-xiii-assembly_en.html.

12. Michael Novak, *Business as a Calling: Work and the Examined Life* (New York: Free Press, 1996), 5.

In any case, there is no such thing as a "Christian economy." Such a system would only have been conceivable in the autarchic monasteries of the Middle Ages that set up a parallel world of exemplary social behavior. Instead, the contemporary challenge for the Catholic Church lies in spreading the Christian message throughout the world and in mutual relationship and dialogue with reality. No nostalgic trip back to the medieval guild system is possible, as Catholic distributist thinkers, such as Chesterton and Belloc, or the social romanticist Karl von Vogelsang still thought in the nineteenth and twentieth centuries.[13] The differentiation and independence between the different subsystems must be maintained insofar as the institutions are concerned. This is endorsed, albeit unclearly, by the Second Vatican Council in its Pastoral Constitution *Gaudium et spes* by dedicating three separate chapters to politics, the economy, and culture and by its *Declaration on Religious Freedom*.

The new evangelization does have an important role to play as regards values; in fact, it has a double relevance: (1) in an ethical perspective and (2) in a theological perspective.

In an ethical perspective, the wish to regenerate the core of shared values in the economy, thereby overcoming the present cultural crisis of the Western civilization, necessitates a revision of speculative analysis as it exists on the scientific level, and practical guidance as it is played out on the level of agency.

On the scientific level, the three systems (politics, economics, and ethics) form overlapping circles. There are questions we would assign to only one field of values and others that belong to an overlapping section. Take price calculation: usually it would only be an economic affair. However, when human life is affected by schemes of cost reduction (e.g., quality control for car tires to prevent casualties, although it might be cheaper to pay the indemnities to victims rather than to maintain the expensive quality control), or racism, or sexual harassment at work (some decades ago, we would have placed it in the ethical field, but today it definitely belongs to the overlapping section), ethics become involved.

On the practical level of economic agency, the circles not only overlap, but the ethical value system becomes the overarching system that

---

13. John Maynard Keynes also proposed a return to the mediaeval conception of separate autonomies. See his book *The End of Laissez-Faire* (New York: Prometheus Books, 2004 [1926]).

governs both of the other two. Every free and conscious act is an ethical act and must be directed to human fulfillment.

In a theological perspective, the question not only is ethical (i.e., following an approach based on reason alone) but also involves the role of the faith. The question is, Can we knead the leaven of Gospel values into the stubborn dough of everyday economic practice? The Second Vatican Council attempted to overcome the preponderantly philosophical approach to morality that had become usual before the council. It wanted to open the rigid system of neoscholasticism to the breadth and depth of the revealed mysteries of faith. This leads to our central questions: What *can* Christianity give to the secularized Western civilization? and What can Christianity give to *secularist humanism* in its social dimension? In his monumental work *A Secular Age*, Charles Taylor defines "exclusive humanism," or "self-sufficient humanism" as "accepting no final goals beyond human flourishing, nor any allegiance to anything else beyond this flourishing."[14] This conception of humanism is characteristic and exclusive to our modern secular societies. Following José Casanova's distinctions,[15] we prefer to call it "secularist humanism" (secularist in the sense of an ideology). We use *secularization* in a positive sense. Secularization is good because the world as God's creation is good. Therefore, all human activities that develop the world in its purely profane and earthly dimension (this is what we call "secular") in accordance with God's will are good. Evangelization is not opposed to secularization but to a secularization that excludes religion and transcendence and their valid contribution to society. The church is not opposed to modernity as such but to the modernity that produced Auschwitz. The church opposes sin that mars the creation's original goodness and beauty.

In this context, Oswald von Nell-Breuning has observed an interesting paradigm shift in Catholic social teaching that culminated during Vatican II. Leo XIII spoke of the relationship between the church and the state, Pius XII of the relationship between the church and society, and the Second Vatican Council of the church *in* the world. This is

---

14. Charles Taylor, *A Secular Age* (Cambridge, Mass.: The Belknap Press of Harvard University, 2007), 18.

15. José Casanova, "The Secular, Secularizations, Secularisms," in *Rethinking Secularism*, ed. Craig Calhoun, Mark Juergensmeyer, and Jonathan Van Antwerpen (Oxford: Oxford University Press, 2011), 54–74.

not only a terminological difference. Whereas the Magisterium of the nineteenth century was still characterized by a top-down approach, the popes of the twentieth century increasingly saw their social teaching as a task for the laity who they called on to make use of the social space of the civic liberties opened up by liberal constitutions. They conceived of Catholic social teaching in a bottom-up or horizontal social perspective. In 1946 Pius XII likened the church to "the vital principle of society," an expression reminiscent of the stoic *animus mundi* applied to the Christians by documents continuing from the letter to Diognetus to the writings of Leo XIII. The Second Vatican Council uses the expression "the leavening of society" to avoid any impression of triumphalism, but the idea of the "vital principle of society" (= soul of the world) is included in the concept of leavening.[16]

Such an idea of the church, in its totality of hierarchy and laity, being the vital principle of society leaves ample room for the conscience of the laity, as the active operators in the secular field, to apply the specific principles of Christian faith to their work and their secular activities. As Pope Benedict XVI states in his encyclical *Deus Caritas Est*, 28f, the church understood as hierarchy does not aspire to power but wishes to contribute to forming a just society by purifying reason and enlarging the concept of reason through the church's Magisterium. It does so by teaching social principles. Since the period of Stoic philosophy,[17] as well as that of the church fathers, justice and benevolence, or love, have been understood to be the two main principles governing social life. In Catholic social teaching, beginning with the publication of the encyclical *Quadragesimo Anno* "social justice" and "social charity" have been generally referred to as a dual concept. The adjective *social* raises some questions. Because both justice and charity in their definitions refer to others, and thus are essentially "social," what does the adjective *social* add? The word *social* adds the modern insight that justice and charity not only study the duties we have within the limits of a preestablished (God-given) social system but also entail the analysis (and perhaps critique) of the structures themselves. The adjective *social* invites us to

16. Oswald von Nell-Breuning, "Die Kirche als Lebensprinzip der Menschlichen Gesellschaft," in *Den Kapitalismus Umbiegen: Schriften zu Kirche, Wirtschaft und Gesellschaft. Ein Lesebuch*, ed. Friedhelm Hengsbach (Düsseldorf: Patmos, 1990), 405ff.

17. Aristotle propounds the same idea when he underscores the importance of friendship for social life.

reflect on the justice or injustice of the social rules themselves, of the norms governing social life, and of the role played by government. The concept of "social justice" has been used by all kinds of political movements, especially the socialist parties. But also in the mouth of a nonsocialist like Otto von Bismarck, it meant that the state should intervene with social laws and policies instead of leaving works of beneficence and aid for the poor to private initiative. But this is not the only meaning of social justice—it can also result in a reduction of government or in reforms as envisioned by Arthur Brooks.[18]

To reiterate, since the time of Stoic philosophy and the church fathers, justice and charity have formed an inseparable twin concept. Gustav Gundlach and Oswald von Nell-Breuning both affirm that social charity does not substantially add anything to social justice. We find this reading unfortunate because charity is *the* contribution of Christianity to the secular world. Whereas justice is a part of natural ethics, or of natural law, cognizable by human reason, charity is an infused supernatural virtue, going beyond benevolence. If we reduce Christianity to mere reason, then we destroy it, and it will not be able to make the contribution to humanism that we refer to as "Christian humanism." Charity, or, more generally, what one can call the "virtues of genuflection," masterly summarized by Saint Francis of Assisi in his famous "salute to the virtues" (wisdom and simplicity, poverty and humility, charity and obedience), are the Christian contribution to the history of ideas: we genuflect before God and his image in every human person; we genuflect before the poor, the sick, the weak, and the lonely.

In an essay published in 2011, Taylor summarized and further developed his *A Secular Age*.[19] Therein, Taylor criticizes the usual rendering of the process of secularization as if it were a subtraction story (i.e., pieces of the public sphere are handed over from religious agents to nonreligious agents as if we were pushing pieces of furniture around in the same room) because this conception overlooks that secularization is not only a change of actors but also a project of transformation of the contents. In the end, secularization does not consist only of different ac-

18. See Arthur C. Brooks, *The Road to Freedom: How to Win the Fight for Free Enterprise* (New York: Basic Books, 2012).

19. Charles Taylor, "Western Secularity," in *Rethinking Secularism*, ed. Craig Calhoun, Mark Juergensmeyer, and Jonathan Van Antwerpen (Oxford: Oxford University Press, 2011), 31–53.

tors; these actors also perform different roles in a different framework.

Taylor identifies two primary vectors in the process of secularization: commitment and disenchantment. "Commitment" means underscoring personal devotion over communal ritual practices. "Disenchantment" is *Entzauberung* in the Weberian sense; it signifies the "buffered" self of the human person—one can rationally explain what is happening to him. Before that people had "porous" selves: the boundary between forces and agents was fuzzy; the boundary between the mind and the world was porous.[20]

Taylor then connects this double vector with the rise and forward march of "axial religions," this pivotal change in the history of religion that occurred during the Axial Age (800–200 BC).[21] In preaxial, archaic religions, religious life was inseparably linked to social life. The whole community as such was the principal agent. Religion was embedded in social ritual and, in existing reality, constituted by the society, the cosmos, and earthly existence. What people prayed for was health, life, wealth, fertility, victory, and other material goods. In preaxial religions, people were not required to go beyond human flourishing. Thus, the embeddedness of religion was a matter of identity.[22]

Axial religions go beyond embeddedness. They go beyond human flourishing: "The paradox of Christianity, in relation to early religion, is that on one hand, it seems to assert the unconditional benevolence of God towards humans—there is none of the ambivalence of early divinity in this respect—and yet, on the other, it redefines our ends so as to take us beyond flourishing." According to Taylor, the axial religions break with all three dimensions of embeddedness: the social order, the cosmos, and human good.[23] Thus, as an axial religion, Christianity helped nudge moral and then social imaginaries, that is, the collective notions of good life and life in society, toward individualism.[24]

---

20. Ibid., 36ff.

21. Karl Jaspers, *Vom Ursprung und Ziel der Geschichte* (Frankfurt am Main: Fischer, 1957). See also Robert N. Bellah and Hans Joas, eds., *The Axial Age and Its Consequences* (Cambridge, Mass.: The Belknap Press of Harvard University, 2012).

22. Taylor, "Western Secularity," 44.

23. Ibid., 45. See also Charles Taylor, "What Was the Axial Revolution?" in *The Axial Age and Its Consequences*, ed. Robert N. Bellah and Hans Joas (Cambridge, Mass.: The Belknap Press of Harvard University, 2012), 30–46.

24. Taylor, "Western Secularity," 49.

The crucial change in the process of secularization, beyond that of axial religions, is the possibility of disbelief in God, a possibility that five centuries ago was inconceivable.

In other words, the crucial change here could be described as the possibility of living within a purely immanent order; that is, the possibility of really conceiving of, or imaging, ourselves within such an order, one that could be accounted for on its own terms, which thus leaves belief in the transcendent as a kind of 'optional extra'—something it had never been before in any human society. This presupposed the clear separation of natural and supernatural as a necessary condition, but it needed more that that. There had to develop a social order, sustained by a social imaginary that had a purely immanent character, which we see arising, for instance, in the modern forms of public sphere, market economy, and citizen state.[25]

Based on these distinctions, we think we can take the relationship between secularity and Christianity a step further. Why should it not be conceivable that Christianity as a postaxial religion contributes to real human flourishing by going beyond it? This is the essence of Christian charity: self-transcendence for others in which alone we can find fulfillment. This is the aim of Christian morality: the clue for true happiness, on earth and thereafter. This key idea had already been intuited by Socratic ethics (another axial spiritual phenomenon) with its distinction between pleasure and happiness (the topic of Plato's *Nomoi*). Only where this distinction is made can there really be ethics. Real human flourishing is brought about by self-transcendence through love. The chapters in the first section examine a series of topics and aspects related to this anthropological and ethical dimension of economic activity. Melé shows the inadequacy of utilitarianism and positivism as a basis, offering, instead, a person-centered ethics. Aranzadi, setting forth from the point of view of the acting person, develops an ethics of the business firm as an institution. Larrivee analyzes the anthropological visions underlying the economic theories of Adam Smith, Karl Marx, and Ayn Rand and the importance of the Christian view on the human person. Wishloff underscores that enterprise is a calling to love.

In its social dimension, love is called solidarity: transcending one's own interests to identify oneself with other people's concerns. Actually,

25. Ibid., 50–51.

in love other people's concerns become one's own interests. Jesus Christ teaches this attitude. Take the multiplication of the loaves of bread. The people are hungry, and Jesus has compassion for the crowd (Mk 8:2) This was not the first miracle of "socialist redistribution," even though Jesus did take away the disciples' seven loaves and two fish, but an act of Divine abundance that foreshadowed the sacraments. He cut short every attempt of the crowd to make him king, a desire based on the hope that he would use his powers to solve the food problem. His Gospel is not a political or an economic program. However, Jesus does teach us compassion and generosity.

On the other hand, Christianity is not libertarian. The central passage for Christian liberty is Romans 8:20–23: for Christ, Saint Paul lays claim to the whole *kosmos* that groans in the pains of childbirth and hopes to be set free from its bondage to corruption and to obtain the freedom of the glory of the children of God. In Pauline theology, *eleutheria* means freedom from Mosaic law, from sin and from eternal death. However, Paul's concept is not negative. The severing of the aforementioned bondages serves the aim of setting the human heart free for love: "Owe no one anything, except to love each other, for the one who loves another has fulfilled the law" (Rom 13:8). The truly Christian challenge is to bring together solidarity and freedom. Christian faith is not exclusive, forcing one to choose either solidarity or freedom. On the contrary, it is inclusive, inviting a combination of complementary principles.

Every virtue is a mean between two extremes, not in the sense of an average or of mediocrity but as a summit. This summit is not in the middle: instead, it tends toward one of the extremes. In the case of Christian humanism in society, the thrust clearly is toward solidarity with the poor. Already the Acts of the Apostles show that from its beginnings, the church never separated *diakonia* (service of the poor, the widows, and the orphans) from *kerygma* and *catechesis*. The church fathers both of Latin and of Greek origin are clear: they certainly defend freedom, in particular, religious freedom, but their main concern is the poor. The great Cappadocians, as well as Ambrose, Leo, and John Chrysostom, are especially outspoken. Throughout the whole of church history, the social efforts of Christians are undeniable. Often enough, the church was the only institution that offered ministry and social services to the poor.

The problem with solidarity arises not from its Christian origins but from its usurpation by the secular state. To Anglo-American ears, solidarity suggests collectivism and sounds a shade excessive. However, in Catholic social teaching, the word *solidarity* or *solidarism* is the exact opposite of what socialism intended with collectivism. It means the virtue that seeks the common good and the societal order that is formed by a virtuous population. This is true for Heinrich Pesch, the founder of Catholic solidarism (who conceived of solidarity as a kind of universal social principle that protects the human dignity of man as a social being oriented to the common good), for the encyclical *Sollicitudo rei socialis* and the *Catechism of the Catholic Church*: solidarity in Catholic social *teaching* never has had a collectivist meaning (although for some Catholic social *thinkers*, it has). Free markets are the only medium in which solidarity can exist as virtue. These times of globalization are the best times for solidarity and gray times for solitary individuals.[26] Thus, in his chapter, Hittinger offers a profound reflection, based on justice, on the link between solidarity and the common good.

This does not dismiss government from its duty to care for social needs. The amount or degree of state intervention is open to debate. It is one of the technical solutions that the church's Magisterium leaves to the laity. There is, however, an indicator for wrong government intervention: massive public debt. Where public debt begins to skyrocket, something evidently has gone very wrong in a moral sense. The debate on the right amount of government intervention is conditioned by the question whether a system that is based on voluntary donations by individuals ("charity society") is better than a system that confers entitlements to government aid (welfare society). It has been masterly analyzed by the political philosopher Avishai Margalit.[27] He argues in a fair and honest way and arrives at the conclusion that there is no clear answer to this question. What he considers is that charity societies can, with the best intention, be humiliating, because pity and almsgiving have something humiliating to them. On the other hand, welfare societies have to cope with the disadvantages of a growing bureaucracy that can even be-

---

26. Michael Novak, *Noi, voi e l'Islam: Lettera aperta all'Europa sulla libertà* (Roma: Liberal, 2005); English original: *The Universal Hunger for Liberty: Why the Clash of Civilizations Is Not Inevitable*), 86–87.

27. Avishai Margalit, *The Decent Society* (Cambridge, Mass.: Harvard University Press, 1996), 222–46.

come a type of "feudal" or "*nomenklatura*" bureaucracy. In the context of the topic we are dealing with, the question is, Is it correct to identify charity (or solidarity) with pity? Or in other words (even though this is not what interests Margalit), must the relationship between charity and justice be expressed in the terms of pity versus entitlement? We think this is unnecessary. Pity is the wrong style of giving; it implies a sense of superiority of the giver over the receiver. Compassion is a different attitude: a compassionate person considers herself equally vulnerable to disgrace. Pity, therefore, is an uncharitable attitude.

Still, the relationship between justice and charity is decisive for the well-functioning of solidarity in free markets. Actually, the debates on solidarity do not focus on whether one should help the poor at all (there is general agreement that one should) but rather on who should help and how it should be brought about. Should it be left to the government (social justice) or to individuals (charity)? To facilitate the development of a response, it can help to distinguish justice from charity. Acts of justice (giving others what is their own) are not directly acts of charity (giving myself to others), even though charity also commands those acts of justice. Charity goes beyond justice; it is architectonical for justice as it is for all of the other virtues, directing them toward the final aim of charity, that is, the love of God and of our neighbor for God's sake. There is, however, a tendency in legally organized societies to regulate the claims of people who consider themselves unjustly disfavored by society through law, that is, by mechanisms of justice and not by charity alone. This regulation converts charitable gifts into benefits, which can be claimed on the grounds of entitlements. This actually reduces the amount of charity in a society but can never make charity superfluous.

Thomas Aquinas consistently denies that charity supersedes natural justice, most explicitly in *Summa Theologiae*, II-II, q. 104, a. 6. Grace does not destroy or replace either nature or natural reason. Grace is not less reasonable than nature. Therefore, natural needs and exigencies remain in force and are neither abolished nor rendered irrelevant to charity.[28] Thus, the natural distinctions between charity and justice should be maintained and respected. Justice that usurps what corresponds to char-

---

28. Cf. Jean Porter, "The Virtue of Justice (IIa IIae, qq. 58–122)," in *The Ethics of Aquinas*, ed. Stephen J. Pope (Washington, D.C.: Georgetown University Press, 2002), 272–86.

ity is false justice, and vice versa, unjust acts cannot be justified in the name of charity. Charity is the condition of the visibility of injustice, the motor that drives the social forces to overcome injustice, the sensitive seismograph of tectonic social shifts and tensions. Without charity, the society would be left in the dark without its sun, to use an expression of Saint Ambrose.[29] Baker, in his chapter, gives concrete examples of how charity could transform the existing paradigm of business and of the consequences of its marginalization.

Catholic social teaching is characterized by a tension between social vectors. These vectors are the social principles which have been formulated during the last 150 years of Catholic social thought: personal dignity, the common good, solidarity, and subsidiarity. These vectors point in different directions and thus create an open space for freedom, justice, and solidarity in society. The relationship among these diverse principles is one of "inverse symbiosis": they can grow hand in hand, but if either one is fostered too much, not only will the other principle collapse, but so, too, will that which has been overprivileged.[30] These and other questions are the object of the chapters written by Dougherty, Grassl, and Schlag. They concentrate on the papal social teachings regarding economic life and responsibility and span the arch between their beginnings and the pontificate of Pope Benedict XVI.

Theory alone, however, would lack the flesh necessary for a substantial discourse. We have therefore added four chapters: two, those by Althammer and Jackson, that present specific models of applied ethics and two, those by Carioca and Flynn, that present specific aspects of business life that are important in an anthropological sense, such as the family and cooperation.

We sincerely hope that this interdisciplinary volume can help to go beyond existing frontiers, in order to open spaces of freedom that only will be sustainable in a culture of solidarity.

---

29. "Remove benevolence from human dealings and you have removed the sun from the world; for without benevolence there are no human dealings: showing a stranger the way, correcting the errant, returning hospitality are all fruits of benevolence. It is like a spring of water which refreshes the thirsty." Ambrose, *De officiis*, ed. Ivor J. Davidson (Oxford: Oxford University Press, 2001), I, 32, 167.

30. Cf. Amitai Etzioni, *The New Golden Rule: Community and Morality in a Democratic Society* (New York: Basic Books, 1996), 35ff, on the relationship between autonomy and the moral order.

As always, our first acknowledgment goes to Jennifer E. Miller, without whose patience, kindness, and untiring diligence this book would not have been completed. We also thank the unknown reviewers for their helpful comments, and the Catholic University of America Press for publishing this volume. And, of course, we are grateful to all contributors for their time and effort in completing and correcting their chapters.

PART I

Constructing Theoretical Foundations

ONE

Love, Sustainability, and Solidarity

Philosophical and Theological Roots

Russell Hittinger

I

Societies formed in the tradition of Roman law once had a clear social, moral, and juridical meaning for solidarity. A person had an *obligatio in solidum* when he or she was responsible—which is to say liable—for the debts or actions of another. Solidarity was not a limited liability partnership. A legal and moral "presumption of solidarity" depended on one's membership in a society (nation, family, religion, guild) that persists over time, allowing everyone else to deem the person a member of a corporate whole. An uncle, for example, could be responsible for the actions and debts of his niece, and Jews could have obligations *in solidum* by virtue of being Jews. Liberation from presumptions of solidarity—especially the odious one pertaining to Jews—was one of the works of the democratic revolutions that spread from France and its former colonies to the rest of Europe. The Napoleonic Code forbade the presumption of solidarities because it threatened the solidarity of citizens based on the new creed of liberty, equality, and fraternity. The code permitted only those liabilities contracted by individuals for limited purposes and times.[1]

1. The Napoleonic Code (1804) expressly forbade the presumption of *solidarité* (art. 1202) in order to underscore the ontology of natural persons bound together chiefly, or only, in the state and secondarily by contracts engaged by individuals. The historical evolution of the term is tracked within the Jewish community by Lisa Moses Leff, "Jewish Solidarity in Nineteenth-Century France: The Evolution of a Concept," *Journal of Modern History* 74, no. 1 (March 2002): 33–61. A more global

Having destroyed the legal notion of presumptive solidarities reducible neither to the state nor to individual contract, the revolutions unintentionally emancipated the word *solidarity*, which quickly acquired a plethora of moral and ideological meanings in the nineteenth century: class solidarity, solidarity of political parties or movements, sex and gender solidarity, and the solidarity of humanity itself.

Martin Schlag reminds us that to American ears, *solidarity* sounds like *collectivism* or *socialism*. He is surely right. Yet, despite the way we Americans hear the word, *solidarity* does not necessarily pertain immediately to the state. Indeed, it often marks modes of association underneath, above, or across state sovereignties. More often than not, it suggests a "human-rights patriotism."[2]

Reading this term in more subtle contexts is especially important in the case of Catholic Social Doctrine (CSD), which appropriated "solidarity" long after it had mutated into these diverse moral and social desiderata. What's more, CSD wanted the word to work in tandem with rather traditional notions of social relationships and the virtues of justice and love.

Although Pope John Paul II was not the first magisterial authority to use the term, he was the first to use it not only persistently but also doctrinally—by which I mean that he defined solidarity as a virtue and that he tried to mark analogous meanings of this virtue.

In *Sollicitudo Rei Socialis* (1987), the "virtue" of solidarity is described (initially) as the willingness to make a moral response to common goods (in the plural): "It is above all a question of interdependence, sensed as a system determining relationships in the contemporary world in its economic, cultural, political and religious elements, and accepted as a moral category. When interdependence becomes recognized in this way, the correlative response as a moral and social attitude, *as* a 'virtue,' is solidarity."[3] Several sections later, a crisper definition is given by the pope:

Solidarity is undoubtedly a Christian virtue. In what has been said so far it has been possible to identify many points of contact between solidarity and char-

---

history is provided by Steinar Stjerno in *Solidarity in Europe: The History of an Idea* (Cambridge: Cambridge University Press, 2004).

2. Hauke Brunkhorst, *Solidarity: From Civic Friendship to a Global Legal Community*, Studies in Contemporary German Social Thought, (Cambridge: MIT Press, 2005), 3.

3. John Paul II, Encyclical *Sollicitudo Rei Socialis* (Vatican City: Libreria Editrice Vaticana, 1987), 9.

ity, which is the distinguishing mark of Christ's disciples.... Beyond human and natural bonds, already so close and strong, there is discerned in the light of faith a new model of the unity of the human race, which must ultimately inspire our solidarity. This supreme model of unity, which is a reflection of the intimate life of God, one God in three Persons, is what we Christians mean by the word "communion."[4]

As we can see, the pope uses a single word to flag a plurality of social virtues perfecting actions regarding what two or more persons have in common. Four years later, in *Centesimus annus* we read, "In this way what we nowadays call the principle of solidarity ... is clearly seen to be one of the fundamental principles of the Christian view of social and political organization. This principle is frequently stated by Pope Leo XIII, who uses the term 'friendship,' a concept already found in Greek philosophy. Pope Pius XI refers to it with the equally meaningful term 'social charity.' Pope Paul VI, expanding the concept to cover the many modern aspects of the social question, speaks of a 'civilization of love.'"[5]

At least four recurring focal meanings for solidarity, as social virtues pertaining to different ways we have something in common, can be gathered:

• The first is anthropological: our common ontological perfections as human.

• The second is instrumental: common utilities or externalities. Often, this commons is simply called *interdependence*. In the words of *Gaudium et spes* §5, "needful solidarity." In short, we are all in the same boat together.

• The third is communicative and irreducibly moral: common activities, which can encompass rather diverse modes of cooperation, partnership, friendship, and associations. In *Centesimus annus*, John Paul II speaks of the "an expanding chain of solidarity" (social virtues exercised in one sphere tend to diffuse themselves).[6] Perhaps this kind of solidarity matches up with what we call civil society.

• The fourth is communion: common love, which means that *the union itself* is what is loved, or *koinonia*—this is what the tradition meant

4. Ibid., 40.
5. John Paul II, Encyclical *Centesimus Annus* (Vatican City: Libreria Editrice Vaticana, 1991), 10.
6. Ibid., 43.

by common good and by friendship in the strict and unqualified sense of the term. Recent magisterial documents emphasize the agapic character of love specific to Christianity, but, of course, there are modes of love that aim at a love of the union without being supernatural.

II

To no one's surprise, CSD holds that the human person is made unto the image and likeness of God. As Saint Thomas said of our participation in the Eternal Law, the human person is capacitated "to be provident for himself and for others" (*Summa Theologica*, I–II:91.2). We imitate the divinity in a twofold manner: first, in the unity of our nature as a rational substance and, second, in our ability to communicate good(s) to others through our actions. What is simple in God is represented diversely in the human creature according to his natural and social unities.

We do not need philosophy or social science to observe how these excellences are unfolded in many different actions and kinds of social cohesion. Our common humanity, our interdependencies, and our enterprises and associations give rise to, and express, various notions of justice, beneficence, and benevolence.

So, what is the problem? The diverse modes of solidarity always sustained by their distinct modes of love. A "society," in the broad sense in which we usually use the term, is brimming with different kinds of solidarity. But the fourth kind of solidarity is not only qualitatively different from the first three but also vulnerable to being confused with or reduced to the others. This poses a problem.

The first solidarity is absolutely fundamental but rather nebulously *social*. Humanity does not exist just as such, only individual human beings exist. We have in common certain ontological perfections at the root of our nature—as what Alasdair MacIntyre calls "dependent rational animals." These perfections (rational, free, communicative) are a wellspring for all recognitions on which the various kinds of solidarity depend and according to which we can understand the love of oneself and one's neighbor. Perhaps we can say that love of beings of ones "own kind" marks an important threshold, allowing us to love other persons we scarcely know and with whom we live in no specific or familiar social order. We have the beginning of duties of beneficence and benevolence even from afar.

The second solidarity is also fundamental, but interdependencies readily suggest solutions based on work, exchange, distributions, and public regulations. To some extent, these, too, can be initiated and appropriated from afar. The third solidarity demands a specifically social predicate, for teamwork is necessary, at the very least. Associations are marvelous creatures of human intentionality, and social life would be terribly diminished without them. Even so, enterprises and associations are temporary and usually are intended for a particular purpose, if not for a private yield either for the individuals or for a group of individuals in a particular association. A society constituted by *koinonia* (or *communio*) has a different logic. It can be corroded by a zealous particularity that proves disrespectful of the humanity in other persons. It can also be corroded by unjust, or even by inefficacious, exchanges and distributions. And it can be deranged by a lack of teamwork, trust, and cooperation. Its distinguishing characteristic, however, is that its union is without qualification the common good, or what the tradition called *bonum commune*. It is sustained by a different species of justice and benevolence.

The Catholic tradition has held that there are three such societies: marriage-family, polity, and church. By nature, human beings are matrimonial and political animals, and, by grace created in the soul, ecclesial animals. These three societies, which are the seats of *eudaimonia*, have their own respective ends and social forms. Here is what they analogously have in common that sets them apart from other solidarities. Each has two common goods: (1) an extrinsic common good, which is to say an end or ends being aimed at (tranquility of order for polity, children for marriage), and (2) an intrinsic common good, a form of order for common action of its members, which is nothing other than the union itself. Both ends are the focus of justice and love.

Let's take marriage. As Saint Thomas taught, "[n]or is the direct object of consent a husband but union with a husband on the part of the wife, even as it is *union* with a wife on the part of the husband."[7] Psychologically, one desires and chooses *this* man or woman. It could also be true that one has in view a mutually agreeable end, such as reproduc-

---

7. Sent., Lib. IV d. XXVII, 1.2, qu^a 1 ad 3. Cf. *Summa Theologica*, Supplement, 45.1 ad. 3.

tion, economic security for the wider family, and so forth. But it is the consent *to the union* that precipitates the societal form and deserves to be called marriage. The other intentions—to consent to *this* man or woman and to consent to a common end—can obtain in the absence of matrimony. Indeed, partnerships of various kinds, including partnerships that create a common pool of resources, will often entail a consensus (this person rather than that person) for such and such an end without implying consent to a societal union.[8]

Moreover, the union is indivisible. Like any true friendship, there is only one way to have it—to participate in it by action. It can have no other mode of existence. The common good never exists as a private good, and therefore, when someone exits a marriage or a polity he or she cannot take away his or her private share. Even in our confused legal cultures, courts understand perfectly well that they can divide and distribute the external properties but not the marriage itself. The matrimonial society, therefore, is not redistributed so much as it is dissolved or annulled.

To be sure, societies having a common good also engage in exchanges and distributions but according to the form and order of their union. A marital union does not merely beget children but does so matrimonially. A polity does not aim merely to secure the peace and security of the city but to do so politically—constitutionally, according to a shared form. When a polity makes available free legal counsel to the indigent, it is not said that the rule of law is distributed to private persons.

When he treats of a common good, Saint Thomas always looks at the solidarity in terms of both love and justice. In the *Disputed Questions on Charity*, for example, he points out that even a tyrant might love the good results of polity as his or her own, but the good citizen is one who loves the union itself with a love of friendship. Even more, the saint is said to love the common good of the kingdom precisely insofar as it is poured forth and shared by many.[9]

---

8. Thus, Thomas insists, with his typical brevity that reaches to the heart of the question, that matrimony is not merely the joining of minds or bodies, but rather that "the joining together of bodies and minds is a result of matrimony." Sent., Lib. IV, d. XXVII 1.1. Cf. *Summa Theologica*, Supplement, 44.1 corpus.

9. Thomas Aquinas, "De Caritate," in *Quaestiones Disputatae* (*Disputed Questions On Charity*), ed. Pio M. Bazzi (Turin: Marietti, 1964–1965), 2.2.

Thomas's understanding of social union helps us to distinguish com-mon-good justice from the other modes of justice that fall under the cardinal virtue of justice. It was a scholastic adage that the cardinal vir-tue of justice always implies relation *sub specie alteritatis*. Justice requires a relation and an obligation to "the other." Justice is done when the right thing is put into the possession of the right person, either by exchange (commutation) and bilaterally or by distribution based on merit. The social world could not be sustained unless each is given what is his or hers due precisely *as other*.

But a distinct virtue orders the myriad acts of the other virtues to a common good. Saint Thomas explains:

[L]egal [or general] justice is said to be a general virtue, in as much, to wit, as it directs the acts of the other virtues to its own end, and this is to move all the other virtues by its command; for just as charity may be called a general virtue in so far as it directs the acts of all the virtues to the Divine good, so too is legal justice, in so far as it directs the acts of all the virtues to the common good. Ac-cordingly, just as charity which regards the Divine good as its proper object, is a special virtue in respect of its essence, so too legal justice is a special virtue in re-spect of its essence, in so far as it regards the common good as its proper object.[10]

This is the practice of virtue "looked at from the social point of view"—*sub specie societatis*. It was called "legal" because law is always for the common good, and "general" because the other virtues are mobi-lized (not reduced) to the good of the union. Common-good justice has a different logic of justice and love than the cardinal virtue does because the common good is not "other."

It might sound paradoxical, but the cardinal virtues of justice in ex-change and justice in distribution would destroy common-good justice *if* the union is depicted as something "other." Let me put it in another way. If we only had the two kinds of cardinal-virtue justice (commutation and distribution), we would still be social animals, but the fourth kind of soli-darity that the tradition calls *koinonia* would not exist. Precisely because it is *not* "other," it would appear to be within the range of justice because there is no private part that anchors the exchange or distribution.[11]

---

10. *Summa Theologica*, II-II, 58.6.

11. The dignity of the human person cannot be interpreted on the premise of methodological individualism—namely, that social unities and relations among members can be reduced to nonsocial

In commutative justice, two or more persons can pool their investments. It takes trust and cooperation. But justice is done when each is giv-
en his or her private yield. Similarly, we can set up a common utility—a
water system—but when the water comes out of the tap in my kitchen, it
is meant for my sake. The distribution is just as it should be. This cannot
be supposed in the case of marriage, polity, and church because the union
cannot go into my account, so to speak. Rather, the maxim of Cardinal
Cajetan holds: *Mihi non propter me*, "for me, but not for my sake."

The original and perpetual interest of any society enjoying a common good is that its union remains distinct from the other justices and
loves mobilized for its sake. Here, we must emphasize the word *distinct*,
lest we fall into the totalitarian premise that common good justice entails the exclusion of the other justices and loves.

In Canto-XIV of the *Purgatorio*, Dante meets up with the shade of
Guido del Duca, a tough politician from the Romagna who laments the
fratricidal politics of the cities in that region. He attributes it to the envy
of Cain. Then, in Canto-XV Dante asks Virgil to explain the teaching:

> I thought I'd gather profit from his words;
> And even as I turned toward him, I asked:
> "What did the spirit of Romagna mean when he said
>   'Sharing cannot have a part'?"
> And his reply: "He knows the harm that lies
> in his worst vice ...
> For when your longings center on things such
> that sharing them apportions less to each,
> Then envy stirs the bellows of your sighs.
> But if the love within the Highest Sphere
> Should turn your longings heavenward, the fear
> inhabiting your breast would disappear;
> For there, the more there are who would say 'ours,'
> so much the greater is the good possessed
> by each—so much more love burns in that cloister.
>   (*Purgatory*, XV:42–57)

---

properties of members or composites thereof. Individualism, so put, is compatible with a broad spectrum of *sociability*; it is not compatible with *koinonia*, which cannot be disaggregated and given to the
individual as *other*.

I take Virgil's teaching to mean something like this. In strict justice, each shall have what is his or her own. The lust for what belongs to the other gives rise to envy. We cannot be right with our neighbor by taking or wishing to destroy what is his. Love needs cardinal-virtue justice for the simple reason that we cannot enjoy unions (*communicationes*) when there is injustice. The cure is not to subvert strict justice, much less to make everything common in the same respect. Things truly divisible must in justice be divided and assigned—to each according to his or her own. What is common, however, requires a different justice and love. And it was Signore de Duca's station in *purgatorio* to learn this lesson.[12]

The lesson, once learned and socially completed, is found in the *Paradiso*, where the saints are grouped, first, in their respective grades of participation and, finally, altogether in the celestial rose (*Paradise*, XXX–XXXIII). There, one espies the unity of order in which a plurality of persons is moved by the same love that moves the sun and the stars. We might say that in the *Commedia* justice has two aspects. The first is distribution according to merit; the second is according to order, in which the common good is the object and goal. The latter comprehends what medieval scholastics meant by *iustitia generalis* (*legalis*). Dante explicitly invokes the Eternal Law for the order of a kingdom in which what is good for the whole is good for each of its parts. (XXXII:55–57). Introduced by Bernard of Clairvaux, it is nothing other than the "cloister" foreshadowed by Virgil in the case of Guido del Duca.

III

In the late nineteenth century, some Catholic scholars—clerical and lay—voiced reservations about the traditional term denoting common-good justice. *Legal* justice, they worried, can suggest that only the state has a *bonum commune*. This was the era of Bismarck, when the church was hard-pressed to sustain its societies—marriage, family, schools, re-

---

12. In this line of thought, Dante proposes something strikingly similar to Thomas, who compares love and envy in this way: "Good is loved inasmuch as it can be communicated to the lover. Consequently whatever hinders the perfection of this communication becomes hateful. Thus zeal arises from love of good. But through defect of goodness, it happens that certain small goods cannot, in their entirety, be possessed by many at the same time: and from the love of such things arises the zeal of envy. But it does not arise, properly speaking, in the case of those things which, in their entirety, can be possessed by many: for no one envies another the knowledge of truth, which can be known entirely by many; except perhaps one may envy another his superiority in the knowledge of it." *Summa Theologica*, I-II 28.4 ad 2. See also III 23.1 ad 3.

ligious orders—against the effort of states to sweep all solidarities into that of citizenship. To avoid a univocal notion of common-good justice, they proposed to call it *social justice*. The tradition, after all, had always spoken of common-good justice *sub specie societatis*. This terminological change took place during the pontificate of Pius XI. For his part, Pius XI made it clear that *iustitia socialis* is nothing other than *iustitia legalis/generalis*: "[I]t is of the essence of social justice to demand from each individual all that is necessary for the common good."[13]

As this terminological change was moved down the field of history and social policy, the ball was almost guaranteed to be fumbled. In the first place, in the Great Depression and its aftermath, economic disorder galvanized everyone's attention on issues of exchange and distribution, especially the state's role in remediating imbalances in this regard. In the second place, the term *social justice* had come to mean distributive justice—especially with respect to the weak and the vulnerable. To speak here only of the Anglo-American world, this meaning of social justice was firmly in place a century ago. It would have been a Sisyphean task to make it mean something different.

The result was predictable. The concept and the term *common good* were not lost; rather, the term denoting its specific mode of justice was confusedly put under distribution. So, rather than having three species of justice, each with its own mode, or modes, of love, we are reduced to two: (1) justice of exchange and (2) justice of public distribution, or, what is more likely, redistribution. On this view, we are compelled to speak of those solidarities having *koinonia* in terms that misrepresent the actions and virtues that truly sustain them. Indeed, marriage-family, polity, and church look more like public utilities, and thus, we debate their equities and efficiencies in just that way.

Take, for example, the debates in Europe and the United States over the issue of marriage. What kind of juridic person is a marriage? In 1992 the Hawaiian Supreme Court defined marriage as "a partnership to

---

13. The Fribourg Union was the center of this debate over the terminological change. See Normand Joseph Paulhus, "The Theological and Political Ideals of the Fribourg Union," PhD diss., Boston College, 1983. For the subsequent history, see my essay "The Coherence of the Four Basic Principles of Catholic Social Doctrine: An Interpretation," Keynote Address Pontifical Academy of Social Sciences, XVIII Plenary Session, in *Pursuing the Common Good*, ed. Margaret S. Archer and Pierpaolo Donati, Pontifical Academy of Social Sciences, *Acta* 14 (Vatican City, 2008), 75–123.

which both parties bring their financial resources as well as their individual energies and efforts."[14] This point was reiterated in the controversial 2003 decision of the Massachusetts Supreme Court, which prohibited the legislature from giving a legal title of marriage only to one man and one woman. Let us put to one side the moral issue of whether marriage ought to be exclusively heterosexual and look instead at the description of marriage and the state's interest in it. "We begin by considering the nature of civil marriage itself. Simply put, the government creates civil marriage ... Civil marriage is created and regulated through exercise of the police power ... Civil marriage anchors an ordered society by encouraging stable relationships over transient ones. It is central to the way the Commonwealth identifies individuals, provides for the orderly distribution of property, ensures that children and adults are cared for and supported whenever possible from private rather than public funds, and tracks important epidemiological and demographic data."[15] What aspects of good order move the state to sanction matrimony? The court mentions economic reasons (property), sociological reasons (stable relationships), health reasons (care for the old or indigent), and scientific reasons (collection of epidemiological data). Although this description does not rule out personal intimacy, that, too, will look like a private exchange, with the value-added status of legal recognition. The question before the court was whether the legislature failed in the order of distributive justice when it made a legal title available exclusively to heterosexuals.

I cannot pretend here to discuss the law or the public morality of marriage. I cite these sentences from the Massachusetts decision only as an example of what happens when three species of justice are reduced to two, which are then separated from the specific and appropriate kind of solidarity that is at stake.

IV

I conclude with the good news. John Paul II's emphasis on solidarity as communion (at least in marriage-family and church) has helped us to see that there are some social entities that can be sustained only by three kinds of justice rather than by two:

---

14. *Gussin v. Gussin*, 73 Haw. 470, 483 (1992).
15. *Goodridge v. Dept. of Public Health*, 440 Mass. 309 (1993).

But the rights of the family *are not simply the sum total* of the rights of the person, since the family is *much more than* the sum of its individual members. It is a community of parents and children, and at times a community of several generations. For this reason its "status as a subject," which is grounded in God's plan, gives rise to and calls for certain proper and specific rights.... In the first place, the family achieves the good of "being together." This is the good par excellence of marriage (hence its indissolubility) and of the family community. It could also be defined as a good of the subject as such. Just as the person is a subject, so too is the family, since it is made up of persons, who, joined together by a profound bond of communion, form a single "communal subject."[16]

Interestingly, he summarizes the rights of the family under the Fourth Commandment, namely, as what deserves *honora*. It is not a dormitory housing individuals having human rights; it is not a set of interdependencies remediated by exchange and distribution; it is not a civic association for this or that munificence. Rather, it deserves to be honored because its solidarity is distinct from the others.

Furthermore, some recent magisterial documents have likewise emphasized rather pointedly that common good cannot be conflated with distribution—indeed, even going so far as to reinstall the original term *legal justice*, for which *social justice* was supposed to be the updated improvement:

One distinguishes commutative justice from legal justice which concerns what the citizen owes in fairness to the community, and from distributive justice which regulates what the community owes its citizens in proportion to their contributions and needs.[17]

Each human community possesses a common good which permits it to be recognized as such; it is in the political community that its most complete realization is found. It is the role of the state to defend and promote the common good of civil society, its citizens, and intermediate bodies.[18]

The common good does not consist in the simple sum of the particular goods of each subject of a social entity. Belonging to everyone and to each person, it is and remains "common," because it is indivisible and because only together is it possible to attain it.[19]

16. John Paul II, *Letter to Families* (Vatican City: Libreria Editrice Vaticana, 1994), 15.
17. *Catechism of the Catholic Church* (Vatican City: Libreria Editrice Vaticana, 1992), 2411.
18. Ibid., 1910.
19. Pontifical Council for Justice and Peace, *Compendium of the Social Doctrine of the Church* (Vatican City: Libreria Editrice Vaticana, 2004), 164.

Supposing that we are capable of thinking about (and using) more precise terms for the justice and love that sustains a common good, what does social justice mean? Perhaps it means the justice governing what a community owes to its members. If that is so, social justice is what the great tradition always meant by distributive justice. It can also have broader contexts, such as international aid to persons and groups who are not members of one's community.

There is a limit on distributive justice, which by the same token must apply to social justice. It is called subsidiarity. Namely, when help is given, the *subsidium* must not destroy or derange the communities being assisted. In other words, the limit on distributive justice is nothing other than the mode of union that sustains a community. Hence, we inevitably find ourselves returning to common-good justice. To the specific kind of solidarity that must be *honored*. To be sure, such *koinonia* includes the justices of exchange and distribution, but the salient point is that the justice and benevolence of such solidarities cannot be assembled merely out of, or reduced to, exchange and distribution.

Leaving behind the Model of Positivism and Utilitarianism for Economic Activity

Toward a Humanistic Approach

Domènec Melé

Economic activity and free markets do not operate within an institutional and ethical vacuum. Market mechanisms do not automatically run through mere economic transactions. On the contrary, they need institutions. In fact, it is widely recognized that there are a number of institutions for the free-market system, such as rule of law, protection of private-property rights, enforcement of voluntary contracts, and limited third-party interference in others' exchanges. Oliver E. Williamson highlighted the importance of some economic institutions for capitalism with special emphasis on contracts and transaction costs and on the role of the law, dealing with vertical integration, corporate governance, and industrial organizations as well.[1] These and other social institutions can favor or hinder freedom, on one hand, and cooperation or solidarity, on the other. The former includes aspects such as personal choice, voluntary exchange, the protection of persons and property, and the freedom to compete in markets. The latter are focused on avoiding abuse of power and, in a positive sense, on favoring participation and solidarity in the market economy.

Institutions are therefore necessary, but they are not sufficient to generate sufficient trust, which is crucial for the well working of mar-

---

1. Oliver E. Williamson, *The Economic Institutions of Capitalism* (New York: Free Press, 1985).

kets. Trust also requires the abiding by agreements and respecting others' rights, even in those cases when they could not be caught, or there would be no identifiable harm or victim if they did not abide by agreements or respect rights.[2]

A deeper consideration of economic activity and the free market leads us to observe that institutions are established within a cultural context. Culture, with its shared ideas and values, can explain why several forms of capitalism exist, as Michel Albert highlighted three decades ago by distinguishing the so-called neo-American model championed by Ronald Reagan and Margaret Thatcher in the 1980s from "Rhine Capitalism," present in Germany, France, and in some of Northern European economies. According to Albert, the latter is more equitable, more efficient, and less violent.[3]

After the financial crisis of 2008 and following years, the debate could be enriched with new arguments, but this is not my purpose here. It is enough for now to point out that culture, which includes shared beliefs, values, and ethical assumptions, plays a relevant role in shaping free markets. However, as Capaldi noted, "too little attention has been given to understanding the relation between markets and the totality of our culture."[4] Within a culture, some philosophical ideas and ethical assumptions frame economics and, in particular, the market economy. Positivism, mainly logical positivism, is the philosophical idea dominant in economics and especially in neoclassical economics. Positivism assumes a type of rationality that solely focuses on the phenomena observed and on measurable facts. Consequently, it affirms that the only possible knowledge is that obtained by a scientific method. It separates facts and values and reduces ethics to subjective values.

However, ethical assumptions, or at least a certain normative framework, are also relevant, because "a market economy depends upon and presupposes a framework of ethical presuppositions."[5] The moral philosophy generally assumed by economists is utilitarianism, although of-

---

2. David C. Rose, *The Moral Foundation of Economic Behavior* (New York: Oxford University Press, 2011).

3. Michel Albert, *Capitalism against Capitalism* (London: Whurr, 1993).

4. Nicholas Capaldi, "The Ethical Foundations of Free Market Societies," *Journal of Private Enterprise* 20, no. 1 (2004): 31.

5. Ibid.

ten with some modifications that include some deontological elements.[6] Utilitarianism, as a social and ethical theory, focuses on the consequences of human action and its evaluation in terms of satisfaction. Positivism often aligns with utilitarianism as a foundation for understanding economic behavior and as a base for economic theory. This alignment is possible inasmuch as utilitarianism presents itself as "value free."

Accepting that positivism and utilitarianism are often presented as frameworks for economics and for theorizing on market economy, in this chapter some criticisms of both positivism and utilitarianism are reviewed, and it is argued that a different moral foundation of economic behavior and the market economy is necessary, one that provides a complete view of human beings and their human flourishing and of how to achieve a good and prosperous society. Then, some insights from Christian humanism are discussed, which will hopefully contribute to improving the moral foundations of economic activity.

POSITIVISM AND ITS INHERENT PROBLEMS

Economic studies often accept *positivism*, a well-known stream of thought initiated by the French thinker August Comte (1798–1857) and that extended through Europe in the second half of the nineteenth century. Positivism holds that the only authentic knowledge is produced through the scientific method. Consequently, as Gilkey pointed out, (1) science is the only way to know reality and so the only responsible means for defining reality for rational people, and (2) there is no room for other modes of knowing, such as the aesthetic, intuitive, speculative, or religious.[7]

In the first half of the twentieth century, scientism found strong intellectual support in the philosophical approach known as "neopositivism," "logical positivism," and "logical empiricism," as developed by what came to be known as the Vienna School. This approach emphasized the importance of the principle of verifiability to the point of asserting that the meaning of a term depends on empirical verification and that the only statements that can be accepted as scientific are those that are publicly observable and "objective," that is, detached from personal

6. Jagdish Bhagwati, "Markets and Morality," *American Economic Review: Papers and Proceedings* 101, no. 3 (2011): 162.

7. Langdon Gilkey, *Nature, Reality and the Sacred: The Nexus of Science and Religion* (Minneapolis: Fortress Press, 1993), 2.

traits. This leads to a careful separation of "facts" and "values" and the restriction of meaningful statements to those subjected to, or straightforwardly reducible to, empirical observation, that is, "facts."

Neopositivism exerted enormous influence on a wide range of economic and management theories. From a practical perspective, Positivism has brought about a widely spread "scientific view of the world."[8] However, neopositivism has come under severe criticism since the second half of the twentieth century.

A number of authors, including Quine,[9] Sen,[10] Searle,[11] Black,[12] Hausman and McPherson,[13] and, above all, Putnam,[14] have criticized the facts-and-values dichotomy. The latter, after showing the falsity of the dichotomy in *The Collapse of the Fact/Value Dichotomy and Other Essays*, advocates an "entanglement of fact and value" and considers that the neat line between prescriptive and descriptive components of evaluative judgments should be considered, at the very best, "a philosophers' fantasy."[15] Among the arguments proposed to prove the falsity of the facts-and-values dichotomy, several can be outlined.

Perception Is an Exercise of Our Concepts

Following Putnam, one can argue that statements about facts are not as objective as it is claimed they are, nor are statements of values as subjective as they seem to be. As to the objectivity of factual statements, first, it must be said that it is not possible to point at something as a fact, as if it were made up of certain "basic" experiences stripped of evalua-

8. Herbert Feigl and May Brodbeck, eds., *Readings in the Philosophy of Science* (New York: Appleton-Century-Crofts, 1953), 4.

9. Willard Van Orman Quine, "Two Dogmas of Empiricism," *Philosophical Review* 60, no. 1 (1951): 20–43.

10. Amartya K. Sen, "The Nature and Classes of Prescriptive Judgments," *Philosophical Quarterly* 17, no. 66 (1967): 46–62; and Amartya Sen, *On Ethics and Economics* (Oxford: Blackwell Publishing, 1987).

11. John R. Searle, "How to Derive 'Ought' from 'Is,'" *Philosophical Review* 73, no. 1 (1964): 43–58.

12. Max Black, "The Gap between 'Is' and 'Should,'" *Philosophical Review* 73, no. 2 (1964): 165–81.

13. Daniel M. Hausman and Michael S. McPherson, "Taking Ethics Seriously: Economics and Contemporary Moral Philosophy," *Journal of Economic Literature* 31 (1993): 671–731.

14. Hilary Putnam, *The Collapse of the Fact/Value Dichotomy and Other Essays* (Cambridge, Mass.: Harvard University Press, 2002); and Hilary Putnam, "For Ethics and Economics without the Dichotomies," *Review of Political Economy* 15, no. 3 (2003): 395–412.

15. Putnam, "For Ethics and Economics without the Dichotomies," 396.

tion. Perception, according to Putman, "is not innocent; it is an exercise of our concepts."[16] Everything visible is so because it has been grasped from a particular perspective, that is, from a particular value scheme. To be able to perceive someone as happy, one needs to know what happiness is. A fish is not the same for a fishmonger as it is for someone looking for a pet.[17] As was expressed by Quine, statements about the external world do not "face the tribunal of sense experience" alone.[18]

Science Is Guided by Epistemic Values

In addition, Putnam also finds that science in itself is guided by epistemic values,[19] such as "coherence," "plausibility," "reasonability," and "simplicity." These are not subject to empirical demonstration but are simply a necessary guide to prevent scientific research from getting lost among the infinite options available.[20]

Scientific Language Is not Observational

The language of natural sciences in itself makes abundant use of terms and principles that are not empirically observable. The expressions "cognitively meaningful" or "nonsense" used in logical positivism are neither observational nor logical, nor are they mathematical terminology.[21] Thus, the positivistic goal would be self-defeating.

Common Language Is Cognitively Meaningful

Putnam abides by our common knowledge to render untenable the idea that scientific language is the only one that is "cognitively meaningful."[22] We must, he says, stop equating objectivity with description because describing the world is one extremely important function of language but not the only function; there are many sorts of statements

16. Putnam, *The Collapse of the Fact/Value Dichotomy and Other Essays*, 102.
17. Cheshire Calhoun, "Emotion, Feeling, and Knowledge of the World," in *Thinking about Feeling: Contemporary Philosophers on Emotions*, ed. R. C. Solomon (New York: Oxford University Press, 2004), 114.
18. Quine, "Two Dogmas of Empiricism," 38.
19. Putnam, *The Collapse of the Fact/Value Dichotomy and Other Essays*, 30.
20. Other authors that argue along the same lines are Mariano Artigas, *The Mind of the Universe: Understanding Science and Religion* (Philadelphia: Templeton Foundation Press, 2000), 279; and Stanley Jaki, *The Relevance of Physics* (Chicago: University of Chicago Press, 1966), 348.
21. Putnam, *The Collapse of the Fact/Value Dichotomy and Other Essays*, 34, 106.
22. Ibid., 34.

"that are not descriptions, but that are under rational control, governed by standards appropriate to their particular functions and contexts."[23]

Rational Character of Evaluative Judgments

Moral judgments are logically independent of one's affective state. In logical positivism, the description of value judgments is a combination of propositions of facts and a volitional (a moral imperative or a normative rule) or emotional state regarding these facts. For example, saying, "Tax evasion is wrong," consists of a description (operation done for tax evasion) and the expression of personal disapproval, or an imperative prescription (this fact is wrong). Putnam rejects such a scheme, following Anderson, because motivational states such as boredom, weakness, apathy, self-contempt, or despair "can make a person fail to desire what she judges to be good or desire what she judges to be bad,"[24] judgments about good or bad (moral judgments) have to be logically independent of our affective state—although their connection to this state can be very important in our daily lives. But what about the normative statement added to the description of facts? A second reason responds to this question. Let us consider, for example, how to identify the "descriptive meaning" of the word *cruel* without using the word *cruel* or a synonym.[25] It seems evident that there are situations, like cruelty, which are understandable only from a moral point of view.[26] Without our resorting to evaluative aspects, some situations cannot be intelligible, and hence, their description is only made available from a moral point of view. Putnam concludes that evaluative judgment functions as a cognitive statement about an action's wrongness or rightness.

Sen's 1967 article "The Nature and Classes of Prescriptive Judgments" also emphasizes the rational character of evaluative judgments by arguing that the rational discussion of evaluative matters is always possible. Only a few basic value judgments cannot be justified on rational grounds. The ability to provide reasons is a distinctive feature of evaluative judgments in contrast to purely prescriptive statements (imperatives), so they cannot be identified with each other.

23. Ibid., 33.

24. John R. Anderson, *Rules of the Mind* (Hillsdale, N.J.: Erlbaum, 1993), 102.

25. Putnam, *The Collapse of the Fact/Value Dichotomy and Other Essays*, 38.

26. Putnam, "For Ethics and Economics without the Dichotomies," 399–400; cf. Hausman and McPherson, "Taking Ethics Seriously," 671.

Some Descriptions Are of Implicitly Normative Content

Searle, by discussing if "ought to" could be derived from "is," argues that some descriptions have a normative content. He provides the following example: If Jones uttered the words, "I hereby promise to pay you, Smith, five dollars," this is a factual statement from which one can deduce the evaluative statement: "John ought to pay Smith five dollars." This is because the very notion of promise is already in itself a normative concept: "To recognize something as a promise is to grant that, other things being equal, it ought to be kept."[27] Thus, a description of a promise entails a normative element. Better said, however odd it might sound, it is an evaluative description.[28]

Descriptions with Teleological Content
Entail Prescriptions

From the description "John wants to see a football match," one cannot logically infer that "one ought to provide him with a ticket for this football match" because this is a pure description of a desire. In statements such as this, *is* does not imply *ought*. However, there are things with which a telos (an end to be achieved, including objective, function, role or goal) is intrinsically associated. Saying "a good knife," "a good watch," or "a good farm" denotes what a knife, a watch, or a farm is

27. Searle, "How to Derive 'Ought' from 'Is,'" 51.
28. A possible objection to this would be that, in cases like the description of someone making a promise, one is dealing with propositions of fact disguised as propositions of value, or the other way around (Searle, "How to Derive 'Ought' from 'Is,'" 54). But this just seems to confirm Searle's argument, because it rather points to the fact that expressions of commitment or obligation cannot be accurately described without reference to a normative framework. To shed some light on that, Searle turns to the distinction between regulative and constitutive rules: the first "regulate activities whose existence is independent of the rules," such as polite table behavior, that regulates eating, while "constitutive rules constitute (and also regulate) forms of activity whose existence is logically dependent on the rules" (ibid., 55), such as chess or promises. The intelligibility of the institution of promising depends on the concepts of obligation and accountability; it is not a "brute fact"—as eating perhaps might be—but derives its very existence and meaning from those concepts (ibid., 54). That is why any factual description of activities placed under constitutive rules *is* an evaluative description. From a different perspective, Black demonstrates that propositions of value, such as "Fischer should move the Queen," cannot be transformed into propositions of fact, such as "The one and only way in which Fischer can win is by moving the Queen," without losing significant undercurrents of meaning: "a speaker who uses this form of words counts as doing something more than, or something other than, saying something having truth value" (Black, "The Gap between 'Is' and 'Should,'" 171).

supposed to do or be in accordance with their function or role: a good knife cuts well, a good watch keeps the time accurately, and a good farm is a productive acreage. If the factual-teleological statement refers to people, one can deduce prescriptions.[29] Of course, one can analyze "technical facts," but the facts are more than technical aspects. Facts entail morality. Thus, you can say that Bernard Madoff used a Ponzi scheme (technical aspect), but the real fact is that Madoff committed fraud by using a Ponzi scheme, a major fraud, incidentally, of some $64.8 billion, according to the estimation of the prosecutors.[30] The facts-and-values dichotomy is no longer defendable.[31]

UTILITARIANISM AND ITS SHORTCOMINGS

Since the nineteenth century, in addition to positivism, many economists have used utilitarianism as the social or ethical philosophy underlying their economic theory. One reason for this is that economics emerged as a discipline in the nineteenth century coincided with the dominance of utilitarianism as social and ethical philosophy. Other reasons could be that utilitarianism poses few restraints on markets, and some defend the position that this theory presents itself as "value free" and respectful of what the mass of the population wants without imposing personal values on others. As a matter of fact, since the nineteenth century, "the social philosophy of economists has almost invariably been grounded in utilitarian social philosophy, whether the laissez-faire creed of the nineteenth century or the statism of the twentieth."[32]

Utilitarianism was introduced by Jeremy Bentham (1748–1832) and refined by John Stuart Mill, although its deep roots began with the Greek philosopher Epicurus, British thinkers Thomas Hobbes and John Locke, and thinkers of Scottish Enlightenment philosophy, mainly Francis Hutcheson.[33] Utilitarianism is a type of consequentialism because it focuses on consequences of the human action. Bentham defined

---

29. See an extended explanation in Alasdair MacIntyre's *After Virtue: A Study in Moral Theory*, 2nd ed. (Notre Dame, Ind.: University of Notre Dame Press, 1984), 56–60.

30. "Madoff Mysteries Remain as He Nears Guilty Plea," Reuters, March 11, 2009, retrieved July 11, 2015.

31. Putnam, *The Collapse of the Fact/Value Dichotomy and Other Essays*.

32. Murray N. Rothbard, *The Ethics of Liberty* (New York: New York University Press, 1998), 201.

33. Julia Driver, "The History of Utilitarianism," in *The Stanford Encyclopedia of Philosophy*, ed. E. N. Zalta, 2009, http://plato.stanford.edu/archives/sum2009/entries/utilitarianism-history/.

the principle of utility as that which "approves or disapproves of every action whatsoever, according to the tendency it appears to have to augment or diminish the happiness of the party whose interest is in question: or, what is the same thing in other words, to promote or to oppose that happiness."[34] According to this fundamental principle, happiness is the good to be pursued. Thus, he follows Epicurus, who assumed a hedonistic view of "good." Utilitarianism understands as useful whatever produces pleasure, and pleasure is equated with happiness. Thus, the Principle of Utility could be formulated as "whatever provides the greatest happiness for the highest number is right."

The starting point of Bentham is observing that all people naturally seek pleasure. This descriptive theory, known as *psychological hedonism*, becomes prescriptive in stating that a right action is productive of pleasure, while a wrong action is productive of pain, and consequently people should pursue pleasure. Psychological hedonism is, therefore, based on the self-interest of individuals and their motivation for obtaining pleasure and avoiding pain. Bentham begins *An Introduction to the Principles of Morals and Legislation*, published first in 1789, with a clear statement of psychological hedonism: "Nature has placed mankind under the governance of two sovereign masters, *pain* and *pleasure*. It is for them alone to point out what we ought to do, as well as determine what we shall do."[35] According to ethical utilitarianism, psychological hedonism combined with the fundamental Principle of Utility, mentioned earlier, is the complete morality. Bentham argued that there are no qualitative differences between pleasures, only quantitative ones. This position was refined by John Stuart Mill by distinguishing between sensual pleasures, which humans share with animals, from intellectual pleasures, which are higher pursuits. However, Mill's view of morality is equally to maximize pleasure while minimizing pain for those affected by the action. Similarly, general happiness is "a good to the aggregate of all persons."[36] Thus, both authors combine empirical data (pleasure/pain and satisfaction/dissatisfaction) with a rationality to calculate what action permits the attainment of maximum pleasure with a minimum of pain, not for a single individual but for a collective.

34. Jeremy Bentham, *An Introduction to the Principles of Morals and Legislation* (Oxford: Clarendon Press, 1907 [1789]), I, 3, http://www.econlib.org/library/Bentham/bnthPML1.html.

35. Ibid., I, 1; emphasis in original.

36. John Stuart Mill, *Utilitarianism* (Peterborough, Ontario: Broadview Press, 2010 [1861]), 81.

The Principle of Utility considers the sum of individual happiness, taking as a given that each person counts equally. Thus, the notion of *social welfare*, or satisfaction of the majority, emerges as a key for a political economy based on "social costs" and "social benefits." Although at first glance the rule of morality in utilitarianism may appear attractive, it exhibits significant shortcomings, and several criticisms can, in fact, be made of utilitarianism, as will be seen. Some of these criticisms regard flaws of its internal structure and of certain practical aspects of the theory. Others involve the inadequacy of utilitarianism in dealing with real economic behavior within a market economy and in certain sociocultural contexts. A third group of criticisms— which, ethically speaking, are the deepest—refer to the concept of morality underlying utilitarianism, including how "good" is understood and the consideration of people, in their dignity, diversity, and rights.

Internal Shortcomings: Practical Difficulties in Applying Utilitarianism

The theoretical framework of utilitarianism requires measuring pleasure and pain and an arithmetical calculation of satisfaction and the quantitative maximization of satisfaction of all people affected by an action, seeking to produce more happiness or to increase the happiness in the world. Projecting the principle of utility to social philosophy leads one to take the individual's worldly happiness as the only valid test of social institutions. This presents a number of difficulties. One is that pleasure is very difficult to measure, and the means that can be used to do so are far from homogeneous. How is one to measure the satisfaction of a cyclist who has just won the Tour de France and the pain of being fired from a good job position? As John Rawls noted, utilitarianism treats a group of many as a single sentient entity, ignoring the separation of consciousness.[37]

Another difficulty is foreseeing consequences in both individual and collective decisions, especially in the middle and long terms. This is the case of well-known accidents in nuclear plants, such as that of Fukushima in Japan in 2011 after a strong tsunami and the accident at the Chernobyl Nuclear Plant in the Ukraine in 1986 during a systems test. Another nuclear accident, occurring at Three Mile Island in the United States in 1979, has been analyzed and given as an example of the difficul-

---

37. John Rawls, *A Theory of Justice* (Cambridge, Mass.: Harvard University Press, 1971), 22–27.

ties in calculating happiness considering the long-term effects.[38] Foreseeable consequences of an accident were the cause of further consequences that were ever more unpredictable. Geach gives two examples. One is the decision by Brutus to kill Caesar. As a consequence, a war breaks out between the armies of Brutus and Antony in which many innocent people were killed. Another example is that of a young man mulling over a marriage proposal by use of utilitarian methodology.[39] The author also stresses the uncertainty of large-scale planning derived from the scientific and technological progress that makes the future unpredictable in many aspects, because one can go only by what has been discovered and not by what will be discovered.[40]

Shortcomings in the Social Sphere: Insufficiency to Create a Good Society

A second shortcoming regards the possibility of a market system based on utilitarianism to create a good society. At this point, Smith's well-known idea of the "invisible hand" recurs: through the universal search for personal self-interest, an "invisible hand" will bring about a more prosperous society than that which is achieved when people seek the common good. Competitive markets, combined with self-interest in terms of the cost/benefit ratio, generate the highest value of desired products at the lowest investment of limited resources. Thus, one could argue that this is the best for the society.

Another utilitarianism-based argument regarding market morality is respect for individual freedom in making choices and the subsequent evaluation of their satisfaction. This entails respect for individual autonomy and allows those who participate in the market to express their beliefs and moral values in making transactions by buying or rejecting goods and services. In line with this idea, many people may consider that such morality is sufficient, thinking that any external standard of right and wrong can be applied to the market. These people "see morality in the market as nothing more than the verdict rendered by the sum of total individual of individual decisions."[41]

38. Daniel Dennett, *Darwin's Dangerous Idea* (New York: Simon and Schuster, 1995).
39. Peter Geach, *The Virtues* (Cambridge: Cambridge University Press, 1977), 99.
40. Ibid., 103.
41. Rebecca M. Blank and William McGurn, *Is the Market Moral? A Dialogue on Religion, Economics, and Justice* (Washington, D.C.: Brookings Institution Press, 2004), 85.

Both arguments are flawed. On one hand, there is no doubt that discussing what a good society is and how free markets can contribute to its realization is crucial, but what would happen if everyone assumed that the only aim of the society was to maximize general prosperity in economic terms? What if such prosperity is not shared by everybody? On the other hand, while such a society of virtuous people would be nice, it seems naïve to assume this and to think that only virtuous choices will be sufficient for market morality. Another objection, related to this narrow view of a good society, has been pointed out by Rose in his pedagogical question: "*If a society's sole objective is to maximize general prosperity and it can choose its own moral beliefs, what kinds of moral beliefs would it choose?*"[42]

Seeking self-interest can justify poor working conditions and a lack of respect for basic human rights, immoderate exploitation of natural resources, a lack of concern for waste and pollution, processes or products that negatively affect human safety, and so on. Regarding transactions, acting with self-interest and in the pursuit of economic prosperity, without any further consideration, can justify selling any type of product, including hard drugs, or the provision of any kind of "services," such as prostitution or the sale of children on the Internet.

A market system exclusively based on utilitarianism can bring about an inhuman society. In contemporary society, many people would accept the need for greater morality than that of utilitarianism and would agree that some legal regulations should be included in the market system. Thus, it is widely assumed that the market system includes the claim that companies should recognize and include external costs (environmental damage, for instance) in such a way that no firm can freeload on society as well as that no single individual or company can achieve economic dominance over others. Some defend a wider vision of utilitarianism, which is not only limited to the evaluation of the outcomes but also includes the process employed to obtain them ("process utilitarianism"). This will exclude, for instance, a market for adopting babies, even though it could be very efficient.[43] However, even so, utilitarianism is insufficient.

David Rose has presented the case for creating trust in the market

---

42. Rose, *The Moral Foundation of Economic Behavior*, 4; emphasis in original.
43. Bhagwati, "Markets and Morality," 162.

by using utilitarianism or other consequentialists approach. He argues in favor of the superiority of a nonconsequentialist deontological approach. One of Rose's basic points is that in many cases, an action that might cause obvious harm in one-on-one interactions and thus would be prohibited by an injunction to "do no harm" either does not cause harm or causes no perceptible harm in larger communities. He gives as an example the employment of deception by one of the parties in an exchange involving two persons, and making a fraudulent claim to an insurance company, for instance, by reporting damage which includes a scratched door, which will cost say $500, even though the accident for which the report is filed did not in fact affect that part of the car's body. No one will notice because no one can reasonably be aware of the true circumstances of the accident. In addition, the figure involved will have a negligible impact on the profits of the insurance company, which might run into the millions, or even billions, of dollars. The perception of the dissatisfaction of each individual shareholder regarding this fraud will be inexistent and, thus, can be completely disregarded. So, in accordance with utilitarian principles, this action is right. However, if this action is widespread among the client base, this behavior can seriously harm the company and lead to an increase in premiums charged by the insurance company to all. Rose concludes that when one wishes to advocate a set of moral beliefs that will maximize general prosperity, he or she should focus on principles rather than on utilitarian calculations, the reason being that this brings about more trust and that trust is essential for doing business and for operating markets properly. He affirms this, stating, "[O]nly when moral restraint is regarded as a matter of duty will it produce unconditional trustworthiness where doing so matters most."[44]

The Major Shortcoming: Morality Underlying Utilitarianism

The first philosophical objection to utilitarianism is *the philosophical anthropology underlying* this theory. As noted, only *feeling* and *calculative rationality* are taken into account in considering the human being, when, obviously, we are much more than this. Human life seems reduced to pursuing pleasure and to avoiding pain.

On the other hand, *utilitarianism is not value free at all*. In reducing

---

44. Rose, *The Moral Foundation of Economic Behavior*, 141.

good to pleasure, this normative theory accepts that the unique value is just this: pleasure, a view that has consequences for shaping a good society. In a recent book, Ross Douthat severely criticized the social situation in the United States, one created by certain preferences and their corresponding economic behaviors. According to him, the United States has become a "nation of gamblers and speculators, gluttons and gym obsessives, pornographers and Ponzi schemers, in which household debt rises alongside public debt, and bankers and pensioners and automakers and unions all compete to empty the public trough."[45] Some may agree and others will not, but what is clear is that some of these behaviors could be justified through utilitarianism, this being based on preferences and on the supremacy of the greatest happiness for the greatest number. Certainly, for utilitarianism, the morality of the product is irrelevant—you may equally well be selling cars, pornography, drugs, or human organs. Likewise, the type of culture and social capital that relationships based on utilitarianism generate does not matter; neither does the risk of corrosion of the character of people involved in doing market transactions come into account.

Both establishing some scale or differentiation of degrees of the intensity of pleasure and distinguishing intellectual from sensorial pleasures (with those of a spiritual order considered superior to those of the sensual and materialistic) may improve utilitarian theory. However, this distinction is made within the category of pleasure without considering what motivates the actor's behavior. It is hard to accept, say, that the sacrifice of a mother caring for her ill child over a long period is the concurrence of spiritual and sensitive pleasures. Similarly, it is striking to affirm that acting with a strong sense of self-giving, as was the case of Mother Teresa of Calcutta taking care of the poorest, is solely a question of "spiritual" pleasure.

In addition to the flawed foundation of the utilitarian notion of "good," the aprioristic statement that a decision is ethically right only when it follows the wishes of the greater number as against those of the lesser number is also questionable. This denies the rights of minorities and even some human rights. In a town in which a vast majority was racist, the happiness of the greater number could involve violating the

45. Ross Douthat, *Bad Religion: How We Became a Nation of Heretics* (New York: Free Press, 2012), 25.

human rights of an ethnic minority. Similarly, utilitarianism could be used to justify slavery, torture, abortion, all kinds of lies, and so on, if the perceived benefits were large enough to outweigh the direct and extreme pain of people who are damaged.

It does not seem acceptable that the greatest happiness or benefit for the greatest number can be obtained by following the wishes of a greater number against those of a smaller number, especially if the minority's wishes are founded on better information or on a more solid rationale. This is the problem of populism, an ideology in which politicians claim the side of "the people" against "the elites," which, in fact, is not always a guarantee of good governance. According to Peter Geach, "the radical difficulty [of utilitarianism] arises from the double superlative, if it is taken seriously and not just a piece of piling-up rhetoric."[46]

From a different perspective, some authors have stressed the inadequacy of utilitarianism in dealing with developing countries because its lack of sensitivity to the diversity and oppressive hierarchy within these countries, suggesting the necessity of deontological values, such as justice, rights, and attention to cultural diversity.[47]

A final objection to utilitarianism is that "third-person ethics," that is, an ethics in which the moral character and the effects on the decision maker, are completely beyond any consideration. In this way, utilitarianism becomes a simple rational tool for making public or corporate decisions, without considering what will or may happen within the agent or how this will condition future decisions.

CHRISTIAN HUMANISM

Christian humanism, especially that presented by Catholic social teaching, which I consider here, contrasts with both positivism and utilitarianism. Facing the narrow rationality of positivism, discussed earlier, Benedict XVI has suggested the necessity of "broadening our concept of reason and its application" beyond scientific rationality and, therefore, without "the self-imposed limitation of reason to the empirically

---

46. Geach, *The Virtues*, 91.

47. Sita C. Amba-Rao, "Multinational Corporate Social Responsibility, Ethics, Interactions and Third World Governments: An Agenda for the 1990s," *Journal of Business Ethics*, 12, no. 7 (July 1993): 553–72; and Cornelius B. Pratt, "Multinational Corporate Social Policy Process for Ethical Responsibility in Sub-Saharan Africa," *Journal of Business Ethics* 10, no. 7 (July 1991): 527–41.

falsifiable."[48] Christian humanism is also opposed to utilitarianism, not only in its way of understanding what is "good" but also on account of its anthropology and the vision of human life. Utilitarianism, wrote John Paul II, is an approach "where the morality of human acts would be judged without any reference to the man's true ultimate end."[49]

The anthropological error of utilitarianism, mentioned earlier, is particularly emphasized by authors aligned with Cristian Humanism. Thus, Wojtyla wrote, "The Utilitarian considers pleasure important in itself, and, with his general view of man, fails to see that he is quite conspicuously an amalgam of matter and spirit, the two complementary factors which together create one personal existence, whose specific nature is due entirely to the soul."[50] As a vision of life, utilitarianism is like a channel "along which the lives of individuals and collectives have [a] tendency to flow throughout the ages. In modern times, however, what we have to deal with is a conscious utilitarianism, formulated from philosophical premises and with scientific precision."[51] As noted, persons are solely considered as subjects of pleasure and pain. Intention, character, personal conscience is left out of this theory. As St. John Paul II wrote, "Utilitarianism is a civilization of production and of use, a civilization of 'things' and not of 'persons,' a civilization in which persons are used in the same way as things are used."[52] Geach reminds us that, in accordance with the Judeo-Cristian tradition, God is not utilitarian. He chose one people from among others for his revelation. In addition, Geach argued, if God were utilitarian, we could not rely on his faithfulness and truth, for he might know that false revelation and promise breaking on his part worked out for the best. All great religions show that they believe God cannot renege on his promises.[53]

Utilitarianism and Christian humanism are both teleological; both focus on the effects of the action, but their respective teleological ap-

48. Benedict XVI, "Faith, Reason and the University: Memories and Reflections," Lecture addressed to representatives of science at the Aula Magna of the University of Regensburg (September 12, 2006); available at http://www.vatican.va/holy_father/benedict_xvi/ speeches/2006/september/documents/hf_ben-xvi_spe_20060912_university-regensburg_en.html.

49. John Paul II, Encyclical *Veritatis Splendor* (Vatican City: Libreria Editrice Vaticana, 1993), 74.

50. Karol Wojtyla, *Love and Responsibility* (San Francisco: Harper-Collins, 1981), 35; first published in Polish as *Miłość i Odpowiedzialnosc: Studium etyczne* (Lublin: KUL, 1960).

51. Ibid., 35.

52. John Paul II, *Letter to Families*, 13.

53. Geach, *The Virtues*, 96.

proaches are completely different. While utilitarianism considers the whole life in the effects of each action in terms of pleasure and pain, Christian humanism considers human flourishing as central to human life and the effects of the action in terms of human dignity and integral human development. Christian humanism is rooted not only in the Christian faith but also in reason. Human flourishing is a finding of reason, and on this point, Christian humanism shares the view of Aristotle and of other pioneers in moral philosophy. On this human level, faith shows that there is also a calling to holiness in living in communion with Christ.

Thus, Christian humanism is not opposed to utilitarianism only as a matter of faith, and even less as a confrontation between science and religion. It is a matter of how reason understands the human being. Utilitarianism is proved neither by science nor by logic; it is on the stage merely through being accepted by many people. On its part, Christian humanism can be explained on a rational basis and be accepted as valid in constructing a social order for large quantities of people.

Utilitarianism has its deep roots in the vision of the modernity shared by Descartes, Hobbes, Locke, Hume, and Mill, among others, which is quite mechanical in nature and very much in contrast to the classical "teleological" vision of Plato, Aristotle, Augustine, and Aquinas, in which purpose or goal directedness is an inherent feature of the world.[54]

Christian humanism proposes a different epistemology from that of positivism. Far from a radical separation of facts and values, and considering economic activity as free-values facts, Christian humanism understands that economic activity is, first of all, human activity. Obviously, it has an economic content, but human acts also imply intentionality and a moral content. From this perspective, economic activity is much more than mere transactions; these transactions are human interactions, which involve values such as the recognition of the other party as a person, trust, and a certain sense of reciprocity. Subsequently, markets are networks of relationships between people.

In addition, Christian Humanism presents *a comprehensive view of the human being* and assumes a more profound teleology, according to which humans are not limited to a set of interests and a search for immedi-

54. Edward Feser, *The Last Superstition: A Refutation of the New Atheism* (South Bend, Ind.: St. Augustine's Press, 2008).

ate satisfaction from the consequences of an action but toward human flourishing. This requires a full consideration of the human good rather than one that reduces it to its utilitarian value. A more complete view of the human being also requires an emphasis upon human relationability and sociability as basic features of the human nature and the necessity of social life for growing in humanity.

Christian humanism *fosters a set of moral values* such as freedom, honesty, transparency, and others that favor trust and lead to a sound free market, operating without distortions. These values, along with concern for people make markets more human. This goal is absent in Utilitarianism but is essential to Christian humanism. What is more, cultures in which Christian humanism is embedded can help economic activity by providing a sense of universal brotherhood and solidarity.

Christian humanism *is transcendent*, which also differentiates it from positivism and utilitarianism, in which God is irrelevant. Being transcendent, Christian humanism provides a high motivation for good behavior. This motivation may be relevant in some actions, in which the victim is not identifiable or the harm produced toward others is little, although multiplied by being distributed among many people. The spontaneous motivation might be to commit such a negative moral action rather than refraining from it, unless you have a strong moral motivation. Here religion, including Christian humanism, can provide this motivation and can lead to the development of moral character and to the creation of moral reputation. This generates trust, because trust appears when I know you will not engage in negative moral actions even when you have the opportunity to do so.

The ethics of Christian humanism is *a first-person ethics* and not the third-person ethics, which characterizes the other two streams of thought I have been considering. A first-person ethics involves seeking prudential judgments beyond aprioristic principles and complex arithmetic calculations and takes into account how decision making influences character and future decisions. This does not exclude, however, a few principles based on human flourishing, such as respect for human dignity, human development, and the common good. The latter is an important concept in Christian humanism drawn from Catholic social tradition. The common good is the reference for the moral legitimacy of any social activity or institution. Within this tradition, the common good "is not simply the sum total of particular interests; rather it involves an assessment and integration of those interests on the basis of a balanced hierarchy of values; ultimately, it demands a correct understanding of the dignity and the rights of the person."[55] The common good is the good "that is linked to living in society ... It is the good of 'all of us,' made up of individuals, families and intermediate groups who together constitute society.[56] It is a good that is sought not for its own sake, but for the people who belong to the social community and who can only really and effectively pursue their good within it."[57]

Consistently, such humanism "recognizes the positive value of the market and of enterprise, but which at the same time points out that these need to be oriented towards the common good."[58]

While Christian humanism fosters values and virtues, such those mentioned previously, which can introduce morality in the choices made in the market economy, it also requires laws and institutions with can frame such an economy. In this respect, Pope John Paul II, speaking on the acceptability of capitalism, wrote,

If by "capitalism" is meant an economic system which recognizes the funda-mental and positive role of business, the market, private property and the result-ing responsibility for the means of production, as well as free human creativ-ity in the economic sector, then the answer is certainly in the affirmative, even though it would perhaps be more appropriate to speak of a "business economy," "market economy" or simply "free economy." But if by "capitalism" is meant a system in which freedom in the economic sector is not circumscribed within a strong juridical framework which places it at the service of human freedom in its totality, and which sees it as a particular aspect of that freedom, the core of which is ethical and religious, then the reply is certainly negative.[59]

CONCLUSION

Positivism is often aligned with utilitarianism to the end of looking at economic activity rationally. In this chapter, I have pointed out the er-

55. John Paul II, Encyclical *Centesimus Annus* (Vatican City: Libreria Editrice), 47.
56. Cf. Vatican Council II, Pastoral Constitution *Gaudium et Spes* (Vatican City: Libreria Edi-trice Vaticana, 1965), 26, where the common good is defined as "the sum of those conditions of social life which allow social groups and their individual members relatively thorough and ready access to their own fulfillment."
57. Benedict XVI, Encyclical *Caritas in Veritate* (Vatican City: Libreria Editrice Vaticana, 2009), 7.
58. John Paul II, *Centesimus Annus*, 43.
59. Ibid., 42.

roneous view of positivism and its narrow rationality, which focuses only on technical or economic facts. In contrast, Christian humanism proposes a wider rationality, which includes empirical data and the scientific method but without reducing knowledge to only this method. It tries to identify what things are from a realistic epistemology and takes into consideration the human being and the meaning of human life.

I have also discussed several shortcomings of the theory of utilitarianism, including its notion of good reduced to pleasure, and the utility principle as the exclusive rule of morality. I stressed that rather than being a tool for decision making, utilitarianism entails a vision of the human being and a whole philosophy of life that stops considerably short of consideration for human flourishing.

I have argued that a different moral foundation for economic behavior is necessary for a good and prosperous society. Christian humanism proposes a broader rationality, a complete view of the human being and a teleology favoring human flourishing. This entails ethical values, principles, and human virtues, beyond focusing on the satisfaction for consequences of the action. Consequently, we suggest advancing toward a Christian humanism that not only avoids the previously mentioned shortcomings of the other two approaches but also allows us a more complete understanding of economic activity beyond measurable data and the application of deontological values and virtues. Christian humanism seems much more appropriate for the generating of trust, something that is crucial for economic activity.

THREE

The Morality of the Market from a Theory of Personal Action

Javier Aranzadi

The current crisis, with its constant corporate and financial scandals, is having a very dangerous effect.[1] It is calling into question the role of the market economy and the importance of the firm as a social institution. As Ghoshal says, "Of far greater concern is the general delegitimization of companies as institutions and of management as a profession."[2] In fact, there is a currently widespread perception that the destructive aspect of the market process dominates the economic reality. The market economy is accused of being essentially greedy and pernicious, as in the critique of the "immorality" or "amorality" of capitalism.[3] Obviously, there are many examples of such greedy and immoral behaviors in the economic system. However, the description of contemporary corporate culture in such destructive terms is a very narrow vision.[4]

In this chapter, I adopt the Aristotelian point of view of the acting person, which understands the human as the generator of positive actions. It presents freedom as the search for excellence in action. In this light, I develop two fundamental aspects of human nature.

Activity is the starting point. Aristotle places heavy emphasis on the

---

1. It should be noted that this chapter follows on a previous article titled "The Natural Link between Virtue Ethics and Political Virtue: The Morality of the Market," which appeared in the *Journal of Business Ethics* 118 (2013): 487–96.

2. Sumantra Ghoshal, "Bad Management Theories are Destroying Good Management Practices," *Academy of Management Learning and Education* 41 (2005): 76.

3. Edward Freeman, "Business Ethics at the Millennium," *Business Ethics Quarterly* 10, no. 1 (2000): 171.

4. John Dobson, "Alasdair Macintyre's Aristotelian Business Ethics: A Critique," *Journal of Business Ethics* 86 (2009): 43–50.

fact that the life of *eudaimonia* is a lifetime of activity: "it is a true and reasoned state of capacity to act with regard to the things that are good or bad for man. For while making has an end other than itself, action cannot; for good action itself is its end."[5] Thus, we know human virtues through human actions; we can use the names of virtues or potencies to represent human nature. Our starting point in the study of economics and ethics is therefore human action, as K. Wojtyla masterfully points out: "from human action we derive knowledge not only of the fact that man is its 'subject,' but also of who man is as the subject of his own action. Action, as man's dynamics understood in their totality, permits us to understand better and more closely the subjectivity of man."[6]

Second, the person is a *zoon politikon*. As Solomon said, "the Aristotelian approach begins with the idea that we are, first of all, members of organized groups ... we are not, as our favorite folklore would have it, first of all individuals—that is, autonomous, self-sustaining, self-defining creatures."[7] Coexistence and common participation in determined values and beliefs where the means and ends that constitute individual action are configured. It is entirely suitable, therefore, to define the human being as the Aristotelian *zoon politikon*. With this expression, the person's essential openness to his or her fellow people by means of society and culture is indicated. Thus, every individual action is social and holds cultural significance.[8]

As a consequence of these two aspects of the formal structure of human nature, we can highlight the inappropriateness of studies that seek to set the individual against society. An opposition between isolated individual natural rights and society conceals the intrinsic relationship between the various dimensions of action. A tension appears between self-

5. Aristotle, "Nicomachean Ethics," in *The Complete Works of Aristotle, Volume 2.* The Revised Oxford Translation, ed. Jonathan Barnes (Princeton, N.J.: Princeton University Press, 1984), 6, 1140b4-6, 1800.

6. Karol Wojtyla, "The Person: Subject and Community," *Review of Metaphysics* 33, no. 2 (1979): 273.

7. Robert C. Solomon, *Ethics and Excellence: Cooperation and Integrity in Business* (New York: Oxford University Press, 1992), 146.

8. As the Spanish philosopher Xavier Zubiri points out: "This with (with things, with other men, with me myself) is not something extra, an extrinsic relation, added to man in the exercise of his life. This would be absolutely chimerical. It is something much more radical. The with is a formal structural stage of life itself and therefore of human substantiveness in its vital dynamism." See Xavier Zubiri, *Dynamic Structure of Reality*, trans. N. R. Orringer (Urbana: University of Illinois Press, 2003), 255.

interest ("liberty from") and solidarity ("liberty for"). Yet, as J. Annas points out, "Eudaimonistic theories do not permit this kind of split to develop. Reasoning about my own interests differs neither in kind nor in its sphere from reasoning about the interest of others."[9] Aristotelian ethics is structured around a system of goods, norms, and virtues that are shaped by means of individual action in the institutions of a particular culture. Such action is substantively individual ("liberty from") but with inseparable social and cultural dimensions ("liberty for"). All individuals choose courses of action by deciding what type of life is worth living. In this view, individual virtue (*areté*) occupies a key position, defining the paradigm that each society and culture sets as the model of life to be lived (*eudaimonia*).

But human action has its social, cultural, and historical facets. As Rhonheimer says, "'Human rights' and 'natural rights' are always historically variable since they can only exist within concrete and ever shifting historical conditions."[10] Obviously, if the person is a *zoon politikon* natural rights do not exist prior to the political reality because there is no such a thing as abstract natural rights. As A. MacIntyre remarks, "this would be like presenting a check for payment in a social order that lacked the institution of money."[11] In other words, an abstract "liberty from" does not exist. As Crisp and Slote[12] comment in their account of virtue ethics, a gap exists between Aristotelian virtue ethics in the ancient Greek city-state, in which the politics were *polis-ethics*,[13] and the modern pluralistic modern democracies,[14] where the abstract individual natural rights ("liberty from") reigns. This great historical difference makes it difficult to apply virtue ethics to modern societies.[15] There is a modern dichotomy between individual rights and social morality. A

9. Julia Annas, *The Morality of Happiness* (Oxford: Oxford University Press, 1995), 323.

10. Martin Rhonheimer, *The Perspective of Morality* (Washington, D.C.: The Catholic University of America Press, 2011), 234.

11. MacIntyre, *After Virtue*, 67.

12. Cf. Roger Crisp and Michael Slote, eds. *Virtue Ethics* (Oxford: Oxford University Press, 1997).

13. See Martin Rhonheimer, "Perché una filosofia politica? Elementi storici per una risposta," *Acta Philosophica* 1, no. 2 (1992): 233–63.

14. Cf. Charles Larmore, *Patterns of Moral Complexity* (Cambridge: Cambridge University Press, 1987).

15. On this point, see Robert Louden, "On Some Vices of Virtue Ethics," *American Philosophical Quarterly* 21 (1984): 227–36; and Jerome Schneewind, "The Misfortunes of Virtue," *Ethics* 101 (1990): 42–63.

true political ethics cannot only be an ethics of virtues; it must also be an ethics of institutions. Despite all the reservations one may have, this is the essence of modern political philosophy from Hobbes to Rawls, by way of Kant. We need to achieve a balance between a virtue ethics and an ethics of institutions that supersedes moralizing fundamentalism confined to individual ends (liberty "from") and that deals with the means leading to the institutional realization of such ends: the common good (liberty "for"). Peace, freedom, human dignity, and justice are the key themes of classical political liberalism. In the perspective of *praxis*, it is impossible to separate ends and means. An end can only acquire form and become effective on the horizon of a particular means; hence, any political morality must take a stand on specifically political questions related to the institutional, legal, and economic requirements necessary in each particular historical situation.[16]

The firm-based market economy has very positive moral content: the possibility of excellence of human action. The market economy is the means to economic development and prosperity. Firms based on people acting together, sharing the culture of the organization governed by virtue-based ethics, create and distribute most of the economy's wealth, innovate, trade, and raise living standards. The firm is an institution that performs a very important practice: fostering new possibilities of individual action.

The structure of this chapter is as follows: First, the object of social institutions is presented. Institutions fulfill three functions: they satisfy needs, coordinate the behavior of individuals, and provide norms of conduct and values to be shared by individuals. Then I set out that entrepreneurship, understood as the human faculty to create new ends and means of action, is the driving force behind the market. Continuing with this same line of thought, I next show the firm's social importance: the firm's

16. Daniel Statman, speculating about the relationship between virtue ethics and political philosophy, suggests that communitarianism might turn out to be the political aspect of virtue ethics. See Daniel Statman, "Introduction to Virtue Ethics," in *Virtue Ethics*, ed. Daniel Statman (Edinburgh: Edinburgh University Press, 1997), 18. In this chapter, I defend another possibility. For me, the political aspect of virtue ethics is liberalism but not the liberalism not based on the mainstream economics of *homo economicus*. My account of liberalism is based on human action and institutional processes following Mises and the Austrian School of economics. On the differences within liberalism between the so-called scientific reductionism of the liberals of the Chicago School (M. Friedman, G. Becker) and the humanistic approach of the Austrian School (Mises, Hayek), see Javier Aranzadi, *Liberalism against Liberalism* (London: Routledge, 2006).

social responsibility is to enhance the possibilities of persons. Then I argue in favor of market morality and of the firm as an organization that fosters a very important social practice—the possibility of excellence in human action—before providing some concluding remarks.

THE OBJECT OF SOCIAL INSTITUTIONS

The term *institution* designates the behavioral modes established by society and introduced into social life.[17] Each culture transmits duties and does so through socializing institutions. It could be said that the structure of these duties is not a mental model for use, but a model for *doing*. As Aristotle says, "The end aimed at is not knowledge but action."[18]

Institutions can be defined as the regular common forms of life for individuals. Thus, any institution performs three functions: It (1) satisfies needs, (2) coordinates the behavior of individuals, and (3) provides norms of conduct and values shared by individuals. As D. North says, "Institutions are the humanly devised constraints that structure political, economic and social interaction. They consist of both informal constraints (sanctions, taboos, customs, traditions, and codes of conduct) and formal rules (constitutions, laws, property rights)."[19]

In principle, people come into contact with firms as institutions that operate for the purpose of satisfying needs. Such firms are stabilized in entrepreneurial cultures, that is, in behavior patterns that allow them to produce goods and services. Here, the homogenizing aspect of firms and the use of individuals as production means are found. However, productive activity is carried out by persons who procure their personal development and transform entrepreneurial relationships to fulfill their aspirations. This leads to the emergence of vital tension in which all human action unfolds, a tension between the stabilization of behavior and

17. The ideas put forward in this section have been further developed in Aranzadi, *Liberalism against Liberalism* and "The Possibilities of the Acting Person within an Institutional Framework: Goods, Norms, and Virtues," *Journal of Business Ethics* 99, no. 1 (2011): 87–100. It has been correctly noted in this context that in modern economic analysis, "given incentives" are central to the discovery of institutional arrangements that shape human behavior. I would like to point out that, following L. Mises, in my model the only real thing that is given is human action (the axiom of human action in Misesian terms) with its societal and cultural dynamic dimensions. In this approach, an alternative to mainstream economic theory, there is nothing "given" to be maximized. On this point, see n. 16.
18. Aristotle, "Nicomachean Ethics," I, 2, 1095a6, 1730.
19. Douglas North, "Institutions," *Journal of Economic Perspectives* 5, no. 1 (1991): 97.

change.[20] That is, persons are productive in a society with an already institutionalized division of labor. In essence, persons achieve fulfillment as such only by living with other persons in social institutions that shape the ordinary world with meaning that I call culture.

In this approach, institutions represent an integrated system in which the expectations of roles are rule governed. This rule must be interpreted as a reciprocal stabilization of conduct. Using this conception of expectations, one can explain the origin of the division of labor, which is the basis of economic progress. The division of labor, a particular case of great importance in the institutionalization process, is the expectation of a role insofar as it enables people to specialize in a task and to expect the exchange of goods produced by each person. This possibility of exchange is the basis of the market economy. This typification of the expectation in the exchange is based on the division of labor has become rule governed; it has become institutionalized. Every person has his or her roles defined by the company. As Solomon[21] says, "buyer" and "seller" are established roles within an organized system.

This rule-governed aspect of social institutions is of the utmost importance. The unity of meaning of institutions enables them to be dynamic. The institution has not only made it possible to achieve the ends desired in the past, but it has to also make it possible, in each present action, to achieve the ends determined by each person. As North points out, "They [institutions] evolve incrementally, connecting the past to the present and the future; history in consequence is largely a story of institutional evolution in which the historical performance of economics can only be understood as a part of a sequential story."[22] This process of competition does not have any negative connotations because social interrelations and market exchanges tend to coordinate expectations, provided that the person complies with moral norms. By using an expression utilized in game theory, it can be said that the interrelationships and the market exchanges are positive sums. The expansion of the possibilities of action, of having greater means, is the consequence of the fact that competition is a positive-sum game. The word *culture*, in

20. See George Brenkert, "Innovation: Rule Breaking and the Ethics of Entrepreneurship," *Journal of Business Venturing* 24, no. 5 (2009): 448–64.
21. Solomon, *Ethics and Excellence*, 163.
22. North, "Institutions," 97.

its general meaning, indicates everything whereby the person develops and perfects his or her many bodily and spiritual qualities. Solomon[23] defines corporate culture as shared knowledge, established experience, and values. It is an established group of people working together. Yet these shared values imply thinking of ourselves in relation to others. In this view, the typical opposition between moral thinking and self-interest disappears because pursuing my personal goods promotes those of others. So moral thinking is not external to self-interest but rather something internal to the logic of personal action. The reality observed is individual action, but action with other individuals is social action. As a consequence of this formal structure, the inappropriateness of studies that seek to set the individual against society can be highlighted. An opposition between the isolated individual and society hides the intrinsic relationship between the various dimensions of action. Such action is substantively individual but with inseparable social and cultural dimensions. As Freeman says, "it does not make any sense to talk about business or ethics without talking about human beings."[24]

THE CREATIVE PROCESS AND ENTREPRENEURSHIP

Among the different well-established theories of entrepreneurship,[25] let us consider Kirzner's definition of entrepreneurship: "that element of alertness to possibly newly worthwhile goals and to possibly newly available resources."[26] This entrepreneurship reveals action to be something

23. Solomon, *Ethics and Excellence*, 125–35.

24. Bradley R. Agle, Thomas Donaldson, R. Edward Freeman, Michael C. Jensen, Ronald K. Mitchell, and Donna J. Wood, "Dialogue: Toward Superior Stakeholder Theory," *Business Ethics Quarterly* 18, no. 2 (2008): 153–90.

25. William Baumol, "Entrepreneurship in Economic Theory," *American Economic Review: Papers and Proceedings* 58 (1968): 64–71; "Formal Entrepreneurship Theory in Economics: Existence and Bounds," *Journal of Business Venturing* 8 (1993): 197–210; *Entrepreneurship, Management, and the Structure of Payoffs* (Cambridge, Mass.: MIT Press, 1996); Israel Kirzner, *Competition and Entrepreneurship* (Chicago: University of Chicago Press, 1973); *Perception, Opportunity and Profit* (Chicago: University of Chicago Press, 1979); *The Driving Force of the Market* (London: Routledge, 2000); Frank Knight, *Risk: Uncertainty and Profit* (New York: Augustus M. Kelly, 1921); Harvey Leibestein, "Entrepreneurship and Development," *American Economic Review* 58 (1968): 72–83; Richard Nelson and Sydney Winter, *An Evolutionary Theory of Economic Change* (Cambridge, Mass.: Harvard University Press, 1982); Joseph A. Schumpeter, *Capitalism: Socialism and Democracy* (New York: Harper and Row, 1934); and *The Theory of Economic Development* (Cambridge, Mass.: Harvard University Press, 1934).

26. Kirzner, *Competition and Entrepreneurship*, 35.

active, creative, and human. Reality, in the widest sense, is liable to be turned into resources. Anything, whether tangible or intangible, may be turned into a resource as soon as someone sees in it an opportunity for profit. In this respect, Kirzner speaks of the world as a reality that surrounds us and one that is full of opportunities for profit. The opportunities are out there. The following quote corroborates this view of entrepreneurship: "Our world is a grossly inefficient world. What is inefficient about the world is surely that, at each instant, enormous scope exists for improvements that are in one way or another ready to hand and yet are simply not noticed."[27]

If we bear in mind these two aspects—the creative capacity of the entrepreneurial function and the worldly sphere in which it is deployed— the definition of pure entrepreneurship as the deployment of the person's creative capacity in the reality around him or her becomes clear. Any reality that makes sense to the actor is a field of action for entrepreneurship. Therefore, the importance of social institutions and culture as constituent elements of personal action is not based on external considerations but on both elements, along with personal action, constituting "what is human," where the actor develops the entrepreneurial function. So entrepreneurship is concerned with the discovery and exploitation of profitable opportunities.[28]

Creativity is not, therefore, a mere whirlwind, but the transcending of a given and established framework. Any innovation needs the established market by which to draw attention to its individuality. That is, every change drives market relationships, making it impossible to attain the state of repose that characterizes economic stability in the neoclassical model of mainstream economics. To understand creativity we must not confine ourselves to the product already produced, to the finished work but, rather, must investigate the creative process that leads to this product. We are taking an interactive view of creativity based on three elements: the person, culture, and social institutions. Put another way, entrepreneurial innovation not only has a personal dimension, that is, the creator, but also has a sociocultural dimension.

It could be said that society is a process of creating possibilities for

27. Kirzner, *Perception, Opportunity and Profit*, 135.

28. See Scott Shane and Sankaran Venkataraman, "The Promise of Entrepreneurship as a Field of Research," *Academy of Management Review* 25, no. 1 (2000): 217–26.

action that are realized in social institutions and transmitted through culture. In this dynamic view, society is a spontaneous process; that is, it is based on the will of persons and is not the product of an arbitrary imposition by a centralizing and regulating body.[29] It is a process of human relationships structured around social institutions such as the family, law, language, the market, and so on. Moreover, this process transmits forms of access to reality from one generation to another. This premise may be reformulated and postulated the following: the more individual possibilities for action it generates, the more efficient an institutional and cultural framework will be. That is, we may venture to propose a criterion of social coordination that allows us to define entrepreneurial efficiency as a social institution according to the possibilities for action that firms generate. I would like to suggest a criterion of qualitative efficiency based on the real possibilities of individuals. Nobel Prize winner for economics Amartya Sen[30] spoke along the same lines: "Individual freedom is quintessentially a social product, and there is a two-way relation between (1) social arrangements to expand individual freedoms and (2) the use of individual freedoms not only to improve the respective lives but also to make the social arrangements more appropriate and effective."[31]

Sen's work is highly significant because it indicates the growing interest of orthodox academic economics in seeking theories to explain social reality without reducing it to a set of variables that may be ma-

29. Cf. Ludwig von Mises, *Human Action: A Treatise on Economics*, 4th rev. ed., ed. Bettina B. Greaves (San Francisco: Fox and Wilkes, 1996); and Friedrich August von Hayek, "The Use of Knowledge in Society," in *Individualism and Economic Order* (London: Routledge and Kegan Paul, 1976 [1945]); "The Pretense of Knowledge," Nobel lecture, *American Economic Review* (December 1989): 3–7.

30. See his books Amartya Sen, *Development as Freedom* (New York: Knopf, 1999); *Rationality and Freedom* (Cambridge, Mass.: The Belknap Press of Harvard University, 2002); *The Idea of Justice* (Cambridge, Mass.: Harvard University Press, 2009).

31. Sen, *Development as Freedom*, 49. It is impossible here to deal with the capabilities approaches developed by Amartya Sen and Martha Nussbaum (Martha Nussbaum and Amartya Sen, eds., *The Quality of Life* [Oxford: Clarendon Press, 1993]). The first point would not indicate the differences—remarkable I would say—between the Sen and Nussbaum approaches. Sen's *The Idea of Justice* presents what he considers to be distinctive of his approach, and Nussbaum, *Creating Capabilities: The Human Development Approach* (Cambridge, Mass.: The Belknap Press of Harvard University, 2011), does the same. For a general and critical assessment of both approaches, see Henry Richardson, "Some Limitations of Nussbaum's Capabilities," *Quinnipiac Law Review* 19, no. 2 (2000): 309–32; and his "The Social Background of Capabilities for Freedoms," *Journal of Human Development* 8, no. 3 (2007): 389–414.

nipulated mathematically as a matter of maximizing utility. The sole message of this chapter is that the study of economics must be based on the persons who produce and generate the process. As Solomon says, "by ignoring such 'intangible' features of business life as company morale and coordination in favor of the measurable quantities listed in the financial pages, we are destroying the corporation as community and, consequently, as a fully functional human institution."[32] An attempt to account for the market by looking merely at what is produced will show only statistical information about amounts of goods and services and prices. It will be vital information in ascertaining the state of the market, but it will not explain the process. To understand the generation of wealth the focus must be on the motivations, wills, preferences and rules of individuals.[33]

THE SOCIAL ROLE OF THE FIRM

Let us use the interactive view of creativity to approach the firm. The first thing we note is that entrepreneurial innovation not only has an individual dimension, that is, the person who creates something—the creator—but also a sociocultural dimension. We now have an interactive view of creativity and entrepreneurship linking the person, the firm, and entrepreneurial culture. We should be clear that these are not three different realities but are three moments in the same process. These three moments are closely interlinked, so a change in any one of them affects the creative process. Rather than speaking of what creativity is, we should ask about the origin of creativity. In this view, the social importance of the firm is huge: *the firm's social responsibility is to enhance the possibilities of persons.*[34] The assertion that any person has the ability to create to a greater or lesser extent is not an exaggeration but, rather, the

32. Solomon, *Ethics and Excellence Cooperation and Integrity in Business*, 151.

33. As Joseph Ratzinger wrote: "A scientific approach that believes itself capable of managing without an ethos misunderstands the reality of man. Therefore it is not scientific. Today we need a maximum of specialized economic understanding but also a maximum of ethos." See Joseph Ratzinger, "Church and Economy: Responsibility for the Future of the World Economy," *Communio* 13 (1986): 204.

34. As has been noted in Wolfgang Grassl and André Habisch, "Ethics and Economics: Towards a New Humanistic Synthesis for Business," *Journal of Business Ethics* 99, no. 1 (2011): 37–49, the encyclical letter *Caritas in Veritate* emphasizes the same two basic ideas. First, business activity must be understood as personal action, and second, management should foster the creativity of employees.

reverse. It highlights a current problem of great importance when firms need to innovate at high speed. It highlights the fact that in firms, there is much wasted talent. Jack Welch, until recently president of General Electric, said, "The talents of our people are greatly underestimated and their skills underutilized. Our biggest task is to fundamentally redefine our relationship with our employees. The objective is to build a place where people have the freedom to be creative, where they feel a real sense of accomplishment—a place that brings out the best in everyone."[35] In this respect, S. Ghoshal and C. A. Bartlett, echoing Welch, define the new social dimension of the firm: "Rather than accept the assumption of economists who regard the firm as just an economic entity and believe that its goal is to appropriate all possible value from its constituent parts, we take a wider view. Our thinking is based on the conviction that the firm, as one of the most significant institutions in modern society, should serve as a driving force of progress by creating new value for all of its constituent parts."[36]

This view implies an extension of economics.[37] Firms occupy a central position as basic institutions in society. It is a dynamic view that shows the firm's importance as a behavior pattern in social relations in which the lead role is played by the person and the driving force is entrepreneurship.

To further elaborate on the criterion of entrepreneurial efficiency, economic efficiency can be defined as the enhancement of persons' possibilities for action.[38] The first aspect of this criterion is that it is dynamic. Its coordination lies in the process of social interaction that gradually eliminates inefficient situations. Thus, an economic, social, and cultural

35. Sumantra Ghoshal and Christopher Bartlett, *The Individualized Corporation: A Fundamentally New Approach to Management* (New York: HarperCollins Publishers, 1997), 21.

36. Ibid., 27.

37. For the development of the humanistic management approach, see, among others: Antonio Argandoña, "Integrating Ethics into Action Theory and Organizational Theory," *Journal of Business Ethics* 78 (2007): 435–46; "Las Virtudes en una Teoría de la Acción," DI-880. IESE Business School, 2010; Domènec Melé, "The Challenge of Humanistic Management," *Journal of Business Ethics* 44 (2003): 77–88; Heiko Spitzeck, Michael Pirson, Wolfgang Amann, Shiban Khan, and Ernst von Kimakowitz, eds., *Humanism in Business* (Cambridge: Cambridge University Press, 2009); Edwin Hartman, "Virtue, Profit, and the Separation Thesis: An Aristotelian View," *Journal of Business Ethics* 99, no. 1 (2011): 5–17.

38. Peter Koslowski, *Ethics of Capitalism and Critique of Sociobiology* (Berlin: Springer Verlag, 1996), states emphatically that the market allows not only freedom of consumption but also of action and production.

system will be more efficient if it increases personal possibilities for action. That is, a situation will be more efficient when a person's prospects of action increase. And, conversely, a social and cultural situation will be more inefficient if the possibilities for action afforded to persons are more limited.

However, this criterion should be supplemented, for if only the first part is inserted and an increase in personal possibilities is stopped, it could be inferred that the more freedom of individual action we have, the better society is coordinated. Thus, the paradoxical situation of asserting that the more murderers, drunks, thieves, and so on there are, the better society coordinated is society could be reached, a conclusion that is obviously unacceptable. That is, this first formulation of the criterion provides an element that is necessary but insufficient in and of itself. This first aspect concerns personal freedom of choice. But in the course of this chapter, I have argued that all individual action has a social dimension and that, as a result, the institutional order is maintained by personal actions. Therefore, it is necessary to supplement the criterion of coordination from the social perspective and to assert that the more entrepreneurial and social coordination it generates, the more efficient personal action will be. Thus, it can be asserted that all behavior we normally regard as antisocial or pernicious, such as theft, murder, fraud, or drug addiction, is inefficient because it makes it impossible for society to function, as would also be true of an economy based on theft. [39]

As we have developed the relationship among personal action, institutions, and culture, the criteria may be formulated in three ways. Each one refers to the contribution of each element to the system presented in this chapter. That is, as Csikszentmihalyi says,[40] when speaking of creativity, a systematic view must be taken. Instead of asking about in-

39. This efficiency criterion requires the two formulations in order to correspond to the two views of human freedom. Our first formulation refers to the conception of freedom as "freedom from." In this view, the person is free from institutions to do what she or he likes. It represents the freedom of indifference. One may do this or that. In this view, a person who chooses to be a thief is as free as one who chooses to undertake a great enterprise. To distinguish between such behaviors, I have introduced the second view corresponding to the concept of freedom as "freedom for." This view presents the person as a generator of positive actions. It presents man's freedom in the search for excellence in action. See Servais Pinckaers, *Les sources de la morale chrétienne* (Fribourg: University Press, 1985).

40. See Mihaly Csikszentmihalyi, *Creativity: Flow and the Psychology of Discovery and Invention* (New York: HarperCollins Publishers, 1996).

dividual creativity in isolation, how to stimulate creativity in personal action, in entrepreneurial culture, and in existing firms should be considered. The coordination criterion may be formulated with reference to each element. (1) Regarding firms, the criterion is that the more personal possibilities for action they afford, the more efficient firms will be. (2) Regarding entrepreneurial culture, the more possibilities for action it fosters, the more efficient cultural transmission mechanisms will be. (3) Regarding individual action, the greater its contribution to the firm and entrepreneurial culture, the more efficient the action will be. If this separation is analytical and the sole existing reality is man in action are borne in mind, the three criteria can be summed up in just one criterion: coordination improves if the process of creating culturally transmitted personal possibilities for action in firms is extended.

This systematic criterion allows a common criticism to be countered. Often, the outcomes of an institution and culture are acceptable only from within which the relevant institutional and cultural prerequisites are objected. Thus, for example, the working of the market is accepted provided that the validity of private property be accepted as an institutional prerequisite. If, for moral reasons, private property is rejected, the outcome of the market is unacceptable, and we must regard its supposed efficiency as fallacious, and above all unfair and greedy.[41] Is this objection valid? With the dynamic and systematic criterion propounded above, it may be rejected, as institutional prerequisites are an essential part of personal action. Institutions and culture are not givens that are external to action, and therefore, they are liable to appraisal. With the efficiency criterion, institutions and cultures may be appraised according to the personal possibilities for action that they afford. The only fact that is irreducible, that is, axiomatic, is action as the primary human reality.[42] This primary reality is human action, which consists of deliberately seeking certain valuable ends with scarce means.

41. Cf. Geoff Moore, "On the Implications of the Practice-Institution Distinction MacIntyre and the Application of Modern Virtue Ethics to Business," *Business Ethics Quarterly* 12, no. 1 (2002): 19–32; "Humanizing Business: A Modern Virtue Ethics Approach," *Business Ethics Quarterly* 15, no. 2 (2005): 237–55; "Corporate Character: Modern Virtue Ethics and the Virtuous Corporation," *Business Ethics Quarterly* 15, no. 4 (2005): 659–85; "Re-imagining the Morality of Management: A Modern Virtue Ethics Approach," *Business Ethics Quarterly* 18, no. 4 (2008): 483–511.

42. See Mises, *Human Action*.

THE MORALITY OF THE MARKET

The market economy is the means to economic development and prosperity. But now the economic crisis is putting the market economy, the firm as institution, and the morality of profits at stake.[43] Throughout this chapter, I have maintained that the market economy is not captured in the neoclassical model efficient price-clearing process based on the *homo economicus*. The market economy is based on the acting person within his or her sociocultural framework. Value creation, the driving force behind modern organization, cannot be reduced to a factor of production or to objective knowledge. Creativity becomes real in the structuring of the means and the ends in projects. But it is fundamentally important to make it clear that the creative capacity of the person is dynamic. Creativity is not dynamic because it develops over time but because it goes beyond what is immediately given. This dynamism developed by creativity is the transformation of reality through action. This basic concept is necessary for understanding the capitalistic process: that the end is an imagined reality and that the means must be constituted through action.

In the previous section, I presented an interactive view of the value creation process linking the person, the firm, and entrepreneurial culture. It should be made clear that these are not three different realities but three moments in the same process. These three moments are closely interlinked, so any change in any one of them affects the creative process. Rather than speaking of what creativity is, the question should be, "From where does creativity originate?" In this view, the social practice of the firm is huge: the firm's social practice is to enhance the possibilities of persons.

As Ghoshal, Bartlett, and Moran say, "corporations, not abstract economic forces or governments, create and distribute most of an economy's wealth, innovate, trade and raise living standards."[44] The social institutions, in this case, firms, have their own dynamism, which depends on the opportunities that enable their members to exercise their creativity and

---

43. Hartman, "Virtue, Profit, and the Separation Thesis," makes a pertinent defense of profits from an Aristotelian point of view.

44. Sumantra Ghoshal, Christopher Bartlett, and Peter Moran, "A New Manifesto for Management," *Sloan Management Review* 43, no. 9 (1999): 9.

capabilities. So following Moran and Ghoshal,[45] the economic process can be defined as a value-creating process based on the following elements: (1) the universe of all possible resource combinations, (2) perceived possibilities, (3) productive possibilities, and (4) productive opportunities. And Moran and Ghoshal affirm that "as many firms of different forms and sizes engage in this process, each broadens the scope of exchange in ways that allow it to focus on some fragmented bits of the knowledge that Hayek (1945) talked about."[46] Creativity action is the result of our ability to project ourselves and to envisage what may exist in the future.[47] The background of action should not be sought in the past but in the attempt to obtain a more profitable present out of a future that does not yet exist.[48]

Any person, however unadventurous, undertakes a project outside his or her immediate area of development. The person has the ability to procure information that motivates him or her to act. If the entrepreneurial function is reduced to mere knowledge, there is no room for creative capacity, a capacity that consists of seeing more possibilities where there is apparently nothing. It is not, as is often said, that persons with great creative capacity need little information in order to create great firms but, rather, the other way round: such persons are able to create more practical information than are others, which means the entrepreneurial function cannot be confined to great geniuses. Any person, by the fact of being a person, has this ability, which is not reducible to objective knowledge.[49]

As I have said, the social function of the firm consists of fostering its employees' creative capacity although not as a form of social benefit. In fact, the firm's essential function is to enhance the real possibilities

45. See Peter Moran and Sumantra Ghoshal, "Markets, Firms and the Process of Economic Development," *Academy of Management Review* 24, no. 3 (1999): 390–412.

46. Ibid., 405.

47. See Scott Shane, "Prior Knowledge and the Discovery of Entrepreneurial Opportunities," *Organizational Science* 11, no. 4 (2000): 448–69; and Sankaran Venkataraman, "The Distinctive Domain of Entrepreneurship Research," *Advances in Entrepreneurship, Firm Emergence and Growth* 3 (1997): 119–38.

48. The same idea was masterfully expressed by Professor Julián Marías in the following words: "My life is not a thing, but rather a doing, a reality projected into the future, that is argumentative and dramatic, and that is not exactly *being* but happening." Julián Marías, *Persona* (Madrid: Alianza Editorial, 1996), 126. More bluntly, Peter Drucker says that "the best way to predict the future is to create it." Peter Drucker, *El gran poder de las pequeñas ideas* (Buenos Aires: Editorial Sudamericana, 1998).

49. Nicholas Dew, S. Ramakrishna Velamuri, and Sankaran Venkataraman, "Dispersed Knowledge and an Entrepreneurial Theory of the Firm," *Journal of Business Venturing* 19 (2004): 659–79.

of its employees. The greater these possibilities, the greater the possibilities of monetary profit. There is a wider range of possibilities to explore. Consequently, the firm's function must not be reduced to that of making money and paying taxes. This is necessary, but it is not enough. Milton Friedman, Nobel laureate for economics, says that "[t]he social responsibility of business is to increase its profits. Few trends could so thoroughly undermine the very foundations of our free society as the acceptance by corporate officials of a social responsibility other than to make as much money for their stockholders as possible."[50]

We may share Friedman's idea, but the following questions arise: How do we increase profits? What is the essence of the productive process? What needs to be encouraged and increased? The answer can be no other than the entrepreneurship of persons. This is the way to increase profits: creating, creating, and creating! But this involves taking account of the efficiency criterion I described in the previous section: entrepreneurial coordination and wealth increase if the process of creating culturally transmitted personal possibilities for action in firms is extended. All the fundamental ideas of Friedman's work on the microeconomic theory of consumption, monetary policy, and his defense of free-market economy can be integrated into a more general and systematic framework. As E. Freeman says, "Better stakeholder theory focuses us on the multiplicity of ways that companies and entrepreneurs are out there creating value, making our lives better, and changing the world."[51] All work cannot be reduced to a technical command. People do not only make shoes or build houses. In every productive act, they seek something else. They seek to carry out those actions with ease, with the perfection of a specific power and confidence of aim. Virtue is in this way a *connaturality* with the acts that belong to the productive domain. It is a second acquired nature that empowers people with ability, brilliance, mastery, competence, and excellence to make shoes or houses. In other words, virtue is the fulfillment of being human in the dynamism of human action: "knowing," "making," or "doing." As Rhonheimer points out, "Virtue in all its types is a habit for carrying out well the actions of a faculty: a *habitus operativus bonus*."[52]

50. See Milton Friedman, "The Social Responsibility of Business Is to Increase Its Profits," *New York Times Magazine* (September 13, 1970).

51. Agle et al., "Dialogue: Towards Superior Stakeholder Theory," 166.

52. Rhonheimer, *The Perspective of Morality*, 193.

In any action there are external effects, *poiesis, facere,* and internal ones of *praxis, agere.* That is, external goods are achieved at the institutional level in our system: institution (goods), culture (norms), and individual action (virtues). In this dynamic system, ethics is the system of goods, norms, and virtues that makes personal action coherent at its societal, cultural and individual levels. The technical virtue (*habitus operativus bonus*) is the fulfillment or excellent of the intelligence in respect to *poiesis, facere,* that is, in respect to the act of "making" external goods. As MacIntyre recognizes, "this making and sustaining of forms of human community—and therefore of institutions—itself has all the characteristics of a practice, and moreover of a practice which stands in a peculiarly close relationship to the exercise of the virtue."[53] Second, as I have expounded previously, economics is not reduced merely to the productive act; it also encompasses the choice of ends and means of production inherent to economic action dynamism. This is the realm of prudence (*phronesis*) that is fulfillment or excellence in respect to *praxis, agere,* that is, the act of "doing" or the choice of good actions. People are not just "making" shoes or houses; they are "doing" good shoes or houses. As the classic Greeks said that to live the good life one must live in a great city, I agree with Solomon[54] when he says "to live a decent life choose the right company."

CONCLUDING REMARKS

This chapter presents the analysis of social institutions and the firm-based market economy from the theory of human action (an agent-based approach). Within action, all facets of the person are displayed: the individual, the social, and the cultural. The essence of the human being is his or her openness to other individuals within institutional structures through culture. This openness is something intrinsic to human action, never something external.

A theory of personal action in societal institutions bridges the way from a virtue-based ethics toward an ethics of institutions. Corporate culture is defined as shared knowledge, established experience, and values. It is an established group of people working together. These shared values imply people's thinking of themselves in relation to others. But

53. MacIntyre, *After Virtue,* 194ff.
54. See Solomon, *Ethics and Excellence.*

the only reality that people observe is personal action within its cultural and institutional dimensions.

The firm-based market economy has a very positive moral content: the possibility of excellence of human action. The market economy is the means to economic development and prosperity. Firms based on people acting together, sharing the culture of the organization and being directed by virtue-based ethics create and distribute most of the economy's wealth, innovate, trade, and raise living standards. The firm is an institution that performs a very important practice: fostering new possibilities for individual action. Economics does not limit itself to the product. It also encompasses the choice of the ends and means of production that generate the product. This realm of prudence (*phronesis*) is the fulfillment or excellence in respect to *praxis*, *agere*, that is, the act of "doing" or the choice of good actions.

With the coordination criteria presented, it can be said that social coordination improves if the process of the creation of individual possibilities of action that is carried out in the social institutions, in this case, the firm, is extended. In that moment, entrepreneurship, the creative tension that expands, maintains, or diminishes the possibilities of action, emerges. Within this process of action enters all the elements that characterize human action as a dynamic, a historical process that is open to the future and, of course, subject to error and failure.

FOUR

Economic Theory Meets Human Nature

How Anthropological Views of the Human Person Shaped Economic Theory in Western History

John Larrivee

Reflecting on what the fall of communism and the other economic experiments taught, Pope Benedict XVI wrote:

The collapse of the Communist systems was due in the first instance to their false economic dogmatics. But there is a tendency to overlook the deeper fact that they broke down because of their contempt for man and because they subordinated morality to the needs of the system and its promises of a glowing future. The real catastrophe that the Communist regimes left behind is not economic. It consists in the devastation of souls, in the destruction of moral consciousness. I see a fundamental contemporary problem for Europe and for the world in that while no one contests the economic failure, and former Communists do not hesitate to become economic liberals, there is an almost total silence about the moral and religious problems that were the real heart of the matter. And this means that the problems left behind by Marxism are still with us. The dissolution of the primal certainties of man about God, about himself, and about the universe—the dissolution of the consciousness of those moral values that are never subject to our own judgment—all this is still our problem.[1]

Demonstrating why abandoning the price or profit mechanisms was "false dogmatics" may explain why former communists embrace eco-

---

1. Joseph Ratzinger, *Values in a Time of Upheaval* (San Francisco: Ignatius, 2006), 145.

nomic liberalism and is standard fare for economics courses. But why did the failure of an economic theory leave us with moral problems? What were the moral/religious problems that were the real heart of the matter Marx attempted (but failed) to solve yet are still with us? What was the link between human nature and economic thought?

As practical individuals, economists want to focus on whether something works, not necessarily the motives or the philosophical understanding of the person behind it. We are trained to examine the system and outcomes, not the philosophy. Unfortunately, this focus leaves us unprepared to understand the enormous battles in the past two centuries that, although they occurred over economic organization, often had more to do with human nature generally than the important, but narrower, question about the efficiency of markets.

The various economic regimes did not merely try to produce more stuff or achieve social justice. They were based on certain assumptions of human existence and human nature: that people are solely material beings and that all human behavior and outcomes must be explainable in material terms. Given the enormous impact of the Industrial Revolution, many people placed a heavy weight on the economic system, theorizing that changes in the system would change people and solve deeper problems in the human condition. The trial of these alternative systems was a test of that theory, and their failure was not merely an answer to the economic question of the efficiency of central planning but a lesson about human nature: people are not simply products of the system; people need more than economic arrangements on which to base their lives.

Alas, most economists have paid little attention to these types of concerns about economic arrangements. To understand the type of critique Benedict XVI made they would need to reread their own history with attention to how debates over human nature entered into economic theory. In this chapter, I seek to do this by using the basic philosophical areas (metaphysics, epistemology, ethics, politics) and then by analyzing how the answers to these questions shaped economic ideas from Smith to Marx to the twentieth century. Doing so demonstrates how answers to these questions about human nature influenced three areas: the values people held, the behavioral models of human action that shaped how people thought different economic systems would work out, and their attitudes toward civil society.

For example, faced with the loss of epistemological certainty (rejecting revelation), Smith used sympathy and the self-interest in the invisible hand to explain how society could work harmoniously. Just two
generations later, the metaphysical foundation had collapsed completely
to materialism. Marx, knowing materialism implied that moral ideals
could not exist, thus developed the supposedly scientific inevitability
of communism to salvage ethics and politics with common ownership.

The same materialism spilled into the behavioral assumptions that
shaped the political/economic experiments of the twentieth century
and modern viewpoints today. De-emphasizing human sinfulness and
free will meant weighting environmental and biological factors more
heavily. This undermined the importance of ideas or values, including
the institutions of civil society (perhaps especially family and religion)
that fostered them, and instead implied the ideal society could only be
achieved with the appropriate political/economic arrangement. Groups
as diverse as fascists, communists, and socialists, as well as more recent
nonreligious libertarians and liberals, disagreed about direction of these
forces and thus the right economic/political mix, but they agreed on
the materialist assumptions behind the theories and their implications
of the power of economic forces. The failure of these variations returns
us to the problems inherent in those shared assumptions, to questions of
"primal certainties."

HUMAN NATURE AND ECONOMIC THEORY
FROM SMITH TO RAND

A useful way to understand the philosophical debates that have involved
both human nature and economic systems is to recognize fundamental
questions facing philosophical inquiry, central questions about human
life:

> Metaphysics: What is being? What is the nature of existence?
> Epistemology: What can we know?
> Ethics: What is good? How/for what should we live?
> Politics: How should we live together, organize society?

This framework clarifies how social science theories connect to an understanding of humankind and the universe, what assumptions theorists
must be making to be consistent, and how Christians can appropriate

the best insights and advances of social science theories, without sac-
rificing the fundamental vision of human nature the Judeo-Christian
heritage offers to the world.

Interestingly, this point was made quite clearly by the Soviet Union
itself. The Communist Party produced several texts for various disciplines, intending to be official statements of the party's positions regarding those areas. They provide unique insights into how the communists
tried to link philosophical assumptions regarding human nature with
their economic principles. One of them, *The Fundamentals of Marxist-
Leninist Philosophy*, commences with the statement "Marxism-Leninism
cannot be properly understood without its philosophical basis ... What
is the essential nature of the world around us? What is the relationship
between nature and spirit? Between matter and consciousness? What is
man and what is his place in the world? Is he capable of knowing and
transforming the world, and, if so, how is it to be done?"[2] It also adds that

[s]ome philosophers try to prove that the basic question of philosophy is man,
human life itself with all its problems. No one would deny that questions of
man's social life occupy a central place in philosophy, particularly Marxist philosophy. But they may be regarded from both materialist and idealist positions.
Thus, the basic question in philosophy is the question that theoretically sets the
direction of philosophical inquiry, that formulates its point of departure and
governing principles. This was the sense in which the classics of Marxism called
the question of the spirit-matter relationship the basic philosophical question.
The basic question of philosophy has two aspects. The first aspect is the question of the essence, the nature of the world and the second aspect is the question of its knowability.[3]

Note that while the existential questions all people must face are the
same, *Fundamentals* already hints strongly at how their answers will dif-
fer from the Christian position.

In the Judeo-Christian heritage of the West, the metaphysical foundation is that God exists; he made man, who is spiritual and physical; he
cares about each person; and he gave the combination of physical and
moral laws. Epistemologically, these laws can be known by reason, observation, and revelation. In terms of ethics, these laws then tell us how

to live for human flourishing, growing in love of God and others, and in virtues. In politics, these involve the creation of a society that encourages these overall and in which people see themselves as brothers and sisters before God, loving others as God loves them.

As the party states, the metaphysical and epistemological positions were assumed to be the foundation: only after knowing what man is could a person speculate on how he or she ought to live. However, this process was difficult because those bases were gradually challenged during the Renaissance and Enlightenment, forcing people to grapple with the problem of rationalizing ethics if the foundations did not exist or could not be known. This was the position in which Smith found himself.

Smith's Descent from the Scholastic Framework

While Smith's role in developing economic theory is well known, his role as a philosopher is less so. He wrote at a critical stage in capitalist development. He both chronicled and explained the enormous changes rocking England and soon engulfed other nations: the rise of larger firms, the working class, and the division of labor in larger firms, trade, and markets, among others. On the other hand, he was not simply studying the self-functioning of the market. He was searching for a united understanding of society, making sense of the physical world and humanity's place in it in light of the eroding consensus about the nature of existence and of what could be known.[4]

As with many others of the time, Smith rejected revelation (the epistemological change from the Judeo-Christian heritage) but retained a belief in God generally. He also rejected the Judeo-Christian concept of natural/moral laws (to which people could be held accountable) and, instead, used a transformed concept that meant something closer to physical laws, to forces, or to inclinations God had placed in people rather than rules they must obey. As Rothschild writes, "Hume's and Smith's systems of moral sentiments are scrupulously cleansed of everything, or almost everything, which is a matter of revelation. They are systems of secular virtue."[5] Similarly, Piedra observes two other philosophers who

---

4. Joseph Schumpeter, *History of Economic Analysis* (New York: Oxford University Press, 1994 [1954]), 182.

5. Emma Rothschild, *Economic Sentiments: Adam Smith, Condorcet, and the Enlightenment* (Cambridge, Mass.: Harvard University Press, 2001), 231.

heavily influenced Smith, Lord Shaftesbury and Francis Hutcheson. "They believed in man's natural goodness and in a wise and benevolent Designer of all nature, including human nature. They were true Deists who rejected Christian Revelation and all religious and moral truths that were not self-evident to natural reason. The concept of original sin was alien to them."[6]

As is evident, these rather critical metaphysical assumptions were about existence and human nature. Rejecting revelation, they turned to nature and reason as grounds for studying how to live. However, this did not solve the problem of human nature. One still needed to make assumptions about what people were and how they behaved. Christianity had assumed that people were good but marred by original sin. Hobbes rejected this thesis and assumed that human nature was inherently bad, and consequently, everyone was the enemy of everyone else. This state of nature, naturally antagonistic and unharmonious, implied that people created the government to restrain one another so that they could get along. On the other hand, many other thinkers of the period rejected both nature and original sin as too negative and too difficult to overcome, assuming, instead, that human nature was inherently good or harmonious. This also had certain implications. In particular, if people are inherently good, then all evil inclinations must be due to factors in society, rather than the people themselves. Rousseau, for example, assumed that private property and commercial society were responsible for the corruption of natural harmony. This type of reasoning created a massive sense of urgency and optimism that if the conditions could correctly resolved, people would get along. For Smith, this general assumption of human goodness fed not into a call for a top-down social solution but for a confidence that the moral and economic mechanisms were adequate to ensure human cooperation.

Importantly, Smith also held an exceptionally strong vision of equality: "The difference of natural talents in different men is, in reality, much less than we are aware of; and the very different genius which appears to distinguish men of different professions, when grown to maturity, is not on many occasions so much the cause, as the effect of the

6. Alberto Piedra, *Natural Law: The Foundation of an Orderly Economic System* (Lanham, Md.: Lexington Books, 2004), 56.

division of labor. The difference between the most dissimilar characters, between a philosopher and a common street porter, for example, seems to arise not so much from nature, as from habit, custom, and education."[7] In an era of crumbling views of revelation and of human souls (which allow for equality in a dimension other than physical), this assumption was critical for new types of moral reasoning (e.g., utilitarian). Equality implied that people should be treated equally.[8]

These assumptions about human nature and existence confronted the enormous changes happening economically. How did Smith manage to connect the two? Interpretations of this project vary widely, from those (often economists and social scientists) who view his work as mechanistic or primarily positive analysis to those who emphasize it as a philosophical engagement with the dangers of commercial society and his efforts to offer a foundation of virtue to counter those threats.[9]

Piedra exemplifies an interpretation of Smith's system as one within a natural law tradition (i.e., that mechanisms originating in nature should be followed) but in which moral, or at least socially beneficial, behavior arises automatically.[10] This automatic nature has been described as a moral Newtonianism, that is, a process intended to simplify ethics and economics to just a few (or one) forces. Sympathy and self-interest are not opposites but different sides of a similar mechanism governing how people behave, as the product of simplified drives whose outcomes can be studied. Smith proposed that God had given people in-

---

7. Adam Smith, *An Inquiry into the Nature and Causes of the Wealth of Nations*, ed. R. H. Campbell and A. S. Skinner, vol. 2 of *The Glasgow Edition of the Works and Correspondence of Adam Smith* (Indianapolis: Liberty Fund, 1981 [1776]), I.ii.4.

8. Sandra Peart and David Levy, *Vanity of the Philosopher: From Equality to Hierarchy in Postclassical Economics* (Ann Arbor: University of Michigan Press, 2005), 3.

9. This variety arises from numerous factors: he revised his *Theory of Moral Sentiments* substantially just before his death and had many of his writings burned, of which some have been reconstructed from student notes from lectures early in his career.

10. Piedra, *Natural Law*, 55–69. See also, Schumpeter, *History of Economic Analysis*, 141–42. Schumpeter describes Smith as one of the last of the natural law philosophers. By this he meant not the natural law of Christian tradition but the sense of his time that natural forces still held a kind of normative implication. The goal was to identify the natural forces and then follow them. Kolakowski notes how this shifted by the 1800s, especially for Marx. The goal was more Promethean: not discovering the natural forces to follow them but to control them and in doing so control man's destiny overall. Leszek Kolakowski, *Main Currents of Marxism*, trans. P. S. Falla (New York: Norton, 2005), 337. See also Frederick Engels, *Socialism: Utopian and Scientific* (New York: International Publishers, 1969 [1892]), 72–73.

born senses which when followed would result in human society functioning harmoniously. He reduced these to two: sympathy (analyzed in
detail in *Theory of Moral Sentiments*) and self-interest (whose economic
component was analyzed in *Wealth of Nations*).

This solves two problems at the epistemological level. First, without revelation, how can people know what is right and what should be
done? The second was more practical: How could people calculate what
to do in every circumstance and do so quickly enough? These challenges
provided justifications for rejecting the rationalist confidence in reason
alone, as well as anything grounded on moral rules (religious or not).
The same God who set the forces of nature, from the planets to the animals, to function automatically, has implanted forces of sympathy and
self-interest in people. Assuming people are equal and generally good
(the metaphysical assumptions) the invisible hand works automatically
for society.

On the other hand, Hanley interprets Smith as offering a virtue ethics based approach to the challenges of rapidly changing commercial society.[11] Hanley believes that Smith did not yet embrace a utilitarian approach developing at the time and regarded the moral reasoning of the
rationalists, deontologists, or the traditional Christian approach as too
complex. In addition, as time went on, Smith increasingly agreed with
many of Rousseau's critiques of how commercial society was largely
driven by status seeking (rather than direct utility from consumption)
and that it could undermine character. Hanley proposes that Smith
sought a middle ground between Mandeville's acceptance of market
gains at the expense of virtue and Rousseau's rejection of the market to
retain virtue.[12]

Hanley argues that, faced with these problems, Smith instead chose
to look back to the Greeks to take a virtue ethics approach, a model
in which sympathy can be retained, even in the face of self-interested
behavior. People care about how they are viewed by others. Although
they are happy to be viewed positively, even if without grounds, they
are more satisfied by earning the praise of others for actually behaving in
a more virtuous and considerate manner. Beyond that stage, people may

11. Ryan P. Hanley, *Adam Smith and the Character of Virtue* (New York: Cambridge University Press, 2009).

12. Ibid., 102–104.

actually come to value the virtues directly. Hanley argues that Smith was encouraging harnessing self-interest as a means to move people to higher levels of virtue and consideration of others. It would be flexible, easily taught, and applied.[13] In that way, people could be enticed, and the status-seeking element of the market harnessed to move people from self-love focused on possessions or perception by others to self-love for having deserved the praise of others for virtuous living to self-love guided by love of living for the virtues themselves.[14]

Others have focused on his use of sympathy as a shift in ethical reasoning. For example, Schumpeter writes that Smith moved from ethics as an examination of normative principles, or even the study of behavior, to study how people made judgments about behavior.[15] Peart and Levy emphasize a more utilitarian interpretation of Smith's reasoning regarding sympathy. Sympathy provided a means by which people obtained utility from the improvement in well-being of others, which occurred both through economic improvement, as well as from some policies. In addition, sympathy tended to induce people to see others as equals about whom they should care.[16] Thus, sympathy provided a mechanism for consideration of others at a time when confidence in eternal moral principles was fading.

Across these explanations is the common thread of Smith's attempt to explore the economic, moral, and social order in light of changed metaphysical and epistemological views. Piedra contends that Smith's view of human nature contributed to an excessive confidence that changes in the economy would be enough to create a harmonious society. Believing this, those who followed Smith concluded that leaving people free of constraints, to follow both impulses, would be enough. Piedra writes that "[i]t cannot be denied that Smith contributed, without realizing it, to the hyper evaluation of the economic which characterized the liberalism of the nineteenth century and which later became known as economism. His faith in the goodness of man, influenced undoubtedly by his deistic approach to life, led him to the naïve conclusion that the free mar-

13. Ibid., 68–77.
14. Ibid., 92–99.
15. Schumpeter, *History of Economic Analysis*, 129.
16. Peart and Levy, *Vanity of the Philosopher*, 7–9. They acknowledge that this thinking grew much stronger across the classical period to Mill.

ket system, guided by individual self interests, could function effectively and bring about the greatest happiness for the greatest number."[17]

I believe Piedra correctly observes that Smith's (excessive) confidence in human nature contributed to an excessive confidence in an automatic market and moral mechanism. However, he may be in error in ascribing it to deism, which assumed more of a clockmaker idea of a creator who started the universe but no longer cares. Instead, Smith appears to have had far more allegiance to a Stoic than to a deist view.

The Stoics viewed the universe as governed by a benevolent supreme being who guided everything according to a grand plan. The Stoic, thus, cultivated self-control as part of accepting the plan of that loving creator. The system could work automatically (naturally) on its own for the un-thinking, but a Stoic wiseman could come to understand the mechanism and to embrace the direction not out of simple natural pressures but out of virtuous regard for what the creator wanted. Note how this merges both an automatic/natural mechanism for most (possibly all), while leaving open the possibility of living virtuously, embracing the creator's plan for deeper reasons than self-interest.

How much this was Smith's view is uncertain, but he clearly devotes far more space to Stoic ideals than to other systems. For example, in *The Theory of Moral Sentiments*, his review of various moral systems dedicates three pages to Plato, two to Aristotle, and twenty-two to the Stoic system, concluding with the sentence "That the Stoical philosophy had very great influence upon the conduct and character of its followers, cannot be doubted; and … its general tendency was to animate them to actions of the most heroic magnanimity and most extensive benevolence."[18]

In the final edition of *The Theory of Moral Sentiments*, published just before his death, Smith added an entirely new and substantial section to the original six, "Part VI: The Character of Virtue." That addition includes a chapter filled throughout with a strong Stoic voice, in particular that belief in a creator is extremely important in encouraging universal benevolence. Smith writes,

17. Piedra, *Natural Law*, 65.

18. Adam Smith, *The Theory of Moral Sentiments*, edited by D. D. Raphael and A. L. Macfie, vol. 1 of *The Glasgow Edition of the Works and Correspondence of Adam Smith* (Indianapolis: Liberty Fund, 1982 [1759]), VII.ii.I.47.

This universal benevolence, how noble and generous soever, can be the source of no solid happiness to any man who is not thoroughly convinced that all the inhabitants of the universe, the meanest as well as the greatest, are under the immediate care and protection of that great, benevolent, and all-wise Being, who directs all the movements of nature; and who is determined, by his own unalterable perfections, to maintain in it, at all times, the greatest quantity of happiness. To this universal benevolence, on the contrary, the very suspicion of a fatherless world, must be the most melancholy of all reflections.[19]

Later, he adds, that "[t]he idea of that divine Being, whose benevolence and wisdom have, from all eternity, contrived and conducted the immense machine of the universe, so as at all times to produce the greatest possible quantity of happiness, is certainly of all objects of human contemplation by far the most sublime. Every other thought necessarily appears mean in the comparison."[20]

This takes a more sophisticated view that the system could work automatically/naturally on its own, but it did not need to stop there. Moral reasoning still required understanding and a person devoted to living virtuously could rise above an animalistic/nonthinking response to incentives mechanisms.

If this is correct, Smith's confidence in the automatic model appears similar to those of others of his time, but his reasoning behind it is very different: a strong view of a benevolent being who controlled everything rather than a creator who made the system and who has since let it go without concern. Seen in this light, faith is not in the mechanism but in the creator. Looking through this Stoic lens gives a very different interpretation of Smith's *intentions*, although not the effects of his ideas. If others of the time were not so committed to such a strong view of a benevolent creator, it is likely that the major impact was primarily as Piedra concluded, that Smith's economic and moral writings contributed to a general sense that everything could work on its own.[21]

---

19. Ibid., VI.ii.3.2.
20. Ibid., VI.ii.3.4.
21. James Halteman and Edd Noell, *Reckoning with Markets: Moral Reflections in Economics* (New York: Oxford University Press, 2012), 56–59; see also Paul Hazard, *European Thought in the Eighteenth Century*, trans. J. Lewis May (Harmondsworth: Penguin, 1965), 177.

The Post-Smith World

However, as the Industrial Revolution ground on, simple optimism gave way to a more sobering reality in the face of a growing working class subjected to dehumanizing and often exploitative working conditions, deprived of human autonomy and decision making. Many reformers, religious or not, sought to address these injustices with a host of responses: moral suasion, individual reforms, and regulations of the worst abuses, as well as calls for common ownership of various forms. For most, the conditions were so horrible that philosophical concerns were mere intellectual games in the face of true horrors. Enough agreed on the final values, the need to deal with the effects of capitalism: that the collapse of the metaphysical and epistemological foundations was not an issue. This made it easier for most not to realize the impact of the loss of those certainties.[22]

But not for all. As Nietzsche made extremely clear in his writings at the end of the 1800s, Christian values required a Christian metaphysical view of the human person. Once that view was removed, these values could no longer be justified. His extremely caustic critiques of those who tried to do so is especially helpful for seeing the challenge of the times: "When one gives up the Christian faith, one pulls the right to Christian morality out from under one's feet. This morality is by no means self-evident: this point has to be exhibited again and again, despite the English flatheads. Christianity is a system, a whole view of things thought out together. By breaking one main concept out of it, the faith in God, one breaks the whole: nothing necessary remains in one's hands ... Christian morality is a command; its origin is transcendent; ... it has truth only if God has truth—it stands or falls with faith in God."[23]

How did Nietzsche get to this point? While the early 1800s seethed with the challenges of changing political arrangements and economic conditions, philosophy had churned onward in rejecting the metaphysical foundation.[24] Materialist philosophers refined their attack to define

---

22. Nietzsche criticized their failure to recognize the problem in his classic statement "for the English, morality is not yet a problem," from *Twilight of the Idols* in *The Portable Nietzsche*, trans. Walter Kaufmann (New York: Viking, 1966), 516.

23. Ibid., 515–16.

24. Henri de Lubac, *The Drama of Atheist Humanism* (San Francisco: Ignatius, 1998 [1949]), 27.

the spiritual experience as the product of material conditions. Central to this was Ludwig Feuerbach, who claimed that God was merely the product of people projecting their ideals onto a hypothetical being. God did not create man; man created God. To this he added the concept of alienation and argued that while people originally developed religions to enable them to cope with their conditions, those religions came to be independent of their creators, ultimately dominating them and leaving the people dominated by and alienated from the concept and institution they had created to make their lives easier.[25]

As de Lubac argues, Nietzsche drew the obvious extension from Feuerbach: if God was made up, merely a fictional being on which to project the best values of people but ultimately the product of material conditions, surely values themselves are merely products of people and, thus, of material conditions as well.[26] And just as the religions people create ultimately come to dominate them, the same occurs with ideals: they acquire an independent existence that, in turn, comes to hinder man himself. This is especially true of the Christian ideal of equality, whose result is to hold back the great.

Marx's Attempt to Save Ideals with Economic Inevitability

How does one avoid such a conclusion? As a follower of Feuerbach, Marx also recognized the challenges that materialist philosophy posed to addressing the economic changes. This point is so critical that Kolakowski starts his monumental analysis of Marxism with the statement "Karl Marx was a German Philosopher.... [L]ogically as well as chronologically, the starting-point of Marxism is to be found in philosophic anthropology."[27]

Marx was not studying the economic question of how to coordinate a centrally planned economy or proposing common ownership to achieve social justice. Others had proposed such schemes, and some were trying them. But Marx agreed with Nietzsche's reasoning that philosophical materialism means that such ideals do not exist. In fact, he was extremely critical of others (whom he called "utopian Socialists")

25. Ibid., 24–42.
26. Ibid., 42–72.
27. Kolakowski, *Main Currents of Marxism*, 8.

who argued for reforms based on ideals but who did not recognize that ideals cannot exist if materialism is true. Moreover, appeals to principles such as "liberty, equality, fraternity" could never be adequate because they were mere ideas, not changes in the economic relations that, alone, could be truly formative.

His solution was to develop a "scientific" (i.e., grounded in what he believed were physical laws about humans and nature) model about how society will ultimately move to communism. Because it is inevitable, it does not have to be based on trying to achieve any specific ideal. Marx, thus, tried to solve the eternal problem of moral choice by using the inevitability of communism to obtain a normative foundation ex nihilo.[28] As Engels wrote, "According to the laws of bourgeois economics, the greatest part of the product does not belong to the workers who have produced. If we now say: that is unjust, that ought not be so, then that has nothing immediately to do with economics. We are merely saying that this economic fact is in contradiction to our sense of morality. Marx, therefore, never based his Communist demands upon this, but upon the inevitable collapse of the capitalist mode of production."[29]

What was needed was the systematic working out of a model of human nature, knowledge, and economic systems that would progress to that result. As Engels described their project, "[T]he Hegelian method was absolutely unusable in its available form. It was essentially idealistic, and the problem here was that of developing a world contemplation more materialistic than any previously advanced."[30] This meant facing, more seriously than ever before, all the implications of philosophical materialism: no God meant no moral law, no ideals, no soul, purely physical causation of human behavior, no providential direction to history, and so on.

Starting with human nature, because people are simply material creatures, no "spirit" can propose or override the material drives. Peo-

28. Thus, solving both the economic and philosophical crises of the 1840s. Alvin W. Gouldner, *The Two Marxisms: Contradictions and Anomalies in the Development of Theory* (New York: Seabury Press, 1980), 58.

29. Frederick Engels, "Preface," in Karl Marx's *The Poverty of Philosophy* (New York: International Publishers, 1992 [1847]), 10.

30. Frederick Engels, "Review of Karl Marx's *Contribution to the Critique of Political Economy*," in *Ludwig Feuerbach and the Outcome of Classical German Philosophy*, ed. Frederick Engels (New York: International, 1941), 77.

ple, including ideas, must be the product of circumstances. As Marx
wrote, this insight had long been a part of French materialism. But it
still lacked several pieces: the historical mechanism, the analytical method, and the scientific approach of explaining everything in terms of material forces, not ideals.

Earlier writers could only argue about reforming the general system, largely in terms of politics, but could not justify why or explain
how. While treating people as material, they did not go far enough to
recognize that principles to which they appealed could not exist, nor
could they provide a mechanism by which purely physical beings could
understand their circumstances in enough mass to change them.[31] Marx
believed that sufficient masses of the people would only acquire a consciousness of their position when circumstances had changed to make
it adequately clear to them. Writing too early, they could not see what
Marx did: that capitalism was finally creating the conditions to demys-
tify the world so that the masses would become aware of the superiority
of socialized ownership and overthrow the current system.

Capitalism does not just improve productivity—although that was
critical to establishing the enormous productivity needed for the future communist society—it transformed people, their relationships, and
their understanding. The profit motive induced the bourgeoisie to pursue the division of labor to reduce costs and maintain profits. This di-
vested workers of private property, and homogenized their identity by
homogenizing their (atrocious) working conditions, with other types of
personal interests fading in comparison. This resulted in an ever-greater
consolidation of people, concentrating them into just two classes: the
proletarians without property and the ever-smaller group of bourgeoisie. The extreme harshness of its conditions also changed people themselves, preparing them to welcome common ownership of the means of
production and ending alienation and exploitation.

31. While pointing out their limitations, he nonetheless praises their metaphysical assumptions
about human nature. For example, he writes, "In Helvetius, who likewise started from Locke, materialism assumed a really French character. Helvetius conceived it immediately in its application to
social life. The sensory qualities and self-love, enjoyment and correctly understood personal interest are the basis of all morality. The natural equality of human intelligences, the unity of progress
of reason and progress of industry, the natural goodness of man, and the omnipotence of education
are the main features in his system." Frederick Engels and Karl Marx, *The Holy Family or Critique of
Critical Criticism: Against Bruno Bauer and Company* (Moscow: Progress, 1975 [1844]), 153.

Only Marx was able to combine the implication of philosophical materialism with a materialist historical mechanism by which a desirable society would occur, not by choice but by the pressure of economic forces. Oddly, Marxism participated in eliminating ideals but preserving their implications by locating them as the inevitable outcome of society. This critical combination of quasi-religious conclusions, making the case for this ideal society without needing any normative grounding, proved enormously attractive to an intellectual class that faced the loss of the Judeo-Christian metaphysical and epistemological understanding. It also implied the place for action must be society itself. The way to affect people must be to change social organization.[32]

As with Smith, this approach recognizes Marx not just as a political figure, social reformer, or economist but also as a philosopher. Although he early concluded that philosophy alone was not enough, that only actual economic reform could change the setting for humankind, he remained grounded enough in his philosophical training to recognize that any economic theories had to be consistent with his vision of the human person and vice versa. Marx offered a comprehensive picture rationalizing commitments to social justice without needing a metaphysical foundation. This was not just trying to use economic theory to solve the social problems of income inequality or injustice but doing so in light of the philosophical problem that ideals cannot exist at all if one adopts philosophical materialism and in a way intended to force social action.

Rand as One Culmination of the Materialist Path

But what if communism turns out to not be feasible or inevitable? Then Marx's neat solution to existential problems is lost. This is Rand's position. Writing in the mid-twentieth century, in the early years of the collectivist economic systems, Rand was not simply in favor of capitalism. She was an unabashed critic of collectivism in all its forms. She believed capitalism was most moral because it encouraged people to live for their own fulfillment and did not require people to sacrifice for others.

What makes this view so interesting is that she is clear about the philosophical grounding for her position. She agrees with Marx and

32. Rocco Buttiglione, *Karol Wojtyla: The Thought of the Man Who Became John Paul II* (Grand Rapids, Mich.: Eerdmans, 1997), 292–305.

Nietzsche on the metaphysical and epistemological foundation: the material world is all that exists. Knowledge can only come through reason and the senses. For her, no authority, thus, could compel a person to sacrifice himself for another. Reason implied each person ought to work for his own fulfillment, not for some collective good.[33] Why did she reach a different conclusion than Marx? Because by the time she was writing, it was obvious that communism is neither inevitable nor liberating. Marx had failed, and we are back to Nietzsche. Thus, for economics, if people are only material, and there is no revelation, reason points them only to their own self-fulfillment, without concern for others, and the free market is best for that.

HUMAN NATURE, ECONOMIC THEORY, AND THE ECONOMIC EXPERIMENTS OF THE TWENTIETH CENTURY

This account explains how the collapse of communism two decades ago is not merely a story of the failure of an economic system of central planning, but of a philosophical project intended to rationalize ethics and political ideals without a metaphysical foundation. The twentieth century was not simply a conflict with Nazism, fascism, or communism but, in part, also demonstrates how shifts in the philosophical vision of the human person shaped theories about which economic systems would be desirable given the values and behavioral assumptions that flowed from those visions.

While today attitudes toward the free market can be classified in numerous ways, (classical vs. modern liberal, individualism vs. collectivism, pro-market vs. pro-government, etc.), adding the metaphysical and the epistemological dimension considered here provides a richer picture that draws out the importance of the Christian view to which Benedict XVI referred. These are presented in table 4-1, which provides two dimensions: a spectrum of views of free-market society (from good to bad) and the choice between the general Judeo-Christian metaphysical assumptions that God exists, there is a moral law, and people have free will to act (the left column) or the materialist alternative that there is

33. Harry Binswanger, "Philosophy, the Ultimate CEO," in *Why Businessmen Need Philosophy: The Capitalist's Guide to the Ideas Behind Ayn Rand's Atlas Shrugged*, rev. and expanded ed., ed. Debi Ghate and Richard Ralston (New York: New American Library, 2011), 31–33.

TABLE 4-1. Metaphysical Views and Attitudes toward Capitalism

Metaphysical Views and Attitudes toward Capitalism	
Metaphysical Views: God, Human Nature, Moral Truth	
Judeo-Christian Framework	Philosophical Materialism
God, Soul, Moral Law All Exist	No God, No Soul, No Moral Law
Markets Good → Bad 1. Religious Conservative	3. Libertarian, e.g. Nonreligious / Rand
2. Religious Liberals (worried about market impact on social justice) and Some Traditionalists (worried about market impact on institutions of society)	4. Fascism, National Socialism, Communism, Socialism, Nonreligious Intellectual Left

no God, no moral law, no free will (the right column). This mirrors the choice alluded to in Marxist thought, as in the *Fundamentals* it states that "[t]here are only two main streams in philosophy: materialism and idealism. This means that any philosophical doctrine, no matter how original, is ultimately either materialist or idealist in content. The struggle between materialism and idealism is closely connected with the struggle between science and religion. Since it is clearly opposed to idealism and religion, materialism rejects faith in God and the supernatural; materialism is inseparable from atheism."[34]

Consider the right-hand column, that is, the materialist perspective (quadrants 3 and 4) of table 4-1. Assuming people are solely material beings implies human behavior is explainable entirely by material factors. Shifting from a Judeo-Christian view, which assumed behavior flowed from personal (spiritual), biological, and social (including economic) factors, the loss of the personal element necessarily implied greater importance to changing the circumstances, especially the economy.[35] This

34. Fedor V. Konstantinov, The *Fundamentals of Marxist-Leninist Philosophy*, trans. R. Daglish (Moscow: Progress Publishers, 1974), 26.

35. The two quadrants here, differing by market attitude but united in metaphysical foundation, mirror that of Solzhenitsyn. He observed that the general perception of the conflict between capitalism and communism ignored the important commonality—their shared philosophical materialism, and that the West might find itself on a different path to the same materialist end. See, for example, his "Templeton Lecture of 1983," in *The Solzhenitsyn Reader: New and Essential Writings,*

approach then became a battle over how economic forces shape people and how one should feel about that.

Quadrant 3 includes many modern nonreligious (e.g., Rand) libertarians who link their ethics of individualism and their behavioral assumptions that the market improves human behavior or, at least, is adequate to handle human failings that arise. Assuming there is no moral law from God, there can be no reason to compel the productive to sacrifice for the unproductive. Thus, the free market is preferable because it not only encourages cooperative behavior; it also enables people to live most freely with fewest economic and social constraints (which cannot be justified anyway).[36]

On the other hand, many of the twentieth century's collectivist views, from fascism and national socialism to socialism and communism, including modern nonreligious liberalism, are in quadrant 4. Despite their different approaches, they all view(ed) capitalism as negatively powerful, its mechanisms causing economic injustices and its emphasis on individual freedom corroding character and undermining social relations and concern for the common good. Thus, they assumed some stronger government or a different ownership arrangement was needed to rein it in, and attempt(ed) to offer some grounds for people to live in more consideration of society.[37] National Socialism and fascism assumed a powerful state and the collective goal of the nation would work (with concern for the nation's interest overriding self-interest), whereas communism and modern liberalism relied on common ownership and/or government control.

Moreover, these common assumptions resulted in a tremendous ur-

---

1947–2005, ed. Edward Ericson and Daniel Mahoney (Wilmington, Del.: Intercollegiate Studies Institute, 2006), 576–84.

36. It would also include some nonreligious libertarians who nonetheless care for others but believe that market effects are on the whole more positive than negative and consequently that little government is needed.

37. Francois Furet, *The Passing of an Illusion: The Idea of Communism in the 20th Century* (Chicago: University of Chicago Press, 1999), 175. "In Fascism, as in Communism, the idea of the future was based on a critique of bourgeois modernity.... It arose from a variety of currents from authors of very different origins, all of whom demonized the bourgeoisie.... It was meant to restore the unity of the people and the nation in the face of a society being disintegrated by money.... Fascism was born not merely to vanquish Bolshevism but to break the divisiveness of the bourgeois world. The same ambition and the same ill-being supported both promises and both movements. The Fascists and the Bolsheviks relied on different and even contradictory supports—the one on class, the other on nation—but both sought to dispel the same curse by the same means."

gency about the system. Whatever political/economic mix is chosen, the arrangement bears the enormous role of ensuring that a society full of people who cannot be moral agents, for whom no purpose or moral law exists, including responsibility for others, nonetheless, will decide to get along harmoniously. Society must make up for lost normative grounds that might have motivated cooperation previously, with increased power from the social organization. Part of the reason secularists placed so much emphasis on economic reform in the twentieth century was in recognition that lost capacity to appeal to moral truth implied the system itself had to carry more weight in organizing society.

On the other hand, if people are both physical and spiritual beings (the left column), then addressing that dimension of human behavior that can be improved by changes in economic arrangements is important, but it is not the whole picture. Those in the left column often hold substantial differences in views over how (and how much) capitalism affects personal actions and effort, material justice or individual character and social relations, and this disagreement results in different prudential views about economic arrangements and policies. Those in quadrant 1 generally think the market is good for a population raised in virtue. Those in quadrant 2 include religious liberals, who tend to worry about the market's effect on economic justice, and some religious conservatives concerned about the market's impact on traditional social arrangements.

But agreement on the metaphysical framework means those in quadrants 1 and 2 know these external conditions are not everything. Because people are also spiritual beings, they also need truth, to know what life is about, to have meaning to live for, to know there are moral laws to follow, to grow in virtue, and to overcome sin. Thus, spiritually equipping people is an important part of a good society. They know that some problems are physical and best dealt with in a physical dimension, perhaps economically or by the government. Other problems are more spiritual and/or philosophical for which spiritual and philosophical means are more appropriate. They also accept some fuzziness on the margins: some physical changes may have a driving impact on people's spiritual lives, while some spiritual changes may affect personal actions or efforts and thus have physical consequences. Similarly, biological or social forces may create pressures on individuals to behave in certain ways, but knowledge of the moral law and growth of virtue may enable people to resist such physical pressures. It is part of the challenge of being both physical and spiritual creatures.

These different beliefs about human nature also shaped how people in the different columns view the role and efficacy of civil society. Although there is disagreement over how adequate this is (given the expected impact of capitalism), people in both left quadrants agree these spiritual factors matter enormously. Thus, those in the left half believe society needs institutions that provide these spiritual resources, particularly families and churches.

On the other hand, economism induces people to undervalue civil society.[38] As materialists, they are boxed in: *everything* must be explainable and solvable physically. As earlier, this position is captured in *Fundamentals*:

Depending on how we answer the basic question of philosophy, we are bound to draw certain definite social conclusions concerning men's relationship to reality, the understanding of historical events, moral principles, and so on. If, like the idealists, for example, we regard consciousness, spirit as primary, as definitive, then we shall seek the source of social evils ... not in the character of man's material life, not in the economic system of society, not in its class structure, but in man's consciousness, his errors, his wickedness. Such a belief gives us no opportunity of determining the main directions in which social life changes.[39]

Trapped by their assumptions of human nature, their only hope was changing the economy. This makes clear how debates about the choice of system had to be about more than just productive efficiency.

CONCLUSION: HOW THE ECONOMIC EXPERIMENTS POINT TO THE IMPORTANCE OF HUMAN SELF-UNDERSTANDING

Communism failed.[40] But what does that mean? For most, it implies simply that capitalism proved itself more efficient. But that does not go

38. Gouldner, *The Two Marxisms*, 346–48.
39. Konstantinov, *Fundamentals*, 22–23.
40. Beyond the economic failure, the social failures of violence, oppression, alienation, crime, distortion of truth, undermining of relationships, moral decay, and so forth are reasonably documented, though not as well as they should, and nowhere near as well known as they ought for their lessons to humanity. Some sources helpful for this are as follows: Leon Aron, *Roads to the Temple: Truth, Memory, Ideas, and Ideals in the Making of the Russian Revolution 1987–1991* (New Haven, Conn.: Yale University Press, 2012). Aron documents the growing recognition that communism had failed

far enough. The greed, individualism, alienation, and moral decay common across economic systems still present in capitalist nations, although worse in communist nations, imply that something more is at stake in the answer. Simple lessons in efficiency do not explain Benedict XVI's interpretation, that the fall of communism points us back not to the invisible hand but to man himself.

While the language is often unfamiliar to economists, from Smith to Marx to the regimes of the twentieth century, each recognized that his or her economic system had to match the vision of the human person he or she held. Their common outcome—that merely rearranging the economy was not enough—thus also challenges their underlying visions of humanity. And it likely points back to a more important role of our answers to what it means to be human and the sense of truth that is so central a part of religion, as well as of institutions religions assist and validate, from charities to families. These ideas, of course, are exactly what the Gospel addresses. Christian action in the world will be more effective if we understand how the failures of such experiments point to the importance of those metaphysical truths of which we are stewards and which are the true gift we have to offer.

---

even to solve the social problems. John Clark and Aaron Wildavsky, *The Moral Collapse of Communism: Poland as a Cautionary Tale* (San Francisco: Institute for Contemporary Studies, 1990). This provides a similar examination for Poland. Stéphane Courtois, Nicolas Werth, Jean-Louis Panne, Andrzej Paczkowski, Karel Bartošek, and Jean-Louis Margolin, eds., *The Black Book of Communism* (Cambridge, Mass.: Harvard University Press, 1999), 4. This gives a historical account of communism in each country. Paul Hollander, ed., *From the Gulag to the Killing Fields* (Wilmington, Del.: Intercollegiate Studies Institute, 2006). This includes numerous first-hand accounts in different countries. Alexander Yakovlev, *The Fate of Marxism in Russia* (New Haven, Conn.: Yale University Press, 1993), 65–100. This ascribes the failures of communism to the materialism inherent in Marxism itself. Alexander Yakovlev, *A Century of Violence in Soviet Russia* (New Haven, Conn.: Yale University Press, 2002). Yakovlev was a member of a commission that investigated atrocities and recounts them here.

FIVE

Free Markets with *Caritas*
A Transformational Concept of Efficiency

Bruce Baker

The principle of gratuitousness and the logic of gift as an expression
of fraternity can and *must find their place within normal economic activity*.

POPE BENEDICT XVI

Where and how does the *principle of gratuitousness* function in the free
market? In this chapter, I suggest that the principle of gratuitousness
can transform prevalent notions of economic efficiency by removing the
ethical blind spots that linger in the popular idea of a free market guided
by an invisible hand. I aim to show that the principle of gratuitousness,
as an expression of *caritas*, can help to distinguish healthy and unhealthy
dynamics within economic transactions, and furthermore, this notion
of health pertains to the sustainability of a free market. This transforms
the conventional concept of efficiency by recognizing and exposing the
erroneous presumption that efficiency per se is a foundational good. It is
not. The concept of efficiency cannot bear the weight of moral scrutiny,
unless and until it is transformed by interpretation within the context of
caritas, which is an authentic foundational good. This transformational
concept of efficiency provides a useful framework within which to evaluate the contribution of economic activities to the overall sustainability
of the free market. *Caritas* makes the difference in an economic pursuit
that adds strength and vitality to the market, as compared to one that
detracts from it. I aim to show by analysis and illustrative examples that
caritas—revealed in the principle of gratuitousness and in witness to the

Epigraph is from Benedict XVI, Encyclical *Caritas in Veritate* (Vatican City: Libreria Editrice
Vaticana, 2009), 36; emphasis in original.

value of solidarity—is present in those economic activities that contribute to and enhance the sustainability of the free market.

Different sorts of economic activities may, therefore, be characterized based on whether they are either *additive* or *extractive*. By "additive" I mean the sort of economic activities that create wealth (or, at a minimum, create wealth-generating opportunities with intentionality) beyond the immediate profit a party may derive from the mere transaction. Additive activities are akin to creation ex nihilo, in the sense that the outcome realizes a benefit that had not existed before the creative act. Such wealth-creating effects display *caritas*, by virtue of bestowing gifts that would not otherwise have existed apart from the intentional creative act. These activities demonstrate an inherent component of generosity, charity or *caritas*, in that they distribute benefits into the larger community represented by the free market.

"Extractive" economic activities, on the other hand, are those that seek to gain a profit yet *without* intentional concern for solidarity or for the sake of beneficent outcomes motivated by *caritas*. Here I examine a few types of business and financial activity to assess the role of *caritas* in economic transactions. My thesis is that additive transactions convey an element of *caritas*, which leads to economic sustainability, whereas negative transactions do not.

Speaking metaphorically of the free market as a living body, we may say that additive transactions contribute to the overall metabolic health of the body: they nourish sustainable wealth creation. Extractive activities, on the other hand, feed off the energy of the body without adding to its overall strength. Economic activity that bears witness to the spirit and the logic of gratuitousness will build solidarity and contribute to sustainability.[1]

DEMYTHOLOGIZING THE INVISIBLE HAND

To make distinctions between additive and extractive activities is no simple matter. Conventional wisdom argues that such distinctions are simply

---

1. Activities that promote solidarity and sustainability might be deemed "socially useful" as opposed to other "socially useless" sorts of activities that do not contribute to solidarity, to borrow the phrasing of Lord Adair Turner, chairman of the UK Financial Services Authority, who has called "socially useless" the sort of hyperspeculative, self-serving activities that led to the subprime mortgage scandal. Rowan Williams and Larry Elliott, *Crisis and Recovery: Ethics, Economics and Justice* (Basingstoke: Palgrave Macmillan, 2010), 12.

impossible prima facie. Hayek has argued famously that no amount of administrative acumen is sufficient for such matters.[2] The questions are too
complex, it is argued, and the valuations too subjective. The suggestion
that the logic of *caritas* might be essential for the health of the free market would seem to fly in the face of the conventional wisdom regarding
the efficiency of markets. In light of the seeming intractability of questions related to worth and goodness, it is argued, the efficiency of prices
in a free market is the only suitable arbiter of value. Here the idea of an
"invisible hand" is invoked: the market is trusted to blindly make practical, beneficial trade-offs, "as though guided by an invisible hand," in the
famous words of Adam Smith.

This invocation presumes a lot. First, it presumes that a calculus
of prices and other quantifiable market forces offers the only rational
means to evaluate the merits and comparative desirability of outcomes.
Furthermore, it presumes to provide a rationale unencumbered by the
irreducible values and complexities of spiritual faith or overarching
value statements. In essence, it presumes to subjugate all values to the
dominion of the profit-driven efficiency of the free market.

The conventional idea of efficient markets trusts the price-setting
function of a mythical invisible hand to set prices that will lead naturally to the optimum outcome. This is a severely reductionist approach,
of course, and its reductionism is most pronounced and most problematic with respect to the significance of human nature, human dignity,
relationship, and spirituality.

Anatole Kaletsky, in his critical assessment of the events leading up
to the recent collapse of financial markets, points to the flaws in such
mythical thinking. He says this conventional wisdom regarding market
efficiency leads to "the imaginary world of market fundamentalist ideology, in which financial stability is automatic, involuntary unemployment is impossible, and efficient, omniscient markets can solve all economic problems, if only the government will stand aside."[3]

This imaginary world is built on the premise that economics may

2. Friedrich August von Hayek, *The Constitution of Liberty* (Chicago: University of Chicago
Press, 1960).

3. Anatole Kaletsky, *Capitalism 4.0: The Birth of a New Economy in the Aftermath of Crisis* (New
York: PublicAffairs, 2010), 156. Kaletsky elaborates on the fundamental problems within this
"imaginary world" by pointing out that the presumption, common in the practice of modern economics, that human nature can be modeled in mathematical formulas is "an act of hubris" (168).

be practiced in a spirit of "scientific asceticism," devoid of moral questions and detached from moral consequences.[4] This premise trusts in the mythical idea of an "invisible hand" that somehow weaves the chaotic movements of human choice into a tapestry of meritorious and beneficial outcomes. The mythological aspect of this premise has recently been critiqued by several observers,[5] including Samuels, who disparages the idea of the invisible hand as "an ambiguous and inconclusive ... feature of a striking theme in which a belief is offered in the absence of truth."[6] Adam Smith, the seminal voice behind this concept, employs the phrase "invisible hand" only rarely and gingerly to fill a gap in the explanation of political economy. Based on his finely tuned reading of Smith, Samuels concludes that Smith is well aware of the semantic risk in such an elliptical expression, knowing that "people settle for propositions that suit the imagination, or set minds at rest, when truth is unattainable."[7] Ironically, the vague or even tautological idea of the invisible hand is sometimes cited in support of analytical explanations for the functioning of a market economy. Such explanations apparently accept it as a matter of faith that the notion of "an invisible hand" can actually explain the free market as a self-organizing principle.

Sedláček describes well the "historic irony" in the development of economics, which leads to acceptance of this mythical power ascribed to the invisible hand. He ties the origins of this myth to the split between ethics and economics. Once moral inquiry is removed from the purview of economics, the latter morphs into an exercise in quantitative methods: "The idea of the invisible hand of the market is, in reality, born of moral inquiry, but another hundred years later the issue of morality is lost and economics is completely emancipated from ethics. An unusual reversal has taken place. Adam Smith, Thomas Malthus, John

4. Luigino Bruni and Stefano Zamagni, *Civil Economy: Efficiency, Equity, Public Happiness* (Oxford: Peter Lang, 2007), 15.

5. Tomas Sedláček, *Economics of Good and Evil: The Quest for Economic Meaning from Gilgamesh to Wall Street* (Oxford: Oxford University Press, 2011); Kaushik Basu, *Beyond the Invisible Hand: Groundwork for a New Economics* (Princeton, N.J.: Princeton University Press, 2011); Marilynne Robinson, *When I Was a Child I Read Books* (New York: Farrar, Straus and Giroux, 2012); H. Woody Brock, *American Gridlock: Why the Right and Left Are Both Wrong* (Hoboken, N.J.: John Wiley and Sons, 2012); Joseph E. Stiglitz, *The Price of Inequality: How Today's Divided Society Endangers Our Future* (New York: W. W. Norton, 2012).

6. Warren J. Samuels, Marianne F. Johnson, and William H. Perry, *Erasing the Invisible Hand: Essays on an Elusive and Misused Concept in Economics* (New York: Cambridge University Press, 2011), xvi.

7. Ibid., xx.

S. Mill, John Locke—the great fathers of classical liberal economics—
were foremost moral philosophers. A century later, economics has become a mathematized and allocative science, full of graphs, equations,
and tables, with no room for ethics."[8]

In the pursuit of mathematical methods and scientific asceticism,
economics has been cut loose from its roots in moral philosophy. This
has profound implications for the concept of market efficiency because
it leads into the expectation that quantitative methods are the best tool
for determining the common good, with the corollary conclusion that
the pursuit of profits, under the mysterious control of the invisible
hand, becomes presumptively the de facto means of making optimal
trade-offs among individuals and within society as a whole.

The problem, however, is that the profit motive does not distinguish
between sustainable and unsustainable activity. The invisible hand does
not discriminate between additive and extractive transactions. It can operate with equal force and efficiency in either direction. It is ambidex-
trous and ambivalent in this regard.

My thesis is that the logic of *caritas* provides the corrective needed to
recognize where and how the forces of free-market efficiency are conducive to sustainability. I argue that the beneficent power of the market
to serve human flourishing is based not in a morally tacit understanding of economic efficiency as a foundational good or cardinal value but,
rather, in the notion of *caritas* as a necessary component of economic
transactions.[9] This transformed notion of efficiency generates and enhances sustainability in the free market.

RELATIONSHIPS VERSUS TRANSACTIONS

The logic of *caritas* is paradoxical. It requires to be understood from
within the context of faith in the greater reality of human dignity that
transcends the logic of prices and preference relations. The principle of

8. Sedláček, *Economics of Good and Evil*, 177.

9. John Paul II draws the connection between human dignity and market freedom: "No free
economy can function for long and respond to the conditions of a life ... unless it is supported and
'enlivened' by a strong ethical and religious conscience" (Vatican Council II, Pastoral Constitution
Gaudium et Spes [Vatican City: Libreria Editrice Vaticana, 1965], 24). Cf. John Paul II, "A Civilization of Solidarity and Love: An Invitation to *Centesimus Annus*," in *A New Worldly Order: John Paul II
and Human Freedom*, ed. George Weigel (Washington, D.C.: Ethics and Public Policy Center, 1992),
section 5.

gratuitousness flies in the face of conventional thinking about the efficiency of the market. The problem is not that conventional thinking
about efficiency is wrong per se but, rather, that it is incomplete. It does
not countenance the greater reality of the relationships that enable the
market to thrive and prosper. The conventional idea of market efficiency does not allow room for the logic of gift/charity. The conventional
wisdom strains to rule out charity, the same way a bilge pump works to
rid a boat of unwanted water that seeps into the vessel. Conventional
wisdom says that if there is any charity in the market system, it must
have arrived there through flaws in the market, just as bilge water arrives
through leaks in the hull. According to the conventional wisdom, therefore, the logic of gift is a contradiction in terms, prima facie.

The underlying problem, of course, is that the logic of market efficiency is incapable of bearing witness to any greater reality. It is con-
strained to the mundane. It can never rise above the rudimentary level
of mathematical approximations. It reduces human behavior to something entirely inhuman.

Richard Sennett points to the quest for ever-greater efficiency, as
measured by corporate profits, as the impetus for the unsavory changes in
corporate bureaucracies.[10] Relationships between worker and employee,
producer and consumer, and seller and buyer have become more transient
and depersonalized. These trends are the consequence of the quest for
more predictability and efficiency in profit engines of business. George
Soros sums it up by saying that transactions have replaced relationships.[11]

The quest for amoral efficiency in transactions drives the human element of *caritas* out of the equation. With the moral aspects of relationship cut off from the metrics of efficiency, there is a ratchet effect that
leads in the direction of the total commoditization of every good and
service. Ultimately, commoditization becomes the arbiter of morality.
Prices are everything, and Pareto optimization rules. In this sense of
market efficiency, there is no room for the transcendent nature of human
relationships to provide realism with respect to justice and the moral dis-
cernment of good and evil.

10. Richard Sennett, *The Culture of the New Capitalism* (New Haven, Conn.: Yale University
Press, 2006), 22–25.
11. George Soros, *The Crisis of Global Capitalism: Open Society Endangered* (London: Little,
Brown and Company, 1998), 73.

Some economists are quick to defend the separation of morality from economics on the basis that moral issues deserve attention in another, separate realm of thought. The troubling aspect of this position is that moral concerns are soon forgotten when attention shifts to the econometric analysis of market functions. This econometric focus excludes moral issues of justice from consideration, reducing such concerns to the lowest common denominator, namely, the quintessential ideal of efficiency in free, open, and perfect competition. The only type of justice that remains explicitly valid in conjunction with this emphasis on the econometrics of efficiency is a sort of *commutative* justice, that is, justice defined as equal and fair exchange, *simpliciter*. When all things of value can be bought and sold, justice will be done when the price is fair. Benedict XVI refers to this sense of commutative justice as "the principle of equivalence" and points out its inability to sustain market health: "If the market is governed solely by the principle of the equivalence in value of exchanged goods, it cannot produce the social cohesion that it requires in order to function well. *Without internal forms of solidarity and mutual trust, the market cannot completely fulfil its proper economic function.*"[12]

Here is the result of the logic of efficiency: justice is relegated to become a mechanistic by-product of efficiency, and morality is reduced to the question of how to make markets more efficient.

Of course, the pragmatic question of establishing fair prices to achieve Pareto optimality fails to account for unquantifiable benefits pertaining to the spirituality and morality of relationships. Duns Scotus recognizes this transcendent component of economics in his treatment of commutative justice. He recognizes that the presence of an indeterminate, yet real, component of gift (donatio) is necessary in order for a transaction to be free and beneficial and, therefore, sustainable in a market economy: "For among men it is hard for contracts to exist where the contracting parties do not intend to set aside something of that exact or indivisible justice owed to one another, so that to some extent a donation accompanies every contract."[13] This donation or gift is not an unintended accident of the economic trade but, rather, is an intentional gifting of one to the other, in recognition of the cardinal value inherent

---

12. Benedict XVI, *Caritas in Veritate*, 35; emphasis original.

13. John Duns Scotus, *Political and Economic Philosophy*, trans. Allan B. Wolter (St. Bonaventure, N.Y.: The Franciscan Institute, 2001), 47.

in the relationship, and in witness to the command, *"do unto another as you would wish done to you."*[14]

CIRCULAR LOGIC

In the absence of the redeeming context for the evaluation of economic outcomes as provided by the theological understanding of *caritas*, efficiency in the sense of Pareto optimization stands in for theology as the sensemaking context. Pareto optimality seems to provide a coherent logic: Justice demands fairness. Fairness results from efficiency. Efficiency, therefore, leads to justice. The problem is that this is circular logic built upon spurious presumptions.

M. Douglas Meeks has a keen eye for what has happened to our concept of morality within the modern market economy:

Market forces, then, are said to be automatic, unconscious, mechanistic, and unintended. As such, the market can take the place of state and church and even the family ... Naturally, the God concepts that provided these institutions with authority systems could also be replaced. The coherence of the system is derived not from tradition or command but from the unintended outcome of self-interested, self-guided activities of individuals. Taking on the character of necessity and inevitability, economic law could seemingly fulfill all public functions that "God" had previously performed. The market, were its law obeyed, promises a free and harmonious way of integrating and coordinating society without authority and coercion.[15]

The fair and efficient operation of the market thus becomes the new theology of capitalism. It becomes the context for not only the power of production but also for justice and morality. Pragmatism trumps transcendence. That is the unfortunate and self-contradictory conclusion of the quest for efficiency. This conclusion is also the fatal undoing that makes markets unsustainable and brings them to the brink of collapse. This is why free markets require a healthy dose of *caritas* if they are to survive.

14. Ibid.

15. M. Douglas Meeks, *God the Economist: The Doctrine of God and Political Economy* (Minneapolis: Fortress Press, 1989), 51ff. Harvey Cox makes the same point with biting and convincing satire, pointing out that "the religion of The Market has become the most formidable rival [to traditional religions], the more so because it is rarely recognized as a religion." Harvey Cox, "Market as God: Living in the New Dispensation," *Atlantic Monthly* 203, no. 3 (March 1999): 18–23.

The logic of *caritas* (i.e., the principle of gratuitousness) transforms the econometric concept of efficiency in the marketplace and makes the market sustainable. The logic of *caritas* restores the crucial element of humanity that is otherwise washed away by the quintessential ideal efficiency. By incorporating the logic of *caritas* into the fundamentals of exchange, human relationships are sustained and restored.

This is a decidedly different concept of human dignity, which flies in the face of conventional wisdom regarding *homo economicus*. In *Caritas in Veritate*, Benedict XVI reminded us that human dignity is ultimately grounded in a transcendent vision of the person, and not in a pragmatic view of the person as contributor to economic transactions: "[I]ntegral human development is primarily a vocation, and therefore it involves a free assumption of responsibility in solidarity on the part of everyone. Moreover, such development requires a transcendent vision of the person, it needs God: without him, development is either denied, or entrusted exclusively to man, who falls into the trap of thinking he can bring about his own salvation, and ends up promoting a dehumanized form of development."[16]

The idea of *homo economicus*, on which econometric models are built, leaves out the essential aspect of relationship in which human dignity is found. The essence of human dignity derives from the mystery of relationship with God. The transcendent vision of the person as one in relationship with God is also the foundation of a relationship with one's neighbors. The transcendent vision of relationship therefore is also the basis for proper understanding of the role of the person in economic activity, as well as the purpose of the market. To arrive at a coherent description of society, whether in politics, economics, or any other realm, requires a transcendent vision of the human person as being created for, and existing within, relationship with God. This requires a doctrine of the whole person, the integrated self, as existing in relationship with God.[17]

The mystery of relationships, between persons and in communion with the Triune God, is an essential foundational good that permits the

16. Benedict XVI, *Caritas in Veritate*, 11.
17. John D. Zizioulas surveys the theological development of this insight. John D. Zizioulas, *Being as Communion* (London: Darton, Longman and Todd, 1985), 18.

market to operate in the first place. A market that exists only to serve itself will eventually collapse under its own weight because the relationships supporting it will wither and die. The warning signals of this dire cycle can be seen in the growing inequality of economic opportunities and wealth. The wealth-producing capacity of capitalism is, of course, a boon to human flourishing. Wealth can bear fruit in the form of a virtuous cycle that generates more economic opportunity and creates more customers to be served. Economic productivity and efficiency are necessary to alleviate poverty. But if wealth is applied solely to the goal of self-preservation and self-magnification, in a winner-take-all game of efficiency, the winner will eventually be the only one left standing, and the market will cease to exist.

Caritas offers the antidote to this dire prospect, by offering a transcendent view of human dignity as the telos of economics.[18]

Economics rested on a foundation of concern for the greater telos of human society for millennia. In the modern era, however, the practice of economics has sought status as an academic discipline severed from questions of morality, and these false presumptions have become problematic. Until the rise of the modern academic discipline of economics in the twentieth century, the study of the economic aims of society fell under the rubric of "political economy."[19] Morality was implicit in the subject of political economy; the aim was to seek the common good, and the concern was how best to govern society for the sake of the common good. The very idea of economic policy was implicitly presumed to be a practical work of moral philosophy. Dirksen grasps the nettle when he calls out the inescapable need for any and all economists to build their theories of economic behavior on some underlying ideas that presume to know something of human nature: "Every economist accepts certain basic characteristics of human nature which is nothing else

18. I have addressed this theme elsewhere in: Bruce Baker, "Human Dignity and the Logic of *Caritas*: The Source and Direction of Economic Justice," *Verbum Incarnatum: An Academic Journal of Social Justice* 5, no. 1 (2012): 1–22.

19. Political economy is the subject of turn-of-the-century studies such as: Philip H. Wicksteed, *The Common Sense of Political Economy* (London: Macmillan, 1933 [1910]); and Alfred Marshall, *Principles of Economics* (London: Macmillan, 1946 [1890]). The implicitly moral context of economic behavior is seen also in John Stuart Mill, "Principles of Political Economy with Some of their Applications to Social Philosophy" [1848], in *Collected Works of John Stuart Mill*, ed. John M. Robson (Toronto: University of Toronto Press, 1963).

than accepting a certain philosophy of man. Whether he accepts one set of characteristics or another doesn't matter; he is dependent upon some kind of philosophy of man."[20]

When the deeper significance of human relationships is removed from consideration, economic transactions become amoral, that is, devoid of moral content. This has sad consequences for the modern moral imagination. The bond is broken between economics and a higher-order understanding of morality based in spiritual goods. This leads to a loss of consideration for personal, I–thou relationships in the study of economic transactions. Bruni and Zamagni have diagnosed the situation accurately in their call for reform, to help reinstate appreciation of civic-minded responsibility as an explicit virtue of political economy: "Economics became a science relegated strictly to the economic sphere in accordance with the *homo oeconomicus* paradigm to explain human action, while sociology as a science was confined to the social sphere and the *homo sociologicus* paradigm."[21]

Deprived of its psychological and social complexities, the definition of human nature was transformed into a caricature that lent credibility to a double error.[22]

The logic of *caritas* is an essential ingredient to bring about this reform. *Caritas* is, after all, a foundational good that pertains to I–thou relationships. *Caritas* is a spiritual reality that imbues transactions with moral significance by recognizing the transcendent value of the other person. The logic of *caritas* is the cathartic antidote to reductionist utilitarian thinking.

A TRANSFORMATIONAL CONCEPT
OF EFFICIENCY

The logic of *caritas* is the catalyst that transforms the conventional wisdom about efficiency. *Caritas* rescues economics from the tyranny of efficiency construed as summum bonum. When *caritas* is recognized as

20. Cletus F. Dirksen, "The Catholic Philosopher and the Catholic Economist," *Review of Social Economy* 4, no. 1 (1946): 15. I am indebted to O'Boyle for this pertinent reference to Dirksen. Edward J. O'Boyle, "Requiem for *Homo Economicus*," *Journal of Markets and Morality* 10, no. 2 (Fall 2007): 321–37. Cf. Sedláček, *Economics of Good and Evil*, 231: "Economics in general has been surprisingly uncommunicative with the ethical sciences it originated from."

21. Bruni and Zamagni, *Civil Economy*, 130–31.

22. Ibid., 132.

a foundational good in the free market, efficiency can no longer be discussed merely in the language of econometrics; instead, it comes to be viewed within the more holistic realm of relationships of transcendent value.

Of course, this flies in the face of conventional wisdom and will be rejected as prima facie foolishness whenever and wherever the presumptions of the conventional wisdom are permitted to linger silently beneath the surface of economic discourse. The conventional wisdom presumes to have an answer to this foolishness: by insisting on value-free concepts, the hypothetical ideal of a perfectly efficient market becomes the embodiment and final arbiter of value. This insistence is grounded in the belief that value-free market transactions are the only way to make progress. But what is "value free" about such a market system? Value has been tacitly imputed to efficiency as the definitive arbiter of "good." The logic of *caritas* transforms this concept of efficiency by offering a more robust and more realistic understanding—albeit messier and trickier to analyze—that good and evil exist and that political economics can both help and harm humanity in ways that elude the antiseptic presumptions of "scientific asceticism" claimed by proponents of the conventional wisdom.[23] Bruni and Zamagni see the issue clearly: "We do not identify ourselves with this type of scientific asceticism because, ... we feel that scientific reason can serve a function in the foundation of values, and that values and scientific knowledge are not necessarily mutually opposed."[24]

Is there a way forward toward a more robust understanding of efficiency? How is the logic of *caritas* to be embodied and nurtured? The first step is to realize that this will remain forever an ongoing challenge and that there are no definitive prescriptions. The struggle against the power of Mammon will go on and on until the new heaven and the new earth have come. Our present struggle is to recognize the transforming power of *caritas* and to devise ways to build it into our political economy. Benedict XVI identified this as the fundamental issue with the transformation of economic power and sustainability of global markets:

23. Hans Jonas, *Il principio di responsabilità: un'etica per la civiltà tecnologica*, trans. Pier Paolo Portinaro (Torino: Einaudi, 1990), 142.

24. Bruni and Zamagni, *Civil Economy*, 15.

The great challenge before us, accentuated by the problems of development in this global era and made even more urgent by the economic and financial crisis, is to demonstrate, in thinking and behaviour, not only that traditional principles of social ethics like transparency, honesty and responsibility cannot be ignored or attenuated, but also that in *commercial relationships* the *principle of gratuitousness* and the logic of gift as an expression of fraternity can and must *find their place within normal economic activity*. This is a human demand at the present time, but it is also demanded by economic logic. It is a demand both of charity and of truth.[25]

To the extent that economic market power is deployed in the spirit of *caritas*—that is, in the spirit of contributing to the common good— then macroeconomic theory has much to gain by relying on the transformational concept of efficiency in view. When the spirit of *caritas* is absent, however, or the logic of *caritas* becomes broken, then efficiency no longer serves as a trustworthy guide toward the aims of society. The invisible hand can become a harmful and illegitimate taskmaster if cut loose from the moral wisdom of the society that seeks to benefit from it.

To illustrate these concepts and propose constructive steps forward, I examine three specific emerging business developments: (1) patents related to pharmaceutical drug design and marketing, (2) "monetization" strategies in recent Internet-based business models, and (3) financialization of speculative debt obligations. In each of these three test cases, I apply the logic of gratuitousness (*caritas*) to distinguish between potentially additive and extractive economic activities, and then propose systemic mechanisms to enhance the solidarity-enhancing aspects of these businesses.

PHARMACEUTICALS AND PATENT
CLIFF AVOIDANCE

Patents are a two-edged sword. The rationale for them is simple enough— to encourage beneficial innovations by granting monopoly power to inventors who might otherwise decide not to risk the time, effort, and resources required to develop new products. Patents work by imposing artificial constraints on an otherwise free market. The whole rationale for them is based in the belief that the efficiency of the market is not capable

---

25. Benedict XVI, *Caritas in Veritate*, 36; emphasis in original.

of bringing about the greatest common good for society. The upside is to bring about helpful innovations. When patents work as intended, the logic of *caritas* is fulfilled because the economic engine is harnessed to bring a boon to society. This is the proper "additive" function of trade in patented products.

The downside of patents occurs when their power is abused by using them as a means of extortion through artificially inflated pricing and profits. This would be an "extractive" use of patent power. To the extent that patent power is used as a means of artificially shifting any social surplus to the supply side, transactions for the products in question will suffer from lack of consideration for the betterment of customers and society at large, which will be the outcome of transactions devoid of *caritas*.

To illustrate the extractive effects that can ensue from this misapplication of market power, I look to the example of Pfizer and their business strategy regarding Lipitor, the best-selling drug of all time and the cash cow that helped to make Pfizer the world's largest pharmaceutical company. Pfizer is estimated to have sold more than $100 billion worth of Lipitor. The drug has accounted for a quarter of the company's profits during most of the past fifteen years. Pfizer's successful business strategy of creating and sustaining a dominant position in a highly profitable market is admirable and their innovation and successful marketing have brought real benefits to society. The health benefits of Lipitor and the good business operations of Pfizer have no doubt contributed to the common good. These outcomes are not the focus of my critique. My concern regards Pfizer's efforts to construct additional barriers to entry in search of cartel power exceeding the scope of the seminal patents on Lipitor. These actions beg the question of whether the corporate strategy has drifted into extractive transactions. This is admittedly a tangled question, for no precise line can be drawn between the fair use of patents to promote innovation and the overreaching use of patents to squash competition. Nonetheless, analysis of this case reveals the need to ask the question, "Where to draw the line?" in recognition that patent tactics can function as either extractive or additive influencers of the economic common good.

Pfizer faced what is known in the industry as a "patent cliff," meaning that when its patent expired in 2010, Pfizer's profit margin would dive as generics rushed in to sell cheaper versions of the identical chemical compound, atorvastatin.

The entry of generic versions into the free market would presumably be a benefit to society, and certainly to the patients taking the drug, as the price would be expected to fall from $3 per dose to less than $1 as competitors established themselves. This restoration of a market-driven price for a hugely valuable product would serve to bring an additive component of *caritas* into the transaction, in that the customers and society at large would be receiving a greater benefit with every dose.

However, this was not quite how this story played out. Pfizer adopted aggressive strategies to extend the patent protection on Lipitor by filing hundreds of additional patent applications in an attempt to concoct new claims on the drug's usage, thereby continuing to reap the extortive prices they were receiving by locking the generics out of the market. Since 1998, these applications have yielded 171 new patents for Pfizer mentioning Lipitor and/or atorvastatin.[26] The huge investment in patent filings was financially justified by the even greater profit potential for the drug—but at what cost to society?

Pfizer did not stop with the flood of patent applications. They also negotiated private deals with generic-drug manufacturers to secure their agreement to stay out of the market for several months. In addition, during the year leading up to the patent cliff, Pfizer was aggressively "forging deals with insurers, pharmacy benefit managers and patients to meet or beat the price of its generic replacements."[27] This was, in effect, an attempt to establish a cartel. These marketing tactics were investigated by the Federal Trade Commission (FTC), but as of the writing of this chapter, the FTC has taken no legal action.

On the patent front, however, Pfizer was successfully able to extend its monopoly on Lipitor for several months beyond the originally expected expiration date by appealing previous decisions of the Patent Office and by negotiating settlements with competitors. The company delayed the introduction of a generic version of Lipitor by Ranbaxy Laboratories of India by up to twenty months later than many analysts had been expecting, according to the *New York Times*.[28] A key factor

26. Based on my research of the U.S. Patent Office database, conducted July 2012.

27. Duff Wilson, "Facing Generic Lipitor Rivals, Pfizer Battles to Protect Its Cash Cow," *New York Times*, November 29, 2011.

28. Stephanie Saul, "Release of Generic Lipitor is Delayed," *New York Times*, June 19, 2008.

in Pfizer's strategy was to threaten patent enforcement of its monopoly into 2017.[29]

Pfizer's tactics illustrate the profit potential in patents that has incentivized the practice of "patent trolling," in which businesses are created for the sole purpose of acquiring patents that can be then be used to threaten other companies and extract profits from the sales of other companies' revenues: "Rogue patent trolls (law firms) can buy sleeping patents (patents that have not yet been used to bring products to the market) at a low price, and then when a firm is successful in the same field, claim trespass, and threaten to shut it down as a form of extortion."[30]

Patent trolling might be seen to be a business strategy motivated by the desire to benefit from extractive transactions. The logic of *caritas* might transform these methods if there were a way to evaluate the justice issues based on the impact on the persons affected most directly rather than based on the income statement of the patent owners.

MONETIZATION OF INTERNET-BASED TECHNOLOGIES

The rising tide of Internet-based business opportunities is largely driven by the monetization of personal data.[31] To attract users, Internet-based services are frequently offered gratis, at no cost to users. Google, of course, has been the bellwether, the first company to earn large, continual profits by monetizing its access to consumers in the mass market. At first glance, the "free" price of Internet offerings might seem to be aligned with the principle of *caritas*, gift, or grace. Indeed, it is true that the free access to these services conveys a gift to society at large. There is a positive additive effect here because access to information, goods, and services contributes to the overall stability and sustainability of markets. The lesser-known and potentially extractive nature of these transactions however also deserves to be noticed. After all, "there is no such thing as a free lunch."

To make a profit and to create a sustainable business model, these companies must devise a scheme to "monetize" their access to users. In

29. Ibid.

30. Stiglitz, *The Price of Inequality*, 203.

31. For a useful summary of the issues related to business tactics based on data-mining, see David Bollier, *The Promise and Peril of Big Data* (Washington, D.C.: Aspen Institute, 2010), http://www.aspeninstitute.org/publications/promise-peril-big-data.

simple terms, this amounts to manipulating and selling access to information about the people who have taken advantage of the free services. As Google, Facebook, and many others have discovered, monetization typically takes the form of targeted advertising, based in data-mining technology.

This new industry of data mining exists for the purpose of digitizing, analyzing, and manipulating the human behavior represented by data gleaned from users' interactions. Some of the most powerful companies in this field value their obscurity and operate with as much anonymity as possible. These include Acxiom, eBureau, Epsilon, ChoicePoint, and TargusInfo—all names that remain generally unknown by the people whose personal data they harvest. While these purveyors of Big Data might prefer to remain invisible and avoid public scrutiny, their customer set includes almost every brand name in the consumer, financial, and industrial markets. The whole purpose of these data miners is to glean profitable predictions of human behavior based on the accumulation of vast amounts of data on individuals. Acxiom is one of the biggest, with more than twenty-three thousand computer servers harvesting data on half a billion people and processing some fifty trillion data transactions per year.[32] The company has revenues of more than $1 billion per year and is poised for rapid growth.

The question at hand is whether this sort of monetization tends to develop in generally additive or extractive directions. This is not a critique of advertising; rather, the issue is whether monetization leads potentially into extractive transactions. The reason for concern is that the drive to monetize relationships leads to tactics that treat users as datasets rather than as persons. This can lead to business strategies based in the premise that the personal data of users are assets to be mined for value, without concern for the human dignity of the individuals represented.

The drive to monetize users' data replaces relationships with transactions. From a business point of view, this means that value resides in the power to monetize a relationship. Persons can thus be treated as commodities. This can be seen in such rubrics as "net promoter score," a measure of the potential profit a business may expect to glean from

---

32. Natasha Singer, "A Data Giant is Mapping, and Sharing, the Consumer Genome," *New York Times*, June 17, 2012.

any given customer's buying habits and socioeconomic metrics. Because datasets do not carry the same ethical implications as relationships with real persons, the logic and the spirit of *caritas* may be more easily neglected.

The financial pressure to take advantage of access to personal data is not a trifling matter. Nonetheless, ethical businesses can strive to protect the individual freedom of their customers by avoiding manipulative tactics that seek to monetize customers without their consent in the bargain.

FINANCIALIZATION OF SPECULATIVE DEBT OBLIGATIONS

Alan Greenspan expects the recent global recession brought on by the collapse of mortgage markets to go down in history as "the most virulent financial crisis ever."[33] The sources and causes of the so-called great recession are many and varied, far exceeding the scope of this chapter. I shall make no attempt to apportion blame for the crisis, or to sort the many complex technical details that contributed to the systemic underpricing of speculative risks in consumer and commercial debt obligations. Suffice it to say that the crisis was brought on by problematic government policies combined with financial industry innovations that pushed portfolio theory to the limit in ever more sophisticated synthetic financial instruments.[34] Ironically, the Community Reinvestment Act of 1977, ostensibly conceived out of concern for low-income homeowners, encouraged lenders to originate toxic loans. These eventually engendered the development of increasingly complex instruments to manage portfolio risks[35] and compounded the moral hazards of the ratings agencies and investment bankers for whom "trading in mortgage-backed securities came to dominate the profits and attention of the brightest minds in the financial industry."[36]

33. Alan Greenspan, "The Crisis," *Brookings Papers on Economic Activity* (Spring 2010): 201–46, 243.

34. Charles A. McDaniel Jr., "Theology of the "Real Economy": Christian Economic Ethics in an Age of Financialization," *Journal of Religion and Business Ethics* 2, no. 2 (2011): Article 1. http://via.library.depaul.edu/jrbe/vol2/iss2/.

35. Carolina Reid, "The Community Reinvestment Act and the Authority to Do Good," *Public Administration Review* 72, no. 3 (2012): 439–441, esp. 440.

36. Michael A. Santoro and Ronald J. Strauss, *Wall Street Values: Business Ethics and the Global Financial Crisis* (Cambridge: Cambridge University Press, 2013), 90.

No matter the origins of the crisis, my thesis suggests that the health of the mortgage markets might have been impaired by the trend in the direction of extractive economic activities that—pushed to the extreme—contributed to the market collapse. As innovations in the financialization of mortgage risks became more complex, the relationships between mortgagees and the eventual holders of mortgage-backed securities became more abstract and obscure. The bundling and rebundling of default risks effectively removed opportunities for even a modicum of *caritas* to reside in the lending relationships. Financialization depersonalized debt obligations, treating personal commitments (i.e., home mortgages) as abstract commodities. Perhaps the most insidious hazard of these innovations was the incentive to originate toxic loans in the first place. Any opportunity for *caritas* that might have been embodied in the interpersonal relationship between lender and borrower was effectively removed by the pressures to write mortgages that would be assimilated into synthetic financial products. In short, relationships were subordinated to financial calculations. The individuals whose financial risks were bundled and traded were treated as commodities rather than as real persons.[37] The opportunity for personal moral commitment was thus eroded, because both lenders and borrowers were enticed by moral hazards, such as "liar loans." Under such circumstances, profit maximization trumps solidarity, and the market eventually suffers the consequences. Joseph Stiglitz describes the unfortunate outcome of these trends: "We have gone far down an alternate path—creating a society in which materialism dominates moral commitment, in which the rapid growth that we have achieved is not sustainable environmentally or socially, in which we do not act together as a community to address our common needs, partly because rugged individualism and market fundamentalism have eroded any sense of community and have led to rampant exploitation of unwary and unprotected individuals and to an increasing social divide."[38]

It would appear that the logic of gratuitousness (*caritas*) was miss-

37. Some of the following remarks come from my essay "Human Dignity and the Logic of *Caritas*."

38. Joseph E. Stiglitz, *Freefall: America, Free Markets, and the Sinking of the World Economy* (New York: W. W. Norton, 2010), 275f. Cf. Thomas B. Edsall, "Separate and Unequal," *New York Times*, August 5, 2012.

ing in the market forces that led to the financial crisis of 2008. The system was unsustainable, yet bankers kept extracting profits so long as the music kept playing, as one infamously put it.[39] These business models led the global economy down the slippery slope of financial efficiency devoid of the logic of *caritas*. Greater concern for *caritas* would have brought more attention to the human dignity of borrowers and lenders alike, but those considerations are not easily factored into the calculations of risk and profit that have come to dominate financial services. The invention and deployment of new derivative instruments generally ignored the rather intractable problem of evaluating the impacts on human relationships and focused instead on the mathematics of arbitrage. To use the biblical example of gleaning, it was as if every last scrap of grain was harvested and the dust of broken husks also was swept up from the threshing floor and packaged for sale wherever even the slightest profit could be made. Bonuses for the winners of the game were similarly maximized. All profits were sucked out of the system, and nothing was given back. It is easy to see in hindsight, of course, but how can these excesses be prevented in the future? Solutions to these problems can be found on a case-by-case basis, and they will invariably embody the logic of gift, to whatever extent possible, and will thereby bear witness to human dignity.

CONCLUSION

The logic of *caritas* provides the corrective needed to recognize where and how the forces of economic efficiency are conducive to the health and sustainability of a market system, and where and how they are not. The beneficent power of the market to serve human flourishing is based not in the morally tacit aim of economic efficiency but, rather, in a gift-bearing efficiency aligned with *caritas*.[40] The latter is the only type of efficiency that generates and enhances sustainability in the free market. *Caritas*, not efficiency, is the cardinal good.

To the extent that economic market power is deployed in the spirit

---

39. Michiyo Nakamoto and David Wighton, "Citigroup Chief Stays Bullish on Buy-Outs," *Financial Times*, July 9, 2007.

40. John Paul II draws the connection between human dignity and market freedom: "No free economy can function for long and respond to the conditions of a life . . . unless it is supported and 'enlivened' by a strong ethical and religious conscience" (*Gaudium et Spes*, 24). Cf. "A Civilization of Solidarity and Love," section 5.

of *caritas*—that is, in the spirit of contributing to the common good—macroeconomic theory has much to gain by relying on the transformational concept of efficiency in view. Conversely, when the spirit of *caritas* is absent or the logic of *caritas* becomes broken, efficiency no longer serves as a trustworthy guide toward the aims of society. The invisible hand can become a harmful and illegitimate taskmaster if cut loose from the moral wisdom of the society that seeks to benefit from it.

SIX

Freedom as the Call of Being
Restoring the Foundations of
Ethical Enterprise

Jim Wishloff

The central question of economics is what to produce, for whom, and how to produce it. The matter is, of course, central to human affairs. As corporeal beings, human persons must win their way in the world by provisioning for themselves as any organism does. We are more than material, or even living and conscious, beings in nature, however. Human persons live not just by instinct but also by rationality. We think ourselves through the question of political economy, as it were, and our enterprises, those organizations we charge with the "solving" of the provisioning problem, rest on or originate from these thoughts.

Because the exercise of freedom is at the core of being human, the formation of markets that allow buyers and sellers to freely engage in trade would surely seem to be an outworking or embodiment of right thinking in economic matters. It is not unfounded to hope that well-functioning markets would deliver the outcomes desired of an effective provisioning system:

People have access to the goods they need to live a dignified existence.

Decent work that uplifts the human personality is available to all people who need employment outside of the home.

This work is done in a spirit of communal solidarity shaping institutions that will extend the work into the future.

Surpluses are generated that are adequate to a continuation or reproduction of the effort of the society.

The integrity of the life support systems of the planet is respected at every point in the economic process.

Yet we know that our current economic world suffers from a grossly uneven distribution of resources (hundreds of millions of people live in a state of utter deprivation while hundreds of millions of people contract physical ill health from being in a state of overabundance), a paralyzing financial instability (untenable levels of indebtedness across much of the industrialized world), an immoral subjection of vulnerable people to indecent working conditions (preteen boys in Bangladesh enduring hellish conditions to break apart the world's exhausted shipping fleet), a senseless destruction of the natural world (one-quarter of the world's mammal species facing extinction due to human takeover of their habitat). The political, economic, and environmental disorder being witnessed is preceded by disorder in our minds. It is imperative to pinpoint the root cause of this failure in our thinking.

It is proposed that both the diagnosis of what has gone wrong in our thinking and the prescription of the way forward to sound thinking can be uncovered by examining the two competing conceptions of freedom presented by Pope Benedict XVI in his encyclical *Caritas in Veritate*. "We must appropriate the true meaning of freedom, which is not an intoxication with total autonomy, but a response to the call of being, beginning with our own personal being."[1]

What is meant by the call of being and how would a renewal of this meaning restore the moral and cultural foundations of an ethical marketplace? What caused an erosion of this understanding and how does this lapse from authentic liberty into license stand in the way of the application of virtue in the conduct of enterprise? In sum, what is the basis of these two conceptions of human freedom, and how do these different understandings necessarily shape the conditions of economic life?

THE MODERN MIND: POLITICAL ECONOMY IN AN AGE OF IDEOLOGY

No folly seems more characteristic of our time than the desire to establish a firm and meaningful temporal order, but without God, its necessary foundation.[2]

The modern world has chosen to go it alone without God. "Ideological rejection of God"[3] characterizes our time, but "without God man neither

1. Benedict XVI, Encyclical *Caritas in Veritate* (Vatican City: Libreria Editrice Vaticana, 2009), 70.
2. John XXIII, Encyclical *Mater et Magistra* (Vatican City: Libreria Editrice Vaticana, 1961), 217.
3. Benedict XVI, *Caritas in Veritate*, 34.

knows which way to go, nor even understands who he is."[4] Little wonder then that the exclusion of God results in an "inhuman humanism."[5]

It is not an accident, however, that the present age has landed in secularism. We flounder in "an illusion of our own omnipotence"[6] because of a nearly four-century cultural drift inaugurated by certain molders of the modern mind and sustained by many other intellectuals acting against reason. Understanding the disjunction in thought that put us on our current course is critical if a humane marketplace is going to be built.

It is the province of philosophy, and beyond philosophy, theology, to take up the question of the ultimate grounding of our existence. From Aristotle, four centuries before Christ's birth, to Aquinas in the thirteenth century, the greatest minds operating from the basic assumption that through thought reality can be understood devoted themselves to gaining metaphysical and moral insight.

In the sixteenth century, a momentous shift took place. Thinkers, beginning with Descartes, turned away from reason to the imagination. Philosophy was supplanted by artistic vision. Reflection would no longer be on the world of real existence that men have not made or constructed. The artist can make his canvas conform to the picture he holds in his mind, and those working with ideas could do the same. Rather than having our thoughts answer to reality, the assumption was that we could will into being any conception we have about our lives and the universe in which we live. Philosophy ceased to be true to its etymological roots; it ceased to be a love of wisdom. As a result we live by schemas we invent whole cloth in our minds. We have given ourselves over to "popularized fancies."[7]

Quite simply, we have lost touch with reality. The self, regarded as pure consciousness, is free to create its own reality. Thought becomes the warden of being. The only world left is the world we make with our ideas. Human beings take God's place determining value and the nature of being. There is no "meaning that is not of our own making"[8] to discover.

Ideological thinking empties the universe of ontological goodness, destroys the anthropological underpinnings of ethics, and plunges hu-

4. Ibid., 78.

5. Ibid.

6. Ibid., 74.

7. John XXIII, *Mater et Magistra*, 213.

8. Benedict XVI, *Caritas in Veritate*, 70.

man culture into a state of nihilism. In the realm of political econo-my, unbound freedom delivers totalitarian rule. Domination is sought through the power that wealth confers (capitalism) or through state power (socialism). Both regimes fail to properly order the world's goods because neither of them starts out from an understanding of the real, "whole"[9] nature of man.

In 1891 Pope Leo XIII wrote that "socialism ... is to be utterly re-jected"[10] and presciently foretold what would come about if socialism was adopted. "The equality conjured up by the Socialist imagination would, in reality, be nothing but uniform wretchedness and meanness for one and all without distinction."[11] Subsequent popes would con-tinue to be scathing in their indictment of the ideology. "[Communism holds] doctrines which seek by violence and bloodshed the destruction of all society ... [unopposed the way is prepared] for the overthrow and ruin of the social order."[12] Compromise between Marxism and Christi-anity is "impossible."[13]

The ideology fails because each person is unique and is given the gift of freedom. Radically unequal endowments between people will lead to unequal results. Forced equality of outcomes works against hu-man nature itself and "all struggling against nature is in vain."[14] When human persons are not required to exercise economic initiative, the hu-man personality is stunted in its growth and the wellsprings of wealth dry up. Socialism leads to inefficiency and privation wherever it is prac-ticed.

The functions of the state are also perverted when it steps in to do the work that only individuals, families, and private associations can do. The human person is not simply "an element, a molecule within the so-cial organism."[15] Individuals have the right to something of their own. The Seventh Commandment would make no sense if they did not. The state acts unjustly, in violation of this commandment, in abolishing pri-vate property. True wealth and prosperity cannot be built on injustice.

9. John XXIII, *Mater et Magistra*, 213.
10. Leo XIII, Encyclical *Rerum Novarum* (Boston: Daughters of St Paul, 1891), 23.
11. Ibid., 22.
12. Pius XI, Encyclical *Quadragesimo Anno* (Vatican City: Libreria Editrice Vaticana, 1931), 112.
13. John Paul II, Encyclical *Centesimus Annus* (Vatican City: Libreria Editrice Vaticana, 1991), 26.
14. Leo XIII, *Rerum Novarum*, 26.
15. John Paul II, *Centesimus Annus*, 13.

Neither can they be built on social disharmony, yet this is what the promotion of class welfare leads to.

The deepest root causes of the ascendance of socialism are philosophical materialism and atheism. The human person is understood based on material production alone. There is no place for God because there are no higher goods than the production of wealth. People find it hard to accept the spiritual void left in the wake of these ideas so the ideology must be forcefully imposed. Such compulsion adds to the alienation people experience. Pope John Paul II offers a deep explanation of socialism's failure: "Marxism had promised to uproot the need for God from the human heart, but the results have shown that it is not possible to succeed in this without throwing the human heart into turmoil."[16]

Like socialism, capitalism, the society that arises when capital accumulation is taken to be the ultimate end of the dominant institution of that social order, is also materialistic, secularistic, and totalitarian. Milton Friedman says people ought to set out in business "to make as much money as they can."[17] This is a corruption of the economic ideal, a perversion of the right use of money. Catholic social doctrine is equally clear on this: "A theory that makes profit the exclusive norm and ultimate end of economic activity is morally unacceptable."[18]

What distinguishes capitalism as a ruling order is the place assigned to gain. Other regimes have been able to generate surpluses (material goods over and above that required for the maintenance and reproduction of society). In these regimes, the value of the surplus was seen in the use to which it could be put—for example, displaying the regime's might, constructing religious edifices, or consuming luxuries. In capitalism, the surplus is used to generate more surplus. Gain is sought as an end in itself. The means became the ultimate end. Money dislodges God as being of primary importance in men's hearts.

The search for more in the regime of capitalism is relentless. New surpluses are continually put to use to generate more surplus. This is capitalism's essential nature, and it began working its way out as a social reality at the same time that the denial of a moral reality independent of

16. Ibid., 24.

17. Milton Friedman, *Capitalism and Freedom* (Chicago: University of Chicago Press, 1962), 20.

18. *Catechism of the Catholic Church* (Vatican City: Libreria Editrice Vaticana, 1992; English version: New York: Image Doubleday, 1994), 2424.

our thoughts was taking hold. Avarice was given a free reign. A science of chrematistics would eventually arise to provide the warrant for this *never-ending* pursuit of more.

Because more can only ever be fulfilled by all, the will is to an unreachable economic totality. Pope Pius XI discloses the real motives directing economic affairs. "Free competition is dead: economic dictatorship has taken its place. Unbridled ambition for domination has succeeded the desire for gain."[19]

Other institutions are coerced by the power of commercial enterprises to do their bidding, to tailor their own practices and ideals to the aims and needs of business. The state is charged with upholding justice and the common good, so the influence economic actors have on those holding political office is especially significant. Pope Pius XI would go so far as to say that the state has become "a slave, bound over to the service of human passion and greed."[20]

Every single aspect of human life in society is examined for its potential as a profit-generating activity. Everything becomes a marketable commodity, even goods that, by their nature, ought never to be bought and sold. All the stops are pulled out to turn things that have always been received as gifts into items that must now be paid for.

Labor, too, is something to be bought and sold. The worker is a commodity like any other. Because the purpose of being in business is to maximize financial margins, however, and because labor is a cost against those margins, it becomes rational to reduce the money spent employing people to a bare minimum. This can be done by paying them as little as possible, a practice antithetical to the generosity of Jesus, or by reducing the need for a human presence through automation. This creates the intractable problem of technological unemployment. In the regime of capitalism, tens of millions of people lack access to productive resources or gainful employment. The technological system does not need them; indeed, it desires their absence. Even though unemployment causes "great psychological and spiritual suffering,"[21] modern industry has no answer for the scourge.

If the human person is a mere tool in the profit-making process, then it is not surprising that work is designed for them without any

19. Pius XI, *Quadragesimo Anno*, 109.   20. Ibid., 109.
21. Benedict XVI, *Caritas in Veritate*, 25.

thought as to the "welfare of their souls" or "their higher interests."[22] Capitalism is humanly inadequate because it holds things to be of more importance than people.

Conflict is endemic. In what should be a harmonious endeavor, labor and ownership clash, like "two armies engaged in combat,"[23] over wages and working conditions. The envy systematically cultivated by the commercial world to keep people unsatisfied with what they have also disrupts social unity. Everyone's desire to have more runs into everyone else's desire for the same.

The key criterion for deciding what to bring to market is *whatever* can be *made* to sell. This need not be something useful to or uplifting of the purchaser. The mission is profitability not answering "real needs."[24] More money can often be made by preying upon human frailty, by exploiting human weakness, so the "lowest human passions"[25] are intentionally aroused as a business strategy. Advertising bombards people with propaganda to keep them consuming what is produced.

All means of wealth acquisition—speculation, rent seeking, financial shadiness—are held to be good. Competitive advantage can be gained by not accepting responsibility for negative externalities generated by the firm. Privatizing the Profits and Commonizing the Costs in this way ignores "the social character of economic life, social justice and the common good."[26] Legitimate financial success is overstated. Another way the Double P Double C game is played is to dispose costs onto future generations. In addition to this, the concentration of economic resources in gigantic corporations allows these economic entities to exclude others from entering the market in the hopes of monopoly profits. Competitors are bought up. The profit margins of suppliers are squeezed to nullity. Vexatious lawsuits are filed against would be entrants. Patents are taken out not to protect one's discoveries but to restrict the inventiveness of others. Annual billion-dollar advertising budgets act as a significant barrier to entry.

All of this results in a moral ratcheting down. Those "who pay the least heed to the dictates of conscience"[27] are able to crush "more cautious competitors."[28] The anonymity offered by the limited liability

---

22. Pius XI, *Quadragesimo Anno*, 135.
23. Ibid., 83.
24. Ibid., 132.
25. Ibid..
26. Ibid., 101.
27. Ibid., 107.
28. Ibid., 134.

corporation dulls a sense of responsibility. People have to struggle to retain their virtue within the "structures of sin"[29] that develop in capitalism.

These structures are not easy to modify or overturn. A "devouring usury"[30] is at the heart of the struggle for profits. This means there is a commitment to an infinite expansion of production since the last money borrowed must be paid off. Unlimited economic growth consumes "the resources of the earth" in an "excessive and disordered way."[31]

As with its ideological companion, socialism, what is missing in capitalism is a comprehensive picture of the human person and an acknowledgment of "God's prior and original gift of the things that are."[32] In the absence of a realistic metaphysics and philosophical psychology, objectively improper "consumer attitudes and lifestyles"[33] are created. People are "ensnared in a web of false and superficial gratifications"[34] in our provisioning system their "one solicitude"[35] being to obtain their daily bread in any way they can.

The challenge is to create an economic world worthy of what we are as human beings. Having more does not redeem the human condition because man is made for the supernatural and the eternal. Our economic striving and the resultant economic structures ought to reflect this fact. For this to happen, a sound metaphysical and moral foundation for enterprise must be restored. Undertaking a Christian reflection on the "meaning of man's pilgrimage through history"[36] can deliver the necessary ground for establishing free markets with solidarity and sustainability.

CHRISTIAN HUMANISM:
THE ESSENTIAL ELEMENTS

The basic diagnosis that has been offered is that the modern world and its economies are in trouble because of a "lack of thinking."[37] Ideological commitments are followed to the point that rationality itself is lost.

What does the use of the two wings of the human spirit, faith and reason, yield as the truth about our being and our actual position in the

29. John Paul II, *Centesimus Annus*, 38.
30. Leo XIII, *Rerum Novarum*, 6.
31. John Paul II, *Centesimus Annus*, 37.
32. Ibid., 37.
33. Ibid., 36.
34. Ibid., 41.
35. Pius XI, *Quadragesimo Anno*, 135.
36. Benedict XVI, *Caritas in Veritate*, 16.
37. Ibid., 53.

order of existence? What are the essential elements of a Christian understanding of being and of human personal being?

Creation

Only by facing the stupendous fact of existence can reason attain a reflective fullness. Aristotle asserts that "all men by nature desire to know,"[38] and this longing takes us to questions of metaphysical import: "Why is there something rather than nothing?" "Why is what exists as it is and not somehow else?"

Wonder at the mystery of creation points to a creator, to an omnipotent god, capable of bringing into being all that exists out of nothing. A creating intelligence is behind the evident design of the universe. The ground of being is the mind of God.

This ensures the reasonableness of creation and means that it can be investigated and understood. In undertaking such study, reality is the measure of the mind, not the other way around. "Truth consists in the equation of the mind to the thing."[39] A basic attitude of receptivity is needed:

> Truth and the love which it reveals, cannot be produced: they can only be received as a gift. Their ultimate source is not, and cannot be, mankind, but only God, who is himself Truth and Love. This principal is extremely important for society and development, since neither can be a purely human product: the vocation to development on the part of individuals and peoples is not based simply on human choice, but is an intrinsic part of a plan that is prior to us and constitutes for all of us a duty to be freely accepted. That which is prior to us and constitutes us—subsistent Love and Truth—shows us what goodness is, and in what our true happiness consists. *It shows us the road to true development.*[40]

Human Nature

Our wonder turns to the essential reality of being human. Uncovering what constitutes the human being qua human requires observation of what human beings uniquely do in the world.

The human species acts scientifically—that is, it is seen to engage the

38. Aristotle, "Metaphysics," in *The Complete Works of Aristotle,* vol. 2, the Revised Oxford Translation, edited by Jonathan Barnes (Princeton, N.J.: Princeton University Press, 1984), I, 1.

39. Thomas Aquinas, *Summa Theologica,* 5 vols., trans. Fathers of the English Dominican Province (New York: Benzinger Brothers, 1948), I, Q.21, A.4.

40. Benedict XVI, *Caritas in Veritate,* 52; emphasis original.

world experimentally to establish scientific principles. These insights
are extended to technological applications. Although animals may use
tools in a rudimentary way, only man designs and builds machines. Phenomenon such as nuclear power plants, space shuttles, and computers
are a result of human agency. Human beings pierce the impenetrable
wall of time with their ability to bind together the experienced present
with the remembered past and the anticipated future—that is, they have
a historical awareness that allows them to establish historical tradition
and develop historically. This means that they do not live by biological
inheritance only but by the cultural and institutional world they bring
into existence. This is made possible by the use of symbolic communication. The universal (e.g., triangularity) can be grasped in the absence
of the particular (e.g., a specific instance of a triangle). Conceptual understanding is possible in a perceptual world of singulars. The pursuit
of the fine arts plays an important role in human existence. There are no
counterparts to Beethoven, Michelangelo, and Shakespeare in the animal kingdom. Man is imbued with natural religion and a moral sense.
Contemplation of life's meaning and purpose accompany an awareness
of personal decline and death, and the difference between morally re-
pugnant and morally praiseworthy conduct can be recognized.

What accounts for this distinctive human splendor? What explains
these remarkable differences in kind that are observed?

What is unique about the human person is that the material and the
spiritual are married in a single creature. The human body is animated
by a spiritual soul, created not by the parents in the process of physical
generation because the soul is immaterial but "immediately by God."[41]
The spiritual soul of every human person survives bodily death and
lives forever because the soul is independent of the corporeal world.

The human person is thus in possession of intellectual powers and
free will. The vocation of being human is to come to the fullest development of these distinctive human faculties. The intellect is perfected
by knowing truth, and the will is fulfilled by loving goodness. The supreme truth is God, and the supreme goodness is God. Therefore, the
ultimate purpose in life is to know God and love God and, because our
immortal soul destines us eternally, to enjoy God forever. God made

41. *Catechism of the Catholic Church*, 366.

human beings for loving fellowship with himself. Indeed, God created the universe to enter into this love relationship with humankind. The cosmos comes first in time but not in divine intention.

The human person is also inherently social by nature. People could not come into existence unless other human beings procreated them, and they could not stay in existence unless other human beings maintained them in it. Human beings enter the world in a state of utter helplessness and are literally loved into being. Throughout their lives they depend on others for their maturation just as others depend on them for their growth.[42]

Natural Moral Law

As a rational animal the human person is uniquely charged with the burden of freedom. To be human is to be consigned to choosing to do one thing instead of another. The endowment of reason makes the human person a seat of responsibility.

Moral realism follows from metaphysical realism. What we ought to be and do is based on what we are. Again, this understanding is discovered or uncovered not produced or invented. A natural moral law applies to the human person as body and soul unity. Authentic liberty is found in adhering to this law, which is preserved in the Ten Commandments and is also reflected in the cardinal virtues. Prudence, justice, fortitude, and temperance are the qualities of character that enable the human person to reach the furthest potentialities of his or her nature. These moral habits ought to be cultivated because they perfect the distinctly human powers and protect against the harm that inordinate desire can do to the human personality.

Human beings "cannot prescind"[43] from their nature. The moral law "etched"[44] on their hearts presses in on them. C. S. Lewis states this fact of human existence as follows: "human beings, all over the earth, have this curious idea that they ought to behave in a certain way, and can-

---

42. Natural theology can yield an understanding of God's existence, but Christian scriptures reveal the mystery of the Trinity—three Persons—Father, Son, and Holy Spirit in one divine substance. The inner Trinitarian life, marked by perfect love, is the model for human relations. Relationality characterizes divine reality and is found at the very heart of human existence. Human life is always a being-from, a being-with, and a being-for others.

43. Benedict XVI, *Caritas in Veritate*, 21.

44. Ibid., 59.

not really get rid of it ... they know the Law of Nature [natural moral law]."[45]

This is not the whole story about the reality of the human condition, however. Lewis goes on to point out a second fact: "[human beings] do not in fact behave that way ... they break [the Law of Nature]."[46] The evidence for this is clear. People act imprudently by not exercising the proper caution or foresight. People commit injustices by not giving to others what is rightfully theirs. People lack the fortitude to face the challenges of their lives directly. People fail to moderate their desires for pleasurable things. Moral failure at the individual level gets reflected in societal breakdown.

The basic problem is a willful rejection of the order to proper to our souls, and because this order has been implanted "deep within"[47] us by our Creator, it is a turning away from God. This denial of our creatureliness makes it impossible for us to attain the happiness for which we were created.

Jesus of Nazareth

Pride turns human beings away from God, but God does not leave them in this lapsed state. The Christian story is ultimately "Good News." There is also the wonder of God's more than amazing grace.

In another act of absolute love, God provides the way by which human beings can reach the ultimate end for which they were created. God sends his Son, the second Person of the Trinity, Jesus Christ, as "Redeemer."[48] Christianity is "the religion of God who has a human face."[49] This is the awesome mystery of the Incarnation. God stepped into history as a man.

In Jesus, God puts himself into human hands and suffers a humiliating death on the cross to bear humanity's transgressions. Jesus's resurrection completes God's saving plan. God's shocking response of love enduring to the end reveals his essence.

It remains for human beings to accept God's invitation to a new life of grace lived in intimacy with the Holy Spirit. This relationship to

45. C.S. Lewis, *Mere Christianity* (New York: MacMillan, 1943), 7.

46. Ibid., 7.

47. Benedict XVI, *Caritas in Veritate*, 76.

48. John Paul II, Encyclical *Redemptor Hominis* (Vatican City: Liberia Editrice Vatican, 1979).

49. Benedict XVI, Encyclical *Spe Salvi* (Vatican City: Liberia Editrice Vatican, 2007), 31.

God in love sustains the Christian in his or her existence and elevates his or her nature to a supernatural level. Freedom is participation in the very being of God through grace.

God's grace is absolutely needed if the most sublime teachings of Christianity, for example, the Sermon on the Mount, are to be lived out. "'Hearts of stone' have to be transformed into 'hearts of flesh' (Ezek. 36:26)."[50] It is quite impossible to perform the Beatitudes by dint of human effort alone. Supernatural help in the form of the theological virtues is required. Faith, hope, and love are "absolutely gratuitous gifts of God" infused "in our souls"[51] by God as a sign of his presence and as a means to make us holy.

The cardinal virtues are not supplanted but neither do they remain just natural. "Grace does not destroy nature, but perfects it."[52] The theological virtues inform and give life to the natural virtues making them more than what they could be without supernatural help.

What it means to be a human person takes on a deeper, fuller meaning. The key to grasping what we are called to be is to look above the level of the mundane to the divine to see what our personhood should be. Jesus realizes humanity perfectly. In doing so, he explains our humanity to us, which is something we cannot do for ourselves because we did not create ourselves. The goal of the Christian life to be nothing less than Christlike becomes entirely understandable. Imitating Jesus brings us to the perfect freedom that was naturally his. God teaches us "through the Son what fraternal charity is."[53] This means that Christian disciples must be prepared to take up the Cross because Jesus showed his love by laying down his life for others.

CATHOLIC SOCIAL THOUGHT:
THE BASIC PRINCIPLES

The social teachings of the church have their basis in natural moral law or in the law of our being. As a proximate endeavor, the fulfillment of political economic aims must abide by or build on the truths of metaphysics, philosophical psychology, and ethics. That is, human nature,

50. Benedict XVI, *Caritas in Veritate*, 79.
51. Ibid., 34.
52. Thomas Aquinas, *Summa Theologica* Q.1, A.8, reply to obj. 2.
53. Benedict XVI, *Caritas in Veritate*, 19.

constituted by matter and spirit, is "normative for culture."[54] A good social order "conforms to the moral order."[55]

The prescription Catholic social doctrine gives for how the goods of the world ought to be ordered is predicated on the deeply social nature of our being. "*A metaphysical interpretation of the 'humanum'*"[56] discloses that associations of greater to lesser intimacy, beginning with the family and extending through intermediary groups to the political community, are demanded by reality. A richly textured social life arises because man by nature seeks to associate.

The good of the human person as a citizen or a member of a community is the common good of the human society in which he lives, where the common good is understood to be the social order that facilitates every person to attain perfection. The common good is not in opposition to any individual person's good, for it is precisely in the social order that the individual develops.

Self-sacrifice for the common good is not the denial of self but is self-fulfillment. Practicing *agape* love, willing the good of others, is not the diminishment of our selves but is the perfection of our personhood. "It is through the free gift of self that man truly finds himself."[57]

Solidarity, defined as "*a firm and persevering determination* to commit oneself to the *common good*; that is to say to the good of all and of each individual, because we are *all* really responsible *for all*,"[58] is the fundamental principle of the Catholic view of social and political organization that operationalizes charity or brings it to bear in creating social reality. Our obligations to others are this expansive. Practically, it means we can never be "indifferent to the lot of another member of the human family."[59]

The principle of subsidiarity is closely linked with solidarity and must remain so. The key idea of subsidiarity is that the internal life of each community should be respected—that is, a community or social body of a higher order should not do for a community of a lower order what it should do for itself. Subsidiarity finds its justification in love. It is not an act of caring to do something for another person that the person should do for him- or herself. "Subsidiarity respects personal

54. Ibid., 48.   55. Ibid., 67.
56. Ibid., 55; emphasis original.   57. Ibid., 41.
58. John Paul II, Encyclical *Sollicitudo Rei Socialis* (Vatican City: Liberia Editrice Vatican, 1987), 38; emphasis in original.
59. John Paul II, *Centesimus Annus*, 51.

dignity by recognizing in the person a subject who is always capable of giving something to others."[60]

Subsidiarity also ensures that solidarity, the moral-organic bond providing unity to the communities naturally formed by human beings will be realized. The two virtues must be taken together because the formation of a community is not a technical problem to be solved once and for all but is a moral struggle to be faced with as much equanimity as possible. Human community is only established if it is desired, generated, and nourished by the people who form the community. Subsidiarity leaves people to this essential work. Solidarity holds everyone's efforts together.

Justice must be present. In its absence, a stable social order is simply not possible. If people are not rendered what is due them, social breakdown inevitably ensues. But justice is merely the "minimum measure" of charity and is completed by "gratuitousness, mercy, and communion."[61] Thus, while justice is the basic social virtue enabling us to shoulder the responsibilities of social life, we must go beyond desert if we are to emulate God's love.

The Catholic vision of the economy is not just for a better-regulated capitalism. Jesus's clear instruction in the Sermon on the Mount is that we "cannot serve God and wealth."[62] Jesus did not say that we should not, or that it would be difficult, but that we *could not*. It is an impossibility not unlike the impossibility of simultaneously taking both paths when reaching a fork in the road. Capitalism can only be healed by addressing the pathology of purpose that lies at its heart. Catholic social thought offers the remedy. "The perfect order which the Church preaches ... places God as the first and supreme end of all created activity, and regards all created goods as mere instruments under God, to be used only in so far as they help towards the attainment of our supreme end."[63]

Particular economic aims must be linked with this universal teleological order. If they were, then a "new order of economic productivity, socially responsible and human in scale,"[64] "a society of free work, of enterprise and of participation,"[65] would result.

How can such a healthy socioeconomic order be built? How can

60. Benedict XVI, *Caritas in Veritate*, 57.

61. Ibid., 6.

62. Mt. 6:24.

63. Pius XI, *Quadragesimo Anno*, 136.

64. Benedict XVI, *Caritas in Veritate*, 41.

65. John Paul II, *Centesimus Annus*, 35.

the basic principles of Catholic social thought be implemented to bring about a system of responsible free enterprise?

THE CONDUCT OF ENTERPRISE:
A VOCATION TO LOVE

Christian humanism holds that we were made in love and for love, that our lives are a vocation to divine charity. The twofold commandment to love (Mt 22:37–40), which "synthesizes the entire law,"[66] is to be fulfilled in enterprise as well. We are to will the good of others in our organizational life just as we do in our personal life. Because a company is a community of human persons, love must be extended in the practice of management and form the firm.

The subject and end of every social institution, including economic enterprise, is the human person. Institutions exist to elevate man because in the Catholic worldview man is a high and holy mystery, made in God's own image. As such, he is infinitely more worthy than any material goods that might be produced or the organizational entities created to generate that production. Pope Benedict XVI explicitly states this. The *"primary capital to be safeguarded and valued is man, the human person in his or her integrity."*[67]

The justification of an enterprise is the correspondence of its economic activity with God's plan for man. Capital resources are to assist in the process of sanctification but are not to be thought of as an end in themselves. "Profit ... [is] a means for achieving human and social ends."[68] The legitimate telos of every work community is the common good.

Of primary importance is what is produced or supplied. Enterprises ought to make a contribution to human flourishing by what they bring into being. Material goods are meant to be a means to our development. What we have should help us to realize our destiny, which ultimately is spiritual not material. Although we are in the world, we are not of it, having been created for eternal happiness with God. Economic production should not deflect people from this end. The "material and instinctive" dimensions of our being should be subordinated to our "interior and spiritual"[69] ones. The goods and services provided by commerce

66. Ibid.
67. Benedict XVI, *Caritas in Veritate*, 25; emphasis original.
68. Ibid., 46.
69. John Paul II, *Centesimus Annus*, 36.

should *really* be goods and services, not bads and disservices, when human well-being in its totality is considered.

The proper objective of marketing is to identify the people who would benefit from these goods and services and provide them with the information they need to make prudent decisions. If the truth about these products cannot be communicated honestly and openly, then the chances are good that the firm is treading on thin ice ethically. Promotional efforts need to do even more today. They need to encourage people to simplify their lives both to reduce the environmental impact of consumption and to help people find a place for leisure and prayer. Business should aid in the shift to lifestyles where consumer choices and financial decisions are determined by "the quest for truth, beauty, goodness, and communion with others for the sake of common growth."[70] The pursuit of wisdom must replace acting on hedonistic impulses.

Goods and services are produced by people using material means. Labor takes precedence over capital in the process because of human dignity. To look on labor as another commodity to be bought and sold at the service of capital expansion is a basic moral perversion. It is to give dead capital priority over sacred human personhood. Laborers must not be "treated like any other factor of production."[71]

People ought to be given meaningful work that utilizes and develops their higher faculties. Responsibility for managing the enterprise would then be broadly diffused. Employees would rightly be seen as associates or partners in the venture. Proper attention should be paid to the work practices in place. The hours of work required, the physical demands put on the worker, and the safety conditions should be humane. Love can never countenance work environments that are harmful to the physical health and moral integrity of the people working in them.

People are owed a living wage for their work. The human race perpetuates itself only in families, so families must, at a minimum, have their material needs met. Parental requests ought to be accommodated to the greatest extent possible. Management should work flexibly with each individual and family, fostering personal and professional relationships that make a good life for employees and their families possible, thereby contributing to the building up of the basic social structures of

70. Benedict XVI, *Caritas in Veritate*, 51.
71. Ibid., 62.

our existence. That is, love is to be expressed not only *in* our families but also *to* all families. Firms have an obligation to put in place policies under which the family can more easily fulfill its mission.

Ethics inheres in all economic decisions. Those owning and managing commercial undertakings, the decision makers in an enterprise, have an obligation to consider the impact their decisions have on the broader social whole encompassing their operations. "*Business management cannot concern itself only with the interest of the proprietors, but must assume responsibility* for all the other *stakeholders who contribute to the life of the business*: the workers, the clients, the suppliers of various elements of production, the community of reference."[72]

Today, the environment presents itself as a particularly salient community of reference. Our love is to extend to the natural world as well. We have an obligation to be good stewards of God-given creation, maintaining it in its integrity, and protecting it by opening it up to God through our own sanctification. Our covenant with the environment should mirror the creative love of God.

As demanding as the sum of these responsibilities is, it really composes a moral minimum. Christianity goes the "second mile" (Mt 5:41). God's love seeks and suffers to save, and this is the love that Christians are called to "pour forth."[73]

Good employment opportunities can be provided to the disabled or hard to employ. Information can be volunteered to legislators if it would aid them in making regulations, even if this is not required by law. Leadership can be shown in building an industry consensus around abolishing unjust practices or achieving positive social change. Human ingenuity and capital resources can be applied to address pressing environmental problems thereby helping to bequeath to future generations a world not depleted of its resources.

A life in business is a "ceaseless pursuit of a just ordering of human affairs."[74] The work of enterprise is to continually will one's greatest contribution to the common good. God's original gift of the earth was to the whole of humankind. Private property rights are not absolute therefore but serve this more primordial reality. There is room on this earth "for everybody to live with dignity."[75] It is our duty, our obliga-

72. Ibid., 40; emphasis in original.   73. Ibid., 5.
74. Ibid., 78.   75. Ibid., 50.

tion in friendship, to use the gift of our lives to ensure that all God's children have a place at the "table of the common banquet."[76]

CONCLUSION

The vocation of business can be entered into in good conscience. In *Centisimus Annus*, Pope John Paul II gives a paean to entrepreneurship. The important virtues of industriousness, diligence, prudence, reliability, foresight, courage, patience, trustworthiness, truthfulness he stresses are apt to be called on in initiating any substantial economic undertaking. Our being calls us to be enterprising in providing for ourselves and our loved ones and neighbors. When private initiative is lacking, political tyranny and stagnation prevail. These are the stakes of not accepting the burden of freedom.

But the proper place for material development in the Christian life must also be kept uppermost in our consciousness. We ought to heed the words of Jesus: "For what does it profit a man, if he gain the whole world, but suffer the loss of his own soul? Or what will a man give in exchange for his soul?" (Mt 16:26.) Generating a vast amount of goods does not justify an economic system. The more important matter is what happens to people in the process. Is there growth in holiness? Is a civilization animated by love being built?

76. John Paul II, *Sollicitudo Rei Socialis*, 33.

PART II

Assessing the Encyclical Tradition

SEVEN

Justice, Charity, and the Political Order

Assessing the Encyclical Tradition

Richard J. Dougherty

The proper relationship between justice and charity is a central concern of the last two centuries of Catholic social teaching and doctrine. Concerns for the right ordering of the political order, which ordering can have a profound impact on the promotion of the life of virtue,[1] are rightly seen in the encyclical tradition as intimately connected with the fundamental concern of the institutional church—the embrace of the theological virtue of charity and, thus, the salvation of souls. The intention in this chapter is to address this critical theme in the tradition, the connection between justice and charity, focusing on some particularly clear considerations of the question as found especially in papal encyclicals.

One can perhaps illuminate the difficulty of navigating this question of the relationship between justice and charity by noting that in the *Summa Theologiae*, Saint Thomas Aquinas treats the issue of the criteria for just war, which seems at first glance to be surely about the questions of justice, under the heading of the virtue of charity.[2] Why the consideration of war would fall properly to the theological virtue of charity

---

1. See, for example, the *Catechism of the Catholic Church*, sections 2236–37. See also Benedict XVI, Encyclical *Deus Caritas Est* (Vatican City: Libreria Editrice Vaticana, 2005), 28: "Justice is both the aim and the intrinsic criterion of all politics. Politics is more than a mere mechanism for defining the rules of public life: its origin and its goal are found in justice, which by its very nature has to do with ethics."

2. Aquinas, *Summa Theologica* II-II, q. 40.

rather than to the cardinal virtue of justice (or even prudence or fortitude) is not immediately clear from the text.[3] Furthermore, the very
placement of the discussion compels us to think more deeply about how
we apply the transcendent teaching of charity to the relatively mundane
concerns of the temporal order. More important, interpreters might
be compelled to think further about whether the temporal order itself
seeks or requires a connection with a charity that is not understood as
merely or solely transcendent.

Pope Benedict XVI noted in his September 2011 address to the German Bundestag that Christianity does not propose a revealed law to the
state: "Unlike other great religions, Christianity has never proposed a
revealed body of law to the State and to society, that is to say a juridical order derived from revelation. Instead, it has pointed to nature and
reason as the true sources of law."[4] This is a theme that Pope Benedict
had sounded out in a number of places earlier, in different ways, perhaps most fully in his first encyclical, *Deus Caritas Est*, issued in 2005:
"The Church cannot and must not take upon herself the political battle
to bring about the most just society possible. She cannot and must not
replace the State. Yet at the same time she cannot and must not remain
on the sidelines in the fight for justice."[5] The church has a special responsibility to the political order, he notes, but it does not overtake the
legitimate function of the state. This principle is, in fact, an articulation
of one of the fundamental aspects of the social doctrine tradition, as we
shall see—that there are proper spheres for moral and political action
and discourse, and each element of the social order has its own responsibilities and duties.

One especially enlightening illustration of the relationship between
charity and justice can be found in Pope Pius XI's 1931 encyclical, *Quadragesimo Anno*,[6] appearing on the fortieth anniversary of Pope Leo XIII's
celebrated *Rerum Novarum*,[7] a document referred to in *Quadragesimo* as
"the *Magna Charta* upon which all Christian activity in the social field

3. A closer examination of the text will perhaps reveal the rationale behind the choice St. Thomas makes in including considerations of just war under the heading of "charity."

4. Address delivered September 22, 2011, in Berlin; available in English at http://www.vatican
.va/holy_father/benedict_xvi/speeches/2011/september/documents/hf_ben-xvi_spe_20110922_
reichstag-berlin_en.html.

5. Benedict XVI, *Deus Caritas Est*, 28.   6. Pius XI, *Quadragesimo Anno*.

7. Leo XIII, *Rerum Novarum*.

ought to be based."[8] *Quadragesimo Anno* indeed takes its starting point from *Rerum Novarum*, as Pope Pius XI declares the intention of the encyclical in paragraph 15: "We deem it fitting on this occasion to recall the great benefits this Encyclical has brought to the Catholic Church and to all human society; to defend the illustrious Master's doctrine on the social and economic question against certain doubts and to develop it more fully as to some points; and lastly, summoning to court the contemporary economic regime and passing judgment on Socialism, to lay bare the root of the existing social confusion and at the same time point the only way to sound restoration: namely, the Christian reform of morals."[9] The connections Pope Pius draws between the economic order and the promotion of sound moral teaching is a matter of real significance, as we see throughout the encyclical.

Early in the encyclical, Pope Pius XI addresses the economic conditions within which *Rerum Novarum* was conceived and written, conditions that produced a widening disparity between the wealthy few and a poor multitude. This circumstance was not seen as problematic by some (i.e., the few); indeed, as he notes, "[q]uite agreeable, of course, was this state of things to those who found in their abundant riches the result of inevitable economic laws and accordingly, as if it were for charity to veil the violation of justice which lawmakers not only tolerated but at times sanctioned, wanted the whole care of supporting the poor committed to charity alone."[10] Pope Pius XI's point is that while charity is, of course, a good and is to be promoted, it in no way is meant to be a complete substitute for the principle of justice. The social and political order has a responsibility to the common good that must point beyond the task of charitable giving.

Thus, as he says subsequently, "the institutions themselves of peoples and, particularly those of all social life, ought to be penetrated with this justice, and it is most necessary that it be truly effective, that is, establish a juridical and social order which will, as it were, give form and shape to all economic life."[11] Although a just social order does not rely simply on charity to relieve the lot of the poor, neither does it undermine the charitable impulse, but must be animated by and promote a concern for true justice in the system as a whole.

---

8. Pius XI, *Quadragesimo Anno*, 40.   9. Ibid., 15.
10. Ibid., 4.   11. Ibid., 88.

QUADRAGESIMO ANNO AND THE
SCIENCE OF ECONOMICS

It is perhaps worth adding here a brief note on the production of the encyclical; Pius XI apparently requested that the German Jesuits take on the task of preparing a draft of the letter, and this task was largely accomplished by Oswald von Nell-Breuning and Gustav Gundlach.[12] (Pius XI seems to have fully authored the section from 91 to 96, specifically criticizing the fascist economic program in Italy.)[13] Nell-Breuning himself later noted that the encyclical is "well-saturated with Gundlach's thought."[14]

At the outset of *Quadragesimo* Pope Pius XI commends *Rerum Novarum* for its success in prompting the development of a new approach to what he calls a "true Catholic social science,"[15] one that promotes "a social and economic science in accord with the conditions of our time."[16] The critical part of that new approach, we discover, is found in applying to the contemporary world the broad principles of Catholic Social Doctrine outlined in *Rerum Novarum*, not allowing these principles to "lie hidden behind learned walls."[17]

The concern with thinking anew about the political and economic order is a matter Pope Pius returns to frequently. In particular, in the context of discussing the necessity of a fundamental reform of the social order, the encyclical takes direct aim at the approach to economics advocated by defenders of the liberal free market. In section 88, in particular, we find a critique of the idea of a "free market" unlimited by a concern for the common good, or, for a science of economics that is not informed by moral principles: "[T]he right ordering of economic life cannot be left to a free competition of forces. For from this source, as from a poisoned spring, have originated and spread all the errors of individualist

12. See, for example, Oswald von Nell-Breuning, "The Drafting of *Quadragesimo Anno*," in *Readings in Catholic Moral Theology*, No. 5, ed. Charles Curran and Richard McCormick (New York: Paulist Press, 1986), 60–68. On Gundlach's contribution, see Anton Rauscher, "Gustav Gundlach, S.J.: One of the Architects of Christian Social Thinking," *Homiletic and Pastoral Review* 103 (October 2002): 30–31.

13. A fuller critique of the Fascist program is found in Pope Pius XI's subsequent letter, Encyclical *Non Abbiamo Bisogno* (Vatican City: Libreria Editrice Vaticana, 1931).

14. Nell-Breuning, "The Drafting of *Quadragesimo Anno*," 62.

15. Pius XI, *Quadragesimo Anno*, 20.   16. Ibid., 19.

17. Ibid., 20.

economic teaching."[18] Time and again the encyclical returns to the necessity of infusing the market with the principles of the moral order.

One might reasonably wonder whether the injection of moral concerns into the order of economic life is a desirable turn. A critique of this approach is sometimes forwarded concerning at least a portion of the tradition of Catholic social thought touching on property ownership and related questions (such as the just wage or living wage), which critique asserts that in this area, the church has abandoned its own laudable tradition of thinking in terms of nature and the natural law tradition. The claim is that there is a science to the study and implementation or workings of the laws of economics and that the church, in trying to impose concerns about wages and access to other labor-oriented goods, is failing to recognize the operative principles intrinsic to the economic realm. The consequence of that approach, it is claimed, is that the church is led to promote policies that are bound to fail, for they are not informed by the laws of the science, and the consequences of that failure will be that its teachings will bring disrepute to the church, leading people to reject its teachings in this area—and perhaps other, unrelated areas—as unserious. Attempts to impose principles on the economic order that are extrinsic to the order itself, it is held, fail to capture the reality of the economic order. One passage of such a critique will suffice: "The primary difficulty with much of what has fallen under the heading of Catholic social teaching since Pope Leo XIII's *Rerum Novarum* (1891) is that it assumes without argument that the force of human will suffices to resolve economic questions and that reason and the conclusions of economic law can be safely neglected, even scorned."[19] It seems perfectly understandable that the church, as with Pius XI here in *Quadragesimo Anno*, would be interested in promoting a humane science of economics. But the challenge that is brought against this effort is that the attempt to "humanize" it leads to a violation of its operative principles. Economics as a science, in this view, must be accepted in its fullness and must not be interfered with by extraneous concerns.

Perhaps we could approach this argument by means of a parallel argument from political science. One might argue, for example, that

18. Ibid., 88.

19. Thomas E. Woods Jr., "Catholic Social Teaching and Economic Law," *Journal des Economistes et des Etudes Humaines* 13, no. 2 (2003): 330.

there is a science of war and that there are certain internal principles to that science that can be discerned by the student of war. If this is so, one could reasonably conclude that any attempt to intervene in those "natural laws" of the science would be an external imposition on the science and perhaps could accuse those who propose such ideas to be violators of the natural law of war. Yet, were the church not to intervene in those internal dynamics, it would have to abandon old and long-established ideas, such as those found in the tradition of just war thinking.[20] What just war principles do, it seems, is precisely to impose on the conduct of war limitations or inhibitions that are not internal to war itself but are, instead, often understood as hindrances upon the conduct of war. Indiscriminate bombing, targeting of civilians, torturing prisoners of war, and the like may be actions that hasten victory in war, or lead to saving the lives of one's own soldiers or civilians, but few (some, but few), charge the church with having violated the natural order and having abandoned natural law by teaching that such actions are a violation of justice.

It is something like this concern that Pope Pius XI is addressing in section 88 of *Quadragesimo Anno*, when he speaks of the deleterious effects of what he calls "individualistic economic teaching":

Destroying through forgetfulness or ignorance the social and moral character of economic life, it held that economic life must be considered and treated as altogether free from and independent of public authority, because in the market, i.e., in the free struggle of competitors, it would have a principle of self direction which governs it much more perfectly than would the intervention of any created intellect. But free competition, while justified and certainly useful provided it is kept within certain limits, clearly cannot direct economic life—a truth which the outcome of the application in practice of the tenets of this evil individualistic spirit has more than sufficiently demonstrated. Therefore, it is most necessary that economic life be again subjected to and governed by a true and effective directing principle.[21]

What we find in the encyclical as a whole is the attempt to balance the principles of economics with the concerns of justice and morality, in par-

---

20. See, for example, the aforementioned passage cited from Thomas Aquinas's *Summa Theologica* on the criteria for the conduct of a just war (II-II, q. 40); see also *Summa Theologica* I-II, q. 105, a. 2 for his treatment of the Old Law's standards for just war.

21. Pius XI, *Quadragesimo Anno*, 88.

ticular within the economic sphere. Put differently, concerns for justice must be intertwined with, and not divorced from, the aims of charity.

This concern with the larger consequences of economic choices is taken up by Pope John Paul II in *Centesimus Annus*, on the one hundredth anniversary of *Rerum Novarum*. There Pope John Paul II addresses the challenge of prosperity brought about by a successful economic system, when the prosperity is not grounded in moral principles: "Of itself, an economic system does not possess criteria for correctly distinguishing new and higher forms of satisfying human needs from artificial new needs which hinder the formation of mature personality."[22] The church does not propose its own models for the political and economic order, except by providing a comprehensive social teaching as an *"indispensable and ideal orientation."*[23]

Pope Benedict XVI, in his 2009 Encyclical *Caritas in Veritate*, notes the ways in which the success of the economic system, in fact, depends on factors extraneous to itself, such as a stable political order that enforces contracts and promotes just laws. In addition, he asserts that besides promoting commutative justice, economic life also needs "works redolent of the *spirit of gift*."[24] A priority within such works would undoubtedly have to be an "openness to life," which, he notes, is "at the center of true development."[25]

JUSTICE AND CHARITY

As stated previously, one of the important principles set forth in *Quadragesimo Anno* is found in the discussion of the relationship between justice and charity. Early on Pope Pius addresses the economic conditions within which *Rerum Novarum* was conceived and written, conditions that produced a division in society between the wealthy few and a poor multitude. Pope Pius XI's concern is to note that while charity is, of course, a good, and to be promoted, it in no way is meant to be a complete substitute for the principle of justice. He notes that "no vicarious charity can substitute for justice which is due as an obligation and is wrongfully denied. Yet even supposing that everyone should finally receive all that is due him, the widest field for charity will always remain open. For justice alone can, if faithfully observed, remove the causes of

22. John Paul II, *Centesimus Annus*, 36.   23. Ibid., 43.
24. Benedict XVI, *Caritas in Veritate*, 37.   25. Ibid., 28; see also paragraphs 44–45.

social conflict but can never bring about union of minds and hearts."[26]
So, even while emphasizing the necessity of promoting an abiding concern for justice, Pius XI wants it to be clear that the strictest justice will
not serve as a replacement for charity, nor can it even provide the true
or full basis for the social and political community. The fullness of communal life, rather, is found only in the bond of charity. Yet, as Pope
John Paul II points out in *Centesimus Annus*, the right ordering of society is not left solely to the realm of charity but is a demand of justice as
well.[27]

Here we are reminded of a passage from Aristotle in the *Nicomachean
Ethics*, where he points to friendship as the true foundation of unity in
the political order: "When men are friends they have no need of justice,
while when they are just they need friendship as well, and the truest
form of justice is thought to be a friendly quality. But it is not only
necessary but also noble; for we praise those who love their friends, and
it is thought to be a fine thing to have many friends."[28] Although Aristotle may not have in mind the sense of charity that Pope Pius XI is
speaking of, he does acknowledge here the limitation of law or justice
in serving as the fundamental grounding point of the community.[29] But
he also notes that in the absence of good law, that is, a proper ordering
principle for the community, friendship is made much more difficult to
foster.[30] As suggested at the outset, this connection between justice and
charity is at the heart of Pope Benedict XVI's writings. In his encyclical
Caritas in Veritate, he draws our attention to the demands of "charity in
truth," which, he notes, "requires that shape and structure be given to

26. Ibid., 137.

27. John Paul II, *Centesimus Annus*, 36.

28. Aristotle, "Nicomachean Ethics," 8, 1155a26–29, 1825–30.

29. We may begin to bridge that apparent gap between Aristotelian friendship and Christian
charity by thinking of charity as the source of friendship between and among human beings, or
between man and God. There is good reason that many recognize as a mark of political tyranny
the attempt to abolish friendship in the city; see Aristotle's "Politics," in *The Complete Works of
Aristotle,* vol. 2, the Revised Oxford Translation, ed. Jonathan Barnes (Princeton, N.J.: Princeton
University Press, 1984); and Thomas Aquinas, *On Kingship to the King of Cyprus*, trans. Gerald B.
Phelan (Toronto: Pontifical Institute of Mediaeval Studies, 1949), 27:17 (original: *De regno ad regem
Cypri*, Lib. I, cap. 4, par. 69927). For St. Thomas, the purpose of law ultimately is to restore one's
friendship with God.

30. As Pope John Paul II notes in his 1987 Encyclical *Sollicitudo Rei Socialis*, when we consider
the question of human development and flourishing, the aim of that development is found in seeking God and living in accord with His law (27–29, cited in *Centesimus Annus*, 29).

those types of economic initiative which, without rejecting profit, aim at a higher good than the mere logic of the exchange of equivalents."[31]

SUBSIDIARITY

One of the fundamental themes animating the encyclical, and the idea most closely associated with it, is the principle of subsidiarity. The teaching on subsidiarity is treated by some commentators as a novel idea, or as the by-product of an odd set of political and social circumstances—a "piece of congealed historical wisdom," as one scholar puts it, or simply a "German legal principle."[32] There may be something to be said for the latter categorization, even if it does not fully cover the provenance of the principle; Nell-Breuning asserts that "both the name 'principle of subsidiarity' and the formulation in which it is expressed in *Quadragesimo Anno* came from Gundlach."[33]

From some perspectives, the principle of subsidiarity can be understood as an adaptation of a much older concept, embodied in a host of earlier political or social arrangements; there is something of an affinity, for example, between subsidiarity and the American principle of federalism. Thus, Publius in the *Federalist Papers* recognizes an important element of human nature that any legislator must keep in mind: "It is a known fact in human nature, that its affections are commonly weak in proportion to the distance or diffusiveness of the object. Upon the same principle that a man is more attached to his family than to his neighborhood, to his neighborhood than to the community at large, the people of each State would be apt to feel a stronger bias towards their local governments than towards the government of the Union."[34] The concern he is expressing here is not Pius XI's concern but does acknowledge a connection between the preference for local knowledge and attention and the possibilities of political and social success, given the natural affections people have for their local community.

---

31. Benedict XVI, *Caritas in Veritate*, 38.

32. Quotations from Josef Pieper and Arthur-Fridolin Uta, cited in Thomas C. Kohler, "Quadragesimo Anno," in *A Century of Catholic Social Thought: Essays on "Rerum Novarum" and Nine Other Key Documents*, ed. George Weigel and Robert Royal (Washington, D.C.: Ethics and Public Policy Center, 1991), 31.

33. Joseph Komonchak, "Subsidiarity in the Church: The State of the Question," *The Jurist* 48 (1988): 298–99, cited in Kohler, "Quadragesimo Anno," 32.

34. Jacob E. Cooke, ed., *The Federalist* (Middletown, Conn.: Wesleyan University Press, 1961), 107.

More significant, one can see in Alexis de Tocqueville's account of the life of the townships in the American colonial era that the persistence of local power is seen to be one of the engines that made democratic government workable. Indeed, the whole of his work, *Democracy in America*, ends with an analysis of what he takes to be *the* great threat to American democracy, which he describes as "soft-despotism."[35] Soft despotism, for Tocqueville, is the combination of governmental centralization, which is desirable (in essence, national and international concerns need to be addressed at the national level), and administrative centralization, which is a disease deadly to democratic governance—the centralizing of the concerns of local communities into the hands of distant bureaucrats whose primary concern is not found in securing the liberty of local communities to direct their destiny. This question is most important for Tocqueville in a broader sense, as one sees clearly in his subsequent study of the ultimately failed and dangerous centralizing tendency in France in his *Ancien Regime and the French Revolution*.[36]

Yet, these earlier iterations do not capture fully the encyclical's intention in utilizing the term, for the language used in introducing the principle of subsidiarity reveals its unique character, recognizing at first some of the consequences of the contemporary age that must be addressed: "As history abundantly proves, it is true that on account of changed conditions many things which were done by small associations in former times cannot be done now save by large associations."[37] Interestingly, Pope Pius does not suggest what exactly these conditions are that have changed, such that one is compelled to turn to larger associations to address certain challenges that formerly were tended to by small associations.[38] And, indeed, this assertion has suggested to some

35. See Alexis de Tocqueville, *Democracy in America*, trans. Harvey C. Mansfield and Delba Winthrop (Chicago: University of Chicago Press, 2000), especially vol. 2, part IV, chapter 6, "What Kind of Despotism Democratic Nations Have to Fear."

36. See, for example, Alexis de Tocqueville, *The Old Regime and the Revolution*, trans. Alan S. Kahan (Chicago: University of Chicago Press, 1998); especially book two, chapter 2, "How Administrative Centralization Is an Institution of the Old Regime, and Not the Work of Either the Revolution or the Empire, as Is Said."

37. Pius XI, *Quadragesimo Anno*, 79.

38. One might note a similar tendency in American constitutional law, of the claim that the complexity of contemporary society calls for a state expanded in scope and size—an analysis often accompanied by a call for abandoning traditional strictures on the exercise of power by government at the national level. For example, dissenting in the 1986 case *Bowsher v. Synar*, Justice William

that there is something of a dichotomy in the encyclical concerning the proper or necessary role of the state. For example, Edward Norman, in citing this passage, argues that "the Encyclical *Quadragesimo Anno* ... accepted the necessity, in modern conditions, of aspects of collectivism."[39] Before addressing that question, however, it is important to see the fuller presentation of the principle of subsidiarity:

> Still, that most weighty principle, which cannot be set aside or changed, remains fixed and unshaken in social philosophy: Just as it is gravely wrong to take from individuals what they can accomplish by their own initiative and industry and give it to the community, so also it is an injustice and at the same time a grave evil and disturbance of right order to assign to a greater and higher association what lesser and subordinate organizations can do. For every social activity ought of its very nature to furnish help to the members of the body social, and never destroy and absorb them.[40]

Thus, while acknowledging some legitimate role for larger or higher associations, there is also a recognition that that role must be closely guarded against, such that it not come to overshadow the "lesser and subordinate organizations," which more rightly play the significant role in the social order.

Pope Pius XI has thus set the context for introducing the fuller sense of subsidiarity, through the role it plays in balancing the authority of multiple associations within society, and he now turns to the substance of his argument:

> The supreme authority of the State ought, therefore, to let subordinate groups handle matters and concerns of lesser importance, which would otherwise dissipate its efforts greatly. Thereby the State will more freely, powerfully, and effectively do all those things that belong to it alone because it alone can do them: directing, watching, urging, restraining, as occasion requires and necessity demands. Therefore, those in power should be sure that the more perfectly a graduated order is kept among the various associations, in observance of the

---

Brennan defends a removal provision under the law by appealing to the complex problem it is meant to address: "Rarely if ever invoked even for symbolic purposes, the removal provision certainly pales in importance beside the legislative scheme the Court strikes down today—an extraordinarily far-reaching response to a deficit problem of unprecedented proportions" (478 *U.S.* 787).

39. Edward Norman, *The Roman Catholic Church* (Berkeley: University of California Press, 2007), 173.

40. Pius XI, *Quadragesimo Anno*, 79.

principle of "subsidiary function"[41] the stronger social authority and effectiveness will be the happier and more prosperous the condition of the State.[42]

What emerges from this characterization of the principle of subsidiarity is not, contrary to what has been suggested, the acceptance of some kind of collectivism. Rather, it is simply a recognition that the existence of associations in society marks both an essential element of protection against an overreaching state, on one hand, and the recognition of the social and political nature of human beings, on the other. As Oswald von Nell-Breuning has put it, in commenting on this passage, "[t]his is the frequently mentioned and famous principle of *Subsidiarity of Social Activities*, also called the principle of *Subsidiarity of Associations*, a fundamental principle of Christian social doctrine which renders it essentially different from every collectivistic and one-sidedly exaggerated universalistic social philosophy."[43] *Centesimus Annus* elaborates on this point, critiquing the totalitarian state for absorbing into itself "the nation, society, the family, religious groups and individuals themselves."[44]

SUBSIDIARITY DEVELOPED

The teaching on subsidiarity as set forth in *Quadragesimo Anno* becomes a central focal point of subsequent Catholic social teaching. In the 1997 *Catechism of the Catholic Church*, for example, we find the principle of subsidiarity treated at some length in part three, in the context of addressing the Life of Christ. The passage commences with a discussion of the social nature of the human person, defending the existence and promotion of "voluntary associations and institutions" that allow social life to flourish.[45]

But the *Catechism* also notes that there may arise some difficulties

---

41. "Servato hoc 'subsidiarii' officii principio"; "subsidiarii" is derived from "subsidium," meaning aid, help, or assistance.

42. Pius XI, *Quadragesimo Anno*, 80.

43. Oswald von Nell-Breuning, *Reorganization of Social Economy: The Social Encyclical Developed and Explained*, trans. Bernard W. Dempsey (New York: The Bruce Publishing Company, 1936), 206; emphasis original. Thomas Kohler addresses the moderating role played by subsidiarity in the following terms: "[S]ubsidiarity condemns as perverse the various strains of libertarian individualism that deny man's social character and that pretend we bear no responsibility toward one another unless we voluntarily assume it. Similarly, the principle denounces communitarian orders that submerge the person into the mass" (Kohler, "Quadragesimo Anno," 38).

44. John Paul II, *Centesimus Annus*, 45.

45. *Catechism of the Catholic Church*, 1882.

from the recognition of the fact that human beings are not autonomous entities and that one has to be watchful of the role to be played by social institutions: "Excessive intervention by the state can threaten personal freedom and initiative. The teaching of the Church has elaborated the principle of *subsidiarity*, according to which 'a community of a higher order should not interfere in the internal life of a community of a lower order, depriving the latter of its functions, but rather should support it in case of need and help to co-ordinate its activity with the activities of the rest of society, always with a view to the common good.'"[46] Protection must be afforded the lower-level associations that assist the individual being in developing a fully integrated human life, and thus any "higher-order" community must be understood as not replacing the functions of the smaller associations but enhancing and supporting what they do. It is important to note, also, that the common good is the guiding standard to be employed, and thus, the protection afforded the lower-level associations is not to be understood as simply providing individuals with an arena within which they can all pursue their idiosyncratic individual conceptions of the human good.

The *Catechism* concludes this passage by noting that human beings are given the freedom to act on their natural capacities, exercising their reason and judgment in caring for themselves and others, and in so doing serve as "ministers of divine providence."[47] "The principle of subsidiarity is opposed to all forms of collectivism. It sets limits for state intervention. It aims at harmonizing the relationships between individuals and societies. It tends toward the establishment of true international order."[48] This opposition to collectivism can itself be seen as a reflection of the assertion in *Quadragesimo Anno* of the natural right to property that each individual possesses, a right that must be protected by society.[49] This point is also found in *Centesimus Annus*, where Pope John Paul II notes that the proper role of the state is found in the promotion

46. Ibid., 1883; the internal citation is to John Paul II, *Centesimus Annus*, 48.4, itself citing *Quadragesimo Anno*.

47. *Catechism of the Catholic Church*, 1884.

48. Ibid., 1885; the *Catechism* does not elaborate on this point here, concerning the connection between the principle of subsidiarity and the international order. The larger passage addresses the relationship between the person and the "human community as a whole" (1877), but this would be a fruitful issue for further reflection.

49. See, for example, Pius XI, *Quadragesimo Anno*, 56 and 61.

of subsidiarity, by "creating favorable conditions for the free exercise of economic activity, which will lead to abundant opportunities for employment and sources of wealth."[50]

In addition, section 2209 of the *Catechism*, in the context of the treatment of the family as the fundamental building block of society, once again acknowledges the importance attached to the principle of subsidiarity within the social order: "The family must be helped and defended by appropriate social measures. Where families cannot fulfill their responsibilities, other social bodies have the duty of helping them and of supporting the institution of the family. Following the principle of subsidiarity, larger communities should take care not to usurp the family's prerogatives or interfere in its life."[51]

One can see here that the *Catechism* has adopted the thought of *Quadragesimo Anno* and its related documents on this principle. And the principle seems to include at its heart the preference for local authority or local control, and—although this is perhaps more arguable, and worthy of discussion—a preference for limited intervention in the local community. For example, the passage in *Quadragesimo Anno* that speaks to the prudential considerations that should be brought to bear in the analysis of matters such as the appropriate pay scale includes some consideration of the just wage. The encyclical notes that a multiplicity of factors has to be taken into account here, including the relative profitability of the business. So Pope Pius says, "But if the business in question is not making enough money to pay the workers an equitable wage because it is being crushed by unjust burdens or forced to sell its product at less than a just price, those who are thus the cause of the injury are guilty of grave wrong, for they deprive workers of their just wage and force them under the pinch of necessity to accept a wage less than fair."[52]

And here, perhaps, is the special significance of the principle of subsidiarity for Pope Pius XI's purposes in the encyclical: the argument seems to be that if one is going effectively to promote the notion of subsidiarity then the only way to do so is to ensure that you, in fact, have the smaller associations around to carry out the functions appropriate to

50. John Paul II, *Centesimus Annus*, 15.   51. *Catechism of the Catholic Church*, 2209.
52. Pius XI, *Quadragesimo Anno*, 72.

them. In the absence of such institutions—often today called "mediating" or "intermediate" institutions—it is hard to see how certain matters could be handled at the lower or more local level that the encyclical commends. The concern for the role of such associations leads the pope to assert that there is a "natural right to form associations" (30, 37) and that these mutual associations serve the function of allowing the people to protect themselves against unjust oppression.[53] Indeed, he says, *Rerum Novarum* schooled many in how to do exactly that (31). As Edward Norman has argued, even in the light of the felt necessity of relying on larger associations at times, "smaller groups within the life of the state still had functions that the state must protect."[54] These associations include unions, and he focuses on them here, but the term will also come to include families and other civic organizations aimed at promoting the common good. Again, Norman suggests, "[h]ere was a species of arts-and-crafts policy that owed inspiration not to twentieth-century Fascism but to medieval guilds."[55] There is also in the encyclical an admonition to the unions to be sure to promote "justice and equity" (35); and, perhaps toward that end, there should be, alongside the unions, "associations zealously engaged in imbuing and forming their members in the teaching of religion and morality so that they in turn may be able to permeate the unions with that good spirit which should direct them in all their activity" (35).[56]

That concern for respecting the limits of state power is reiterated in Pope Benedict XVI's *Caritas in Veritate*, where he categorizes subsidiarity among the concerns of charity. Subsidiarity is "first and foremost a form of assistance to the human person via the autonomy of intermediate bodies."[57] The assistance of larger entities, when provided, is properly aimed at promoting the emancipation of these "intermediate bodies." Only in this way can human dignity be respected, and in so doing, subsidiarity emerges as "the most effective antidote against any form of all-encompassing welfare state."[58]

53. See, for example, ibid., 30 and 37.
54. Norman, *The Roman Catholic Church*, 173.
55. Ibid.
56. A particularly moving depiction of the role such associations might play, for good or bad, can be seen in Elia Kazan's 1954 movie *On the Waterfront*.
57. Benedict XVI, *Caritas in Veritate*, 57.
58. Ibid.

CONCLUSION

Chapter 4 of the *Compendium of the Social Doctrine of the Church*, specifically treating the "Principles of the Church's Social Doctrine," for good
reason, commences with a consideration of the common good.[59] The
common good, it notes, does not consist in simply the sum of the particular goods of individuals, but rather can better be understood as the
"social and community dimension of the moral good."[60] Because the
common good is, in fact, common, each member of the society has a
function to play in cooperating in "attaining it and developing it."[61] As
Pope Paul VI notes in *Octogesima Adveniens*, "[t]o take politics seriously at
its different levels—local, regional, national and worldwide—is to affirm
the duty of man, of every man, to recognize the concrete reality and the
value of the freedom of choice that is offered to him to seek to bring
about both the good of the city and of the nation and of mankind."[62]
This individual and communal effort is achieved through a proper use of
talents and possessions (including the "universal destination of the earth's
goods"[63]) and the promotion of the principles of subsidiarity and solidarity.[64] The actualization of the common good includes as well an important role for the church and the church's teaching role.

Quadragesimo Anno articulates a defense of the authority or legitimacy of the church in addressing public or social affairs, even when the
institution's primary concern is something different, the salvation of
souls: "Certainly the Church was not given the commission to guide
men to an only fleeting and perishable happiness but to that which is
eternal. Indeed, 'the Church holds that it is unlawful for her to mix
without cause in these temporal concerns'; however, she can in no wise
renounce the duty God entrusted to her to interpose her authority,
not of course in matters of technique for which she is neither suitably
equipped nor endowed by office, but in all things that are connected

59. Pontifical Council for Justice and Peace, *Compendium of the Social Doctrine of the Church*,
166–70.

60. Ibid., 164.

61. Ibid., 167.

62. Paul VI, Apostolic Letter *Octogesima Adveniens* (Vatican City: Libreria Editrice Vaticana,
1971), 46.

63. The language is taken from John Paul II's *Centesimus Annus*, 31.

64. Pontifical Council for Justice and Peace, *Compendium of the Social Doctrine of the Church*,
185–96.

with the moral law."[65] Although this may be perfectly legitimate, and desirable, and even perhaps necessary, in some instances, it is also true that it is difficult at times to do so and to do it well, and sometimes, it may even appear to prove counterproductive.

Of course, the fact that it might cause some difficulties to the church is not sufficient grounds to argue that the church should not undertake the role. It is, so it seems, one of the challenges that simply accompanies the project, and once one perceives a problem arise, there may be some complications in addressing it that one has to be willing to accept to address the situation at hand. A parallel might be drawn here between the question of the church addressing the social order and the church addressing philosophical principles. For example, as Pope John Paul II put it in his 1998 encyclical, *Fides et Ratio*, the church does not see fit to enter into and pronounce on every philosophical dispute, but does so only when the dispute tends to the undermining of the belief of Catholics, or challenges the philosophical premises necessary for proper theology.[66] When that does occur, John Paul argued, it is necessary that the church state clearly its own commitment to the pursuit of the truths of philosophy, defending—for example—the existence of nature and the human capacity to come to know the truth.[67] Indeed, much earlier in the encyclical tradition, Pope Leo XIII in his 1879 *Aeterni Patris* noted the important role that the church plays in defending philosophy by forwarding the teaching of divine revelation: "But the natural helps with which the grace of the divine wisdom, strongly and sweetly disposing all things, has supplied the human race are neither to be despised nor neglected, chief among which is evidently the right use of philosophy."[68] The papal claim is that the church does not intervene in this way to supplant philosophy but, rather, to allow it to flourish on its own terms.

---

65. Pius XI, *Quadragesimo Anno*, 41; the internal quotation is taken from Leo XIII, *Rerum Novarum*. See also John Paul II, *Centesimus Annus*, 53. Redemption is the end of the church's social doctrine.

66. See, for example: "[I]t is the Magisterium's duty to respond clearly and strongly when controversial philosophical opinions threaten right understanding of what has been revealed, and when false and partial theories which sow the seed of serious error, confusing the pure and simple faith of the People of God, begin to spread more widely." John Paul II, Encyclical *Fides et Ratio* (Vatican City: Libreria Editrice Vaticana, 1998), 49.

67. See John Paul II, *Fides et Ratio*, 50: "It is the Church's duty to indicate the elements in a philosophical system which are incompatible with her own faith."

68. Leo XIII, Encyclical *Aeterni Patris* (Rome: Acta Sanctae Sedis 12, 1879), 2.

The compulsion, or felt need, to engage in the political, social, and cultural questions that are part and parcel of the encyclical tradition, however, seems to emanate from a somewhat different quarter. Here the question is one of justice and the right ordering of society, the concern for establishing good order, and the relief of suffering and oppression in the political and social realms. And although this concern is always seen in terms primarily of the happiness of man and the salvation of souls, it still takes its task as addressing some of the most crucial, yet contested, issues of the day. In his own recognition of the issuing of *Rerum Novarum*, Pope Paul VI in 1971, in *Octogesima Adveniens*, notes that the church has a "specific message to proclaim" but that it also has an interest in seeing a just outcome emerge from the "social, political, and economic changes" that were being promoted in societies around the world.[69]

One might contemplate the challenge facing the church in this regard by considering one of many possible circumstances it could face. It may occur, for example, in the desire to promote the rights of workers, that certain church leaders might embrace a particular solution to, say, the problem of unemployment or of stagnant wages. It may happen that the action promoted by the church is adopted but turns out to be a failure in practice. Or, perhaps, the measure supported by the church does not get enacted, but the problem that had arisen somehow satisfactorily resolves itself anyway. It might be fairly easy to come up with such scenarios that, in fact, have arisen that fit the description here but that is not the point in bringing it up. Rather, the suggestion is simply that there may be some consequences to engaging in such an enterprise, consequences that may not always seem to redound to the benefit of the church and its reputation.

Now, partly that problem—if it is one—can be avoided by not addressing very particular issues at all, or by not recommending, say, one political choice over another when it comes to matters about which prudential judgments have to be made. This is why Pope Pius XI, even in the course of defending the church's intervention into the political or economic sphere, notes that this does not include "matters of technique for which she is neither suitably equipped nor endowed by office."[70] Thus, what is at stake, in part, is how one ought to address important

69. Paul VI, *Octogesima Adveniens*, 4–5.
70. Section 41.

social matters without alienating those of good faith who could be open to the fuller teaching of the church on social and moral matters.[71]

This is not meant in any way to be a suggestion that the church should abandon the attempt to provide guidance for the social and political order, to enter into what Pope Pius XI calls the realm of justice in addition to the realm of charity. That is an important and essential role for the church, for just as the church might be criticized for misjudging some aspect of its analysis of the political or economic realm, so it might be criticized by others for appearing to be indifferent to the plight of the poor and the dispossessed. Father James Schall has described the situation in the following terms, having in mind the issues addressed in the encyclical: "Even when grace builds on nature, it is designed to complete the intrinsic purpose of nature, not to eradicate it. The poor generally want and are expected to have some title for their incomes that comes from their own dignity, from themselves. This system of mutual contribution is what Catholic social thought has called, since Pius XI's Encyclical *Quadragesimo Anno*, 'subsidiarity.'"[72]

In his 1937 encyclical, *Divini Redemptoris*, Pope Pius XI again returns to the question of the relationship between justice and charity, in part, by reference back to his earlier analysis: "If, therefore, We consider the whole structure of economic life, as We have already pointed out in Our Encyclical *Quadragesimo Anno*, the reign of mutual collaboration between justice and charity in social-economic relations can only be achieved by a body of professional and interprofessional organizations, built on solidly Christian foundations."[73] Yet, even when recognizing the importance of the structure of and protections for organizations within society, Pope Pius XI never loses sight of the final goal of such considerations, as is made clear toward the end of *Quadragesimo Anno*:

All experts in social problems are seeking eagerly a structure so fashioned in accordance with the norms of reason that it can lead economic life back to sound

71. Consider here the reflections found in Vatican Council II, Pastoral Constitution *Gaudium et spes*, 43, on the role of the laity; for example: "Let the layman not imagine that his pastors are always such experts, that to every problem which arises, however complicated, they can readily give him a concrete solution, or even that such is their mission." I thank my colleague Mark Lowery for pointing me to this passage.

72. James V. Schall, *Roman Catholic Political Philosophy* (Lanham, Md.: Lexington Books, 2004), 64.

73. Pius XI, *Divini Redemptoris*, 54.

and right order. But this order, which We Ourselves ardently long for and with all Our efforts promote, will be wholly defective and incomplete unless all the activities of men harmoniously unite to imitate and attain, in so far as it lies within human strength, the marvelous unity of the Divine plan. We mean that perfect order which the Church with great force and power preaches and which right human reason itself demands, that all things be directed to God as the first and supreme end of all created activity, and that all created good under God be considered as mere instruments to be used only in so far as they conduce to the attainment of the supreme end.[74]

This point we are prepared for, in fact, by a couple of earlier comments in the encyclical concerning the genesis of the contemporary problems being explored in the document. At one point, for example, Pope Pius XI notes that the difficulties we face could have been dealt with earlier, but were not, in part because "the seeds of a new form of economy were bursting forth just when the principles of rationalism had been implanted and rooted in many minds, and there quickly developed a body of economic teaching far removed from the true moral law."[75] In addition, he notes that the demise of the concern for the common good and the importance of the natural sociability of human beings have been undermined by contemporary liberalism and that "[l]iberalism is the father of this Socialism that is pervading morality and culture and that Bolshevism [which] will be its heir."[76] *Centesimus Annus* contains a similar critique of strains of modern thought: "The atheism of which we are speaking is also closely connected with the rationalism of the Enlightenment, which views human and social reality in a mechanistic way."[77] Finally, Pope Pius XI has noted that this is a ubiquitous problem, not confined to open critics of the church, for there are many professing Catholics, Pope Pius XI asserts, who "are almost completely unmindful of that sublime law of justice and charity that binds us not only to render to everyone what is his but to succor brothers in need."[78] Once again, then, we are reminded of the intimate connection between justice and charity, and of the necessity of a fruitful and collaborative unity of purpose in public action.

74. Pius XI, *Quadragesimo Anno*, 136.
75. Ibid., 133.
76. Ibid., 122.
77. John Paul II, *Centesimus Annus*, 13.
78. Pius XI, *Quadragesimo Anno*, 125.

EIGHT

Freedom and Solidarity

A Catholic Model of
Economic Organization

Wolfgang Grassl

In recent decades, Catholic discussion on economics has been deadlocked between defense and rejection of free markets. This was not always so. In fact, between the papacy of Leo XIII and that of Paul VI, what exactly was the proper Catholic position on society and its economy was little disputed. The tendency to abide by secular ideological agendas rather than listening to the church—*sentire cum Ecclesia*—is the principal reason for the divergence of positions claiming to be Catholic. This intellectual reductionism is deplorable because it dilutes the richness and the wisdom of Catholic social teaching (CST), which has always sought to formulate a position that is not only scripturally and dogmatically correct but is also made for the human scale by supporting what recent papal teaching calls "integral human development" (CA, § 43; CV, §§ 4, 8f, 11, 17f, 30).[1]

A truthful position on the *vexatissima quaestio* of the Catholic debate on economics is quite straightforward. As a matter of fact, CST recognizes that markets can foster creativity and make a positive contribution to economic development and social well-being (CA, §§ 19, 34; CV, § 35). Yet CST has never conceded exclusivity to markets as an instrument of social coordination nor has given a wholesale endorsement of capitalism as an economic system, simply because the moral limitations on private

---

1. The following abbreviations will be used for papal encyclicals: John Paul II, *Centesimus Annus*, CA; Benedict XVI, *Caritas in Veritate*, CV.

property and free markets—the social obligation of property and the duty of care for those who are marginalized within this system—are not generated by the system itself (CA, §§ 33, 35, 42; CV, §§ 35f, 38). For capitalism to be a morally acceptable arrangement, the values that must guide economic agents are instilled from outside—from the broader sphere of civil society in which Benedict XVI saw the economy embedded. Rather than seeing philanthropic businesspeople volunteer to correct the negative effects of free markets through charitable action alone, the pope explicitly endorsed his predecessor's call for a systemic solution, by civil society reappropriating the sphere of the economy (CV, §§ 38, 46). Already John Paul II had demanded "that the market be appropriately controlled by the forces of society and by the State, so as to guarantee that the basic needs of the whole of society are satisfied" (CA, § 35). CST does not sustain divided solutions but aspires at a productive economy that integrates the best moral inclinations of entrepreneurs, managers, consumers, and workers without relegating them to corrective action outside the system: "The Church's social doctrine holds that authentically human social relationships of friendship, solidarity and reciprocity can also be conducted within economic activity, and not only outside it or 'after' it" (CV, § 36). But CST, as a matter of fact, also does not support any form of socialism, as an ideology built on stifling individual initiative, infringing the right to private property, and using the state as an overpowering redistributive mechanism that numbs individual moral inclinations.

Neither the partisans of free markets and of "democratic capitalism" nor those of statist solutions and of "liberation theology"—to use these labels simply for describing ideal types that admit of several adumbrations—have found exclusive support for their positions in recent CST as expressed in the encyclicals of John Paul II and Benedict XVI. These documents uphold solidarity and subsidiarity as equally important—and, indeed, as coordinated—principles of a good social order (CV, § 58). Both are required by human dignity: without solidarity, life would be, in Hobbes' phrase, "solitary, poor, nasty, brutish, and short"; without subsidiarity, it would be at best ineffective and at worst subject to intrusions by the powerful that violate the proper autonomy of human affairs. The first deficiency implies a horizontal, and the second, a vertical disorder of social life. Solidarity provides the material element of sociality as the glue that binds human society together; subsidiarity is the formal principle for the proper ordering of love, where, as Saint Augustine had pointed out in defining virtue, the *ordo amoris* ought to accord to every object that kind and degree of love that is appropriate to it.[2]

The dynamics of CST derive from the interaction between these two principles in social life. The flat rejection of *Caritas in Veritate* by exponents of both contending camps in Catholicism, particularly in the United States, in favor of one of the two coordinated principles neglects the richness, complexity, and depth of this document, which does not support simple solutions and in no way aligns with secular political categories. The encyclical does indeed suggest a third way as the proper Catholic view of the economy. However, contrary to much misunderstanding, Benedict XVI made it clear that his solution is not one *between* the market and the state as alternative and mutually exclusive social arrangements. The pope does not present a "third way" between traditional capitalism and traditional socialism but a new model uniting three poles animated by three types of social agents—the market, the state, and civil society. He dispenses with any dualistic opposition by suggesting a civil economy in the image of the Holy Trinity—as qualitatively different from the reductionist, intractable, and unproductive extremes of market versus state.[3]

This chapter reconstructs the counterproposal CST formulates to traditional views of social thought. It is based on substituting triadic relations for dichotomies, and these relations may then (but need not be) understood against the background of a Trinitarian model. The Catholic view that emerges from recent papal teaching is in line with long-standing CST. Although emphases may be placed differently, the underlying generative forces of CST—a particular view of God, man, and society—are constant, and all positions on the proper nature of economic organization can be measured by this standard.

THE LIBERAL VIEW OF SOCIETY

Classical liberalism has posited the individual person as the only source of meaning and value in human experience. Social institutions are then

---

2. Cf. St. Augustine of Hippo, *The City of God*, Books 8–16, trans. Gerald G. Walsh and G. Monahan (Washington, D.C.: The Catholic University of America Press, 1952), XV.22, 469.

3. On the conception of a "real third way" in the sense of Benedict XVI, cf. John Milbank, "The Real Third Way," in *The Crisis of Global Capitalism*, ed. Adrian Pabst (Eugene, Ore.: Cascade Books, 2011), 27–70.

in some sense derivatives of individual properties. Liberalism has thus framed social reality as being in a dichotomous opposition: individual versus society, individual versus government, economics versus politics, or freedom versus coercion. Communities have of course always existed, but the "enlightened" liberal tradition that formed Western thought increasingly saw them as medieval remnants the functions of which should be assumed either by individuals or by the state.[4] Society was understood as an accidental aggregate of atomistic individuals and government as a coercive institution necessitated by the antisocial propensities of human nature. The idea that these are the only agents and that their relationship is contradictory rather than merely one of contrast or tension originates with Hobbes, and via Locke and the philosophy of the Enlightenment, it has influenced American political thought.[5] Locke assumed a clear opposition between individuals and government, or the private and public spheres. Any intermediary institutions of civil society are unstable and will come either under the sway of commercial exchange or under the hegemony of bureaucratic control.[6] In the United States, this bipolar social ontology has been tenaciously defended across all political camps, assuming that issues of power, distribution, and representation must be seen as zero-sum games, with any marginal weakening of the individual benefiting government and any marginal weakening of government benefiting the individual: "it is *autonomous action of each individual versus the exclusive action of the government.*"[7] Economic activity is located at the level of the individual by assuming markets to emerge spontaneously in response to supply and demand and markets being but forms of how a society of individuals cooperates. Markets and societies are basically the same, whether (in the economicist view) society is seen as a complex of market transactions or whether (in the sociological view) markets are rather treated as organizational forms of society. Under the first perspective, all social phenomena originate from the

4. See Robert Nisbet, *The Social Philosophers* (New York: Thomas Crowell, 1973).

5. See John B. Davis, *The Theory of the Individual in Economics* (London: Routledge, 2003), chapter 2. Even Rawls's two principles of justice "presuppose that the social structure can be divided into two more or less distinct parts, the first principle applying to the one, the second to the other." In their separation and lexical ordering, they reflect the social dualism of the liberal tradition. John Rawls, *A Theory of Justice*, 61, 302.

6. Cf. Karl Polanyi, *The Great Transformation: The Political and Economic Origins of Our Time* (Boston: Beacon Press, 1944).

7. Mises, *Human Action*, 731.

voluntary acts of individuals who seek to produce public goods at lower cost. However, by ignoring the great complexity of modern society, which has several types of agents that cannot simply be attributed to one of two poles, this view of social and political life is narrowly reductionist. Its underlying dualism, which is stronger in American economic thought than elsewhere, is untenable from several perspectives, not least from those of sociology, philosophy, and theology. But, even more important, it has failed to provide good explanations of economic life itself. Economic reality cannot, as macroeconomic models still maintain, neatly be divided into a "private" and a "state" sector; microeconomic theory cannot clearly be separated into private and public choice. There are hybrid forms of goods besides private and public goods; the size and power of some "private" corporations exceed that of entire states; and the increasingly fractionalized public sphere is no longer dominated by governments but at least shared with interest groups and media organizations. Consequently, the assumption of a dichotomous structure of social reality has become less credible.

The liberal tradition of social thought has understood humans as individuals whose lives take place in a flat world of horizontal conflicts and zero-sum games. Modernity relies on this type of social dualism.[8] Society consists of individuals who define their relations in a more or less autonomous and free manner even if they use intermediate bodies (such as chambers of commerce, trade unions, or charities) to do so. This view rests on three fundamental assumptions: (1) society and politics are based on a dichotomous opposition (of individual versus society, or individual versus government); (2) markets are identified with civil society, and social relations are subsumed under economic relations; and (3) freedom is typically defined *ex negativo*, as absence of some constraint. From Hobbes via Locke, Montesquieu, and Smith to Mill, Hayek, and Nozick, individuals and governments are the only social agents, and their relationship is contradictory rather than one of contrast, complementarity, or tension. Markets are a form of human cooperation and thus seen as a function of (and sometimes as constitutive of or even identical with) society. Mises consequently argued that "there is no kind of freedom and liberty other than the kind which the market

8. Davis, *The Theory of the Individual in Economics*, 2–6.

economy brings about."[9] Freedom is understood negatively, as the absence of restraint or coercion. It is to protect a sphere of untrammeled personal autonomy "within which a man can act unobstructed by others."[10] This concept of freedom has its origin in Ockham, for whom it applied to the will, which he saw as free exactly if it was indifferent to contraries and could freely choose between them.[11] For exponents of the liberal tradition in its various forms, individual choice rules supreme as long as it does not infringe the freedom of others. Both contending camps in (American) Catholicism subscribe to this tradition in different ways. It is antithetical to long-standing CST.

THE CATHOLIC VIEW OF SOCIETY

CST does not understand the stuff of society to be composed of individuals but of persons. They are defined by relations of which many may be contingent, but some are necessary (in a biological, moral, legal, or theological sense). Personality expresses the human property of resembling God, which individualism completely ignores.[12] CST therefore rejects all three propositions of the classical liberal tradition and presents an alternative to them—a Catholic model of social life in freedom and responsibility. The three counterproposals are (1) social ontology is tripartite, with the same persons (rather than individuals) cooperating on markets, in civil society, and in the state (a term that CST prefers to the rather more diffuse "government"; CA, § 35; CV, §§ 38, 41); (2) civil society with its values of solidarity, reciprocity, and fraternity must impregnate both markets and the state by creating hybrid structures of businesses that transcend divisions between public and private, for-profit and not-for-profit, and even consumer and producer and are thus directed at "civilizing the economy" (CV, § 38; CA, § 15f); and (3) freedom must be seen *ex positivo* as the *"possibility of integral human development"* (CV, § 9; CA, §§ 17, 19, 25) and clearly as a gift from God that involves responsibility.

At the heart of the Catholic vision lies a relational view of the person. This view constitutes society as the sum of stable relations. Where-

---

9. Mises, *Human Action*, 283.

10. Isaiah Berlin, *Four Essays on Liberty* (Oxford: Oxford University Press, 1969), 122.

11. See Servais Pinckaers, *The Sources of Christian Ethics* (Washington, D.C.: The Catholic University of America Press, 1995), 242f.

12. Cf. Jacques Maritain, *The Person and the Common Good*, trans. John J. Fitzgerald (New York: Charles Scribner's Sons, 1947), chapter 3.

as economists in the liberal tradition saw individuals related to each other by markets—as consumers and producers, or as workers and employers—Benedict XVI rejected such extrinsicism. Human beings must not be reduced to their social rôles, which are merely contingent and do not define their essence. He replaced it with the vision of an immanentist (or intrinsicist) relatedness. Like the persons of the Nicene Creed, the three social agents—markets, civil society, and the state—have different identities and functions and are therefore different entities, yet they are of the same substance, because they are ultimately but different forms of human organization. It is persons who exchange on markets, build institutions of society, and embody functions of the state. Civil society is constituted by the various communities, which John Paul II called "real communities of persons" (CA, § 49) such as families, companies, clubs, and charitable organizations. The "civil economy" referenced by Benedict XVI (CV, §§ 38f, 46f) is then civil society using cooperation that aims at reciprocity among producers and consumers.[13] The multiple relationalities of persons translate into an interconnected social *cosmos* as composed of human associations at various levels, from the family and the household via communities to a common polity and to the family of nations. These associations have different ends, are hierarchically ordered, and are governed by the highest common good.[14] The mutual interpenetration of society gives each form of organization its proper task, in accordance with subsidiarity, while directing all of social life toward one goal: integral human development.[15] The institution of marriage provides a good example: it is not a contract between individuals but, by its nature, a social relationship characterized by reciprocity that exists prior to and beyond the persons who enter into it. The contribution it makes to the human flourishing of persons called to marriage is not that of utilitarian "happiness," nor is its place in a hierar-

13. Reciprocity in the sense of CST is not the *do ut des* ("I give so that you may give") of reciprocal exchange. Cf. Luigino Bruni, *Reciprocity, Altruism and the Civil Society* (Abingdon: Routledge, 2008).

14. Cf. Aquinas, *Summa Theologica* I-II, q.113, a.9, ad 2; II-II, q.47, a.11, resp.

15. Cf. Wolfgang Grassl, "*Pluris Valere*: Towards Trinitarian Rationality in Social Life," in *The Whole Breadth of Reason: Rethinking Economics and Politics*, ed. Simona Beretta and Mario Maggioni (Venice: Marcianum Press, 2012), 313–48; "Hybrid Forms of Business: The Logic of Gift in the Commercial World," *Journal of Business Ethics* 100, Suppl. 1 (2012): 109–23; "Integral Human Development in Analytical Perspective: A Trinitarian Model," *Journal of Markets and Morality* 16, no. 1 (Spring 2013): 135–55.

chy of relationships substitutable. Human institutions are therefore not legitimized—and, indeed, not even able—to alter it.[16]

At the heart of this vision lies a distinctively Catholic anthropology, and for Benedict "the social question has become a radically anthropological question" (CV, § 75). Persons are defined by relationships and are "made for gift" (§ 34) as the recipients of grace, and their freedom lies in the pursuit of excellence (or of human flourishing).[17] All components of this view are *positive* by expressing what persons (or social institutions) *are*, they are *teleological* by stating what they are called to *be*, and they combine *horizontal* with *vertical purposes* for which persons have been created. Whereas in the liberal tradition, freedom was understood as absence of coercion, and individuals were left to define their own goals, CST supports a positive notion of freedom as the ability of man to grow into his given end. It is no longer a "freedom of indifference" but a "freedom for excellence" with a twofold root: first, a sense of the true and good and, second, a desire for knowledge and happiness.[18]

But at a deeper level, the Catholic vision differs from the principles of liberalism not only on anthropological and axiological but already on metaphysical grounds as well.[19] For partisans of "democratic capitalism" and of "liberal socialism" (or, for that matter, "liberation theology"), their advocacy of markets and of the state, respectively, as regulative principles of social life is based on zero-sum assumptions: less market means more government control, and less government intervention means exposing vulnerable people to the brutal forces of the market. A distinctively Catholic metaphysics desists from such categorical divisions in favor of rejecting both contradictories, without negating differences, and for different reasons.[20] This would seem to leave no room for a "third way" between capitalism and socialism. However, the near-Catholic philosopher Simone Weil pointed out that a "between" (μεταξύ) need not indicate some point on the same level as the extremes, for it can both separate and connect.[21] Aquinas repeatedly emphasized that human beings are between different

---

16. Cf. *Catechism of the Catholic Church*, §§1603ff, 1639f, 1644f.

17. Cf. Pinckaers, *The Sources of Christian Ethics*, chapter 15.

18. Ibid., 357.

19. Cf. Adrian Pabst, *Metaphysics: The Creation of Hierarchy* (Grand Rapids, Mich.: Eerdmans, 2012), 32ff, 246ff.

20. Cf. *Catechism of the Catholic Church*, §2425.

21. Simone Weil, "Metaxu," in *Gravity and Grace*, trans. Thomas R. Nevin (New York: Putnam, 1952), 200–204.

vertical levels of reality such as between animals and angels because they are ordered toward God.[22]

However, it would be easy to misunderstand the bridging of a "between" as an arbitrary movement in either direction. Benedict XVI did not postulate just any "interpenetration" of social actors or a random integration of the social sphere, nor did he support a super-corporatism, which was still present in Pius XI's *Quadragesimo Anno*. Although market, civil society, and the state are each propelled by their own "logic," he defined a clear direction of causality: civil society must extend the principles that are germane to it—gratuity, reciprocity, and solidarity—to the sphere of markets, where other principles predominate, and even to that of public administration. Intermediate bodies are then not in any linear sense *between* individuals and the state but are the glue that holds all of human society together by being its wellspring of pro-social values.

The Catholic vision is thus more complex than that of the liberal tradition: it sees humans as persons necessarily defined by social relations, and it assumes a stratified reality, with vertical relations—hierarchies of values, of excellence, and of sin—coexisting with horizontal relations within these levels in what mathematically would be a lattice structure.[23] The autonomy of man in the liberal view is replaced by the acceptance of a radical (and thoroughly vertical) dependence on grace as reflected in Benedict XVI's insistence on man's reception of absolutely gratuitous gifts from God in the forms of love and truth (CV, §§ 5, 34). Because we receive everything gratuitously and can truly attribute nothing to our own devices, we must give without counting on favors being returned. Utilitarian calculation, autonomy, and choice are replaced by calling, by a "job description" for humans in the implementation of which they are indeed free.

The limitation of such a complex multilevel configuration lies in the fact that there are vertical relations between and horizontal relations within levels of reality. A single entity transcends this limitation and unites at once vertical and horizontal relationships: the Holy Trinity.

22. Aquinas, *Summa Theologica* I, qq.66, 72; cf. also I, q.93.

23. Benedict XVI indeed suggested that the four main principles of CST—human dignity, solidarity, subsidiarity, and the common good—structure social reality along horizontal and vertical axes. See *Address of His Holiness Benedict XVI to the Participants in the 14th Session of the Pontifical Academy of Social Sciences*, Vatican City, May 3, 2008, http://w2.vatican.va/content/benedict-xvi/en/speeches/2008/may/documents/hf_ben-xvi_spe_20080503_social-sciences.html.

Trinitarian dogmatics assumes no hierarchy between the three Persons, although the Son proceeds from the Father and the Holy Spirit proceeds from both Father and Son (*filioque*). The three Persons have their individual identity and yet are all God, bound together by mutual love. Their mutual indwelling (*perichōrēsis*) thus sublates vertical and horizontal differences in an *Aufhebung* that indeed reflects Hegel's three senses of the term: it abolishes them yet preserves them, and most of all, it lifts them up to a level of sublimity that is accessible more to the mystic than the everyday faithful. This "economic" model of the Trinity is found in a more rudimentary form in John Paul II's teaching (*Christifideles Laici*, §§ 6, 18f, 40), but it is been further developed in *Caritas in Veritate*, which holds it up as the ideal of social relations (§ 54).

The most far-reaching contribution of the encyclical may be its unambiguous dissociation from a dichotomous model of social ontology and, by implication, from not only liberalism and much of modern economic thought but also from all kinds of social constructivism. In perhaps his most radical passage, Benedict XVI lamented this bipolar opposition: "The continuing hegemony of the binary model of market-plus-State has accustomed us to think only in terms of the private business leader of a capitalistic bent on the one hand, and the State director on the other. In reality, business has to be understood in an articulated way" (CV, § 41). He went to great length in explaining this articulation. Like CST before him, and with explicit reference to his predecessor, the pope pointed to civil society "as the most natural setting for an economy of gratuitousness and fraternity" (CV, § 38; CA, § 35). But the three "subjects" obviously do not perform at the same levels: "economic life must be understood as a multi-layered phenomenon" (CV, § 38). Markets, civil society, and the state are therefore not in a horizontal conflict over the same goods—in this may lie the strongest deviation from the liberal view of society. Because he rejected the dichotomy of individual versus state, the pope did not relegate the civil economy he supported to a "third sector" but saw it at work throughout society, as "a broad new composite reality embracing the private and public spheres, one which does not exclude profit, but instead considers it a means for achieving human and social ends" (CV, § 46). Persons, as relational individuals, make up the civil economy, and reciprocity, as its defining characteristic, must extend to the state. The pope thus challenged the policy recommendations of modern economics not least because he rejected its underlying social ontology.

A TRIADIC (AND TRINITARIAN) SOCIAL ONTOLOGY

The general argument of *Caritas in Veritate* is not new, for it has been used in previous papal teaching and in various forms in the works of theologians and social scientists. But only occasionally have triadic structures been recognized as more fundamental to society than dichotomies. The French counterrevolutionary statesman and political thinker Louis de Bonald envisaged a truly Catholic society as consisting of triadic relations between components—domestic, public, and religious—that in turn were of a triadic nature, thus reflecting the Holy Trinity.[24] The sociologist Georg Simmel argued that more complex social relationships go beyond the basic dyad, which allows individuals to maintain their identity and to have control over it by withdrawal. Triadic groups change the form of interaction by allowing for strategies of competition, alliances, or mediation. Triads are likely to develop a group structure independently of the individuals in it, which makes them the true building blocks of society.[25] At a higher level of aggregation, the communitarian tradition in social thought has long recognized communities as a third agent besides individuals and government. Some of the literature on civil society may be attributed to this camp. Alexis de Tocqueville already in the 1830s described a vibrant community life in the United States. However, when appreciating the self-help actions of citizens, he described them as spontaneously formed groups of citizens rather than as stable intermediate structures; his account does not present a civil society as envisaged by communitarian thought.[26] Unlike the stable guilds, corporations, confraternities, or municipalities of the Middle Ages, sheriff's posses did not mediate between individuals and government. American political thought has counted such citizen action toward the sphere of individuals, and the bipolar model has been

24. Cf. Jacques Alibert, *Les triangles d'or d'une société catholique: Louis de Bonald théoricien de la Contre-Révolution* (Paris: Pierre Téqui, 2002).

25. Cf. Georg Simmel, *Soziologie: Untersuchungen über die Formen der Vergesellschaftung* (Leipzig: Duncker and Humblot, 1908), chapter 2.

26. Cf. Pawel Zaleski, "Tocqueville on Civilian Society: A Romantic Vision of the Dichotomic Structure of Social Reality," *Archiv für Begriffsgeschichte* 50 (2008): 260–66.

retained. Few thinkers indeed have stepped outside it regardless of their own political leanings—mostly philosophers, anthropologists, or sociologists, but hardly an economist.[27] Based on his work on economic history, Karl Polanyi identified two alternative nonmarket mechanisms of economic organization: redistribution and reciprocity.[28] Redistribution is typical of state actors whereas reciprocity, which is common particularly within ties of kinship, ethnicity, or religion, amounts to sharing with others in the expectation that when needed the action would be reciprocated. Societies thus have three basic options for producing and transferring value. It is crucial to appreciate the distinctions between altruism and reciprocity and between reciprocity and exchange of equivalents (i.e., market exchange). Reciprocity in this sense is gratuitous and does not rely on a calculated *do ut des*. Among the economists, a rare exception was Kenneth Boulding, who divided the social system into three large, overlapping and interacting sub-systems: markets (based on exchange), government (based on threat), and an "integrative system" that establishes community.[29] Representative of the latter is the "grants economy," which is characterized by unilateral transfers between social agents.

Some approaches in economics have recently moved beyond dichotomous categories, such as those between private and public goods, by allowing for impure public goods, club goods, and so forth or by recognizing that much social value is created through relational goods. Empirical work has documented that economic agents are as much motivated by pro-social as by purely egoistic incentives.[30] Communitarian thinkers admit of three agents of society ordered toward different ultimate ends, with markets aiming at producing profits through exchange, the state maintaining order through regulation and redistribution, and civil society fostering values of fraternity through cooperation and reciproc-

27. Cf. Rick Wicks, "A Model of Dynamic Balance among the Three Spheres of Society—Markets, Governments, and Communities—Applied to Understanding the Relative Importance of Social Capital and Social Goods," *International Journal of Social Economics* 36, no. 5 (2009): 535–65.

28. Karl Polanyi, *The Livelihood of Man* (New York: Academic Press, 1977), 35–43.

29. Kenneth E. Boulding, *The Economy of Love and Fear* (Belmont: Wadsworth, 1973), 5, 27f.

30. The literature in this field is voluminous. See, for example, Serge-Christophe Kolm, *Reciprocity: An Economics of Social Relations* (Cambridge: Cambridge University Press, 2008); Leonardo Becchetti, Alessandra Pelloni, and Fiammetta Rossetti, "Relational Goods, Sociability, and Happiness," *Kyklos* 61 (2008): 343–63; Pierpaolo Donati and Riccardo Solci, *I beni relazionali* (Turin: Bollati Boringhieri, 2011).

TABLE 8-1. Three Sectors of Social Life

	Markets	Civil society	State
Ultimate end	Profit	Fraternity	Order
Proximate end	Efficiency	Solidarity	Equity
Means	Autonomy, exchange, contracts	Cooperation, reciprocity, gratuitousness	Regulation, control, redistribution
Goods produced	Private	Relational	Public

ity. Markets achieve their ultimate ends through efficiency, civil society through solidarity, and the State through equity (table 8-1). Most notably, with relational sociology, a new paradigm has emerged that sees neither the *homo oeconomicus* nor any aggregates as the ultimate components of social reality but, rather, persons characterized by relations and networks of interaction.[31] It also captures the empirical finding that for many people, God resides in relations—because he *is* relationality.[32]

Of course, triadic configurations cannot automatically be given a Trinitarian meaning. Despite the scholastic dictum, *omne trinum est perfectum*, capturing an aspect of the uniqueness of the Trinity depends on transcending the focus on the merely static composition of the social whole. The parts must also be related functionally and dynamically to each other, in analogy to the structure of the Trinity, which is bound together by mutual love: "The Trinity is absolute unity insofar as the three divine Persons are pure relationality. The reciprocal transparency among the divine Persons is total and the bond between each of them complete, since they constitute a unique and absolute unity" (CV, § 54). Aquinas's notion of connaturality may apply here: elements constituting a hybrid must resonate with or be attuned to each other just like the Persons of the Trinity.[33] Each divine person, Aquinas argues, is a whole rather than a part;[34] by analogy, a society composed of human persons created *in imagine Dei* is also a whole composed of wholes rather

31. Cf. Mustafa Emirbayer, "Manifesto for a Relational Sociology," *American Journal of Sociology* 103, no. 2 (1997): 281–317; Pierpaolo Donati, *Relational Sociology: A New Paradigm for the Social Sciences* (London: Routledge, 2010).

32. Cf. Pierpaolo Donati, *La matrice teologica della società* (Soveria Mannelli: Rubbettino, 2010).

33. Aquinas, *Summa Theologica* I, q.93, a.6, ad 3; see also I-II, q.26, a.1, ad 3 and a. 2; I-II, q.31, a.8, ad 2.

34. Ibid., q. 30, a.4.

than of individuals.[35] The doctrine of the Trinity says that God is Himself community, and every human institution seeking to grow into the perfection of God must by necessity transform itself into a community of persons. Because people are becoming "members one of another" (Rom 12:5) and "servants of one another" (Gal 5:13), they are giving of themselves to "build up each other" (1 Thes 5:11) and "do good to one another" (1 Thes 5:15). To the extent that they do so and emulate unity in diversity, businesses and other social organizations can indeed capture some of the divine substance, if ever so imperfectly.[36]

NEW FORMS OF ECONOMIC ORGANIZATION

From an economic viewpoint, the three great themes Benedict XVI proposed are the following: relationalism (which builds on John Paul II's personalism), a civil economy embedded in society, and new hybrid structures in corporate organization and governance.[37] Together these principles amount easily to the greatest innovation in CST regarding economic organization since Leo XIII. Yet these new cornerstones of CST are in perfect harmony with the traditional core principles of human dignity, solidarity, subsidiarity, and the common good, of which they are applications to the reality of contemporary business and society. Indeed, common goods are produced if solidarity at the horizontal level is ordered according to subsidiarity in the vertical sense, which makes it most effective while safeguarding human dignity. Common goods as lying in "the totality of social conditions allowing persons to achieve their communal and individual fulfilment" are then, as Benedict XVI argued, always located in the vertical dimension of the social order, because they aim at a qualitatively higher state rather than at a mere expansion of human possibilities at the same level.[38]

The past decades have seen many developments in business life that

35. Cf. Maritain, *The Person and the Common Good*, 46f.

36. Cf. Enrique Cambón, *Trinità modello sociale* (Rome: Città Nuova, 1999); Grassl, "Pluris Valere."

37. Cf. Wolfgang Grassl, "Ekonomia obywatelska: Trynitarny klucz do odczytania ekonomii papieskiej," *Pressje* 29 (2012): 58–82; Grassl, "Hybrid Forms of Business"; Grassl and Habisch, "Ethics and Economics."

38. Benedict XVI, *Address of His Holiness Benedict XVI to the Participants in the 14th Session of the Pontifical Academy of Social Sciences*.

go in the direction of what Benedict XVI advocated. There has been an erosion of the categorical divide between profit-based and nonprofit enterprises, as various types of businesses have emerged that embody characteristics of both. Different forms of social enterprises competing on markets are examples, as are models of mission-related investing, community development, civil society organizations, and social entrepreneurship.[39] Comparative economic analysis has of course long pointed to a multiplicity of trade governance mechanisms in which trust, personal norms, and social codes are determining factors. The idea of a clear demarcation between markets and states as solely determining economic organization has become a fool's errand.[40] Another of the most entrenched social dichotomies—that of market participants being either consumers or producers—is breaking down as co-creation of value allows consumers to participate in the production of goods, and particularly of services.

The obliteration of categorical divides in economic life has a long tradition. European countries, and particularly those with strong Catholic cultures, already in the nineteenth century developed cooperative movements for farmers, craftspeople, shopkeepers, and consumers that have become formidable players on factor and consumer markets. They allow smaller suppliers to bundle their otherwise atomistic market power to compete with multinational corporations and thus at least partially to overcome diseconomies of scale. Household buyers can thus approximate the purchasing power of corporate buyers, although the success of this movement has, for organizational reasons, always been greater on business than on consumer markets. Several institutional and legal forms have been created ranging from limited partnerships, registered cooperatives, and marketing consortia based on rules of both efficiency and equity to corporate-nongovernmental organization collaboration and, under the "new public management" movement, to public-private partnerships and the outsourcing of government functions.[41] These models have spilled over to Latin America, where Brazil is now home to a

---

39. Cf. David Billis, ed., *Hybrid Organizations and the Third Sector* (Basingstoke: Palgrave Macmillan, 2010); Wolfgang Grassl, "Business Models of Social Enterprise: A Design Approach to Hybridity," *ACRN Journal of Entrepreneurship Perspectives* 1, no. 1 (2012): 37–60; Grassl, "Hybrid Forms of Business."

40. Cf. Elinor Ostrom, "Beyond Markets and States: Polycentric Governance of Complex Economic Systems," *American Economic Review* 100, no. 3 (2010): 641–72.

41. Cf. Wolfgang Grassl, "Cooperative Marketing: Efficiency Conditions for Alliances," in

thriving cooperative movement (*economia solidária*), and to Africa, where microlending on the model of Bangladesh has facilitated the emergence of a new class of business owners. Ethical investment funds, fair-trade organizations, and alternative forms of travel complement this trend. All these businesses use a wide variety of governance models. Under globalization, it is entirely predictable that different cultures will bring about different business models for the civil economy.

To a large extent, CST stood at the origin of this movement in the nineteenth century and often has the church supported the development of cooperatives, mutuals, unions, and other membership-led organizations.[42] Benedict XVI mentioned credit unions as a positive example (CV, § 65). The worldwide Economy of Communion as a project of the Focolare Movement is a network of businesses that freely choose to share their profits according to three principles of equal importance— to grow their businesses, to help people in need, and to spread the culture of giving.[43] Benedict XVI supported exactly these endeavors when he proposed the civil economy (CV, §§ 38f, 46f) and the Economy of Communion (§ 46) as models to be followed.

Reciprocity is at work in many for-profit operations as well, for example, in cooperatives, family businesses, social enterprises, or employee stock ownership plans. There is, then, no reason to privilege nonprofit enterprise by crediting it with a higher moral value, for the more important task is that of infusing all forms of business with what economists call "pro-social" attitudes and theologians simply call "love": "Charity in truth, in this case, requires that shape and structure be given to those types of economic initiative which, without rejecting profit, aim at a higher goal than the mere logic of the exchange of equivalents, of profit as an end in itself" (CV, § 38). Neither is there reason for making nonprofit goals the hallmark of social enterprise, which would again tap into the extrinsicist trap of separating domains, for the mode of organization is clearly secondary to the purpose of a business.

Canada/Caribbean Business: Opportunities and Challenges for Management, ed. T. Brunton and T. Lituchy (Port-of-Spain: University of the West Indies Press, 1998), 87–101.

42. Cf. Peter Davis, "Co-operative Management as a Catholic Vocation," in *Business Education and Training: A Value Laden Process*, vol. 4, ed. S. M. Natale (Washington, D.C.: University Press of America, 2000), 157–80.

43. Cf. Lorna Gold, *New Financial Horizons: The Emergence of an Economy of Communion* (Hyde Park, N.Y.: New City Press, 2010).

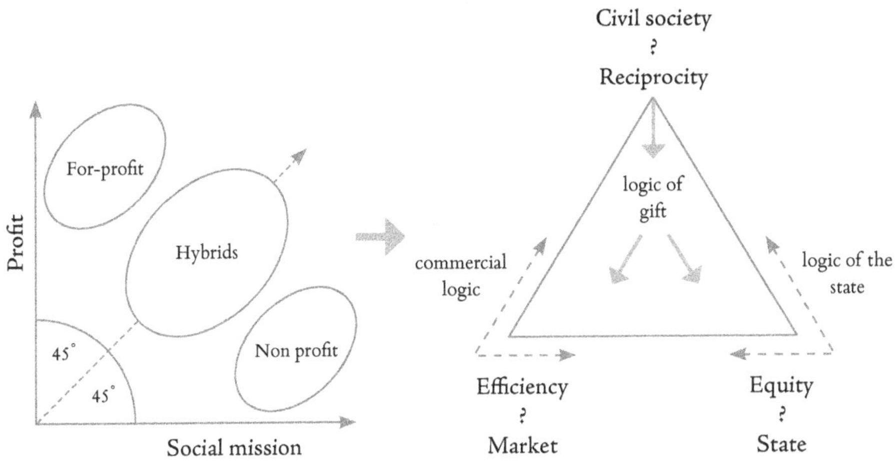

FIGURE 8-1. Change in Models of Society

Benedict XVI rejected mere spillovers of gratuitousness into the market sector, as practiced in the American form of philanthropy (CV, § 42). Philanthropic activity in this model remains extrinsic to the market, because the relationship is one-sided, as between a charitable donor and a recipient. Nor are public welfare programs enough—paternalistic social assistance can be, the pope declared, "demeaning to those in need" (CV, § 58). The self-organization of civil society is preferable over any of these extrinsic solutions, and the real challenge is not to provide food aid but employment that allows poor people to develop their own lives in dignity (CV, § 63). Both the economy and the state must be subordinated in value to civil society, which is the appropriate agent to provide opportunities for the marginalized, by using markets and State institutions wherever they best serve the purpose of human development. The direction of causality is important here: the values of civil society must shape markets and the public sector, not vice versa, for hybridization to be a "civil" process. Whereas the classical view of society saw divisions by sectors, CST proposes integration—but integration in a particular direction and for a particular purpose. From its "natural home" (CV, § 39) in civil society, the "logic of gift" must infuse "commercial logic" and the "logic of the State" in a dynamic process that shifts equilibria in a force field between three competing institutional logics by influencing the other spheres internally. The static model of separate spheres must give way to a dynamic model in the spirit of the Trinity (figure 8-1).

Recent CST recognizes the role of markets in harnessing human creativity. In fact, their function of facilitating exchange is indispensable. But they do not by themselves produce the personal virtues that are required for them to function well (CV, §§ 32, 35), and "commercial logic" has the tendency of placing all human relations under economic calculation. Markets must not be reduced to one historically contingent form of economic organization—capitalism as practiced in the early twenty-first century (CV, § 41). Market economies existed long before the Industrial Revolution brought about capitalist forms of production and, to extend the argument much beyond that of Karl Marx, of consumption.[44] Even within capitalism, there are different economic cultures with variegated models of industrial organization, management styles, and roles for the public sector.[45] It is a mistake to reduce capitalism to one form that has emerged only over the past century, with joint-stock corporations dominating and corporate policy therefore being directed at maximizing shareholder profits over the short term. It is this model of capitalism that recent papal teaching criticized, but not the market economy as such. Benedict XVI expected "that business enterprise involves a wide range of values, becoming wider all the time" (CV, § 41). But these values are not generated by markets; they are human possibilities infused by grace that are transmitted through civil society. Benedict XVI sounded a clarion call for devoting more creative energy to safeguarding institutions such as craftsmen, family farms, and other family businesses, which already John XXIII had explicitly endorsed (*Mater et Magistra*, § 85) and which had been a concern of CST since Leo XIII. CST calls on states to "enact policies promoting the centrality and the integrity of the family" (CV, § 44), which is the most important "intermediate" form of social organization and needs a solid economic foundation. However, CST does not condone American-style capitalism with its tendency to foster financialization and corporate over personal forms of organizing companies (CV, §§ 24, 40, 65). It recognizes the "human inadequacies of

---

44. Cf. Fernand Braudel, *Civilization and Capitalism: 15th–18th Century,* vol. 2, *The Wheels of Commerce* (New York: Harper and Row, 1982).

45. Cf. Wolfgang Grassl, "L'entreprise européenne—inéxistante, moribonde, ou modèle pour l'exportation?" *Géoéconomie* 28 (2003): 153–80.

capitalism" and rejects "the resulting domination of things over people" (CA, § 33).

As a novelty in CST, *Caritas in Veritate* also states that the consumer "has a specific social responsibility" in parallel with that of businesses (§ 66). The pope calls for new models of consumption, "for example, forms of co-operative purchasing like the consumer co-operatives that have been in operation since the nineteenth century, partly through the initiative of Catholics" (CV, § 66). Here, too, creativity is needed, and the pontiff's call is partially being answered. Better access to information and greater transparency of corporate decisions have reduced the asymmetry of information and thus price-setting power on which traditional forms of consumption and retailing relied. A business landscape is developing that exhibits many properties of a civil economy.[46] Consumer movements have created new models of household production, direct distribution, and quality-conscious consumption. Under the cover term *collaborative consumption*, various models of sharing, bartering, trading, and renting, have been invented and have been facilitated by advances in social media and peer-to-peer online platforms.[47] The transformation of passive consumers into collaborators through social media harbors the opportunity of creating new human communities (although the quality of these still remains to be seen).

On the other hand, Pope Benedict XVI did not ignore the limitations of the state. Not only did he point to the questionable record of aid to developing countries; he also emphasized that "subsidiarity is the most effective antidote against any form of all-encompassing welfare State" (CV, § 57). Yet there is a necessity for the state to introduce regulation through which market behavior leads to monopolies, or the protection of consumers is required. Similarly, Benedict XVI called for a "strategic revitalization" of agriculture. He deplored how particularly in less-developed countries, the agricultural sector is being crowded out by low-value manufacturing only then to import foodstuff from "dynamic economies." These, however, "are tempted to pursue advantageous alliances," and an increasing oligopolization of large industrial

46. Cf. Michael E. Porter and Mark R. Kramer, "Creating Shared Value: How to Reinvent Capitalism—and Unleash a Wave of Innovation and Growth," *Harvard Business Review* 89, no. 1/2 (2011): 62–77; Grassl, "Hybrid Forms of Business."

47. Cf. Rachel Botsman and Roo Rogers, *What's Mine Is Yours: The Rise of Collaborative Consumption* (New York: HarperBusiness, 2010).

producers in a few developed countries leads to higher prices and a growing dependency for developing countries that used to be largely self-sufficient. The pope concluded that "a new balance between farming, industry and services is necessary so that development may be sustainable."[48] But recognition of economic or social ills does not *eo ipso* invite State intervention. More responsible consumption and more enlightened business practices are as important as is government regulation to solve the problem. Much entrepreneurship, management capacity, and social imagination is needed toward this end, and market solutions and the engagement of civil society have priority over the merely subsidiary action by the state. But CST declares that there is a solution and that humans can at least in principle find it. If we look for perfection, the Trinity is still the paragon from which to learn.

CONCLUSION: ECONOMIC REVIVAL AND FREEDOM

What would it take to recover, at least in certain pockets of society, some of the rich artistic and commercial culture of the Renaissance that still serves as a model for a civil economy? Both arts and crafts are individually appropriated skills that are socially recognized and transmitted. They require for their flourishing a community of practitioners, institutions of training and adjudication, systems of patronage and sponsorship, supply chain networks for raw materials and tools, and distribution channels to intermediaries and final consumers. Even all of these would be insufficient were it not also for the social appreciation of individual accomplishment, and of beauty and individual style within path-dependent traditions; they create incentives to enter an art or a craft, which typically implies joining a guild or self-regulating community of practitioners. Crafts from carpenters to cooks and from roofers to goldsmiths, if they are truly meant to flourish, require standards that are produced by communities but cannot be generated by markets of anonymous consumers.[49] The workers employed in the building of French cathedrals in the twelfth century organized themselves as Les Compa-

48. Benedict XVI, *Angelus message*, November 14, 2010, http://w2.vatican.va/content/benedict-xvi/en/angelus/2010/documents/hf_ben-xvi_ang_20101114.html; see also Benedict XVI, *Caritas in Veritate*, 27.

49. Richard Sennett, *The Craftsman* (New Haven, Conn.: Yale University Press, 2008).

gnons du Devoir, and this labor union, the oldest still in existence, has supported the development of a strong artisan culture in France not least because of its being deeply embedded in civil society.[50] From the state is needed protection against fakes and counterfeits. Last, the humus of creativity depends on inspiration and talent, which are products of divine grace. Artistic talent and exacting standards of perfection must be nurtured by communities building on individually received grace; they are not factors of production tradable on markets.

CST rejects "corner solutions" such as exclusive reliance on markets or the State to organize economic activity and yet does not position a better solution just anywhere on a continuum *between* these, as a "third way." There can be no doubt that recent CST has given much credibility to the creative power of markets, and yet the task of *"civilizing the economy"* (CV, § 38) will continue to make public action necessary where human virtue fails. As with other matters, a genuinely Catholic view is anagogical by suggesting that a civil economy—influenced by the positive forces of society—transcend both market and state. Ultimately it is to serve integral human development: the human person is "constitutionally oriented towards 'being more'" (CV, § 14) than what may be the prevailing state of social, economic, technological, or political development. The real challenge *Caritas in Veritate* places before us is to combine economic revival with intellectual, moral, and spiritual growth. Benedict XVI proclaimed that our failings to support integral human development and a just society are grave, but that they are all the more serious because we have not even created a truly efficient economy by our own standards. The ongoing financial crisis on both sides of the Atlantic is a case in point, as is our inability to see globalization as more than a zero-sum game. Before our moral failings come our intellectual failings—"man's darkened reason" (CV, § 36). One of these may be our continuing incapacity to understand that CST does not abide by the secular divisions that interests, tradition, or politics have erected. A moral failing is then our persistence in neglecting the good counsels of magisterial teaching, which are too easily relegated to "merely prudential opinions." Although "the Church does not have technical solutions

50. Cf. Birgit Kleymann, Hedley Malloch, Tom Redman, and Jacques Angot, "The Dynamics of a Variably Coupled Social System: The Case of Les Compagnons du Devoir," *Journal of Management Inquiry* 17 (2009): 381–96.

to offer" (CV, § 9), the truth CST proffers about man and society is as compelling as that about morality. Prudential choices *are* moral choices, because prudence, or practical wisdom, is a virtue necessary to living a moral life.[51]

The Catholic vision of economic organization is then largely incompatible with the model emerging from the tradition of liberalism. Dogmatic commitment to ontological atomism, as it reverberates in individualist social philosophy from Ockham via Locke to Hayek, cannot accommodate the idea of both creation and human associations sharing in intra-Trinitarian relations.[52] CST does not share in the abstract, vacuous notion of freedom as unrestrained choice that is the mark of liberalism. For it, social bonds and intermediary institutions with corresponding levels of responsibility provide a setting within which—but not against which—human action is free. The continuing hybridization of business that ensues from the erosion of the binary divides of the liberal tradition opens up new opportunities and thus enhances a positive freedom to create value in new and creative ways. It is a path toward the *"society of free work, of enterprise and of participation"* that John Paul II advocated: "Such a society is not directed against the market, but demands that the market be appropriately controlled by the forces of society and by the State, so as to guarantee that the basic needs of the whole of society are satisfied" (CA, § 35). The freedom to engage in entrepreneurial activity and to make profits is as necessary for a good society as is human solidarity based on responsibility for one another: "Integral human development presupposes the responsible freedom of the individual and of peoples: no structure can guarantee this development over and above human responsibility" (CV, § 17).

Among the Catholic faithful, the somewhat inane debate over "free markets" will continue, as partisans of both sides will claim Catholicity for their agenda. There is a great gulf between such discussions at the macro-level—about "systems" and "policy"—and developments at the micro-level of businesses, where many of the developments recent papal teaching supported are in full swing. In many countries, divides between sectors, profit status, ownership, or agents of value creation are being bridged, and sometimes—though certainly much too rarely—civil

51. Cf. Aquinas, *Summa Theologica* I-II, q.47, aa.4f, 6f.
52. Cf. Pabst, *Metaphysics*, 442ff.

society indeed influences markets and the state. In some cases, civil society truly harbors and fosters the values of cooperation, reciprocity, and gratuitousness, and in others, less so or no longer. For all cases, however, CST offers a challenge of qualitative growth, as persons in their roles of citizens, market participants, or government representatives live up to their vocation to transcend perceived limitations by "being more" and thus grow into the likeness of a Trinitarian God. This positive freedom to strive for integral human development—or human flourishing—by embracing the whole truth about man, society, and God and by acting on it in freedom and responsibility, is a far cry from the mere shedding of restraints that lies at the heart of the liberal tradition.

NINE

Catholic Social Teaching on the Economy
Pope Benedict XVI's Legacy

Martin Schlag

PROLEGOMENA

In this chapter, by paying special attention to Pope Benedict XVI's legacy to social ethics in the economic sphere and indicating possible future contributions to Christian humanism from his thought, I attempt to demonstrate in what ways Catholic social teaching (CST) can and is making a contribution to contemporary society. Obviously, there is a great legitimate breadth in this field among scholars and movements because of different sociocultural circumstances and personal preferences. However, at least for Catholics, the Magisterium of the Popes constitutes a unifying impulse for reflection. Therefore, I concentrate on papal documents. The possible contributions to be drawn therefrom are divided into three points of general interest that affect CST and three points of special interest that concern the economic field in particular. Such a chapter presupposes a basic understanding of the relationship between the economy and ethics, and it is here that I start.

In the popular literary culture that surrounds the economy and economic affairs, the surprising thing about Michael J. Sandel's book *What Money Can't Buy: The Moral Limits of Markets*, is the importance he attaches to the human meaning of gift. He states, "Economists don't like gifts. Or to be precise, they have a hard time making sense of gift giving as a rational social practice."[1] Against such an attitude, he defends the

---

1. Sandel, *What Money Can't Buy* (N.Y.: Farrar, Straus and Giroux, 2012), 99.

giving of gifts as something ingrained in human character: "Some gifts are expressive of relationships that engage, challenge, and reinterpret our identities."[2] Anybody acquainted with Pope Benedict XVI's social encyclical *Caritas in Veritate* will recognize the similarity between the pope's teaching in that document and Michael J. Sandel's affirmations.[3]

Similarly, in January 2011, Michael E. Porter and Marc. R. Kramer published their article "Creating Shared Value: How to Reinvent Capitalism—and Unleash a Wave of Innovation and Growth."[4] Therein, they advocated a new form of economy. Capitalist in essence but irreducible to the mere creation of wealth, this economy incorporates social benefits and ecological sustainability within the idea of financial profit, thus simultaneously creating economic and social value. CST has been repeating these same ideas for decades.

In May 2011 I participated in the annual conference of the Transformational Business Network, a group of about four hundred firms that put capitalism at the service of development. The belief of these firms is that the economy is not a zero-sum game but that the economic growth of the poor is also to the advantage of the rich.[5]

What these three protagonists have in common is that they repeat key ideas contained in the 2009 encyclical *Caritas in Veritate* but seem to be oblivious to its existence. CST does appear to be one of the better-kept secrets of the Catholic Church.[6] Given its character as a very balanced and mature body of ethical teaching, this is certainly a pity. In reality, it is exactly what is needed in the present crisis. Several nations are in the middle of a crisis that is neither purely economic nor global. It is a financial, economic, political, and social crisis of the Western world, especially of Europe. At its roots, it is a cultural crisis: something has gone wrong with those elements that allow our societies to function well and that have to do with the core of our shared values.

2. Ibid., 102.

3. Its full title is "Encyclical Letter *Caritas in Veritate* of the Supreme Pontiff Benedict XVI to the Bishops, Priests and Deacons, Men and Women, Religious, the Lay Faithful, and All People of Good Will on Integral Human Development in Charity and Truth," June 29, 2009. Available online at http://www.vatican.va/ holy_father/benedict_xvi/encyclicals/ documents/hf_ben-xvi_ enc_20090629_caritas-in-veritate_en.html.

4. Porter and Kramer, "Creating Shared Value."

5. See Brian Griffiths and Kim Tan, *Fighting Poverty through Enterprise: The Case for Social Venture Capital* (Guildford: Transformational Business Network, 2009).

6. Cf. the evocative title of Edward DeBerri, James E. Hug, Peter J. Henriot, and Michael J.

What has gone wrong? On one hand, it would be too easy to blame everything on greed or on a lack of individual virtues. It would also be too easy for Catholic teachers to affirm that the church had always taught the correct solution and that—had it been put into practice—things would have gone better. This is not correct, because the church upholds principles but does not offer technical solutions. There is no such thing as a "Christian economy." In a certain sense, it is even healthy to be "anticlerical" in the economic sphere:[7] priests should talk about theology and philosophy and limit themselves to the ethical aspects of economics. Even only speaking about business ethics, however, presupposes a basic understanding of how the world and the economy function. In any case, the laity is called to be the principal agent in discovering the specific ways and means of shaping the secular sphere in a morally sound way, compatible with Christian faith.

On the other hand, however, it would also be too easy to think that the crisis of the West was just a technical mistake and that once we had the system fixed, we could return to "business as usual." The time is ripe for a paradigm shift in the economy. The economic crisis is not a mechanical flaw in an otherwise perfect machine. On the contrary, the cause of the crisis has to do with this understanding of the economy as a machine, as a mechanical system, which functions according to technical laws and has nothing to do with ethics.

The consequences of such an erroneous conception are manifold. They become manifest in deceitful financial products, in a lack of personal entrepreneurship, in growing public debt, in a gross expansion of government, and in the general idea that people who let themselves be cheated deserve to be cheated. John XXIII's description of injustice in the economic system remains true: "Justice is to be observed not only in the distribution of wealth, but also in regard to the conditions in which men are engaged in producing this wealth. Every man has, of his very nature, a need to express himself in his work and thereby to perfect his own being. Consequently, if the whole structure and organization of an economic system is such as to compromise human dignity, to lessen a

---

Schultheis, eds., *Catholic Social Teaching: Our Best Kept Secret* (Maryknoll, N.Y.: Orbis Books and the Center of Concern, 2003).

7. The meaning to which I allude is the one used by St. Josemaría Escrivá, cf. *Conversations with Monsignor Escrivá de Balaguer* (Dublin: Ecclesia Press, 1972 [1968]), n. 47.

man's sense of responsibility or rob him of opportunity for exercising personal initiative, then such a system, We maintain, is altogether unjust—no matter how much wealth it produces, or how justly and equitably such wealth is distributed."[8]

Democratic capitalism or the social market economy (or however one calls the market economies in which we live) is a tripartite system, or a society composed of three subsystems. The reality goes beyond the classical definition of capitalism as an economic system based on private property, the free market, and the accumulation of wealth.

These three subsystems are

1. the political system, consisting in a democratic republic based on the consent of the people, the separation of powers, and the rule of law;

2. the economic system, an inventive economy based on personal initiative, private property, and open and free markets; and

3. the cultural-moral system, primarily a culture of self-government, based on virtues essential for free people, such as self-discipline, respect for others, courage, and other fundamental values or virtues.

Each of these systems consists of both a set of values and of certain institutions that protect them. Although the different spheres are each institutionally independent and relatively autonomous, and yet interrelated, the cultural–moral system is meant to pervade and to animate the other two, to be kind of the "soul" of the society. The problem is that the moral–cultural system is the weakest link, because the success of capitalism can destroy its foundations. Consumerism and practical materialism tend to destroy the foundation of virtues that make capitalism work.[9] As Michael J. Sandel has formulated, "Markets crowd out morals."[10]

What solutions can be found? First, with regard to institutions, it is vital for the social market economy that the three systems remain institutionally independent but check and balance one another's power. Religious leaders should not have direct political power, political leaders should not meddle in religious affairs, and individuals and businesspeople should have enough economic independence and power to pursue their self-interest without state interference. However, businesspeople

---

8. John XXIII, *Mater et Magistra*, 82–83.
9. Cf. Novak, *The Spirit of Democratic Capitalism*.
10. Sandel, *What Money Can't Buy*, 93–130.

should also pursue the common good; in a similar vein, political leaders are obliged to foster religious freedom and religious leaders to regenerate public morality.

This leads us, second, to values. Skills and knowledge are not enough for good business. A simple example illustrates this fact. A car manufacturer produces one million cars per year. Despite strict quality controls, there are fifty casualties every year. The indemnity the car manufacturer has to pay amounts to $200,000 per casualty. The economic consequence is that the manufacturer must add $10 to the cost of each car. This economic approach is perfectly valid and does not mean that the car producer values human life at $10. He could, however, be tempted to scrap the very expensive quality control, save the money, and just pay more indemnity for more casualties. However, this would be unethical because human life has no price but dignity.[11]

Thus—as speculative sciences—politics and economics overlap with ethics. However, there are two different consequences of including ethics in the economic sphere that must be distinguished. The first refers to economics as a science, the second to the economy as economic activity or practical agency. With regard to the science of economics, ethics modifies the underlying epistemology insofar as ethics excludes certain actions as destructive of human happiness. If economics "studies human behavior as a relationship between ends and scarce means which have alternative uses,"[12] this does not mean that all ends are interchangeable or indifferent, or that any efficient means may be used. Economics as a science would become inhuman or make no positive sense if all aims were equally valid. Of the virtually infinite number of possible alternatives of action, those that infringe on human dignity are destructive. Economics, as a science, does not study such actions as its object. Marketing for narcotics, for instance, is not and should not be taught at business schools, not only on the grounds that these kinds of drugs are unethical but also because it would not be economic in the full sense of the word to traffic drugs. Narcotics do not serve the happiness of the human person, and even though the narcotic trade is financially profitable, such trade is not

11. A similar case, taken from an actual business, is described by Andrew Crane and Dirk Matten, *Business Ethics: Managing Corporate Citizenship and Sustainability in the Age of Globalization* (Oxford: Oxford University Press, 2010), 143–44.

12. Lionel Robbins, *An Essay on the Nature and Significance of Economic Science* (London: Macmillan, 1935), 16.

business. The same would be true for politics: a despotic tyrant who treads on human rights is not "doing politics" but is committing crimes.

When practical agency in the field of economic activity is considered, ethics supplies the overarching values that influence each and every political and economic action. Ethics are the rules of human action insofar as an act is human, and every free human action is subject to ethical evaluation. The question is, of course, "which" or "whose" overarching ethics should be recognized. Here I propose that Christian humanism, embodied in CST, can make an important contribution to real human flourishing, precisely *because* it transcends the merely immanent goals of the good life. The key idea for human flourishing is found in the distinction between pleasure and happiness. Only when this distinction is made can there really be ethics. It is here that we can truly begin to appreciate Pope Benedict's legacy and his contribution to CST and possible future contributions to Christian humanism that can be drawn therefrom.

Pope Benedict XVI's social encyclical *Caritas in Veritate*, the primary text published on our subject, was received far less enthusiastically than his first encyclical, *Deus Caritas Est*. Some Catholics, especially in the United States and among businesspeople, have had great difficulties comprehending its contents or accepting some of the solutions given to certain questions, such as creating a true world political authority and stronger international organizations, the spirit of gift and gratuitousness, large-scale redistribution of wealth, and the importance given to the environment and to immigration. Yes, it is true: *Caritas in Veritate* is very long, and it probably deals with too many topics. However, it deserves lasting attention, because over time it can help reflect on the economy and economics in a way that many agents in the field and in business education consider both necessary and urgent.[13]

The pope's reflection on the economy and economics is focused on the concept of "integral human development in charity and truth." This is the title of the encyclical. It is a consequence of the church's conviction that the human person is the center, the measure, and the aim of all societal organization and that human dignity is its fundamental principle. Integral human development is not identical with economic

---

13. See, for example, Ursula Nothelle-Wildfeuer, "*Caritas in Veritate*: Globalisierung, Wirtschaft und Entwicklung," in *Der Theologenpapst: Eine kritische Würdigung Benedikts XVI*, ed. Jan-Heiner Tück (Freiburg/Basel/Wien: Herder, 2013), 83–96.

growth, although economic growth is an important element of development. In the wake of the great optimism unleashed by the victory of the American political model after World War II, faith in the possibility of unlimited progress and growth prevailed. The sobering report of the Club of Rome in the 1970s, as well as the oil shock, altered this tendency. Progress and growth were no longer seen as unlimited but, rather to the contrary, were even treated as potentially dangerous if separated from other criteria. In this line of thought, Amartya Sen combined economic growth with health and education to reach a richer definition of development; such a definition was both requested and accepted by the United Nations for their Human Development Index. Pope Benedict XVI manifestly uses a parallel concept. He combines economic growth (the topic of Paul VI's encyclical *Populorum Progressio*) with openness to life and families (the theme of Paul VI's encyclical *Humanae Vitae*) and education in the Christian faith (the subject of Paul VI's encyclical *Evangelii Nuntiandi*). Thus, he also unites three different aspects of the teaching of Paul VI, which are often separated, aspects that reaffirm the dignity and the importance of the human person. Pope Benedict XVI's primary contributions to contemporary society with regard to CST, and his focus on the human person, can be divided into three points of general interest that affect CST and three points of special interest that concern the economic field in particular.

GENERAL POINTS OF INTEREST

"The Church's social doctrine came into being in order to claim 'citizenship status' for the Christian religion."[14]

The first general point of interest refers to the epistemological status of CST. John Paul II underscored the fact that the social teaching of the church was not a "third way" between capitalism and communism, an immediately applicable economic or political program, but rather theology, and to be precise, moral theology.[15] John Paul II thus stressed pluralism and freedom of political thought among the Catholic laity in the West and supported freedom of religion in the East, exonerating Catholics from the accusation of dependence on the church, and thus in the

---

14. Benedict XVI, *Caritas in Veritate*, 56.
15. Cf. John Paul II, *Sollicitudo rei socialis*, 42.

eyes of their communist oppressors, on foreign powers in their political and social decisions.

In an altered social environment, Pope Benedict XVI did not stress the theological character of the social teaching of the church but alternatively underscored the traditional conception of *duplex ordo cognitionis* (double order of cognizance). Faith and reason, in particular, the natural law, are the sources of the church's social documents. We are confronted not only with a growing marginalization of religion, especially of the Christian faith in the public sphere, but also with a marginalization of reason in its character as natural law. In the optimism of the 1960s and the wave of renewal desired by Pope John XXIII and the council fathers, it was not foreseeable that the ethical conformity of society by and large, together with the natural law teaching of the Catholic Church, would so soon disintegrate. John XXIII's encyclical *Pacem in Terris* and important documents of the council had placed great emphasis upon the concept of the "rule of law," meaning the limitation of legislative power by metajuridical norms of natural justice. Civil law is aimed at protecting human life, other human rights, and natural institutions like heterosexual marriage and large families. We are now in a situation in which the rights language and the idea of the rule of law have been reinterpreted and are being used to promote ethical relativism and ways of life diametrically opposed to Christian notions of justice in society.[16]

In response, Pope Benedict XVI has stated that the church does not aspire to any form of power over states or societies, either direct or indirect, but wishes instead to offer its message as an *officium intermedium*:[17] a service to widen the concept of reason and to enable it to recognize and put into practice what is just with greater ease. This is very much in line with the social teaching of the church as it emerged from Leo XIII's encyclical *Rerum Novarum*. The relationship between faith and society was formerly viewed as a relationship between the church and the state, which was to be solved in a manner similar to the relationship between two sovereigns who, in friendship, sign a treaty or, as it is more prop-

16. See Russell Hittinger, "Introduction to Modern Catholicism," in *The Teachings of Modern Roman Catholicism on Law, Politics, and Human Nature*, ed. John Witte Jr. and Frank S. Alexander (New York: Columbia University Press, 2007), 1–38.

17. Benedict XVI, *Deus Caritas Est*, 28f.

erly called in this context, a concordat. With this concordat, the state allowed the church, as an institution, to enter into its territory with its hierarchy and its religious orders, who set up schools, hospitals, universities, orphanages, and so on. This is no longer the model of modern liberal societies. Today, members of the Christian laity are called on to use their own freedom to give testimony to Christ, spreading the Gospel in the sphere of freedom opened up by human rights, putting into practice the program of the Second Vatican Council's Pastoral Constitution *Gaudium et Spes*: the church in the modern world. Through "voluntary disestablishment," the church has positioned itself in civil society, without, however accepting "privatization."[18] This position does not reduce the church to a mere association or society among others, subject to civil government, as a misinterpretation of the slogan "a free Church in a free society" might render. The church must maintain independence and a critical distance from civil power to fulfill its prophetic mission of critiquing injustice. Therefore, in a certain sense, the church is above the state, insofar as it is called to teach the moral limits of all earthly power. On the other hand, it does not possess any political power, and it does not aspire to any. Its authority is purely moral and is directed toward enabling and empowering men and women of good will to discover what is right and just in the historical circumstances in which they live. This is the meaning of the pope's assertation that "[t]he Church's social doctrine came into being in order to claim 'citizenship status' for the Christian religion."[19] The task of the lay Catholic faithful, together with people of other denominations and of other faiths, is to put these teachings into practice, not as an extension of the hierarchy but in their own name and conscience. Politicians, entrepreneurs, and other operators in society must therefore, in general, not expect directives from the Magisterium but must discover them in their own conscience, guided by the principles of natural law as taught by the church. Another aspect of the future development of the social teaching of the church will certainly be the growing importance attributed to lay Christians working in society and, more particularly, in the economic and political spheres. Hand in hand with such an emphasis, it is to be expected and hoped that

18. Cf. José Casanova, *Public Religions in the Modern World* (Chicago: University of Chicago Press, 1994), 62–63.

19. Benedict XVI, *Caritas in Veritate*, 56.

the Magisterium will increasingly limit itself to giving principles and refrain from entering into details, as expressed by Pope Benedict XVI in his declaration that the church does not offer "technical solutions."[20]

"The social question has become a radically anthropological question"[21]

The very title of the encyclical expresses the pope's concern with placing the human person at the center of all economic transactions. This is the second general point of interest I would like to underscore. Benedict XVI understood the market not as a mere exchange of goods, and even less as a mechanical system, but as an encounter between persons.[22] He condensed this conviction into a significant sentence: "The social question has become a radically anthropological question."[23] The "social question" was the question of the blatantly unjust treatment of workers that gave rise to Leo XIII's encyclical *Rerum Novarum* in 1891. It is the essence of the church's social teaching. By redefining the social question, Pope Benedict XVI has actually refocused CST, directing its attention to the preeminence of the human person and therefore to the prominence of ethics over technology. Although the centrality of the human person receives renewed attention, the object of concern is no longer that of workers' rights (even though this certainly remains an important concern in many parts of the world) but, rather, the human person's right to truth and love, in need of defense before an all-embracing wave of technology. This wave, considered ethically neutral and scientifically objective, instead often facilitates the creation of a culture of death. One of the future elements in the CST will thus presumably be an insistence on a holistic, ethical approach to the social sciences.

"This is the institutional path—we might also call it the political path—of charity"[24]

The third general point of reflection that Pope Benedict XVI has left to CST is the importance he attributed to "institutional ethics." Individual ethics is the branch of ethics that reflects on the human actions of individuals, whose aim is personal happiness in heaven. In contrast, social

---

20. Ibid., 9.   21. Ibid., 75.
22. Ibid., 35.   23. Ibid., 75.
24. Ibid., 7.

ethics reflects on the community as such and the rules by which the social life as a whole is directed toward the earthly common good (peace,
liberty, and justice). The agent of social ethics, rather than an individual
person, is collective: it is the community. Within the field of social ethics is institutional ethics, which focuses on the role of institutions. Unfortunately, in the Catholic tradition, there has been a certain blindness
for the importance of the institutions of the liberal state and the liberal
economy. The reason for this, in my opinion, has to do, among other
reasons, with the neoscholastic revival of the natural law. This revival
strove to base its social teachings on the metahistorical foundation of
human nature rather than on the romantic backlash against rationalism,
which reaction had led to a social nostalgia of the Middle Ages (with
rather bizarre ideas for a modern industrial society: no wages, only one
large industrial corporation with owners and workers equally entitled
to participation, etc.). Opposed to romanticism, neoscholasticism attempted to deduce eternal ethical laws from human nature.[25] Now, this
can be quite successfully done as far as individual ethics is concerned
because human nature is astoundingly uniform. When applied to society, however, this method quickly becomes ideological: it deduces
what it has previously introduced. The result was that some Catholic
authors criticized the division of power and the idea of popular sover-
eignty as contrary to the "essence of the State," which they conceived
in an organic sense, analogous to the "mystical body of the Church."
They contested that the State was also a body, composed of different
organs.[26] Hence, before Pius XII, the utmost the Catholic Magisterium
could concede toward political liberalism was "neutrality." The bitter
experiences under Hitler and other forms of totalitarian government (as
well as other factors) radically altered this stance. The church was able
to reconcile herself with a renewed and a more mature form of political liberalism that was no longer hostile to the Christian faith.[27] It took
much longer for it to accept economic liberalism, and in fact, the func-

25. See Ratzinger, "Naturrecht, Evangelium und Ideologie in der katholischen Soziallehre,"
24–30; Arno Anzenbacher, *Christliche Sozialethik* (Paderborn: Schöningh, 1997), 126–49; Uertz, *Vom
Gottesrecht zum Menschenrecht*, 193–218.
26. Cf. Uertz, *Vom Gottesrecht zum Menschenrecht*, 155–61.
27. Cf. Benedict XVI, *Address of His Holiness Benedict XVI to the Roman Curia Offering them His
Christmas Greetings*, December 22, 2005; available online at http://w2.vatican.va/content/benedict
-xvi/en/speeches/2005/december/documents/hf_ben_xvi_spe_20051222_roman-curia.html.

tioning of liberal economic institutions was, and in part still is, seen in a
rather negative light.[28] John Paul II strove to overcome this attitude by
accepting the logic of the modern liberal economy and distinguishing
between different kinds of capitalism in his encyclical *Centesimus Annus*.[29] While *Caritas in Veritate* fully accepts and presupposes *Centesimus
Annus*, it calls for a more profound reflection on its ethical and cultural
presuppositions and conditions. Such a reflection constitutes an important exercise in the development of CST: for their well-functioning institutions require preconditions they cannot themselves create. Institutions are social enactments of values that are exercised and built jointly.
They cannot exist for a long time without the values they are meant to
institutionalize.

Benedict XVI applied these thoughts to economic activity and economic institutions. We can list three special points of interest in his
Magisterium on economic ethics that I have structured following the
three stepped focus underlying *Gaudium et spes*: seeing (understanding)
—judging—acting.

SPECIAL POINTS OF INTEREST

Reconnecting with the Catholic Current of "Civil Economy" and Overcoming Negative Attitudes toward Commerce, Wealth, and Finance in the Catholic Tradition

For centuries, there has existed what one might call a "Catholic antagonism" toward economics, finance, and money, the fundamental factors
of the modern economic system. I have analyzed this in some detail
elsewhere.[30] I think that Pope Benedict XVI's writings can help to overcome this lingering antagonism.

As has already been said, at the Second Vatican Council, particularly in its documents *Gaudium et Spes* (*On the Church in the Contemporary
World*) and *Dignitatis Humanae* (*On Religious Liberty*), the church positioned itself within civil society. It also further developed its method
of engagement with the secular society. From an exclusive attitude of

28. Cf. Reinhard Marx, *Das Kapital: Ein Plädoyer für den Menschen* (München: Pattloch, 2008), 82.
29. Cf. John Paul II, *Centesimus Annus*, 42.
30. Cf. Martin Schlag, "The Encyclical *Caritas in Veritate*, Christian Tradition and the Modern
World," in *Free Markets and the Culture of Common Good*, ed. Martin Schlag and Juan Andrés Mercado (Berlin: Springer, 2012), 93–109.

magisterial superiority in its role as teacher, the church has moved to an attitude of dialogue. The church certainly teaches, because it has been endowed with the Christian revelation under the guidance and protection of the Holy Spirit, but it can also learn from society and from the world about life, rationality, and the mechanisms and laws governing earthly affairs, which it wishes to understand and vivify from within by means of the Gospel's leaven. When it participates in public discourse on these topics, it does so in an open, public, and rational way; its authority with regard to Catholics is rooted in the faith while its authority with regard to non-Catholics is rooted in its wisdom. The church's social teaching is an applied form of hermeneutics. It strives to understand and to give meaning to facts by widening the modern scientific notion of reason that has been rejected by postmodernism, the attempt to decompose all universal systems of meaning. However, the question of the significance of facts in the dimension of the transcendentals, the true, the good, and the beautiful, cannot be avoided. Human beings, by necessity of their rational nature, aspire to grasp the implications of these notions, even and especially, amid their earthly, quotidian affairs. They yearn for meaning. The social teaching of the Catholic Church can contribute immensely to this pilgrimage of discovery. Therefore, pastors and theologians, first and foremost, need an attitude of love and empathy toward the different secular spheres and the culture by which they have been shaped. Evangelization always begins with love and friendship. A person who does not love his or her own culture is incapable of understanding, and, even less so, of evangelizing, it.

However, we also have to make the discovery of sin that mars and spoils the beauty of human activity in secular work. Spreading the Gospel in the secular sphere also means cleansing it of sin. This is not an alienation of temporal affairs, as if something unfitting and alien were forced onto it from outside. Nature, culture, and grace are intrinsically connected, not opposed. The autonomy of earthly spheres is a relative autonomy, relative because they are conditioned by God's law, which is the condition of its flourishing. Redemption, grace, and reintegration presuppose, heal, and ennoble secular activity. We reaffirm the secular sphere in its secularity by overcoming sin and sinful structures.

In the economic field, the time has come for Catholics to speak out with self-confidence, to proclaim that capitalism, first and foremost, has

Catholic roots.[31] They must be capable of demonstrating that the version of the market economy Catholicism developed was superior to its Calvinist version, because it was based on the church fathers' notion of the unity of nature and grace, instead of the Reformers' dichotomy between the sinful world and Christ's almighty predestinating grace.[32] The modern market economy originated where the "paleo-capitalistic" tendency was strongest: at its beginning, during the thirteenth-century Commercial Revolution in Northern Italian and Flemish towns; then in the fourteenth- and fifteenth-century city-states of the early Renaissance; and, later, during the Enlightenment, in the chairs of the universities of Naples and Milan. All of these places were Catholic. And the Catholic thinkers and authors on the economy of the time were able to combine a deep unity between the technical aspects of business with its ethical and religious dimension. Benedetto Cotrugli (1416–1469), for instance, in his famous book on commerce from 1458[33] dealt with the businessman's obligation to save time and money, to keep meticulous business records, and so on and, at the same time, to pray and go to daily mass. The Catholic cultural movement connected to this premodern form of capitalism has come to be known as the "civil economy."[34] From this school of thought stem the concepts in the Pope Benedict XVI's social encyclical, concepts we might find surprising in the context of economic theory: gratuitousness, the logic of gift, fraternity, public happiness, reciprocity, and relationality. Before dealing with these concepts, however, I would like to point out the underlying epistemological conception Pope Benedict XVI proposed.

Overcoming the Methodological Fragmentation in Modern Economics

In *Caritas in Veritate*, Pope Benedict XVI spoke of "the excessive segmentation of knowledge"[35] in fields that have reached a high degree of

31. For a Catholic defense of the free market, see Thomas E. Woods Jr., *The Church and the Market: A Catholic Defense of the Free Economy* (Lanham, Md.: Lexington Books, 2005).

32. For the unintended social and economic consequences of the Reformation, cf. Brad S. Gregory, *The Unintended Reformation: How a Religious Revolution Secularized Society* (Cambridge, Mass.: Harvard University Press, 2012).

33. Benedetto Cotrugli, *Il libro dell'arte di mercatura* (Venice: Arsenale Editrice, 1990). The book was originally written in 1458; the first print edition was in 1573.

34. See Luigino Bruni and Stefano Zamagni, eds., *Dizionario di economia civile* (Roma: Città Nuova, 2009); Oreste Bazzichi, *Dall'usura al giusto profitto: L'etica economica della Scuola francescana* (Torino: Effatà Editrice, 2008).

35. Benedict XVI, *Caritas in Veritate*, 31.

specialization. A good and necessary development inherent in the process of differentiation that constitutes modernity, such segmentation
can also result in loss of the human meaning of the object studied, if the
method of each individual science or sphere is absolutized. Confronted
with this situation, the pope called for "a further and deeper reflection
on the meaning of the economy and its goals."[36]

Michael Novak has correctly characterized Adam Smith as a "philosopher of practice."[37] It is typical of the Anglo-Saxon liberal tradition
in which we live and work that its main founders (e.g., Locke, Smith,
Hume) do not insist on ultimate foundations and metaphysics but limit
themselves to discovering pragmatically functioning systems. In this
sense, with the aim of helping the poor, Adam Smith wished to overcome mercantilism and state-regulated, controlled trade, including monopolies, by lowering prices through competition. A highly simplified
but brief summary can hardly do justice to the many-sided, plurisecu-
lar, and plurisemantic phenomenon of mercantilism or the position of
Adam Smith. However, the main thrust of his ideas, as I understand it,
is thus. In mercantilism, the subject of economic activity was the state
(the king or the nation), which, by means of the "visible hand," steered
all economic activity. In the liberal, or classical, conception of Adam
Smith, the subjects of the economy are the individuals who use the factors of production (land, labor, and capital) guided by their own self-
interest. An invisible hand makes them and their individual activities
converge in the common good. In his formulation, Smith was influenced by the Newtonian conception of natural sciences; applying this
framework to the social sciences, he elaborated an idea of the market
as a mechanism which we can describe scientifically. Hence the origin
of what we can call the "grand lacuna" between economics before and
after Adam Smith. Until Adam Smith, economics was a part of ethics.
The questions scholastic authors posed were, How can I be just? How
can I avoid sin? and How can I reach heaven working in commerce and
trade? They had a prescriptive approach and stated what ought to be
done. In doing so, they obviously also had to state what is, and thus,
they discovered a series of actual economic laws. Adam Smith also considered economics to be a part of moral philosophy. He certainly did not

36. Ibid., 32.
37. Novak, *The Spirit of Democratic Capitalism*, 19.

intend to separate economics from moral philosophy—quite to the contrary. However, perhaps as a consequence of the reduced normativity of Adam Smith's moral system, as a matter of fact, economics after Adam Smith became descriptive instead of prescriptive. Adam Smith's moral philosophy was more a moral psychology or sociology of the feeling of propriety and rule-following than a normative system. Smith tried to explain the kind of human behavior called moral. His concern was to discern how people made moral assessments of their own behavior and of that of other people, and he was not proposing his analyses as criteria for moral rightness but as a "feature of how people judge moral rightness."[38] In the sway of this method, the economy was increasingly described as a "mechanism," functioning by the principle of self-interest, in a manner analogous to the planetary system, which functions according to the law of gravitation. The modern science of economics states what is, not what ought to be.[39] In such a system, one is a long way from Plato, who wrote that he would be tempted to apply the death penalty to anyone who said, "[B]usiness is business, and therefore, business has nothing to do with justice."[40]

There is an obvious flaw in confusing the epistemology of social and natural science: social laws are not the same thing as natural laws. Knowing a natural law does not change it whereas the knowledge of social laws modifies our behavior. We adapt to the social law we have discovered, thereby changing the social regularity of conduct and thus the law itself. Hence, the philosophical difficulty primarily indicated by Pope Benedict XVI with regard to modern economics is that it is the result of a methodological reduction. It is a model in which not all of the elements of reality can be duly considered. Modern economics eliminates the moral perspective, which considers our actions not only as means to achieve a goal but also as conducive to happiness. It is no coincidence that in neoclassical political economy, the term *public happiness* (refers to a moral aim), used in the civil economy, has been substituted by *utility* (refers to means and can be understood in a technical sense). Economic activity, however, is free human activity, that is, actions judged by our

38. Knud Haakonssen, "Introduction: The Coherence of Smith's Thought," in *The Cambridge Companion to Adam Smith*, ed. Knud Haakonssen (Cambridge: Cambridge University Press, 2006), 15.

39. Odd Langholm, "The Legacy of Scholasticism," in *Economic Thought: Antecedents of Choice and Power* (Cambridge: Cambridge University Press, 1998), 158–63.

40. Nomoi II, 662 B-C.

conscience and guided by our convictions and virtues or vices. In such an activity, moral principles are not bothersome limitations opposed to economic benefits. Ethics and benefits are connected: what is ethically bad is also an error in economic terms and vice versa; what is an error regarding the economy is also such from the ethical point of view because it would constitute mistaken human behavior. What does not lead to honest profit is either an error or a sin because it is a waste of resources. As Benedict XVI wrote, "The conviction that the economy must be autonomous, that it must be shielded from 'influences' of a moral character, has led man to abuse the economic process in a thoroughly destructive way. In the long term, these convictions have led to economic, social and political systems that trample upon personal and social freedom, and are therefore unable to deliver the justice that they promise."[41] This is not a condemnation of the modern distinction of sciences and their autonomy but is a call for a more holistic approach. Scientific models are necessarily reductive; they leave out certain elements of reality. From hence stems the danger of absolutizing a scientific method, as well as the need for scientific humility. Science must remain within the limits of its own epistemological presuppositions. Religion, on the other hand, must respect the validity of scientific analysis. Its contribution to knowledge and wisdom is the relationship with God and the reference to an ultimate goal, and thus the meaning of all created reality. The influence of faith therefore, as already has been stated, tends to be holistic, widening the concept of reason to include all dimensions of life, particularly the necessary field of meaning, circumscribed by the transcendentals.

Facing the Challenge of Introducing Fraternity (Charity, Solidarity) in Macro-relationships

Charity is at the heart of the Church's social doctrine.... it is the principle not only of micro-relationships (with friends, with family members or within small groups) but also of macro-relationships (social, economic and political ones).[42]

Because love is the central Christian commandment and the distinguishing element of Christian faith, this challenge is at the core of CST. Let

41. Benedict XVI, *Caritas in Veritate*, 34.
42. Ibid., 2.

us ask ourselves, "What does it mean to sanctify work in the economic sphere?" "What does it mean to Christianize, to evangelize the economy?" "What is the result we hope for once we have finished the new evangelization of the economy?" and "What is the aim of our apostolate in the economic sphere?"

The answer seems to begin with the recognition that there is no such thing as a "Christian economy," because the Christian faith is not directly and immediately applicable as a social, economic, or political program. However, indirectly and consequently, it does make a difference to be a Christian in all dimensions of life, and thus in the economic dimension. The difference consists in conduct that is honest and impeccable, or just, simultaneous with the awareness that justice is not enough. There must be a way to include fraternity[43] in the public sphere from where it has been ousted, not only theoretically by Max Weber, but practically by a criterion of exclusion. This exclusion becomes apparent in the terminological shift from *civil economy* to *political economy*, which took place in the eighteenth century. The word *civil* derives from the Latin *civilis*, the Roman *civitas*, which consisted of all living persons, including women and slaves. The Greek *polis* in contrast, from whence stems our word *political*, was formed by free men only; women and slaves were excluded from the concept. The terminological shift in economics implies an element of exclusion. The criterion of exclusion in the modern economy is efficiency. If you are efficient, you can participate in the economy, and thus you belong to the private sector. If you are inefficient, you are a social case and are hence entrusted to the State for public care. There is something true and necessary in this division, but the extreme attitude of leaving everything social to the State and the public sphere is not good. "Solidarity is first and foremost a sense of responsibility on the part of everyone with regard to everyone, and it cannot therefore be merely delegated to the State."[44] Pope Benedict XVI opposed both the idea that politics is a machine of redistribution of wealth and the idea that economic activity is aimed only at the creation of wealth, which can then be redistributed for charity. "The exclusively binary model of market-plus-state is corrosive of society, while economic forms based on solidarity, which find their natural home in civil society without being restricted to it, build

43. In this context, I use fraternity, charity, and solidarity as synonyms.
44. Benedict XVI, *Caritas in Veritate*, 38.

up society."[45] What the pope is alluding to in this context is the "third sector": private initiatives for socially beneficial aims should possess a specific public standing that does not equate them to profit-oriented private enterprises but grants them legal and fiscal protection. However, his appeal is not only aimed at this form of social entrepreneurship, a very small percentage of all economic activity, but is meant as a challenge to the entire business world: "The great challenge before us ... is to demonstrate ... that in *commercial relationships* the *principle of gratuitousness* and the logic of gift as an expression of fraternity can and must find their place within normal economic activity."[46]

CONCLUSION

In many aspects, Pope Benedict XVI's teaching on the economy is innovative and thought provoking. Such a provocation must be well understood. In this chapter, I have tried to make a contribution toward a better comprehension by showing the general framework and some details of his teaching. Pope Benedict XVI did not advocate a return to the gift economy, typical of primitive societies, or other premodern or collectivist models. He did not ask businesspeople to give up capitalism, to make presents of their goods, or to give services away for free. What he has attempted to capture in words is that the economy is not only a mechanical system of exchange of goods but, first and foremost, is a relationship between persons whose needs and wants create value and have to be adequately addressed. Gift means giving a human sense to economic relations; gratuitousness means discovering "relational goods" and realizing that the human person is priceless. It is the same idea expressed by Gregory of Nyssa and long after him by Kant: the human person has no price but dignity. This is at the heart and the core of Christian humanism, an ideal dear to Pope Benedict XVI: the Christian faith makes human life happy on earth, not only in heaven.

45. Ibid., 39.
46. Ibid., 36.

PART III

Offering Practical Models
and Education

TEN

Economic Efficiency and Solidarity

The Idea of a Social Market Economy

Jörg Althammer

The market mechanism is generally recognized as the most efficient way of economic organization. After decades of controversy, both academic and public, the productive efficiency of the market system is no longer under dispute. However, the predominant view still holds that free trade is in stark contrast to the principles of justice and solidarity. The insinuated incompatibility of a competitive market with higher-ranking societal goals has been approved by critics of the market system and its proponents alike. To the critics, a competitive economic environment leads to a fragmentation of society that imperils social cohesion. The pursuit of personal interests unswayed by a superior moral order is held to be incapable to comply with social norms, as individual actions are no longer channeled toward a common goal. Although the efficiency of a competitive economic environment is generally recognized, the market is nevertheless held incapable of achieving collective goals such as justice and solidarity. As the German theologian and influential social philosopher Oswald von Nell-Breuning once put it, in capitalist societies workers are "means to achieve certain goals, not human beings, and are thus recognized and treated as objects."[1] Thus, the free market has to be curtailed by political rules to sustain basic ethical norms.

Critics of the market system are not the only ones to see competi-

---

1. Oswald von Nell-Breuning, *Kapitalismus—kritisch betrachtet: Zur Auseinandersetzung um das bessere "System"* (Freiburg: Herder, 1974), 178.

tion as incompatible with societal goals. Nobel prize–winning economist and social philosopher Friedrich August von Hayek stresses that
norms such as solidarity and altruism are concepts that evolved in small
groups (the "microcosmos"), whose members "share particular habits,
knowledge and beliefs about possibilities."[2] These values are no longer
applicable in large, anonymous groups (the "macrocosmos") that constitute modern market economies. He named the attribute "social" a
"weasel word," one of the expressions that "deprive of content any term
to which they are prefixed while seemingly leaving them untouched."[3]
To him, in an open society where the income distribution is driven by
anonymous market forces and not the outcome of purposeful individual
action, the ideas of solidarity and social justice are analytically meaning-
less and destructive for the economy.

Philosophers arguing from a social contract theory hold a still different point of view. They understand specific arrangements of the welfare
state as an institution that evolved to preserve the market as the social organization of economic affairs. Solidarity and social justice are therefore
essential requirements for the approval of society to the market economy.

Quite obviously, these authors have different and presumably contradictory concepts of solidarity in mind. This lack of analytical precision makes it difficult if not futile to analyze the interrelationship between free trade and solidarity and the market economy. As long as the
precise meaning of solidarity is not clarified, any attempt to apply this
concept to the analysis of social interaction and organization is to no
avail. In this chapter, I try to shed more light on the principle of solidarity and its relation to the market economy. After developing an analytical concept that comprises different manifestations of the principle of
solidarity in divergent social contexts, I outline the concept of a social
market economy as the organization of solidarity under a competitive
economic environment.

A CONTEXTUAL THEORY OF THE
SOLIDARITY PRINCIPLE

A detailed analysis of the relationship between the market economy
and solidarity requires an analytical clarification of the concepts under

2. Friedrich August von Hayek, *The Fatal Conceit: The Errors of Socialism* (London: Routledge, 1988), 19.
3. Ibid., 114.

consideration.[4] From an etymological point of view, the principle of
solidarity stems from Roman law (*obligatio in solidum*) and constitutes the
legal concept of joint liability. However, as Nothelle-Wildfeuer points
out, the idea of solidarity can be traced further back to the Aristotelian
notion of cohesion and stability of the Greek *polis*, based on the virtue
of friendship between free and equal men.[5] In social science, solidarity
stands for "the mutual coordination of units and their integration into
some larger whole."[6] Solidarity is often interpreted as a certain feeling
of togetherness, the willingness to stand by each other in times of need.
In this understanding, solidarity corresponds to the French Revolution's
concept of *fraternité*. The German sociologist Alfred Vierkandt defines
solidarity as a society's "attitude of strong inner relatedness; all support
society, and society supports all."[7]

Although intuitively perspicuous, the definitions of solidarity mentioned earlier are insufficient insofar as they circumscribe a certain social
attitude that can be interpreted either as a positive description of social
behavior (*solidarité de fait*) or as a normative plea to individual's attitudes
in society (*solidarité devoir*). Furthermore, they lack a theoretical underpinning that allows us to understand the motives and the social forces
that ultimately lead to social inclusion via the principle of solidarity.

Mechanical versus Organic Solidarity

The French sociologist Émile Durkheim offers a framework that allows
us to analyze the motives of solidaristic behavior and the interrelations
between the market economy and solidarity in more detail. According
to Durkheim, the conscience of an individual is dual in nature.[8] One element is "personal and distinct," whereas the other element "is common
to our group in its entirety." In his famous volume *On the Division of La-*

4. On the origins and implications of the solidarity principle, see Hauke Brunkhorst, *Solidarity* (Cambridge, Mass.: MIT Press, 2005); Ursula Nothelle-Wildfeuer, "Die Sozialprinzipien der
Katholischen Soziallehre," in *Handbuch der Katholischen Soziallehre*, ed. Anton Rauscher, Jörg Althammer, Wolfgang Bergsdorf and Otto Depenheuer (Berlin: Duncker and Humblot, 2008), 143–
63; Kurt Bayertz, "Begriff und Problem der Solidarität," in *Solidarität: Begriff und Problem*, ed. Kurt
Bayertz (Frankfurt am Main: Suhrkamp, 1998), 11–53.

5. Nothelle-Wildfeuer, "Die Sozialprinzipien der Katholischen Soziallehre," 150.

6. Whitney Pope and Barclay D. Johnson, "Inside Organic Solidarity," *American Sociological
Review* 48 (1983): 681–92.

7. Alfred Vierkandt, *Gesellschaftslehre: Hauptprobleme der philosophischen Soziologie*, 2nd ed. (Stuttgart: Enke, 1928), 184.

8. Pope and Johnson, "Inside Organic Solidarity," 681.

bor, Durkheim differentiates two modes of social integration: mechanical and organic solidarity. Mechanical solidarity emerges based on the similarities of members of society. These similarities generate a strong awareness of common goals and shared living conditions that ultimately lead to the emergence of a collective consciousness among members of a community (*Kollektivbewusstsein*). According to Durkheim, mechanical solidarity is the predominant mode of social inclusion in "primitive societies." This has been criticized as "stereotyped and historically mistaken,"[9] but this analytical imprecision is not relevant in our context. It should be noted, however, that Durkheim's concept of "primitive societies" analytically corresponds to David Hume's "small communities" and von Hayek's "microcosmos." These communities comprise only a limited number of actors, and the outcome of social interaction can be unambiguously traced back to the originator of an action. The problem of unintended consequences of intentional action is of minor importance. Social norms and values that evolve in the course of repeated interaction help to stabilize expectations concerning the action of others.[10] This mutual stabilization of expectations is the main premise that renders social interaction possible.[11]

Anonymous and functionally differentiated modern societies lack most of these prerequisites. Since the "Great Transformation," society can no longer be regarded as being homogeneous with commonly shared beliefs and effective norms channeling self-interest to the pursuit of a common goal.[12] Social interaction becomes depersonalized. Functionally differentiated societies do not "present individuals to one another, but social functions."[13] The mode of social collusion is not *similarity* but *complementarity*. A complex society is a "system of different organs each of which has a special role, and which are themselves formed of differentiated parts."[14] Social inclusion is based on self-interest and

9. Ibid., 682.

10. The evolution of fairness norms in the course of instantaneous and repeated social interaction has been documented exhaustively by experimental game theory. In repeated games, tit-for-tat strategies proved to be superior to any other strategy; see Robert Axelrod, *The Evolution of Cooperation* (New York: Basic Books, 1984); and Ken Binmore, *Natural Justice* (Oxford: Oxford University Press, 2005), for an analysis of the normative implications of cooperative bargaining.

11. Niklas Luhmann, *Die Moral der Gesellschaft* (Frankfurt am Main: Suhrkamp, 1988).

12. Karl Polanyi, *The Great Transformation* (Boston: Beacon Press, 1944).

13. Émile Durkheim, *De la division du travail sociale* (Paris: Presses Universitaires de France, 1893), 407.

14. Ibid., 129.

is steered by comparative advantages and mutual benefit in exchange. Durkheim labels this process "organic solidarity." This conception of solidarity is analytically equivalent to Herbert Spencer's model of contractual solidarity. It goes without saying that this concept of solidarity is apparently in line with the economic analysis of social behavior and the institution of a free market. Émile Durkheim's conception of solidarity is relevant for our analysis insofar as it comprises the social relations of small communities as well as those of functionally differentiated modern societies. Furthermore, the phenomenon of functional differentiation thus the emergence of a competitive market economy is not an obstacle to solidaristic behavior but, rather, its necessary prerequisite.

Although Durkheim's distinction between mechanical and organic solidarity offers distinct merits, it has shortcomings as well. Besides the questionable stereotype of "primitive" versus "modern societies" and the implicit normative content underlying the concept of evolutionary motion from mechanistic to organic solidarity in the course of social development, there are mainly two analytical weaknesses. One is the stereotype idea that societies—be they "modern" or "primitive"—are organized by one mode of social inclusion alone.[15] This assertion is certainly flawed empirically. Another conceptual weakness is the fact that market exchange is put on the same level with solidarity. Although it is indisputable that competitive interaction has an impact on overall well-being that ultimately leads to a better fulfillment of individuals' goals in society, it has to be recognized that these mutual benefits accrue mostly to the productive members of society. Only those who are able to participate in the process of production and trade are able to benefit from mutual exchange. Thus, for a fuller understanding of solidarity, personal indigence has to be recognized as well.

Reciprocal versus Unidirectional Social Activities

The German philosopher Wolfgang Kersting analyzes social interaction from a different point of view. He differentiates two alternative modes

15. Durkheim himself is not consistent in his use of the concept of social evolution from mechanical to organic solidarity. While he employs this model as a universal explanation of social inclusion in *Division*, he approves the existence of various forms of social cohesion such as "traditions," "common beliefs," and "collective life" in his later work, especially in his analysis of religion and the French Revolution. See Émile Durkheim, *Les formes élémentaires de la vie religieuse* (Paris: F. Alcan, 1912). His modified perception of solidarity is most pronounced in his attitude toward the family. See Pope and Johnson, "Inside Organic Solidarity," 690.

of social inclusion: cooperation and solidarity. Cooperation is an "in all respects useful enterprise of the division of labor for mutual benefit." Cooperative communities can be either competitive or noncompetitive. Noncompetitive cooperative communities pool their resources to pursue a specific, predetermined common goal. In contrast, competitive cooperation is based on the diversity of talents and productive powers in society. The action of an individual is not directed toward a prespecified common goal. In fact, the common good evolves by channeling self-interested activities to the needs and demands of others through the process of competition. Again, competitive cooperation finds its ultimate expression in the competitive market economy.

Cooperation, however, is not the only way of social inclusion in modern societies. The paradigm of cooperation is completed by the alternative paradigm of solidarity. Kersting defines solidarity as a "compensatory system of mutual care, predominantly directed towards the needy and the weak."[16] This definition comprises two modes of solidarity. Mutuality in care refers to the reciprocal character of solidarity that is likewise inherent in the concept of mechanical and organic solidarity. The reference to "those in need" sheds new light on the concept of solidarity that has not been mentioned yet. It breaches the reciprocal character of social interaction and induces a unidirectional, or altruistic, element to social analysis.

The Analytical Concept

Putting these different notions of solidarity together, one gets a broader picture of the different manifestations of solidarity in diverse social settings, which allows us to analyze the meaning of solidarity in modern market economies in more detail. Using the concepts of specificity and reciprocity as an analytical framework gives us four distinctive modes of solidaristic cohesion. Table 10-1 exhibits the specific characteristics of the goods produced and consumed under the different modes of social integration and interaction as well as the relevant institutions for the provision of these goods. The different modes of solidarity are outlined in this section. The relation to the market economy is detailed in the third section.

The most arcane form of solidarity is that of abstract solidarity

16. Wolfgang Kersting, *Theorien der sozialen Gerechtigkeit* (Stuttgart: Metzler, 2000), 23.

TABLE 10-1. Notions of Solidarity in Divergent Social Settings

		Mode of social integration (concept of solidarity)	
		Mechanistic (specific)	Organic (abstract)
Mode of social interaction	Reciprocal	Club goods (unions, mutual insurance associations)	Private goods (markets)
	Unidirectional	Gifts, alms (family, private charity organizations)	Public or publicly provided goods (welfare state)

based on reciprocal social interaction. This understanding of solidarity is what Durkheim and Spencer had in mind when they spoke of "organic" or "contractual" solidarity. As mentioned previously, this notion of solidarity is best realized in a competitive market environment. Under abstract reciprocity, solidarity can only be negative. That means that the individual's legal and political positions are mutually acknowledged in society, but there is no direct action for the benefit of others. Mutual economic and social improvement is the unintended results of trade and exchange.

The second mode of social inclusion is that of specific (mechanistic) solidarity under the condition of reciprocity. This structure of social interaction is what social scientists have in mind when they speak of social inclusion in small-scale communities.[17] In this case, social transactions have a prespecified goal and are predominantly carried out via face-to-face interactions. Group formation and the evolution of social norms arise from rational individual action by sharing resources to pursue common material or ideological interests. The reciprocal nature of social interaction can be either explicit or implicit. Explicit reciprocity means a direct and unmoderated equivalence between individual investment and the corresponding outflow from the common pool of resources. The true character of implicit reciprocity is somewhat more concealed. In this case, the individual acts pro-socially without receiving any reimbursements on predefined terms. But what seems to be altruistic behav-

17. Michael Hechter uses the term *group solidarity* in this context. See Michael Hechter, *Principles of Group Solidarity* (Berkeley: University of California Press, 1987).

ior at first sight is essentially reciprocal in nature, as interaction occurs repeatedly among a given set of prespecified and identifiable actors and altruistic behavior is fully compensated over time. The main challenges to social interaction—the holdup problem and the falling apart of individual and collective rationality—is solved via the reciprocal structure of repeated and well-identified interaction.

It is worth noting that specific reciprocity requires a concrete opposite (the *aliud*) against which the group's common action is addressed. This *aliud* can be impersonal (e.g., a dire economic environment or the exposure to a common social risk) or personal (e.g., a social group competing for the same resources). Either way, resources are being pooled to enhance the individual's social position via improving the welfare of the group as a whole. Thus, this understanding of solidarity is not an open concept like that of abstract reciprocity; besides the social inclusion of the group members, it is necessarily associated with social closure and the exclusion of those who do not belong to this group. The goods produced and consumed are typical "club goods."[18] The implications for social policy are developed further in the next section.

Unidirectional social actions comprise activities that cannot be conceptualized as reciprocal, whether explicit or implicit. This concept presupposes altruistic preference structures. Thus, activities of that kind cannot be analyzed in a theoretical setting that draws exclusively on rational egoism. But they are nevertheless analytically traceable in a rational choice setting, as long as altruistic preferences are not ruled out on axiomatic grounds.

The third quadrant of table 10-1 contains unidirectional actions aimed at specific and predetermined members of society. Social interaction of that kind is predominant in families, but can be found in other social contexts such as private charity of nongovernmental organizations as well, albeit not as pronounced. Finally, the fourth quadrant of table 10-1 represents unilateral acts of solidarity conducted in a depersonalized, anonymous context. Goods produced and consumed in that manner are public or publicly provided goods. This mode of solidarity is best represented by the modern welfare state. The evolution of the

18. On the economic analysis of club goods, local public goods, and common pool resources, see Elinor Ostrom, Roy Gardner, and James Walker, *Rules, Games and Common-Pool Resources* (Ann Arbor: University of Michigan Press, 1994).

modern welfare state represents a fundamental turn in the provision of third-party assistance in two ways. On the one hand, the act of solidarity is depersonalized, a matter of public service. The voluntary act of the donor is substituted by a juridic act of political authorities, and altruism is substituted by coercive political rules. As Wolfgang Kersting puts it, the welfare state "socializes private charity and gives the Samaritan the status of a civil servant."[19]

But this is only one aspect. On the other hand, only political institutions and the public regulation of welfare arrangements allow the beneficiary to lead a self-determined and purposeful life consistent with basic requirements of human dignity and self-agency. The needy individual is no longer the object of altruistic attitudes prevalent in society, but a self-contained person endowed with positive rights. The juridification and the depersonalization of welfare arrangements are simply the flip side of this emancipatory process.

A Comprehensive View of Solidarity

Putting these various notions of solidarity together, we are in the position to formulate a capacious and comprehensive (i.e., "catholic") understanding of solidarity that embraces all notions of solidarity mentioned earlier. The papal encyclicals *Sollicitudo Rei Socialis* (SRS) and *Populorum Progressio* (PP) tell us that solidarity is a moral concept and a duty on both the personal and the societal level (SRS 9, PP 48). Solidarity is based both on the mutual dependence of individuals and on the prescriptive premise that "all men should constitute one family and treat one another in a spirit of brotherhood" (*Gaudium et Spes*, 24). Solidarity is "not a feeling of vague compassion or shallow distress at the misfortune of so many people, both near and far. On the contrary, it is a firm and preserving determination to commit oneself to the common good; that is to say to the good of all and of each individual, because we are all really responsible for all" (SRS 38). This overarching concept of solidarity is based on the notion of the human being as a person: "Solidarity helps us to see the 'other'—whether a person, people or nation—not just as some kind of instrument, with a work capacity and physical strength to be exploited at low cost and then discarded when no longer

19. Kersting, *Theorien der sozialen Gerechtigkeit*, 23.

useful, but as our 'neighbour,' a 'helper' (cf. Gen 2:18–20), to be made a sharer, on a par with ourselves, in the banquet of life to which all are equally invited by God" (SRS 39).

The principle of solidarity is one of the "building blocks"[20] of Catholic social teaching that proposes *an integral and solidary humanism capable of creating a new social, economic and political order, founded on the dignity and freedom of every human person, to be brought about in peace, justice and solidarity.*"[21]

THE IMPLEMENTATION OF
SOLIDARITY IN THE CONCEPT OF A
SOCIAL MARKET ECONOMY

Modern societies are not restricted to one single mode of solidarity. On the contrary, they encompass all notions of social cohesion and inclusion mentioned earlier. The value society places on the solidarity principle depends on the relative status attached to these various phenomena of solidarity and the public management of their interrelationship. To reach a maximum of social inclusion, the various potentials of solidarity have to be organized not only in a nonconflicting but also mutually reinforcing way. A "social market economy" is a way of social organization that aims to reconcile these various modes of solidarity. This implies a twofold task. First, the crowding out of one form of solidarity by another is to be avoided, provided that the different modes under consideration operate on different functional levels. The debate on the welfare state crowding out private activities or endangering family relations falls under this category. The demand for a nonconflicting arrangement of the modes of solidarity does not imply the conservation of social structures, as the terms and general conditions of social interaction may change, which has implications for the adequate mode of solidarity as well. But whenever one mode of solidarity is—in part or entirely—replaced by another, the net effect on social cohesion has to be reassessed. Second, the different modes of solidarity have to be organized in a way that is mutually reinforcing. Here, the subsidiarity principle may serve as a practical guideline.

20. Oswald von Nell-Breuning, *Baugesetze der Gesellschaft. Solidarität und Subsidarität* (Freiburg: Herder, 1990).

21. Pontifical Council for Justice and Peace, *Compendium of the Social Doctrine of the Church*, 9.

Reciprocal Communities

The Market as Abstract Reciprocal Solidarity   As mentioned previously, the competitive market is not only the place of production and distribution of goods and services. It is also an institution that ensures social inclusion in an open society. The market system has proved to be a powerful force that brings together diverse capabilities and sets free the productive and innovative resources of a society. The free exchange of goods and services is not only the prerequisite for the pursuit of individual goals that forms the basis for a self-contained and purposeful life. It is also open to the heterogeneity of social actors, their differences in skills and moral attitudes. In closed and stratified societies, these disparities are, at best, innocuous, yet are most likely a peril to social cohesion. The market economy is thus the natural corollary of what Popper calls an "open society."[22] Insofar, the market is an intrinsic pro-social institution with social benefits of its own. The integrating function of the market has always been recognized by the proponents of the social market economy.

But contrary to Durkheim's notion, a well-functioning market economy does not evolve organically in the course of society's development. The modern market economy is, moreover, embedded in a set of social institutions that are shaped by political forces and are the result of a cultural process of its own. For its proper functioning, a market economy needs a political framework that enforces the right of ownership and at the same time regulates the legitimate use of private property. Laws against the restraint of competition are as necessary as regulations correcting market failure. And finally, any cooperative society has to set rules that generate a just division of the cooperative surplus between the actors involved.

These insights form the basis of the sociopolitical paradigm of the social market economy. It is first and foremost based on the competitive economic paradigm. Although the social market economy is often referred to as a "third way between Socialism and Capitalism" (Alfred Müller-Armack), this does not mean that this concept constitutes a deliberate combination of elements of the free market and central planning. The economic and social benefits of the market system have

22. Karl Popper, *The Open Society and Its Enemies* (London: Routledge, 1966).

always been accepted by the ordoliberal school and—with some qualifications—by Christian social ethics, the two pillars of this concept. The principles of private property and the allocation of goods and services by a system of free prices were never seriously cast in doubt. But the process of free trade and exchange has to be embedded in a social framework. Private property and the free exchange of goods and services are a necessary, albeit not sufficient condition for a social market economy.

Associations of Mutual Interest   Because of its open character and liberality, the framework of competitive cooperation leaves room for the free association of individuals pursuing a common goal. In this case, solidarity is based on the specificity of the common goal and the reciprocal character of social interaction. Again, the agent's motivation can be represented by self-interested preferences that are best achieved by a combination of resources and the coordination of individual plans. But in this case, the coordination is conducted by purposeful planning by the actors or their respective agents. Examples that apply to different notions of this concept are mutual insurance associations or labor unions.

Mutual insurance associations are solidaristic communities based on specificity and reciprocity. The contribution rate is calculated based on the individual's risk and his or her desired insurance cover. Insurance communities of mutual benefit nevertheless constitute specific (mechanistic) solidaristic organizations, as insurance payments are only handed out to those members of the association who suffer a certain loss. These payments are made on predefined terms of the insurance contract. The insurance principle plays a dominant role in the concept of the social market economy, because it is the basis not only of private insurance contracts but of the social security system as well.

An example of group solidarity addressed against other members of society is the formation of labor unions. Workers unite to pursue a goal common to the members of the group, that is, the amelioration of working conditions or an increase of the labor share. Actions of union members are ultimately reciprocal in nature. In the case of labor unions, the *aliud* is easily identified with the firm owners or their agents, the management of the firm. Unionism poses profound and yet unsettled normative questions to social scientists. To liberals, unionization is simply the cartelization of labor supply and thus stands in stark contrast to the idea of a free and liberal economic order. Major proponents of ordoliberalism strongly opposed the idea of collective bargaining. To proponents of solidarism, the formation of labor unions is in accordance with the social nature of humankind and is an act of exercising one's (natural) right of engaging in cooperative associations.[23] Finally, welfare economists pay attention to the allocative outcomes of collective bargaining. Whether individual or collective bargaining is superior in terms of efficiency is still an open question. The concept of the Social Market Economy, however, is unequivocally solidaristic in nature. The free association of unions and their distinguished role in wage formation are unquestioned. In Germany, labor unions are even protected by basic law.

Another powerful and influential mode of solidaristic organization that has to be mentioned in this context is the profession. It has influenced the institutional arrangement of continental European welfare states for decades and is still prevalent in some of its structures. Similarities in the social position and the resulting common interest offer the basis for the evolution of occupational morals and a specific notion of solidarity. The profession as a basis of mechanistic solidarity for modern societies has been recognized not only by Durkheim, but by scholars of Catholic social thought as well.[24] With respect to the welfare state, this manifested itself in a social security system that is structured along the lines of profession.[25]

23. Catholic social teaching falls in this category. The right of workers to join unions has consistently been recognized. The associated problem of unilateral market power has never been addressed in detail; by and large, workers are assumed to be in a weaker bargaining position, and unionism is approved without reserve. On the treatment of labor unions in the social encyclicals, see *Rerum Novarum* (49), *Quadragesimo Anno* (35), and *Sollicitudo Rei Socialis* (9, 15, 26).

24. The system of "solidarism" favored by Heinrich Pesch, Johannes Messner, and Oswald von Nell-Breuning predominantly relied on the profession as the main factor of integration in society. The "professional order" (*berufsständische Ordnung*) served for some time as an alternative draft to the liberal economic order. See Heinrich Pesch, *Lehrbuch der Nationalökonomie* (Freiburg: Herder, 1905); Johannes Messner, *Das Naturrecht: Handbuch der Gesellschaftsethik, Staatsethik und Wirtschaftsethik*, 6th ed. (Berlin: Duncker and Humblot, 1984); Nell-Breuning, *Baugesetze der Gesellschaft*.

25. This is especially true for the German welfare system. Besides the traditional differentiation of security systems between blue- and white-collar workers, there exist independent and self-contained systems for public servants, farmers, seamen, miners, and freelance professionals. However, the last three decades have shown a process of intense harmonization and standardization that occurred almost unnoticed by the public.

Influential as it was at the turn from the nineteenth to twentieth century, this mode of social inclusion has lost its significance to a great part. In the course of social and economic development, social stratification with respect to occupation has eroded, and similarities in the social position and with respect to common social risks have aggravated. For example, the occupational differences between blue-collar and white-collar workers, the associated social status, and their respective self-recognition have narrowed significantly in the last decades. The same holds true for wage earners and particular modes of self-employment. The universality of social risks in less stratified societies demands universal arrangements for social protection, which is an ongoing process in most European welfare states. This may ultimately lead to a completely universalized system of social security, which is nevertheless in full accordance with the stipulations of solidarity.

Unilateral Communities

The Family   No theory of social interaction can do without an explicit analysis of the family, the interrelation of its members and the social position of this institution in society. It is well known that the family is the basis of any society by generating the human and social capital that is necessary for social development and economic growth.[26] Furthermore, in countries with a well-developed, unfunded social security system, the family creates a fiscal externality that has to be compensated for equity and efficiency reasons alike. But the family is not only the primal institution of socialization and the development of social skills and attitudes. It is also a basic institution of social cohesion and mutual support that constitutes an indispensable correlate to the fragmented modern society. In social life, the recognition and the social position of an individual are based mainly on his or her functions and capabilities. Especially in nonstratified societies, a person's social position is directly related to his or her functional prominence to society. The family forms a contrast to that. Here, a person is respected in his or her full entirety, with all of his or her capabilities and deficiencies. Mutual respect is not gained by specific aspects of the person but is devoted to the individual

---

26. James S. Coleman, "Social Capital in the Creation of Human Capital," *American Journal of Sociology* 94 (1988): 95–120; Robert D. Putnam, *Bowling Alone: The Collapse and Revival of American Community* (New York: Simon and Schuster, 2000).

in total. The German sociologist Franz-Xaver Kaufmann speaks of the
"full inclusion" (*Vollinklusion*) of a person that only takes place within
the family.[27] As such, the family contains an element of premodernity
that remains essential for the social inclusion in functionally differentiated societies.

In the course of socialization, families endow the members of society with certain attitudes trained and educated within familial interaction. These personal convictions are relevant to the social cohesion
and the proper functioning of any free and democratic society. This
is because private contracts, as well as any social order, are necessarily
incomplete. Even classical liberals accept the necessity of overarching
norms and values, such as honesty, truthfulness, and the restraint from
fraud and deception, that are indispensable for a frictionless functioning
of social interaction.[28] These norms and values are basically learned and
practiced in the course of socialization and are transmitted from generation to generation. Intact families endow society with the "prerequisites
a free and democratic society relies on, but which it is unable to ensure
by itself."[29]

The correlation between intrafamily solidarity and the public provision of welfare can be taken as the blueprint for the interrelationship
between factual and political solidarity. It goes without saying that the
welfare state still relies on intrafamily social support to a large extent.
Any social system would by far be strained too much, economically and
morally, if it had to take over the social activities accomplished by the
family. According to the subsidiary principle, families should be self-
determining and be granted sole responsibility for all activities concerning intrafamily relations. It is predominantly the task of the welfare state
to enable families to accomplish their specific social functions. For that
reason, the social market economy is often denoted as "familiaristic,"
and justifiably so. The tax system takes account for intrafamily support
by deducting subsistence expenses from the tax base. The social security

27. Please note that I use the term *family* for any social institution that undertakes this process
of full inclusion of an individual, and not for a certain arrangement codified by law or social norms.
Thus, this must not necessarily refer to the traditional construct of the family, although in reality
it predominantly does.

28. Hayek, *The Fatal Conceit*.

29. Ernst-Wolfgang Böckenförde, "Die Entstehung des Staates als Vorgang der Säkularisation," in *Säkularisation und Utopie*, ed. Ernst Forsthoff (Stuttgart: Kohlhammer, 1967), 78.

system accounts for child and old-age care provided by family members. And benefits depend on the number and age of dependent children.

On the other hand, the nuclear family has lost its capability of insuring its members against social risks such as old age, health, long-term unemployment, or care. The welfare state or functionally equivalent institutions had to step in and fill that gap.[30] But whenever possible, welfare arrangements should aim at safeguarding and enforcing intrafamily provision of social assistance.[31] A persuasive example is the provision of long-term care. Traditionally, long-term care was provided by family members, predominantly women. Because of the significant increase in longevity, the ascending severity of dependency, and the changing social structure of the family, this arrangement of care provision was no longer sustainable. After the installment of a public insurance program for long-term care, a competitive market for outpatient services developed, thus facilitating home care of relatives. The same holds true for child-care facilities. All these social services are not to be designed as a substitute but as assistance and encouragement to the intrafamily provision of welfare and solidarity.

Private Charity For centuries, the provision of social assistance has been organized by private institutions. Religious and other mission-driven organizations sheltered the homeless, took care for the impoverished and disabled, and handed out alms for the needy. Welfare provision in premodern societies was based entirely on intrafamily aid and on complementary private charity. According to their specific structure, these communities were disposed with the necessary prerequisites for an efficient arrangement of social assistance based on private charity, such as manageable community size, unambiguous social stratification, and an overarching moral code accepted by the overwhelming part of society. It should be kept in mind that because of this authoritative moral code, the provision of private charity was never based on mere

30. It is often argued that the installation of welfare arrangements has caused the erosion of the enlarged family, as having children is no longer necessary for old-age security. It can be shown, however, that in Western societies the decline of family size happened prior to the installment of public welfare arrangements. The tendency to the nuclear family has to be recognized as a consequence of the demands of the Industrial Revolution, and the establishment of the welfare state as a reaction to the institutional vacuum caused thereby.

31. Martin Kohli, "Private and Public Transfers between Generations: Linking the Family and the State," *European Societies* 1 (1999): 81–104.

voluntarism in a modern understanding but on a commonly shared notion of duty and responsibility. With the disruption of orthodox social inclusion in the course of modernization, all these preconditions were lost, and functional equivalents had to be established. Although private charity is still prevalent in modern societies, its social function has changed considerably. Charitable giving is incapable to solve the social problems of the "extended order," that is, to safeguard the social inclusion of those unable to meet the requirements of a market society. But private charity fills the gaps the anonymous and bureaucratic welfare state leaves behind. Charitable contributions provide the fabric of altruism on which any society relies. Furthermore, social entrepreneurs find new and innovative ways to solve social problems that are not yet tackled by public programs or that are beyond the reach of any welfare arrangement. Thus, a social market economy aiming at the inclusion of all members of society has to shape its institutions and public programs in a way to foster these private initiatives and not to crowd out the private provision of charitable gifts and donations.[32]

CONCLUSION

Modern societies comprise plural ways of solidarity that manifest themselves in various social interactions. It is the main shortcoming of functionalist social theory to have replaced one mode of social inclusion by an alternative single and unique mode. In practice, solidarity based on complementary differences is as relevant as solidarity based on similarities is. The classical but somewhat superseded dichotomy between the market and the state—the one being responsible for economic efficiency and an increase in the overall living standard, the other for solidarity

32. On the crowding out of private charitable contributions by governmental transfers, see Burton Abrams and Mark Schmitz, "The Crowding Out Effect of Government Transfers on Private Charitable Contributions," *Public Choice* 33 (1978): 29–39; and Bruce Kingma, "An Accurate Measurement of the Crowding-Out Effect, Income Effect and Price Effect for Charitable Contributions," *Journal of Political Economy* 97 (1989): 1197–1207. There is, however, evidence that welfare programs might even have a positive effect on private transfers, especially if provision of charity is not only measured in monetary terms but if private services and in-kind transfers are recognized as well; see Martin Kohli, "Private and Public Transfers between Generations," and Harald Künemund and Martin Rein, "There Is More to Receive Than Needing: Theoretical Arguments and Empirical Explorations of Crowding In and Crowding Out," *Ageing and Society* 19 (1999): 93–121; as well as Harald Künemund and Claudia Vogel, "Öffentliche und private Transfers und Unterstützungsleistungen im Alter—'crowding out' oder 'crowding in'?" *Zeitschrift für Familienforschung* 18 (2006): 269–89.

and social justice—is untenable from an analytical point of view. The market and the welfare state, families and free associations of mutual benefit are deeply interrelated and interdependent social arrangements. The generosity of the welfare state rests on the efficacy of the economic system. And the economic efficiency of the market system depends on the arrangement of welfare provision. The role society attaches to families, associations of mutual benefit, and unilateral associations influences the value of solidarity in that society. Furthermore, solidarity and social inclusion cannot be measured by social expenditure or by the share of public consumption. Solidarity is not a function of the level of welfare programs but, rather, of its organizational structure and arrangement. For an empirical assessment of solidarity in society, comprehensive measures that encompass social embedding are necessary. Although measures of that kind exist, there is still much research to be done, both empirically and theoretically.

ELEVEN

Are Work–Family Practices Socially Responsible?

Differing Perceptions in Portuguese Enterprises

Fátima Carioca

The role of the market is crucial for social and economic development. From housing to employment, this fact is irrefutable. However, "[t]he free market cannot be judged apart from the ends that it seeks to accomplish and from the values that it transmits on a societal level."[1] Thus, the free market needs an ethical and legal framework and a responsible behavior of business. Yet, what firms consider to be a responsible behavior depends on what they consider to be the social responsibility of business, commonly known as corporate social responsibility (CSR). In that sense, CSR should comprehend not only the corporate philanthropic initiatives but also the social impact of activities inherent to the business mission in society, such as providing jobs and maintaining as much employment as possible in a free and competitive market, designing organizations favorable to human dignity and development, providing a valuable service to customers, and so on. The contribution of the firm to the human flourishing (or deterioration) of those under its influence has an unquestionable social dimension and strong implications for human sustainability.

Examples of such practices are the internal social practices such as those related to the harmonization of work and family life (WFL). Most firms have been framing these policies not as a CSR case but as a human resources management (HRM) case aiming at the well-being and person-

1. Pontifical Council for Justice and Peace, *Compendium of the Social Doctrine of the Church*, 348.

al development of their employees. This approach is somehow reductive. Its scope is limited to a single stakeholder group—the employees—and the inner mission of the firm. Broadening such a scope seeing families, namely the employees' families as both a stakeholder and a social concern fundamental for sustainability will pave the way to the reframing of the firm's social policies.

Some authors have already claimed the need for recasting the WFL agenda as a social responsibility of the firm.[2] Indeed family plays a crucial role in social sustainability. Family is a social reality based on relationships that support and promote personal development and community life. Therefore, firms as corporate citizens should consider their direct social responsibility in what concerns theirs employees' families, and, indeed, some business leaders have already done so.[3] For instance, Muirhead et al. presented the results of three corporate surveys conducted between 1999 and 2001 according to which the majority of the seven hundred respondent firms declared that work–life balance was among the top priorities for the companies as corporate citizens.[4]

This chapter confronts both the literature and practices—WFL issues and CSR—providing evidence of a strong relation between them. It also demonstrates the value of a holistic view of the organization and its role for its people and society, meaning one embedded with ethical values while integrating other aspects or dimensions such as economics, politics, and social ones.[5]

WORK–FAMILY LIFE AND CORPORATE SOCIAL RESPONSIBILITY

According to WFL literature, Work and Family realities are not independent scopes of human life in general.[6] There is a relationship of

---

2. Marcie Pitt-Catsouphes and Bradley K. Googins, "Recasting the Work-Family Agenda as a Corporate Social Responsibility," in *Work and Life Integration: Organizational, Cultural and Individual Perspectives*, ed. Ellen E. Kossek and Susan J. Lambert (Mahwah, N.J.: Lawrence Erlbaum, 2005), 445–68.

3. Ibid.

4. Sophia A. Muirhead, Charles J. Bennett, Ronald E. Berenbeim, Amy Kao, and David J. Vidal, eds., "Corporate Citizenship in the New Century: Accountability, Transparency and Global Stakeholder Engagement," New York: Conference Board, 2002.

5. Domènec Melé, "Corporate Social Responsibility Theories," in *The Oxford Handbook of Corporate Social Responsibility*, ed. Andrew Crane, Abagail McWilliams, Dirk Matten, Jeremy Moon, and Donald S. Siegel (New York: Oxford University Press, 2008), 47–82.

6. Rosabeth M. Kanter, *Work and Family in the United States: A Critical Review and Agenda for Research and Policy* (New York: Russell Sage Foundation, 1977).

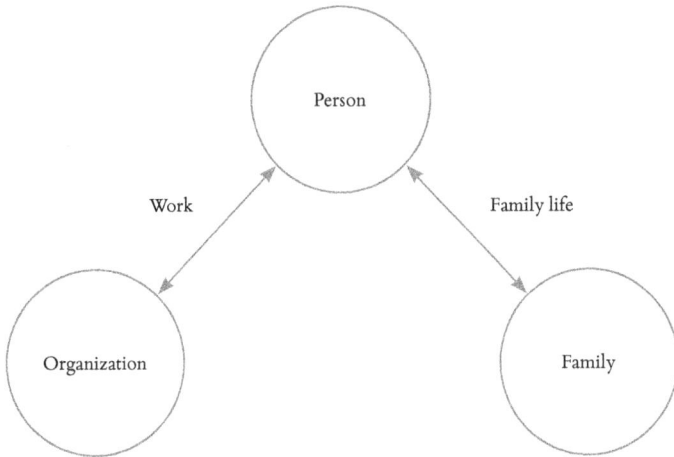

FIGURE 11-1. Integration of Work–Personal–Family Life

mutual spillover between work and family fields. Moreover, as Kanter points out,[7] both worlds and the interrelationship between them are essential, constituent, and intrinsic to personal life. Time, tasks, attitudes, stress, emotions, and behavior developed in one role spread out to other scopes of life.[8] The emotional climate at work affect families and so can a family's emotional climate and demands affect its members as workers.[9] Family situations can define work orientations, motivations, abilities, or emotional energy. Take, for example, the willingness to take risks or to travel previously and after a child is born. Concluding, individual aspirations, work demands, and family concerns across time are

7. Ibid.

8. Ellen E. Kossek and Cynthia Ozeki, "Work-Family Conflict, Policies and the Job-Life Satisfaction Relationship: A Review and Directions for Organizational Behavior–Human Resources Research," *Journal of Applied Psychology* 83, no. 2 (1998): 139–49; Sylvia A. Hewlett and Carolyn Buck Luce, "Off-Ramps and On-Ramps: Keeping Talented Women on the Road to Success," *Harvard Business Review*, March 2005, 43–54.; Nuria Chinchilla and Elizabeth Torres, "Why Become a Family-Responsible Employer?" in *Occasional Paper No 06/3* (Barcelona: International Center Work Family, IESE Business School, University of Navarra, 2006).

9. Linda T. Thomas and Daniel C. Ganster, "Impact of Family-Supportive Work Variables on Work-Family Conflict and Strain: A Control Perspective," *Journal of Applied Psychology* 80, no. 1 (1995): 6–15; Cynthia A. Thompson, Laura L. Beauvais, and Karen S. Lyness, "When Work-Family Benefits Are Not Enough: The Influence of Work-Family Culture on Benefit Utilization, Organizational Attachment, and Work-Family Conflict," *Journal of Vocational Behavior* 54, no. 3 (1999): 392–415.

equally determinants of one's professional trajectory as schematized in figure 11-1.[10]

Research on CSR became rather relevant after World War II, when health insurance and pension programs that represented the essence of the welfare capitalism became standard HRM practices in large corporations and, in many European countries, were taken up at governmental level. This evolution, in parallel with the rising of the corporate form of business organization, led to the awareness of the research questions, "What is a business for?" and "What contribution does it make to society?"[11] Indeed, since the beginning it was difficult to differentiate what businesspeople were doing for business reasons (e.g., to increment productivity) and what they were doing for social reasons (e.g., to make workers better and more contributing members of society).[12] Most of the decisions resulted, probably, from a mix of business and social motivations.

Despite a degree of ambiguity and disagreement on the answer to the previous questions, academic literature on CSR vastly flourished since then, reflecting a growing attention to the subject from different perspectives such as business, government, and society in general. The range of stakeholders became wider, and the issues researched under the CSR umbrella have also broadened in recent past.

However, literature on CSR, whether it elaborates on the definition of the concept[13] or discusses the incorporation of operational and

10. Lotte Bailyn, "Involvement and Accommodation in Technical Careers: An Inquiry into the Relation to Work at Mid-Career," in *Organizational Careers*, ed. J. van Maanen (London: Wiley International, 1976), 109–15; Lotte Bailyn and Edgar Scheln, "Life/Career Considerations as Indicators of Quality of Employment," in *Measuring Work Quality for Social Reporting*, ed. Albert D. Biderman and Thomas F. Drury (Newbury Park, Calif.: Sage, 1976), 151–65.

11. Charles Handy, "What's a Business For?" *Harvard Business Review* 80 (2002).

12. Archie B. Carroll, "A History of Corporate Social Responsibility: Concepts and Practices," in *The Oxford Handbook of Corporate Social Responsibility*, ed. Andrew Crane, Abagail McWilliams, Dirk Matten, Jeremy Moon, and Donald S. Siegel (New York: Oxford University Press, 2008), 19–46.

13. Abagail McWilliams and Donald Siegel, "Corporate Social Responsibility: A Theory of the Firm Perspective," *Academy of Management Review* 26, no. 1 (2001): 117–27; Archie B. Carroll, "A Three-Dimensional Conceptual Model of Corporate Performance," *Academy of Management Review* 4 (1979): 497–505; Mark S. Schwartz and Archie B. Carroll, "Corporate Social Responsibility: A Three-Domain Approach," *Business Ethics Quarterly* 13, no. 4 (2003): 511–12; William C. Frederick, "The Growing Concern over Business Responsibility," *California Management Review* 2, no. 4 (1960): 54–61; Keith Davis, "Can Business Afford to Ignore Social Responsibilities?" *California Management Review* 2 (1960): 70–76; Howard R. Bowen, *Social Responsibilities of the Businessman* (New York: Harper, 1953).

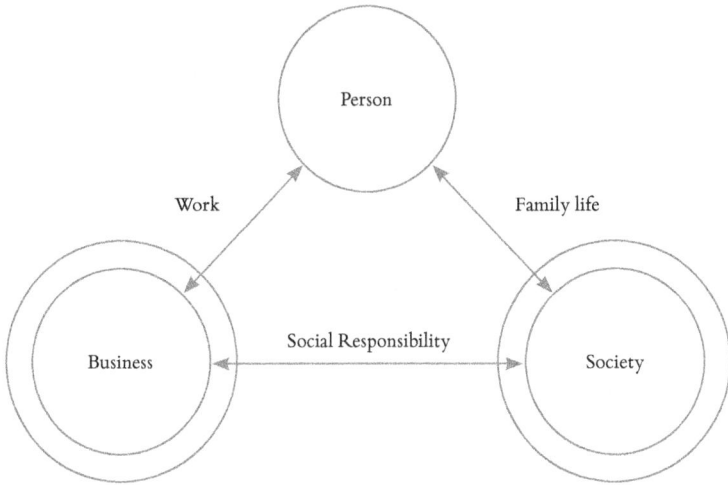

FIGURE II-2. Social Responsibility—Linking Business and Society

behavioral aspects of corporate strategy and practices,[14] always situates CSR at the interface between business and society. No matter which purpose or approach is considered, CSR is rooted in the relationship between business and society.[15]

Returning to the WFL theme, work characterizes the relationship between the individual and the organization. People work for organizations to achieve personal and organizational goals. Organizations are embedded in business as they are designed and structured to provide goods or services to consumers or society in general. The wide term *business* is used independently of the economic model, the ownership, and whether it is a for-profit, not-for-profit, or state-owned firm.

14. Dirk Matten and Jeremy Moon, "'Implicit' and 'Explicit' CSR: A Conceptual Framework for a Comparative Understanding of Corporate Social Responsibility," in *Academy of Management Review* 33, no. 2 (2008): 404; Thomas Donaldson and Lee E. Preston, "The Stakeholder Theory of the Corporation: Concepts, Evidence and Implications," *Academy of Management Review* 20, no. 1 (1995): 65–91; R. Edward Freeman, *Strategic Management: A Stakeholder Approach* (Boston: Pitman Publishing 1984); S. Prakash Sethi, "Dimensions of Corporate Social Performance: An Analytical Framework," *California Management Review* 17 (1975): 58–64; John Elkington, *Cannibals with Forks: The Triple Bottom Line of 21st-Century Business* (Oxford: Capstone Publishing, 1997); Donna J. Wood, "Social Issues in Management: Theory and Research in Corporate Social Performance," *Journal of Management* 17, no. 2 (1991), 383–406.

15. Elisabet Garriga and Domènec Melé, "Corporate Social Responsibility Theories: Mapping the Territory," *Journal of Business Ethics* 53, no. 1/2 (2004): 51–71.

On the other hand, family is a social institution that is instantiated in society, and this reflects the society where it is inserted. Naturally, it shapes its members. As part of society, it affects and is affected by the relationship between business and society. For example, in places where there is a major employer, family, and community life are daily affected by the policies and practices of such a firm. And the reverse is also true: the firm's performance, productivity, and practices are affected by the cultural context where it is implanted.

By applying this rationale and overlaying the different arenas, it is possible to visualize the evolution from the schema in figure 11-1 to the schema in figure 11-2.

It is worth noting that when the interface employer/employee/family, or better, organization/person/family, is framed as business/person/society, these relationships can no longer be considered internal and private to the firm.

CONCEPTUAL FRAMEWORK

The conceptual framework for this research included a set of variables of analysis from the two domains: WFL and CSR. Two major components characterize a family-supportive work environment in an organization:[16] family-supportive policies and family-supportive culture. Both components measure organizational efforts to support employee needs to balance work and family responsibilities. The existence of both components emphasizes the fact that the implementation of formal policies is necessary but not enough to achieve results. The process of work–family policies implementation needs to be supported by the presence of a work–family culture.[17]

Formal family-supportive policies and benefit packages take many forms but can generally be grouped into job flexibility policies and support, benefits, and services packages. One type of job flexibility policy is the offering of alternative work arrangements that include, for example, flexible time, telecommuting, or job sharing. The second type

16. Tammy D. Allen, "Family-Supportive Work Environments: The Role of Organizational Perceptions," *Journal of Vocational Behavior* 58, no. 3 (2001), 414–35; Thomas and Ganster, "Impact of Family-Supportive Work Variables on Workfamily Conflict and Strain: A Control Perspective."

17. Paula Brough and Thomas J. Kalliath, "Work-Family Balance: Theoretical and Empirical Advancements," *Journal of Organizational Behavior* 30, no. 5 (2009): 581–85; Thompson, Beauvais, and Lyness, "When Work-Family Benefits Are Not Enough."

of support, benefits and services packages, may include a multitude of supports, such as dependent care referral services, on-site day care,[18] or even a fitness center and professional counseling.[19] Some policies—for example, paid parental leave[20]—are difficult to categorize because they can be seen as a job flexibility policy and a benefit.

The literature suggests that there are at least three possible components of a family-supportive culture or a work–family culture as defined by Thompson et al.: time demands and expectations on how employees prioritize their work and family commitments, perceived negative career consequences associated with utilizing work–family benefits or devoting time to family responsibilities and managerial support, and sensitivity to employees' family responsibilities.[21]

To characterize a family-supportive work environment, Allen mentions that in addition to studying the existence of a work-family culture, it is crucial to examine the employees' perceptions regarding the extent their organization is family supportive.[22] More global measures of organizational supportiveness, in the sense that they are not restricted to the work–family life domain, are also related to a similar and overlapping set of employee outcomes, say Allen and Benson.[23] According to these authors, commonly used organizational context measures are perceived organizational support, perceived fair interpersonal treatment, and trust in management

In what concerns CSR, as the aim was to understand the organizational approach and categorize it to compare it with others, the Garriga and Melé classification was used.[24] Garriga's framework was used as a lens for the analysis of the different stances adopted by the participating institutions as regards WFL practices. The main reason for choosing such a frame is that it is a comprehensive one and that it reflects the

18. Barbara L. Taylor, Robert G. DelCampo, and Donna M. Blancero, "Work-Family Conflict/Facilitation and the Role of Workplace Supports for U.S. Hispanic Professionals," *Journal of Organizational Behavior* 30, no. 5 (2009): 642–64.

19. Susan J. Lambert, "Added Benefits: The Link between Work-Life Benefits and Organizational Citizenship Behavior," *Academy of Management Journal* 43, no. 5 (2000): 801–35.

20. Ibid.

21. Thompson, Beauvais, and Lyness, "When Work-Family Benefits Are Not Enough."

22. Allen, "Family-Supportive Work Environments."

23. Ibid, Scott J. Behson, "Coping with Family-to-Work Conflict: The Role of Informal Work Accommodations to Family," *Journal of Occupational Health Psychology* 7, no. 4 (2002): 324–41.

24. Garriga and Melé, "Corporate Social Responsibility Theories."

purpose and the way corporations view their role in society. It divides CSR approaches and theories into four groups: instrumental approaches, in which the corporation is seen only as an instrument for wealth creation, and its social activities are only a means to achieve economic results; political approaches, in which corporations recognize the business and social power they have in society and the inherent responsibility for the use of this power in the social and political arena; integrative approaches, in which the corporation is focused on the satisfaction of social demands, arguing that business depends on society for its existence, continuity and growth, and ethical approaches, based on ethical responsibilities of corporations to society, and as a consequence, firms ought to accept social responsibilities as an ethical obligation above any other consideration.

METHODOLOGY

The research, although predominantly qualitative, combined quantitative and qualitative methods in a multiparadigm approach that included the following:

• A survey, aiming to outline WFL policies and initiatives and to characterize the work–family culture, as seen from the organization's and the employees' viewpoint

• Semistructured interviews with HR/CSR managers, line managers, and employees from the participating firms, aiming to understand their perception of WFL policies value, on the organizational environment as being family-supportive and the frame and organizational drivers in what concerns WFL and CSR initiatives

The triangulation of multiple perspectives from different stakeholders— the institutional perspective and the employees' perspectives—and with different research methods enhanced the vision of insightful concepts and enlightened the nature of the link between WFL practices and the CSR approach.

The research was based on a national cross-sectional set of firms, because of its originality, the accessibility of data sources, and the fact that WFL policies and CSR strategies are issues with a significant cultural component.[25]

25. Ellen E. Kossek and Susan J. Lambert, eds., *Work and Life Integration: Organizational, Cultural, and Individual Perspectives* (Mahwah, N.J.: Lawrence Erlbaum Associates, 2005).

A set of twelve Portuguese firms, aggregated in four clusters grouped by economic activity (banking and financial services, wholesale and retail, transport and utilities services), was formed. The participating firms were from different categories (economic activity, employment size, etc.), medium-sized to large (more than 250 employees, according to the "staff headcount criterion"),[26] and featuring initiatives to support employees to balance their work and family responsibilities. These requirements were intended to assure that there was sufficient diversity of practices, contexts, scale, and relevant material. The survey was answered by the HR managers, who were also interviewed, and by 2,472 employees. Besides HR managers, sixty interviews were also performed with the employees (five per firm).

The base survey (see figure 11-3) included two components:

• WFL Policies—measures the availability[27] and the degree of formalization of various work-family institutional policies.[28] While some authors argue that the total number of supports may not be an ideal measure due to the perception that employees may be penalized for using these supports,[29] the majority find that even offering supports (regardless of usage) can have positive effects on the organization and the individual employee.[30] Thus, the total number of supports available was used as a measure of the availability of formal work–family policies.

• Work–Family Culture—measures the existence (absence) of practices that usually obstruct or promote a family-supportive culture in three main dimensions, according to Thompson et al.:[31] time demands or expectations on how employees prioritize their work and family commitments and perceived negative career consequences associated with utilizing work–family benefits or devoting time to family responsibilities and managerial support and sensitivity to employees' family responsibilities. Promoters and hindrances questions were adapted from a

26. 2003/361/EC, "Commission Recommendation of 6 May 2003 Concerning the Definition of Micro, Small and Medium-Sized Enterprises," *Official Journal of the European Union*, no. 124/36 (2003).

27. Taylor, DelCampo, and Blancero, "Work-Family Conflict/Facilitation and the Role of Workplace Supports for U.S. Hispanic Professionals."

28. Lambert, "Added Benefits."

29. Thompson, Beauvais, and Lyness, "When Work-Family Benefits Are Not Enough."

30. Michelle M. Arthur and Alison Cook, "Taking Stock of Work-Family Initiatives: How Announcements of Family-Friendly Human Resource Decisions Affect Shareholder Value," *Industrial and Labor Relations Review* 57, no. 4 (2004): 599–613.

31. Thompson, Beauvais, and Lyness, "When Work-Family Benefits Are Not Enough."

Measures the availability of work–family life policies		Measures the existence of common practices that pave the way toward a work-family culture		
Work–Family Life Policies		Work–Family Culture		
Job Flexibility	Support, Benefits and Services	Time Demands and Expectations	Perceived Negative Consequences	Managerial Support
31 Questions		8 Questions		
WFP		WFC		

FIGURE 11-3. Base Survey on Work–Family Culture

study by Kossek and colleagues about sharing concerns and caregiving decisions[32] while managerial attitude questions were used, among others, by Lambert,[33] in a study between work–life benefits and organizational citizenship behavior.

The WFL Policies scale was considered reliable as it presented a Cronbach alpha coefficient of 0.9022 (firms' data) and 0.9163 (staff data) and the work–family culture one presented a coefficient of 0.8475 (firms' data) and 0.8699 (staff data).

The firms' survey, as well as the employees' survey, was extended with some demographic questions. These included known antecedents of WFL conflict such as gender, age, and educational level;[34] the fact of having children at home; and, in general, having a working spouse.[35]

32. Ellen E. Kossek, Jason A. Colquitt, and Raymond A. Noe, "Caregiving Decisions, Well-Being, and Performance: The Effects of Place and Provider as a Function of Dependent Type and Work-Family Climates," *Academy of Management Journal* 44 (2001), 29–44.

33. Lambert, "Added Benefits."

34. Terri A. Scandura and Melenie J. Lankau, "Relationships of Gender, Family Responsibility and Flexible Work Hours to Organizational Commitments and Job Satisfaction," *Journal of Organizational Behavior* 18, no. 4 (1997): 377–91; Linda E. Duxbury and Christopher A. Higgins, "Gender Differences in Work-Family Conflict," *Journal of Applied Psychology* 76, no. 1 (1991): 60–74; Behson, "Coping with Family-to-Work Conflict."

35. Rosalind C. Barnett and Robert T. Brennan, "Change in Job Conditions, Change in Psy-

The design of the interviews covered the relevant subject areas, based on the themes identified in the literature. The three key areas to gain insight were the following:

- work–family culture, previously described
- family-supportive organizational context, which examines the employees' perceptions regarding the extent their organization is family-supportive,[36] based on perceived organizational support; perceived fair interpersonal treatment and trust in management
- CSR approach, aiming to understand the organizational approach and categorize it to compare with others; where possible, the Garriga and Melé[37] categorization was used

The interviewed employees were representative of the diversity of workforce including male/female, married/other marital status, with/without dependents, representative of various functions (e.g., line managers, supervisors, coworkers), jobs (e.g., operations, administrative, front office, logistic, commercial), and work arrangement organization (e.g., full-time, part-time, shift work). They did not have to be using WFL flexibility arrangements or other benefits, but they had to be permanent employees, not temporary workers, preferably with a certain number of years of work in the firm.

Finally, the cross-analysis of the data led to results that, while not entirely unexpected, were surprisingly unambiguous.

FINDINGS

The fieldwork provided evidence that a gap exists between the organizations' and the employees' perception of the existence/absence of WFL policies, as well as the perception that the work environment is family-supportive (see figure 11-4). In general, the institutional perception transmitted by the HR managers ranked their organization's family supportiveness higher than their employees did.

A notorious exception within the set of the surveyed firms is RT3. The reason may be found in the very informal climate. This very informal

---

chological Distress and Gender: A Longitudinal Study of Dual-Earner Couples," *Journal of Organizational Behavior* 18 (1997): 253–74.

36. Allen, "Family-Supportive Work Environments."

37. Garriga and Melé, "Corporate Social Responsibility Theories."

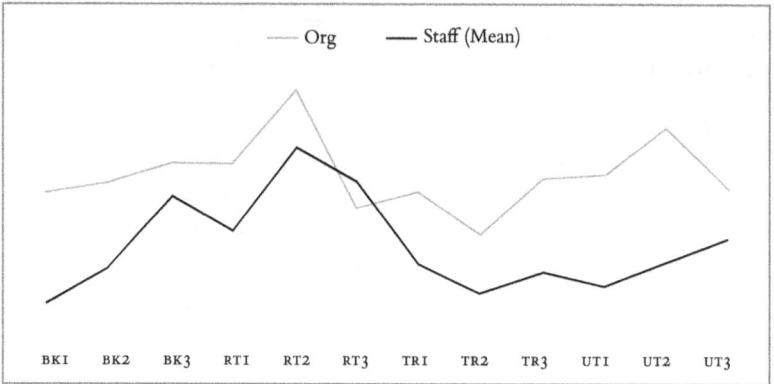

FIGURE 11-4. Overall Perception Gap of Work–Family Culture

climate is based on a young workforce, a vigorously growing business and a strong global corporate entourage associated with a spirit of enthusiasm and simplicity, among other values. This culture not only makes communication easier and more efficient, but it also makes employees believe that there are no inaccessible policies. "There is always lots of news on the walls: in the canteen, in the changing rooms.... When a new policy is implemented, it is spread" (product team leader, logistics team leader, and store manager of multinational home furnishing retail group).

Moreover, after splitting the overall indicators in work–family life policies and family-supportive environment indicators, the perception gaps that are observed (see figures 11-5a and 11-5b for the respective gaps) are significantly different, confirming that these concepts are different and that they depend on different variables.[38]

Not only are they different, but it is also possible to detect that the family-supportive environment gap based on the culture and the organizational environment is much more similar to the overall gap than the one related to the policies. This fact demonstrates the predominance of a family-supportive environment over the simple existence of social policies in the WFL arena, as already studied by Thompson.[39]

38. Thompson, Beauvais, and Lyness, "When Work-Family Benefits Are Not Enough."
39. Ibid.

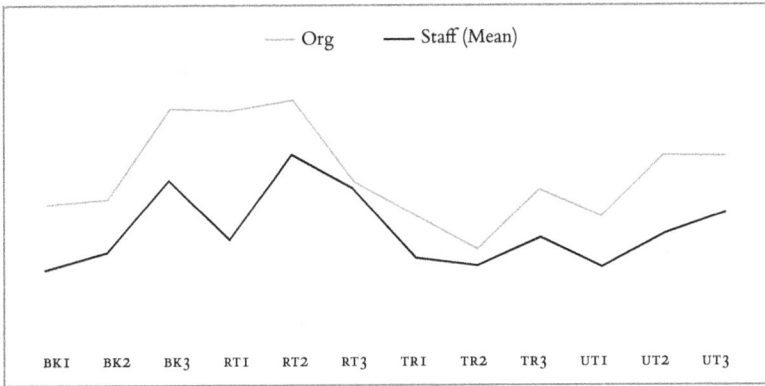

FIGURE II-5A. Work–Family Life Policies Perception Gap

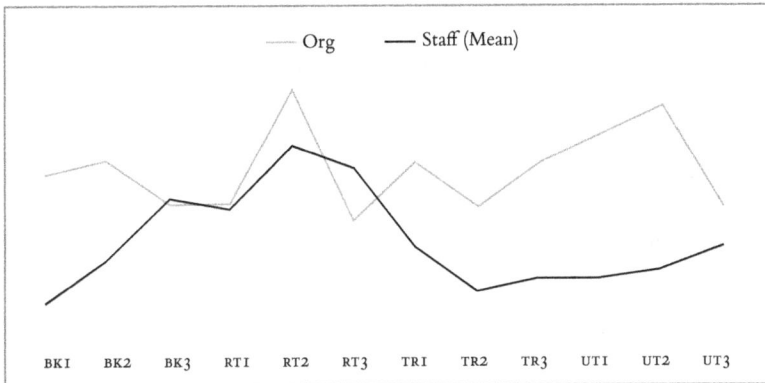

FIGURE II-5B. Family-Supportive Environment Gap

Regarding policies, problems of internal communication were one of the highlighted justifications for the gap, for reasons such as

• formal policies exist, but the employees do not know: "We are too far away from the central department. Of course, there is an intranet where we have all the information and there is also a monthly internal newsletter. But we normally do not have time to have a look at it. When I need to solve a special situation, I ask the central department which are the available policies. Most of the times I am surprised with the quantity of policies we have" (distribution engineer of National Energy Group).

• or they do not know who can access them: "Sometimes we hear that there are, at RT1, certain policies, but we are not sure if they are applicable to us. If our manager doesn't inform us, we assume that they are not for us" (customer assistant of national food retail group).

The policies gap can also corroborate the problem of managers as gatekeepers, as cited in the literature:[40]

• Sometimes, they serve as a barrier to the employees as they have to authorize, agree or, at least, deal with the situation when the employees have access to certain policies (e.g., to reorganize the team): "I know that certain policies exist at RT1 but I also know that it is our manager who has to allow us to access them. So, at the end, I know that, in my situation, I cannot have access to them" (corporate engineer of National Energy Group).

• But they also serve as a barrier to the organization, as managers have a key role to promote the permeability, in order that values, policies, and information reach everyone: "When we ask them [the middle managers] to communicate some policies, some of them will communicate and some others will not do so. We are not sure that the message reaches everyone. That is why we bypass the situation. We send a personal letter to each employee" (HR manager of national food retail group).

To further analyze such differences, I created a scatter chart, as presented in figure 11-6. The graph represents on one axis the staff perceptions of work–family culture values, and on the other axis, the organizational perception values. The graph is divided into four quadrants introduced by the lines indicating the mean value of the staff and the organization perception values.

When examining the chart, it is important to have in mind that all the participating institutions have implemented some WFL policies. For a larger sample with no such precondition, the graphic would surely be different because the lower-left quadrant would be more populated.

40. Michael P. O'Driscoll, Steven Poelmans, Paul E. Spector, Thomas Kalliath, Tammy D. Allen, Cary L. Cooper, and Juan I. Sanchez, "Family-Responsive Interventions, Perceived Organizational and Supervisor Support, Work-Family Conflict, and Psychological Strain," *International Journal of Stress Management* 10, no. 4 (2003): 326–44.

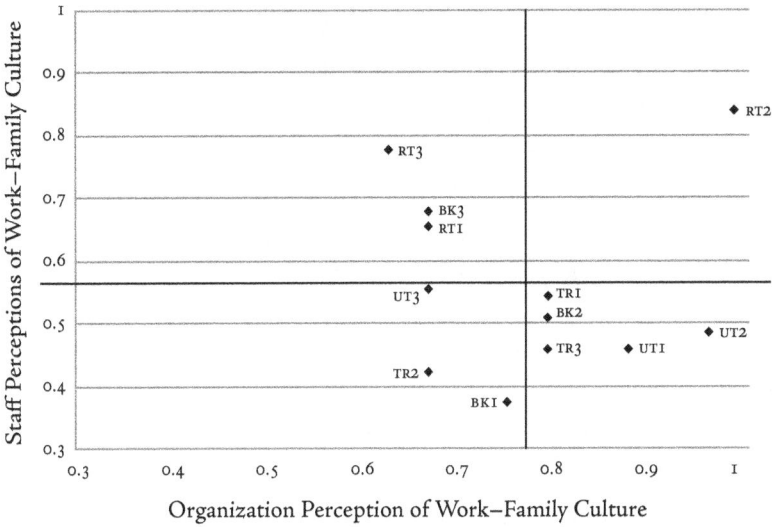

FIGURE 11-6. Staff Perceptions versus Organization Perception of Work–Family Culture

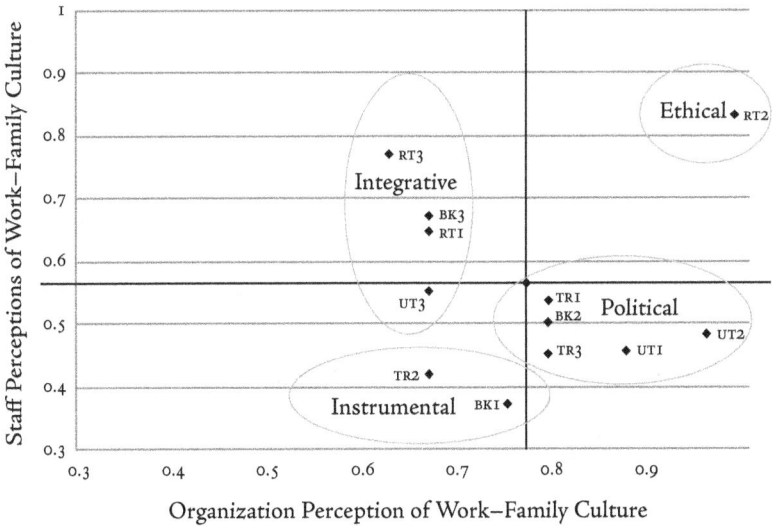

FIGURE 11-7. Staff Perceptions versus Organization Perception of Work–Family Culture (with CSR classification)

After the interviews, the firms were classified according to the CSR approach classification of Garriga and Melé.[41] When overlaying the results, the vision that such groups are similar to the quadrants drawn in the chart clearly emerges (see figure 11-7).

Further conclusions can be established:

• Social policies, such as those concerning WFL harmonization, are an instantiation of the more general corporate approach to CSR.

• The match between the two arenas confirms the hypothesis that the employees' perception is the perception of the consistent corporate behavior while addressing social responsibility issues, either externally or internally.

• Firms from lower quadrants (instrumental and political approaches) indicate that the corporate role (either a financial or a societal one) is their major orientation, even when they offer a comprehensive set of social policies. Firms from higher quadrants (integrative and ethical approaches) complement such an orientation with a more humanistic one that employees perceive and value.

• Ethical and instrumental approaches tend to be clearly perceived by the employees. Political approaches tend to fail to be appreciated by the employees while integrative approaches tend to be overestimated by the employees.

After each quadrant is analyzed in more detail, some further considerations can be made:

• Instrumental approaches to CSR apply when firms consider that wealth creation is their sole responsibility with regard to society, the implementation of WFL practices mainly aims at the maximization of profit, and neither employees nor the corporation greatly values such policies. "Social policies and benefits are an important tool for team motivation but, at the end, we are all driven by goals, targets and results" (branch manager of national financial group).

In general, employees realize that such policies are an instrument for increasing productivity, thus profit. "Though most of the policies are implemented in order to respond to their needs, their performance is

41. Garriga and Melé, "Corporate Social Responsibility Theories."

the ultimate target of such policies" (chief operating officer of national rail services firm).

Focused on performance improvement, corporations see the implementation of social policies as "an obligation essential for employees' satisfaction and motivation" (HR manager of national financial group), as a "pacifier to deal with labour unrest" (HR manager of national rail services firm) or even as talent management instrument: "If we want to attract and retain the best people, we have to offer a variety of WFL policies" (HR manager of national financial group).

Not only aggressively market-oriented firms are found in this group, but also firms struggling for survival tend to adopt such a posture. "In times of economic crisis, you have to survive. That is your main duty as a firm. That is our main Social Responsibility. In order to achieve that one has to forget some other humanistic considerations" (chief executive officer of national rail services firm).

• Integrative approaches to CSR build from the principle that business depends on society for its existence, continuity, and growth, and thus, the corporation is focused on the satisfaction of social demands.

In line with the model of corporate social performance, firms within this group are characterized by three common aspects.[42] First, they demonstrate a very strong sense of identification with the firm's mission, values, and culture but also with expected consistent behaviors personalized by the owner, the founder, or top management—"[O]ur story began a long time ago with our founder" (product team leader of multinational home furnishing retail group); "[W]e have a story of more than a century" (key account of national food retail group).

Second, they establish stakeholder dialogue processes to determine what should be an appropriate corporate social behavior—"We know that everything we do makes a difference. And some things are no longer wanted or accepted by a client or an employee" (sustainability manager of national telecommunications group). They also, proactively, report on economic, social, and environmental performance, following the idea of a triple-bottom line:[43] "We know that sometimes we are part of the

---

42. Donna J. Wood, "Corporate Social Performance Revisited," *Academy of Management Review* 16, no. 4 (1991): 691–718.

43. Elkington, *Cannibals with Forks*.

problem. But we work hard to be part of the solution" (sustainability manager of national telecommunications group).

Third, they tend to separate business, whose goal is basically economic, and social responsibility. They do not deny that business has a social impact, but their basic decision criterion is economic performance. Business leadership is a quite important driver of these firms—"We are leaders within domestic market in all business segments" (commercial manager of national telecommunications group, logistics manager of national food retail group).

Indeed, the major difference between an integrative approach and the instrumental approach to CSR is translated into a more proactive strategy to address the different stakeholders' expectations, including the workers. The normative foundation is not ethics but social expectations and, thus, greatly dependent on the cultural context—and the implementation of practices is pushed by coercive pressures of all stakeholders—"Our mission is devoted to fulfil people's needs and preferences" (store manager of multinational home furnishing retail group). Employees embedded in such a culture demonstrate a great capacity for adaptation to market changes and competitiveness to make a difference and to contribute positively to business. These same attitudes are expected from the firm, namely, in the implementation of new social policies and benefits.

• Political approaches to CSR are identified with the notion of corporate citizenship,[44] as evoking the idea having duties and rights within a community. Firms in this group considered themselves as being part of the society, and they ought to contribute to the common good of that same society. Although certain citizenship activities can be considered as strategic investments,[45] in general, these firms place their participation beyond the economic rationale and consider it critical for the development and well-being of society.

This logic of service is emphasized when the firms are state owned (TR1, TR3, and UT2), domestic major employers (BK2 and UT2), or

44. Dirk Matten and Andrew Crane, "Corporate Citizenship: Toward an Extended Theoretical Conceptualization," *Academy of Management Review* 30, no. 1 (2005): 166–79.

45. Naomi A. Gardberg and Charles J. Fombrun, "Corporate Citizenship: Creating Intangible Assets across Institutional Environments," *Academy of Management Review* 31, no. 2 (2006): 329–46.

public services providers (TR1, TR3, UT1 and UT2)—"We are obliged to reach the whole country, so we have the goal to reach and serve everyone. Integrated as part of this goal, we help local social and cultural organizations that support the community and our local employees and their families. We also give national visibility to local municipal initiatives in order to leverage them" (sustainability manager of national telecommunications group).

The fact that this notion of public service is embedded in their mission creates a strong sense of duty that frames all social policies, either internal or external ones—"We have the obligation to give back to society by the fact of being a big banking institution, at all levels. We give back by being a good firm, profitable and sustainable, but also by giving time to our employees so they can be involved with their families and social initiatives, supporting them and their families and supporting community responses to social needs. For example, we normally sponsor local crèches and recreational institutions" (HR manager of national commercial bank group).

Compared to firms with an instrumental approach, the difference is essential as they redirect their focus to their contribution to society, not only on business. Firms with integrative approaches, although they reflect on their role as an organization, are mainly focused on integrating expectations of individuals, either citizens, clients, shareholders, or employees.

• An ethical approach to CSR in the line of Garriga and Melé could only be recognized in RT2.[46] They believe in ethical norms, as they "render a primordial, indispensable and immensely valuable service not only to the individual person and his growth, but also for society and its genuine development" (planning manager of multinational food and beverages retail group). In line with political approaches, the core notion of the firm is participation in and contribution to the common good of society, primarily to the community in which they operate but also beyond national boundaries, presenting a global sense of citizenship. On the other hand, according to integrative approaches, they recognize the individual rights and duties of their stakeholders, namely their employees. However, not only do they respond and integrate stakeholder ex-

---

46. Garriga and Melé, "Corporate Social Responsibility Theories."

pectations, even proactively, but the firm sees itself as a participant in a stakeholders' network cooperating with each other.

This notion evokes stakeholder management theory as defined by Freeman:[47] "[W]e seek to produce goods and services according to plans aimed at efficiency and to satisfy the interests of the different stakeholders involved. We believe that business creates wealth for all society, to all subjects involved in it. It has to. Otherwise it is not sustainable in the long-term" (plant manager of multinational food and beverages retail group). Moreover, they attend the stakeholders' rights and legitimate interests, not only what is strictly required by law. These firm develop cross-cultural policies even in countries where law and public obligations are much softer: "As a multinational to which society should we be responsible—locals, home or all of these? We try to adopt local country's values but there is a set of core values that is universal, and those we do not discard ever" (HR manager of multinational food and beverages retail group).

This twofold focus—society and the individual person, short term and long term, local and global—is perceived by the employees as credible, consistent, and genuine: "I think that, at this firm, social responsibility is not just a nice and fashionable expression. It is taken seriously, from the top to the bottom. It gives long-term purpose to all our activities" (distribution team leader of multinational food and beverages retail group).

CONCLUSION

This chapter has provided empirical evidence on the similarities between and the differentiating aspects of various medium-sized to large Portuguese firms in what concerns WFL policies and culture and CSR approaches. The analysis situated them, according to their approaches, within a general map describing the way firms considered their role in society. The adopted map, "Corporate Social Responsibility Theories: Mapping the Territory" from Garriga and Melé, classifies the most relevant theories on and approaches to CSR and related concepts into four

47. Freeman, *Strategic Management*; R. Edward Freeman, "The Politics of Stakeholder Theory: Some Future Directions," *Business Ethics Quarterly* 4, no. 4 (1994): 409–22; R. Edward Freeman, "Managing for Stakeholders: Trade-Offs or Value Creation," *Journal of Business Ethics* 96, no. 1 (2010): 7–9.

groups, which the authors have called instrumental, political, integrative, and ethical theories.[48] The map proved valid and useful.

This research allowed the conclusion that a holistic view of CSR, spread through the organization, was desirable to promote the firm as a community of engaged people,[49] not only a holistic approach but one embedded in ethical values, emphasizing the intrinsic rights and dignity of every person, while integrating other aspects or dimensions such as economics, politics, and social ones.[50]

Moreover, the study demonstrated that organizational and employee responses showed some commonality of perceptions, but a divergence of perceptions was also evident. Hence, and in line with the literature, there is evidence of a gap between the institutional and the employee perceptions of the value and accessibility of work–family initiatives and the rated organization's overall family-supportiveness.[51] Not only does that gap exist, but it also varies from firm to firm.

The research recognized the relationship between the organizations' and employees' perceptions gap on WFL culture and the different CSR stances. Moreover, it ascertained that when these are not aligned the gap was significantly higher leading to situations of discredit/lethargy or overconfidence/euphoria, both of them undesirable and posing their own risks.

Whereas inconsistency between both themes was penalizing for the perception of the employees regarding organizational supportiveness, alignment between them proved to reinforce perceptions regarding initiatives in both fields. Thus, an important conclusion is that trust, credibility, and veracity are values that promote the alignment of the employees not only toward strategies but also toward such values and virtues.

Finally, a major conclusion derived from the previous ones, is that "one size does not fit all," meaning that although some companies had the same policies, employees perceived institutional WFL strategy and initiatives differently. One reason was the cultural attributes of the or-

48. Garriga and Melé, "Corporate Social Responsibility Theories."

49. Kanter, *Work and Family in the United States.*

50. Garriga and Melé, "Corporate Social Responsibility Theories."

51. Lauren Parker and Tammy D. Allen, "Work/Family Benefits: Variables Related to Employees' Fairness Perceptions," *Journal of Vocational Behavior* 58, no. 3 (2001): 453–68; Allen, "Family-Supportive Work Environments"; O'Driscoll et al., "Family-Responsive Interventions, Perceived Organizational and Supervisor Support, Work-Family Conflict, and Psychological Strain."

ganization, as explained earlier, but another was the singularities of the workforce (e.g., age, education, work dynamics). This finding requires firms to adopt an attentive and thorough strategy in what concerns the overall management of their people. In fact, not only new work dynamics, based on empowerment, participation, and entrepreneurship, take more time and energy and, thus, present new problems for both men and women juggling work and family commitments, but employees' personal and family needs and expectations also vary according to the individual and time. "In fact, the purpose of a business firm is not simply to make a profit, but is to be found in its very existence as a community of persons who in various ways are endeavoring to satisfy their basic needs, and who form a particular group at the service of the whole of society."[52]

This is also relevant for the free-market economy. First, the free-market economy depends on such cultural and ethical foundations. Second, markets live by embracing new ideas and strategies but also by tackling the hard work of making something happen. To make things happen in the organization, loyal, committed, diligent, and innovative people are needed. These virtues flourish in firms which respect the dignity, freedom, and fundamental rights of the individual and contribute to social well-being and a harmonious way of living together in just, peaceful, and friendly conditions, both in the present and in the future,[53] both inside the firm and in society at large.

52. John Paul II, *Centesimus Annus*.

53. Domènec Melé, "Integrating Personalism into Virtue-Based Business Ethics: The Personalist and the Common Good Principles," *Journal of Business Ethics* 88, no. 1 (2009): 227–44.

TWELVE

Global Capitalism and Values-Based Businesses

The Case of Cooperatives and Benefit Corporations

Patrice Flynn

Global interest in businesses that expand the bottom line beyond profit maximization has exploded in the past decade. Many citizens are searching for business models that take into account a triple bottom line that places measurable value on profits, people, and the planet. Can the market system adapt in ways that allow businesses to make a profit while integrating values-based practices into business charters? Is a new integrative economic system in the works that will strengthen global capitalism?

Global capitalism has never been a static system despite its core, immutable building blocks founded in classical and neoclassical economic theories. As Kaletsky documents, "capitalism is an adaptive social system that mutates and evolves in response to a changing environment."[1] For the market system to avert chaos and create wealth, adaptation is necessary. Most often, adaptation emerges from systemic crises such as war, natural calamities, or financial panics. At such moments, society initially clings to existing ways of self-organization with the expectation that the crisis will pass and the economy will return to the familiar steady state. During crisis, however, new ideas surface and, if integrated, may make the dominant market system economic model stronger and perhaps more suitable to a new era.

This chapter begins with a brief history of the underpinnings of

1. Anatole Kaletsky, *Capitalism 4.0* (N.Y.: Public Affairs, 2010), 2.

global capitalism and then moves into an examination of recent trends that suggest shifts in the operationalization of capitalism through the introduction of two values-based business models: member-owned cooperatives and benefit corporations.

Member-owned cooperative enterprises have an estimated one billion members in ninety-six countries.[2] The United Nations designation of 2012 as the International Year of Cooperatives reflected a groundswell of interest in cooperative businesses that promote the triple bottom line of profits, people, and the planet. The cooperative movement originated in England in the early 1800s, then moved to the United States in the 1900s and to Latin America today, where women in impoverished rural regions are coming together to create cooperative microenterprises.

The benefit corporation was introduced in the United States in 2010 and is now legal in twenty-seven states and pending in another thirteen states. This new form of for-profit business allows firms to legally incorporate long-term social and environmental goals alongside profit maximization. Today, more than 1,600 firms are certified benefit corporations, representing 60 industries.[3] Similar legal frameworks are under consideration in Europe to integrate environmental stewardship and social welfare into the corporate model.

Both member-owned cooperatives and benefit corporations are contemporary innovations in the market system that may have a lasting impact on how capitalism is operationalized moving forward. What is innovative is the incorporation of values into the for-profit business model that allows society to create and distribute wealth, provide meaningful work for young and old alike, honor the human being in the production process, steward natural resources to fuel the production–consumption cycle, leverage human ingenuity with computer and robotics technology, pursue socioeconomic goals efficiently, and enable global capitalism to continue its expansion across the planet in novel ways.

The market system is more complex than ever before and does not fit neatly into the economic constructs of efficiency, rationality, and general equilibrium. A new economic system is in the works. Can the traditional market system adapt and integrate innovations to meet the

2. United Nations, "United Nations Launches 2012 International Year of Cooperatives," *UN Cooperative News*, http://www.social.un.org/coopsyear.

3. B Lab, *2014 B Corporation Annual Report*, http://www.bcorporation.net.

demands of society in the twenty-first century? Serious consideration
of what values-based businesses bring to the marketplace may be wise
given that "nothing is preordained in history, nor anything immutable
in economics."[4]

THE MARKET SYSTEM

To examine advances in global capitalism, it is important to remember its
roots in Europe during the tumultuous period from the sixteenth to eighteenth centuries when tradition-based economies and command-based
economies were challenged and ultimately replaced with Adam Smith's
treatise that became the economic blueprint for the United States.[5]

Economics provides a valuable perspective from which to examine
globalization. Economists share an understanding about how the world
operates based on a set of assumptions grounded in classical and neoclassical economics. Fundamental to the economic way of thinking is the
notion of the market system that holds together a capitalist economy.

The market system is a relatively new type of economy that solidi-
fied during the late eighteenth century and replaced tradition-based and
command-based economies. A tradition-based economy presupposes that
one's socioeconomic position in life is determined at birth. Girls follow in
the footsteps of their mothers; boys, in their father's footsteps. Destiny
was considered a right of birth. In command-based economies, emperors,
kings, and queens determined one's livelihood and, hence, socioeconomic
standing. Vestiges of command economies are visible today in nations
such as China and Saudi Arabia, where central planning and authoritar-
ian control characterize the organization of society. Like tradition-based
economies, command-based systems do not allow an individual the freedom to choose one's family status, trade, craft, or occupation.

The transition away from tradition and command economies to
the market system economy occurred in fits and starts. Historians and
economists recount tremendous resistance to capitalist behaviors such as
mercantilism and profit maximizing, which were not well received by
all, especially feudal monarchies and the church.[6]

---

4. Kaletsky, *Capitalism 4.0*, 16.
5. Adam Smith, "An Inquiry into the Nature and Causes of the Wealth of Nations."
6. Robert Heilbroner, *The Worldly Philosophers* (New York: Simon and Schuster, 1953); Charles
Lindblom, *The Market System* (New Haven, Conn.: Yale University Press, 2001).

RULES OF THE GAME

The Market System

| Interaction of Individuals | → | Choice | → | Expected Costs & Benefits |

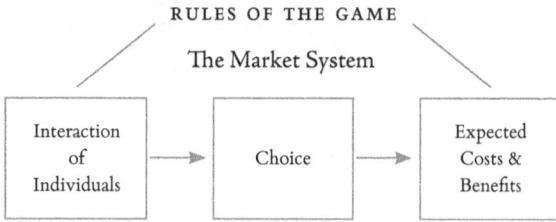

© 2002 Patrice Flynn

FIGURE 12-1. The Market System

The market system is characterized by a host of factors, including the existence of private property rights, economic freedom, profit motive, division of labor, a flow of wealth into production, and the notion that wealth begets power. A market system is a way that society chooses to organize itself to coordinate human behavior and ultimately survive.

As illustrated in figure 12-1, the market system begins with the *interaction of individuals* who enter into voluntary exchange with each other as buyers and sellers. Such transactions occur for some type of private gain that could not otherwise be achieved. The exchange encourages and enables a division of labor across society. The process requires a high level of social coordination, albeit one in which individuals do not have to confer with each other at all times. Chaos is kept at bay because participants and potential antagonists are financially vested in the system. Out of this interactive process, wealth is created, which is the ultimate goal of capitalism.

The second aspect of the market system is *choice*. People make choices to mediate constraints of money, energy, volition, and time. Choices are made based on the *expected costs and benefits* of an action, the third aspect of the market system. Embedded in each choice is a trade-off, the measurement of which requires assessing relative values through marginal analysis, one of the hallmarks of neoclassical microeconomic analysis.

Last, and most important, the market system with all of its intricate components operates under a set of guidelines or *rules of the game* governing exchange, choices, and decision making. Each industry and community determine the rules under which the market system operates. The rules are not static but change as society develops. Here we are reminded of the inherent flexibility built into Smith's market system economic model because the rules of the game are constantly adapting to contemporary society.

No nation operates under the pure market system model. Nonetheless, throughout the world today, the dominant economic model in place is capitalism. Although vestiges of precapitalistic command and traditional economies remain, all nations operate to a greater or lesser degree within the market system model. Until a new economic model comes into existence, the most effective way to have an impact on the global economy is to engage in the crafting and recrafting of the rules of the game, which is where politics, psychology, religion, and sociology enter the discussion about capitalism. Meanwhile, the three-step system illustrated in figure 12-1 will continue unabated as global capitalism grows in size and scope.

It is interesting to recognize innovations in the market system and consider the degree to which such changes have a fundamental impact on the model or simply reflect marginal changes in its operationalization. In this framework, member-owned cooperatives and benefit corporations are examined below. The history, concept, and novelty of each are discussed with an eye toward assessing their relative impact on the operationalization of global capitalism today.

THE CASE OF COOPERATIVES

The prototype of the modern cooperative business model emerged out of the experience of farmers and weavers in northern England during the early 1800s when trade in raw materials and finished goods across the Pennine Pass boomed during the Industrial Revolution. The small towns of Rochdale, Lancashire, Yorkshire, and Manchester were particularly impacted when new cotton mills displaced local cottage industries in woven cloth.

The ensuing unemployment and poverty forced people to migrate to neighboring towns, where work in the mills paid subsistence wages and demanded thirteen-plus-hour workdays.[7] Demonstrations, strikes, and riots broke out in the 1810s and 1820s, along with calls for help from

---

7. David Thompson, *Weavers of Dreams: Founders of the Modern Co-operative Movement*, 150th anniversary ed. (Davis: University of California Press, 1994).

Parliament for factory inspections, limited work hours, and livable wages, which fell on deaf ears.

People took matters into their own hands in the 1830s when a group of sixty weavers formed the Rochdale Friendly Cooperative Society, a worker-owned joint-stock company. The members pooled resources to buy food in bulk to feed themselves. They kept prices low and paid themselves small wages. Within two years, the cooperative closed because credit extended to some members went unpaid, reflecting growing poverty in the region.

Several wealthy members of the business community took note of the cooperative business model and its potential for alleviating the disease and poverty afflicting most of the countryside and burgeoning factory towns in England. Robert Owen, a Welsh owner of one of the largest cotton mills in Scotland, published a book in 1821, *The Cooperative Society,* edited by his friend, John Stuart Mill, the renowned classical economist. Owen's core message in promoting the cooperative business model over the rest of his lifetime was of solidarity: all for one and one for all.

Public attention to worker-owned cooperative companies raised awareness about living and working conditions in England. In the summer of 1843, Charles Dickens visited Manchester and was overwhelmed with the human suffering. Within six weeks of his visit, he wrote *A Christmas Carol,* a story that reflects living conditions of the mill workers and displaced tradespeople he witnessed in northern England during the Industrial Revolution.

Just as Dickens's novel ends on a joyful note one Christmas morning, so does the story of member-owned cooperative corporations. The Rochdale Cooperative reopened on December 21, 1844, and successfully led the way for a cooperative movement that now has one billion members across the industrialized world.

Cooperative Enterprise Principles

A cooperative business is defined as "a voluntary group of people who have joined together to meet their common economic, social, and cultural needs and aspirations through a jointly-owned and democratically controlled business."[8] Cooperatives embody the Catholic social doc-

8. International Co-operative Alliance and European Research Institute on Cooperative and Social Enterprise, *World Co-operative Monitor: Explorative Report,* Manchester, England, October 31, 2012.

trine of subsidiarity by allowing and encouraging people to help themselves and demonstrate self-responsibility through democratic and equitable processes. On the principle of subsidiarity, Pius XI wrote, "Just as it is gravely wrong to take from individuals what they can accomplish by their own initiative and industry and give it to the community, so also it is an injustice and at the same time a grave evil and disturbance of right order to assign to a greater and higher association what lesser and subordinate organizations can do."[9]

Thompson summarized the desire for self-determination among cooperative members as follows: "The Co-operative Movement began as a working class movement in Europe intent on creating a different world. The Rochdale Pioneers made two important choices when they chose power over philanthropy and prosperity over pity. Without capital and economic independence, they would be a slave to charity and beholden to a society controlled by a wealthy few. With capital they would accumulate power, and with power they could make choices and bring freedom and a democratic economy to their members."[10] This spirit is reflected in the writings of Pope John Paul II, who acknowledged the importance of workers taking ownership of capital in an industrial society, a critical component of subsidiarity and human dignity.[11]

The Catholic doctrine of subsidiarity encourages families, communities, unions, businesses, and governments to create new mediating structures in society to contribute to the common good and "warns against the overbearing action of any large social actors and also demands that they render assistance, *subsidium*, when problems are too large to be handled by smaller, local actors."[12] In the case of the Rochdale Pioneers, the people of community took it upon themselves to initiate actions that would sustain dignified livelihoods, a concept that found its way into cooperatives in the United States in the twentieth century.

The core cooperative beliefs are summarized in seven principles adopted worldwide: education, participation, independence, cooperation, voluntary membership, democracy, and concern for community. The

---

9. Pius XI, *Quadragesimo Anno*, 23.

10. Thompson, *Weavers of Dreams*, 138.

11. John Paul II, Encyclical *Laborem Exercens* (Vatican City: Libreria Editrice Vaticana, 1981).

12. Vincent J. Miller, "Saving Subsidiarity," *America: The National Catholic Review*, July 30, 2012, 1.

principles are manifest in the wide array of cooperatives, including consumer, producer, purchasing, and shared services cooperatives.

Since 1895, the International Co-operative Alliance (ICA), based in Geneva, Switzerland, has served as a clearinghouse for information on cooperatives around the world. ICA estimates that one billion people owned shares in cooperative businesses in 2012, the largest three hundred of which reported $2.2 trillion in revenues.[13] During the 2012 International Year of Cooperatives, the ICA and the United Nations showcased advancements and innovations in cooperatives to demonstrate how "Cooperative Enterprises Build a Better World" through the promotion of socioeconomic development and collective self-help.

One of the keys to the success of the cooperative model is having a business vision set by the owners themselves who know best what is needed in a given locale and industry. Engagement of and leadership by citizens within a community is therefore essential. Individuals may become co-op members through the purchase of equity shares or voluntary service. Thus, during times when money is scarce, people can become part of a cooperative by donating time, energy, and skills. This option is valuable for people with low incomes in impoverished communities who may otherwise be disaffected from the formal economy.

The triple bottom line of people, profit, and the planet is manifest in cooperative business decisions. People benefit from community educational programs, collective buying programs, humane human resource management, and other socially responsible business practices. Profits are returned to equity owners through annual dividends and/or patron rebates and, hence, are recycled through the community. A common refrain among cooperatives is "We don't make a profit and run, we make a difference."[14] The planet is served through practices such as purchasing products within a tight geographic radius of the cooperative to minimize the firm's ecological footprint. Such practices reflect cooperative values.

Cooperatives in the United States

Each year, the National Cooperative Bank (NCB) collates data on the number, revenues, and assets of cooperatives in the United States to

13. International Co-operative Alliance and European Research Institute on Cooperative and Social Enterprise, *World Co-operative Monitor: Exploring the Co-operative Economy—Report 2014*, Québec City, October 2014.

14. The Common Market Co-op. http://www.commonmarket.coop.

showcase the "business activities and economic power of these member-owned, member-controlled businesses." The *NCB Co-op 100 List* indicates that co-ops with the largest revenues in 2013 were in the following industries: agriculture (62 percent), grocery and food distribution (16 percent), energy and communications (9 percent), finance (5 percent), hardware and lumber (4 percent), health care (3 percent), recreation (1 percent), and pharmaceutical distribution (less than 1 percent).

The largest annual revenues were reported by CHS Inc. ($40.6 billion) and Land O' Lakes, Inc. ($14.1 billion), both agricultural co-ops located in St. Paul, Minnesota, followed by Dairy Farmers of America in Kansas City, Missouri ($12.1 billion), and Wakefern Food Corp. in Elizabeth, New Jersey ($11.0 billion). Other recognizable businesses not as commonly known to be cooperatives include Ace, True Value, and Southern States hardware stores; Navy Federal Credit Union; Ocean Spray, and Sunkist Growers.

Agricultural cooperatives were among the earliest type of cooperatives and remain the largest today. Food cooperatives, including the Rochdale Friendly Cooperative Society, addressed several key problems including compromised food (i.e., bulk food lined with weight-adding fillers, such as ground bonemeal in flour) and noncompetitive pricing. By buying from local producers and establishing face-to-face relationships, product quality is monitored and costs contained. Today cooperatives no longer rely solely on local producers, although most cooperatives strive to purchase fresh fruits and vegetables from suppliers located within a 150-mile radius of the store.

To promote the cooperative principles beyond a given locale, co-ops purchase and sell fair-trade products that have been certified by reputable organizations. Such practices result in a ripple effect that expands cooperative principles throughout the economy vis-à-vis capacity building for producers, family-scale farming, democratic and participatory ownership and control, labor rights, equality, direct exchange, fair and stable pricing, affordable credit, long-term trade relationships, sustainable agriculture, transparency and accountability, and education.

Cooperative businesses pride themselves on being as innovative as possible to compensate for the lack of economies of scale in production. Continuous quality improvements are key to success. A case in point is cooperative banking in the United States since the Great Recession.

Following the massive government bailout of the financial industry that began in 2007, public interest in cooperative credit unions and community banks grew. Within a week of Bank of America's September 29, 2011, decision to initiate a $5 debit card fee (after receiving a $163 billion backstop from the Federal Reserve and U.S. Treasury), 650,000 customers joined credit unions and transferred $4.5 billion from large commercial banks into the nation's 7,000 credit unions and cooperative banks.[15] Some of the benefits consumers find at member-owned credit unions compared to commercial banks are lower fees, innovative products, local branches, higher interest rates on savings accounts, lower rates on loans, democratic control of capital, and member-driven services.

The results have not escaped the eyes of financiers interested in investing equity in cooperatives. Private investment firms are promoting changes in the Uniform Limited Cooperative Association Act (ULCAA) to extend historic limits to the role of outside investors in member-owned cooperatives. In the past decade, several states have passed legislation that allows for the establishment of Limited Cooperative Associations (LCAs) to provide more flexibility in how co-ops raise money in Wyoming, Iowa, Wisconsin, Minnesota, Tennessee, Texas, Kentucky, and Colorado.

This shift is significant because historically, cooperatives subordinated the interests of outside capital investors in favor of member-patrons who are the primary source of equity capital and the beneficiaries of net earnings. Subsidiarity is central to the operation of traditional cooperatives through the privilege of self-determination and the existence of an underlying belief in solidarity with others through the pooling of financial, human, and other resources. Under new laws, nonlocal investors may buy equity shares in cooperatives, vote in elections, and have a stake in cooperative governance.[16] Limited liability investors are thus allowed to put money into cooperative businesses without knowledge of the local community or the responsibility that comes with day-to-day management of a business.

The Limited Cooperative Association (LCA) model diverges from

15. Credit Union National Association, "CUNA Survey: 40k Members, $80m in Savings on BTD," http://www.cuna.org.

16. Lynn Pitman, "Understanding the ULCAA: A Report from the University of Wisconsin Center for Cooperatives," *Cooperative Grocer Network* 151 (November–December 2010).

core cooperative principles and, hence, is controversial by virtue of undermining self-autonomy, a critical part of the notion of subsidiarity
whereby it is an injustice to take from people something they could do on
their own. The cooperative concept places primacy on self-determination
by restraining outside control.

In Europe, cooperatives have expanded considerably since the early days of the Rochdale Pioneers. Cooperatives are recognized as legal
business forms through article 54 of the Treaty on the Functioning of
the European Union[17] and Council Regulation No. 1435/2003 on the
Statute for the European Cooperative Society.[18] The laws aim to guarantee equal competition between cooperatives and capital companies
and to facilitate cross-border activities of cooperative societies, which in
the European region of the International Co-operative Alliance represents 123 million members, owning 160,000 cooperative businesses that
provide 5.4 million jobs to European citizens in 34 countries. Charles
Gould, the International Co-operative Alliance director-general, notes
that the cooperative sector "is no side player but a major, global, economic force," despite adverse economic conditions during the financial
crisis that began in Europe in 2010.[19]

Cooperatives in El Salvador

Latin America is home to activities that promote rapid growth in global
capitalism while at the same time focus on local needs and conditions.
El Salvador provides an example of how local communities are building
new values-based businesses that allow participants to gain ownership,
pool resources, expand occupational skills, and earn money to feed their
families. The outcome is the establishment of government-sanctioned,
member-owned and -operated cooperatives that exemplify subsidiarity
and solidarity.

The following is the story of a remarkable group of women who
live in a very isolated mountainous region of El Salvador. Names and
places are withheld because of the risk of violence and extortion in the
nation with the highest crime rates in Central America. The story ex-

17. European Union, *Treaty on the Functioning of the European Union*, Brussels, March 30, 2010.
18. European Union, *Council Regulation No. 1435/2003 on the Statute for the European Cooperative Society*, Brussels, July 22, 2003.
19. International Co-operative Alliance, 2014.

emplifies modern innovations in cooperative entrepreneurialism that expand the traditional market system model by incorporating nonmonetary values into the model.

Women in El Salvador face numerous challenges in securing the basics of food, clothing, and shelter. The nation sits on volcanic rock, making subsistence farming difficult, especially in the mountains. Families suffered personal hardships during and after the 1980–1992 war and lost uncounted numbers of family members. With the signing of the peace accords in 1993, Salvadorans set out on a path to rebuild their nation.

To earn money to raise their children, Salvadoran women can either risk immigrating to the United States or moving to large cities to work in *maquila* assembly plants or private homes as domestics. Immigration is risky, and city work is dangerous, especially for women living on their own. Both options result in a separation from one's children. An alternative is to join in solidarity with other women in a village to start a microenterprise or small business.

The concept of microenterprise is rooted in the seminal work of economist Muhammad Yunus, who established Grameen Bank in 1974 in Bangladesh.[20] Grameen Bank provides traditional banking services for depositors in addition to small loans to women with very low incomes who want to start small businesses. Seed money is offered as a noncollateralized loan that charges below-market-rate interest. Women quickly demonstrated that they are attractive customers, with loan repayment rates from 95 to 98 percent.[21]

Empowerment through microenterprise development is the aim of Salvadoran Enterprises for Women (Microempresas Salvadoreña Para Mujeres), established informally by women religious in the aftermath of the Salvadoran war and formally as a 501(c)(3) public charity in 2003 under the leadership of Sister Anne Marie Gardiner, School Sisters of Notre Dame. Salvadoran Enterprises for Women (SEW) nurtures the establishment of women's groups that serve as mediating institutions to enrich civil society and create employment alternatives for women with low incomes. In contrast to microenterprise loans, SEW provides seed money in the form of grants that create no future financial obligations for the recipients.

20. Muhammad Yunus, *Creating a World without Poverty* (New York: PublicAffairs, 2009).
21. Patrice Flynn, "Microfinance: The Newest Financial Technology of the Washington Consensus," *Challenge: The Magazine of Economic Affairs* 50, no. 2 (2007): 110–21.

One of many success stories of SEW businesses is a cooperative effort in an isolated, mountainous village where, after several years of self-organizing, a group of seven women approached SEW in 2006 for assistance to form an indigo-dye business. The women wanted to capitalize on the global demand for clothing made with dark blue indigo. For three hundred years under Spanish colonial rule, Salvadorans produced some of the world's finest indigo. Blue dye from the indigo-producing plant is one of the rare dyes that absorbs well into vegetable and animal fibers and stays fast (i.e., does not run). Through hard work, training, and practice, the women resurrected a lost art and became proficient in making indigo dye, so much so that in 2009, the group decided to learn how to sew the cloth they were dying to provide themselves more work and income. With the aid of sewing classes and donated sewing machines, twenty women became semiskilled tailors.

In 2010 the Salvadoran Ministry of Education recognized the business by awarding a contract to make school uniforms, a steady and lucrative contract that has attracted more women to the business. The government's choice to employ local tailors, not just maquila factories, supports the women's vision of self-determination. As the indigo-dye business advanced, the group sought funds to purchase a small building to expand production. A building was purchased and outfitted in 2010 for the indigo dye and sewing cooperative.

The women are delighted to have meaningful work, in a nice location, close to their children. The women humbly share their gratitude and joy: "Thanks to God, I feel happy now." "No one believed we could reach such a marvelous outcome." "We are blessed to have this team." "Sometimes I look around and ask, did we really do this?" "We've learned a lot. It doesn't take us as long to make a shirt or skirt now. We've practiced a lot!" "I was scared at first because I didn't know how to sew, but others were enthusiastic. Despite problems, we succeeded." "Even the American Ambassador visited us!"[22]

On May 31, 2011, the women received news that the Salvadoran government granted the business legal status as a cooperative. The experience has transformed the lives of these women who now have mean-

---

22. Transcribed from a visit to the cooperative in May 2011 by the author, who is a founding board member of Salvadoran Enterprises for Women since 2003. For more information, see http://www.SEWinc.org.

ingful work, marketable skills, and financial equity in a member-owned cooperative business. The benefits are many. Some women have used the profits to buy bedding for their homes. Others have purchased books and uniforms for their children to attend school. Five women were elected to the local city council. One young woman noted that "some of the youth wondered what they'd do when they finished school. Now they see some possibilities." All the participants feel empowered from the enhanced well-being of the owners, customers, and community.

This indigo dye and sewing cooperative—while a small story about a small group of women in a small nation—is testimony to the power of collective action and member-owned cooperatives to change lives in meaningful ways inspired by Catholic ideals and labor market theories. The women feel proud of their accomplishments and a renewed sense of dignity through service to their community.

Many more examples of successful cooperatives are provided on the United Nations website as part of the 2012 International Year of Cooperatives.

THE CASE OF BENEFIT CORPORATIONS

In contrast to the more established cooperative model, benefit corporations are a new type of values-based business introduced in the United States in 2010. The aim is to harness the power of private for-profit corporations to expand the bottom line beyond profit maximization by incorporating social and environmental goals into business charters.

The concept is an extension of the socially responsible investment (SRI) movement in the financial sector during the 1980s when asset management firms introduced screens on individual portfolios to ensure investors that their money is allocated only to firms adhering to specified environmental, human rights, and/or labor practices. One of the first SRI firms was the Calvert Group LLC, based in Bethesda, Maryland. When the founders introduced the SRI concept in the early 1980s, the old guard on Wall Street mocked the idea. Thirty years later, SRI firms manage an estimated $6.57 trillion in investor funds, up from $3 trillion in 2010.[23] Even the most conservative investment firms offer socially responsible mutual fund options for clients, suggesting that values-based investment is now mainstream.

23. U.S. SIF Foundation, the Forum for Sustainable and Responsible Investment, *2014 U.S. Report on Sustainable, Responsible and Impact Investing Trends*, Washington, D.C., 2014.

Today, a new movement is taking place to expand the triple bottom line (i.e., people, profit, and the planet) beyond the financial sector. The movement is legally driven. In the United States, an entrepreneur who incorporates a business must choose what type of entity to establish. Large transnational firms usually are established as C corporations that have a legal obligation to demonstrate to shareholders that the directors and officers make every effort to maximize profits each quarter. If not, shareholders may sue the corporation on the grounds that potential earnings were forfeited.

For example, if a C corporation decides to invest a portion of retained earnings to protect an ecosystem in one of the towns in which it operates to foster positive community relations, the firm risks being sued by shareholders for breach of contract. The onus is on the firm to demonstrate that the expenditure directly contributed to increased earnings, share price, or dividends. In some cases, proof is available; more often, the benefits are not directly tied to shareholder wealth. Enhanced societal well-being does not qualify as enhanced shareholder well-being from a legal perspective.

The benefit corporation offers an alternative form of private for-profit enterprise that makes it legal for firms to take into consideration community, employee, and environmental interests when making decisions. The concept redefines success beyond quarterly shareholder profit maximization and focuses on what is called *high-impact* investing, a concept of growing interest to large financial institutions.

To qualify as a benefit corporation, three requirements must be met pertaining to purpose, accountability, and transparency. First, the corporation must have an explicit social and/or environmental mission (purpose). Second, the corporation has a fiduciary responsibility to consider the interests of workers, community, and the environment (accountability). Third, the corporation must issue annual data on overall social and environmental performance against a credible independent third-party standard (transparency). All other business operations remain the same, as do the corporate tax obligations.

Firms elect benefit corporation status to insert mission into the profit model and allow more flexibility with regard to long-term strategic planning. B Lab, a nonprofit entity based in Pennsylvania, has certified more than 1,600 benefit corporations to date. Jay Coen Gilbert (cofounder of B Lab with Bart Houlahan and Andrew Kassey) argues that certification helps consumers and investors differentiate between bona fide impact businesses and those with good marketing.[24]

Currently there are twenty-seven states (including the District of Columbia) with benefit corporation laws and an additional thirteen states (including Puerto Rico) with pending legislation. The first state to legislate benefit corporations was Maryland in April of 2010, followed by New York, New Jersey, Vermont, Virginia, and Hawaii in 2011. Another six states passed benefit corporation laws in 2012: California, South Carolina, Illinois, Massachusetts, Louisiana, and Pennsylvania. Between 2013 and 2014, the following states adopted benefit corporation laws: Colorado, Florida, Connecticut, Arizona, Nevada, Oregon, Nebraska, Delaware, Arkansas, Minnesota, New Hampshire, Rhode Island, Utah, West Virginia, and Washington, D.C. At the time this chapter went to press, similar legislation was pending in Alaska, Alabama, Georgia, Idaho, Indiana, Iowa, Kansas, Kentucky, Michigan, Montana, Ohio, Wisconsin, and Puerto Rico.

The types of firms that have sought benefit corporation status include finance, real estate, law, agriculture, cosmetics, photography, apparel, information technology, tourism, management consulting, media, furniture, bookstores, and more. It will be interesting to empirically assess the performance of these firms once data become available.

While benefit corporations do not fundamentally alter the operationalization of capitalism through the market system (see figure 12-1), they do offer a platform from which socially and environmentally oriented corporations can legally provide value and create wealth, thus redefining the bottom line of wealth creation in the market system model. The Benefit Corporation is the most significant change to the notion of the corporation since its inception in 1819 in the United States. The idea is to balance short-term and long-term thinking to satisfy investor demand for immediate profits while planning for the future through stewardship of the planet and attention to human welfare.

CONCLUSION

Values-based businesses that promote subsidiarity and solidarity are not new. Businesses have experimented with wholly employee-owned

24. Jay Coen Gilbert, "On Better Business," presented at TED X, Philadelphia, December 1, 2010.

firms, customer-owned cooperatives, and socially responsible investing over the years. But these strategies have not protected firms from the demands of short-term strategic planning. Regardless of mission, ownership, and incorporation status, every business is subject to the same forces of global capitalism and its unwavering dual mandates of short-term profit maximization and cost minimization.

Member-owned cooperatives provide some protection from the conditions of the open market for small producers and allow for values-oriented business practices. Cooperatives encourage solidarity and subsidiarity by pooling money, skills, knowledge, time, and goodwill toward a shared goal for a group of people who do not want to be dependent on large institutions for their well-being. Although cooperatives are for-profit private entities, their mission includes stewardship of the planet and care of citizens. When people work in solidarity to start and run a cooperative, they expand local employment options and engage in joint production and consumption. The cooperative model illustrates the ability of the market system to adapt in ways that allow for the incorporation of values beyond profit maximization.

Benefit corporations provide one of the only mechanisms to protect owners and managers from legal challenges if retained earnings are diverted from short-term profit-maximizing strategies in an effort to promote environmental stewardship and fair-labor practices. This in itself provides a means for a more flexible market system, one that incorporates social welfare and environmental sustainability goals along with profit maximization.

Why consider alternatives? Because global capitalism has never been a static system. Because entrepreneurs have always pushed the boundaries of the market system to create wealth in new and creative ways. Because increasingly traders are whispering that modern-day global capitalism has lost its moorings, that we are entering an era of grinding instability. Broker dealers are advising wealthy clients to reposition their portfolios for a fundamental geopolitical shift; large commercial banks are closely tracking the new generation of impact businesses, including microfinance technologies in growth markets. Perhaps investing in member-owned cooperatives and benefit corporations may soon become mainstream. Meanwhile, innovations in values-based businesses may help make global capitalism more resilient and adaptable to a new era.

THIRTEEN

Epistemology in Business Education

Challenging the Ideologies

Kevin Jackson

Thinking over critically and reflectively what practitioners, management theorists, and economists take for granted is a crucial task for philosophy; the moral crisis underneath economic collapse reveals it is time to confront this challenge.[1] Even in the popular press, we hear calls for rethinking business and business education.[2] Many pleas suggest a need to formulate a game plan for integrating sustainability into business schools. A widely shared assumption underlying such discussions is that we need a reorientation of the epistemological foundations of teaching and learning, along with a questioning of received approaches to business. The mandate for reorienting business education follows broader trends calling for, on one hand, reenvisioning of education for sustainability across a range of fields, expressed in the United Nations' Decade of Education for Sustainable Development,[3] and, on the other hand, recasting accounts of the nature and purpose of business itself.

While not the only culprit, business school education has contradicted sustainability by cultivating leaders of economic systems that inflict damage on ecological systems supporting life on our planet, exacer-

---

1. Kevin Jackson, "The Scandal beneath the Financial Crisis," *Harvard Journal of Law and Public Policy* 33 no. 2 (2010): 735–78.

2. Ray Fisman and Adam Galinsky, "Training the Liars and Cheaters of Tomorrow," *Slate Magazine*, September 4, 2012.

3. UNESCO, "United Nations Decade of Education for Sustainable Development: Reorienting Programmes," http://www.unesdoc.unesco.org/images/154093e.pdf.

bate climate change, and create a widening gap between rich and poor, such that two-thirds of the world's people suffer malnourishment. In addition, critics implicate mainstream business education for contributing to the global financial crisis.[4] If the status quo of business education perpetuates unsustainability, it is time for business schools to do an about-face and promote sustainability in the curriculum.

EPISTEMOLOGICAL BREAKDOWNS

Mainstream business education splinters knowledge and apportions it into isolated disciplines that fuel interpersonal, ideological, and national conflict;[5] domination of the environment; and rampant industrialization of the Earth.[6]

The prevailing conceptual architecture for business education is patterned after quantitative economic and scientistic managerial models that provide its first principles. This is not to say nonhumanistic fields lack legitimacy, autonomy, and importance as disciplines. Rather, a threat of epistemological corruption renders these disciplines incompatible with the proper end of any sustainable economy—to serve humanity and not the other way around.

QUANTITATIVE OBSESSION

A point of concern is the limitations stemming from business education pursuing the quantitative trajectory economics has followed. Mathematically driven economic theorizing reinforces an illusion that business and economics are value-free and that a distant, even contradictory, relationship exists between economics and ethics—the "separation thesis."[7]

As economics becomes engulfed in mathematization, the human element gets left behind.[8] After the financial crisis, the economic conceptual model embraced by the business world has demonstrated deficiency

4. Mark Dodgson, "An Enterprising Concern," *The Australian*, August 25, 2010, 27.

5. Charles Birch, "Whitehead and Science Education," in *Process, Epistemology and Education: Recent Work in Educational Process Philosophy*, ed. Garth Benson and Bryant Griffith (Toronto: Canadian Scholars' Press, 1998).

6. David Orr, *Ecological Literacy: Education and the Transition to a Postmodern World* (Albany: State University of New York Press, 1992), x.

7. The separation thesis states that economics and ethics constitute distinct discourses for managerial decision-making and business practices. Freeman, "The Politics of Stakeholder Theory."

8. This critique of the mathematization of economics has been advanced by Friedrich Hayek, Robert Heilbroner, and John Maynard Keynes.

in that it overlooks the complexity of human nature at the core of economics and business, properly understood.

In a trend dating back to the early twentieth century, ordinary economic theorizing has become oriented toward mathematics and quantification.[9] A random walk through a library to survey peer-reviewed economics journals reveals the superfluity of quantitative formulas, statistical analyses, and algebraic equations.[10] The profusion of quantitative detritus issues forth whether its instigators are neo-Keynesian disciples or adherents of the efficient markets hypothesis.[11] Yet a shortcoming of this intellectual trend is that it conflates the study of economics with but one instrument of economic examination. In Albert Einstein's words: "Not everything that can be counted counts, and not everything that counts can be counted."

As a symbolic language, mathematics is well suited to study the natural world. It is also an effective means of representing comparatively steady and straightforward economic patterns. But mathematics is not as suitable for a broad range of phenomena—such as institutions, values, culture, and traditions—that have enormous bearing on economic life. It is dubious that quantitatively oriented economics is an adequate intellectual framework for understanding the full scope of economic life, given its instabilities, complexities, and unpredictabilities.

To be sure, economics can reach sound results by deploying mathematics when explaining relationships having distinctively quantitative dimensions. But as economics examines the world in quantitative terms, it passes to the human side, the part that is nonmathematical and that does not behave according to fixed laws. In the words of Wilhelm Röpke: "Economics is no natural science; it is a moral science and as such has to do with man as a spiritual and moral being."[12] Röpke's in-

9. Paul Samuelson, *Foundations of Economic Analysis* (Cambridge, Mass.: Harvard University Press, 1947), 5–6.

10. As Röpke puts it: "When one tries to read an economic journal nowadays, often enough one wonders whether one has not inadvertently picked up a journal of chemistry or hydraulics." Wilhelm Röpke, *A Humane Economy* (Chicago: Henry Regnery, 1960), 247.

11. Nobel Prize economist Myron Scholes states: "There are models, and there are those who use the models," referring to the distinction between "ivory tower" economists who concoct models and financial engineers who apply the models to the actual business world. "Efficiency and Beyond," *The Economist*, July 18, 2009, 368. A number of economists embracing the efficient markets hypothesis posit modifications to it as a consequence of their readiness to accept findings from other fields, such as psychology, to account for seemingly irrational economic behavior of individuals and institutions.

12. Röpke, *A Humane Economy*, 247.

sights point to a drawback of the mind-set of the contemporary economist. In its quest for formulas, the "new economics," especially as en-
shrined in "financial engineering," is eroding our comprehension of
economics as a "moral science."[13]

TUNNEL VISION

Scientism in business management theory has accompanied mathematization in economics.[14] Business researchers shortchange inquiry when
they assume the subject of their investigations—business world—matches physical sciences. They proceed from a mistaken assumption that business unveils itself as an objective phenomenon governed by repeatable
and predictable processes. Associated with this positivism is the dogma
that the only legitimate objective of business is the maximization of
shareholder value.[15] How did such a restrictive epistemological stance on
business come about?

Consider points emerging from a study of business education by
Rakesh Khurana.[16] He maintains that the need to "professionalize" business schools was connected, as in engineering and medicine, with a need
to convey knowledge that would erect a wall, keeping amateurs out.[17] Yet
unlike engineering or medicine, the content of that specialized knowledge remained obscure until 1959, when the Rockefeller, Carnegie, and
Ford Foundations devoted resources to developing technical subjects at
business schools such as linear programming and statistical quality control.[18] The idea was that introducing mathematics-infused social science
into the business curriculum would accord academic respectability. Business faculty would be recruited, hired, and tenured according to production of scientific publications. Khurana points out the irony that, from the
1970s on, this scientific turn led innovative business schools to embrace

13. Ibid.

14. *Scientism* refers to a philosophical notion that refuses to accept the validity of any knowledge other than positive science. Scientism deems values mere by-products of emotions and rel-
egates the question of the meaning of life to the realm of the irrational or illusory.

15. R. Edward Freeman and David Newkirk, "Business as a Human Enterprise: Implications
for Education," in *Rethinking Business Management*, ed. Samuel Gregg and James Stoner (Princeton,
N.J.: ISI, 2008), 138.

16. Rakesh Khurana, *From Higher Aims to Hired Hands* (Princeton, N.J.: Princeton University
Press, 2007).

17. Ibid., 176–92.

18. Pablo Triana, "Why Business Schools Are to Blame for the Crisis," *Bloomberg Business*,
July 13, 2009.

agency theory—an outgrowth of neoclassical economics. The widespread acceptance of agency theory's seductive language, seen as useful for understanding a world in which business organizations, ownership, markets, and technologies are in flux, dissolved traditional ideas of responsibility. Managers are agents whose interests are not necessarily aligned with those of the principals, meaning the owners of a firm, the shareholders. The company is a mere legal fiction, a "nexus of contracts."[19] Here there is no place for a corporate ethos or corporate responsibility. Managers pursue their own advantage rather than the good of the company, much less community welfare.[20] Managers have incentives to magnify their compensation by increasing the size of the enterprise and expanding the reach of their responsibility, even when there is no profit to be gained from this kind of arrangement.[21]

Agency theory emphasized monitoring management performance and providing incentives for managers to improve business performance. Financial innovations emerging in the 1970s and 1980s, such as deployment of leveraging and debt in restructuring business organizations, enjoyed justification in terms of heightened efficiency.

As a legacy of this approach, the focus of business management today is on large, publicly traded corporations that present a complex agency problem whereby managers occupy the role of shareholders' agents. Within business management, theories of social science take center stage. Businesspeople act as if corporations and agency problems are immune from consideration other than shareholder value. According to Sumantra Ghoshal: "In courses on corporate governance grounded in agency theory, we have taught our students that managers cannot be trusted to do their jobs—which, of course, is to maximize shareholder value.... In courses on organization design, grounded in transaction-cost economics, we have preached the need for tight monitoring and control of people to prevent opportunistic behavior."[22]

Underpinning much management discussion is a positivistic and de-

19. John Boatright, *Ethics in Finance* (Malden, Mass.: Wiley-Blackwell, 1999), 176.

20. Kelley Holland, "Is It Time to Retrain B-Schools?" *New York Times*, March 15, 2009, BU1.

21. But see Christopher Avery, Judith Chevalier, and Scott Schaefer, "Why Do Managers Undertake Acquisitions? An Analysis of Internal and External Rewards for Acquisitiveness," *Journal of Law, Economics and Organization* 14, no. 1 (1998): 24, in which executives pursue prestige rather than extra compensation.

22. Ghoshal, "Bad Management Theories Are Destroying Good Management Practices," 75.

terministic outlook. This mind-set is persuasive in consulting, securities trading, and investment banking, which hire graduates from premier business schools in droves.[23] Investors and consultants undertake diagnostics and analysis. So there is a tendency for practitioners to adopt a reductionist mindset, regarding businesses as independent, determined phenomena. In the business school curriculum, the components of analysis are products and services, cash flows, processes, brands, and other stylized ideas that acquire their own metaphysical stature. The narrow, functionalist thinking that produced the orthodoxy surrounding the notion of agency, the restrictive view that value only means economic value to shareholders, and the myopic perspective that regards the purpose of the firm as shareholder centered, all constitute the dominant narrative in business education.

George Anders explains Khurana's assessment: "M.B.A. training has deteriorated into a race to steer students into high-paying finance and consulting jobs without caring about the graduates' broader roles in society. [According to Khurana,] 'The logic of stewardship has disappeared.'" Anders contends that "[p]anoramic, long-term thinking has given way to an almost grotesque obsession with maximizing shareholder value over increasingly brief spans."[24]

According to this received view, what counts is "winning the war" against competitors and maximizing the bottom line. The idea of applying moral principles to business conduct is inconceivable. As the cliché goes, business ethics is an oxymoron. Such a mental model rejects the notion that economic value is in any way related to moral conduct in business. Economics and morality are viewed as incompatible forms of discourse for managerial decision making and business practices. According to this view, the expectation that corporations exercise moral behavior beyond the requirements of law shows confusion about the nature of a free economy, unnecessarily imposes restraints on corporate activity, and squanders corporate value on social initiatives of unsubstantiated value.[25] The only plausible case for obeying legal and ethical standards, under this position, is to avoid monetary costs of noncompliance.

23. John Rolfe and Peter Troob, *Monkey Business: Swinging through the Wall Street Jungle* (New York: Warner Books, 2000), 8–9.

24. George Anders, "Business Schools Forgetting Missions?" *Wall Street Journal*, September 26, 2007, A2.

25. Friedman, *Capitalism and Freedom*, 133–34.

Not only has business management theory been misdirected by scientist assumptions, it fails to capture what business actually is. For all of the technocratic gabble it often generates, business theory gives little attention to basic human interactions that make business a human enterprise.[26] Yet business is fundamentally about human relationships addressed to the proximate objectives of building wealth and fostering exchange and to the broader objective of human fulfillment. Business is incapable of occurring, much less flourishing, outside of interpersonal moral–social matrices. It is astounding that most theories of business premised on shareholder theory divorce business decisions from this human sphere. Not only have the mental models of economics and business management likely played a significant role in bringing about the financial crisis, to the extent they neglect the moral and human dimensions they are ill equipped to provide guidance for leadership. Providing such guidance requires reframing management practices to be concordant with human nature and enduring moral values.

Although not ordinarily acknowledged, classical economic theorists such as Adam Smith espoused principles much in line with the robust pursuit of the common good that sustainability requires. Barely one hundred years have passed since economic theory changed tracks and began developing an individualistic mind-set grounded in the notion of scarcity and the view that people participate in the market purely as self-regarding profit maximizers.[27]

Notwithstanding this relatively recent transition in economic thought, three key ideas on which a human focus and classical economic theory come into agreement are the concepts of virtue, human dignity, and public happiness or the common good. The term *public* underscores the reciprocal character of happiness, as opposed to affluence. One can be affluent

26. Thomas Donaldson and R. Edward Freeman, eds., *Business as a Humanity* (New York: Oxford University Press, 1994).

27. Throughout the history of Western civilization, one finds business ventures embodying humanitarian endeavors. Monasteries dating to the Middle Ages were incipient institutions of economic activity, in which *ora* (culture) and *labora* (work) were coupled. As far back as the fifteenth century, the Franciscans had established the *Montes Pietatis*, precursors of modern banks, which grew up not directly seeking profit but battling usury and providing the impoverished with new beginnings. The nineteenth century brought with it a merging of economic and humanitarian objectives as European welfare establishments and hospitals emerged out of spiritual associations. Luigino Bruni and Amelia Uelmen, "Religious Values and Corporate Decision Making: The Economy of Communion Project," *Fordham Journal of Corporate and Financial Law* 11 (2006): 657–58.

alone, but to be happy requires others.[28] Public happiness is diagnosed in a stream of economics literature stressing the concept that commodities and profits engender prosperity only when situated within a broader context of meaningful interpersonal relationships within which human dignity is accorded respect. In the eyes of many classical economists, the market did not contravene civil society but was the embodiment of it. Proper functioning of the market depended on contracts, cooperation, institutions, and trust. These, in turn, promoted reciprocity. Economic activity provided a setting where humans manifest their social being and reveal their desire for camaraderie in relationships of equality and civility.[29]

The crucial insight is this: the market reveals itself as a manifestation of social life when we discern its dependence on the exercise of virtue, respect for dignity, and a shared sense of the common good. Logically, these moral elements exist before bargaining. By building good and just institutions, by forming agreements grounded in authentic trust rather than based on deceptive and disingenuous transactions, market interactions take on a wider, more virtuous role. This human-centered conception of business is supported by a long tradition of thought common to ancient cultures.[30] That intellectual tradition emphasized the dependence of commercial life on human characteristics taken to be ennobling and immutable.

AN EPISTEMIC TURN TOWARD SUSTAINABILITY

Through a *cura personalis* orientation, business schools can contribute to cultivating such characteristics in business leaders of present and future generations. *Cura personalis* means "care for the entire person," a holistic emphasis on formation of students with attention to how their views, lifestyles, and behaviors influence their well-being and that of others.[31]

28. Research indicates that donors experience benefit from giving. Economists and psychologists find that charitable giving makes people healthier, happier, and financially successful. Giving is, in and of itself, a source of value for those who donate to charity. See Arthur Brooks, *Who Really Cares: The Surprising Truth About Compassionate Conservatism* (New York: Basic Books, 2006); Stephen Post and Jill Neimark, *Why Good Things Happen To Good People* (New York: Broadway Books, 2008).

29. See Samuel Gregg, *The Commercial Society: Foundations and Challenges in a Global Age* (Lanham, Md.: Lexington Books, 2007), 9.

30. Ibid., 3.

31. In Jesuit education, *cura personalis* sometimes carries a more specific reference to a Magis

The ascendancy of scientism in business education has led to a suppression of humanist dimensions, including creativity, compassion, ethics, and spirituality. A *cura personalis* orientation is a corrective to such tendencies.

The model of scientism has led business education in its quest for value-free knowledge, the glorification of the goals of efficiency, and technocratic approaches to problems. Yet at its heart, business is a human enterprise directed at the creation of value and relationships of exchange for mutual benefit that are built on trust and take place within human cultural institutions. Such institutions are where social capital is created (or destroyed) forming the lifeblood of business so conceived. The traditional trajectory of business education has missed the very point of what business is. A malaise in business education has arisen from immunizing the core curriculum from the existential human condition and neglecting holiness, narrative, virtue, social attachment, and meaning.[32]

Yet in their detachment from the human condition, business schools have not delivered a value-free program; to the contrary, business school curricula are value-laden with unspoken assumptions of egoistic individualism, materialism, short-termism, and scientism.[33] One scholar comments that "it is time to ask what we need to know to live humanely, peacefully, and responsibly on the earth, and to set research priorities accordingly."[34]

It would be a mistake to presume that more learning, more information, and more technology are per se capable of ensuring sustainability. Rather, what is at stake is the promotion of business education of a particular kind and quality, an assertion of humanistic values in the face of the realization of the dangers of an overreliance on scientism, accompa-

---

approach, which centers around cultivating the following dispositional elements: *communia* (relationship to others), *caritas* (love as responsibility for others), *creatio* (work as creative act), *dignitas* (respect for dignity of the human person), *fides* (faith in someone or thing), *humilitas* (humility in being and doing), and *vocatio* (work as a calling or vocation). Although the Jesuit approach is largely harmonious with ideas developed in this article, the author intends to be inclusive, not restricting the concept of *cura personalis* to any particular faith tradition but to broadly encompass the world's wisdom traditions, including secular ones.

32. Anne Phelan, "Rationalism, Complexity Science and Curriculum: A Cautionary Tale," *Complicity: An International Journal of Complexity and Education* 1, no. 1 (2004): 9–17.

33. George Posner, *Analyzing the Curriculum*, 3rd ed. (Boston: McGraw-Hill, 2004); William Schubert, *Curriculum: Perspective, Paradigm, and Possibility* (New York: Macmillan, 1986).

34. Orr, *Ecological Literacy*, xi.

nied by what John Ralston Saul terms the pervasive ideology of "corporatism" that "claims rationality as its central quality" yet "leads to our adoration of self-interest and our denial of the public good."[35]

NEW DIRECTIONS

There is an opportunity to redirect business education to cease engendering unsustainable reality—characterized by ecological, financial, and social crises—and educate future business leaders for a sustainable reality where social justice and ecological care prevail. Moving away from propagation of social ills, teaching for sustainability in business education necessitates embracing new ways of conceiving the nature of business itself as an existential human enterprise centered on the creation of value through relationships of exchange.

A TRIAD OF EMERGING SCHEMATA FOR BUSINESS AND SOCIETY

This line of thought may be extended by reference to three alternative frameworks for understanding business' contribution to society. Prahalad's bottom-of-the-pyramid (BOP) approach,[36] Yunus's social enterprise,[37] and Porter and Kramer's shared value have developed alongside the corporate social responsibility (CSR) paradigm.

One advantage of the social enterprise and shared value approaches is that they target social need. By contrast, Prahalad's BOP, rather than targeting social needs, arguably leads to creating new and unnecessary needs. Seen in the best light, social enterprise centers on important social needs, deploying business to address them. Because profit and corporate self- interest are not propelling the business, the temptation to opportunistically use the poor for self-interested motives is reduced. However, in the absence of profitability, enterprises might be less attracted to the social business model. As nonprofits adopt the "business" side, they may loosen bonds with community networks of volunteers, donors, and the like, leading to reduced social capital.[38]

---

35. John Saul, *The Unconscious Civilization* (Ringwood: Penguin Books, 1997), 2.

36. Coimbatore K. Prahalad, *The Fortune at the Bottom of the Pyramid* (Philadelphia: Wharton School Publishing, 2009).

37. Muhammad Yunus, *Building Social Business* (New York: PublicAffairs, 2011).

38. Janelle A. Kerlin, "Social Enterprise in the United States and Europe," *Voluntas: International Journal of Voluntary and Nonprofit Organizations* 17, no. 3 (2006): 247–63.

Porter and Kramer urge bringing business and social good together in the service of creating shared value. Stressing that business, operating within the traditional capitalist paradigm, has forfeited social legitimacy, they propose reinventing capitalism geared not exclusively toward corporate profits, with bolted-on CSR, but instead at shared value between corporations and community. Currently business is mired in an outmoded approach in which it conceives of value creation narrowly, optimizing short-term financial performance in a bubble while missing the most important customer needs and ignoring the broader influences that determine their longer-term success. How else could companies overlook the well-being of their customers, the depletion of natural resources vital to their businesses, the viability of key suppliers, or the economic distress of the communities in which they produce and sell?[39]

The conclusion is that an altered perspective is needed to restore business legitimacy. Under the old model, business distinguished between profit and social responsibility. According to the "doing well by doing good" version of CSR, only CSR that generates economic value for the firm is adopted by firms. After all, fiduciary duties to shareholders often impose a constraint on the quality and quantity of the contributions that an enterprise can make to society. Shared value, by way of comparison, is about "creating economic value in a way that also creates value for society by addressing its needs and challenges."[40] The authors assert that, unlike corporate philanthropic efforts, this alternative approach "is not on the margin of what companies do, but at the center."[41] Unlike CSR, shared value mandates that all an enterprise's budget be dedicated to shared value. For it is within shared value that business converges with social needs. Because it brings about a positive impact on a community, shared value turns out to be good for the company as well.

Certainly significant changes would have to come about in paving the way for shared value. In this regard, business education can play an important role, which is discussed later. For now, it may be noted that, among other alternative competencies, companies and their leaders would need to be capable of identifying social needs, and be equipped to work collaboratively with members of society toward ends within the scope of their shared interest. Enterprises with a commitment to shared value

39. Porter and Kramer, "Creating Shared Value," 62.
40. Ibid., 64.   41. Ibid.

need to channel efforts at building economic value by creating social value. Some of the areas where shared value can be generated include health care, adequate housing, better nutrition, assistance for aging populations, enhanced financial security, and environmental preservation.[42]

Insofar as enterprises embarked on creating shared value need to pinpoint social needs, benefits, and harms relevant to their respective products, Porter and Kramer endorse creating clusters, "geographic concentrations of firms, related businesses, suppliers, services, providers and logistical infrastructure in a particular field such as [information technology] in Silicon Valley, cut flowers in Kenya, and diamond cutting in Surat, India."[43] Cluster building improves company productivity, competitiveness, and innovation while at the same time enhancing the local community. As an illustration, Yara, a leading mineral fertilizer manufacturer, recognized that a dearth of infrastructure in many parts of Africa was an obstacle to farmers obtaining the fertilizers and other farm products they need, as well as an impediment to getting their crops to market. To address this need, they invested sixty million dollars to build agricultural growth corridors in Mozambique and Tanzania.[44]

Although hundreds of examples could be provided, one illustration of how shared value operates is provided by the case of m-pesa, a mobile banking system that Safaricom introduced into Kenya. M-pesa enabled Kenyans to transact financial services via cell phones, which became readily available in the region. The phones reduced risks of carrying and storing cash, which customers turned into e-money. Spouses working at a distance could transmit money home over the phones, reducing transportation expenses. Thanks to the arrival of m-pesa in Kenya, saving patterns ascended, and employment was invigorated when m-pesa agents were hired. Before m-pesa, large traditional banks had neglected the poorer population, deeming it too risky and insufficiently profitable. The World Bank lauded m-pesa and Safaricom for investing in the indigent, and one study by the Consultative Group to Assist the Poor reports that, as a result of the service, rural income rose by 30 percent.[45]

42. Ibid., 67.   43. Ibid., 72.
44. Ibid., 74.
45. Nduta Mbarathi, "Kenya: Poverty Eradication Goes Hi Tech with M-PESA," *The Africa Report*, http://www.theafricareport.com/News-Analysis/kenya-poverty-eradication-goes-hi-tech -with-m-pesa.html.

The m-pesa initiatives exemplify shared value in the sense that Safari-com identified a business niche within which to address social needs of the poor, resulting in substantial amelioration of their lives while simultaneously creating profit for the company.

SOCIAL AND CULTURAL CAPITAL

How does this discussion of the shared-value approach to the relationship between business and society pertain to business education? Because shared value appears a dubious candidate as an immediate paradigm shifter in the current social context of commercial life in which norms of egoistic self-interest and hedonistic materialism dominate, business education can serve an important role as change agent in introducing alternative norms into the disciplinary mix. Business schools can gear efforts toward curriculum changes that endorse the vital importance of sharing and of creative collaboration, and seek pedagogical approaches for cultivating a variety of higher-order dispositions congruent with such norms. Richard Thaler and Cass Sunstein have shown how, by understanding how people think, it is possible to adjust choice environments, helping them choose in more beneficial directions.[46]

The constellation of moral norms and principles, as well as associated virtues and dispositions that undergird sustainability themselves make up a part of the choice architecture. To play a part in nudging corporatist ideology in the direction of shared value (and associated concerns like reducing global poverty, raising environmental awareness, promoting peace and justice, and so on) and to mitigate against unsustainable influences occasioned by greed, excessive risk-taking, egoistic individualism, business education's involvement in bringing about changes in the moral–cultural architecture can be substantial.

It is vital to recognize that business schools are not simply training grounds on how to manufacture economic capital. The time has arrived for business schools to play a role in the development of social and cultural capital. Indeed, social capital—composed of social networks and norms of reciprocity and trust—and, alongside it, cultural capital—composed of forms of knowledge, skills, education, and other advantages that a person has, are both powerful frameworks for supporting

46. Richard Thaler and Cass Sunstein, *Nudge: Improving Decisions about Health, Wealth, and Happiness* (New York: Penguin, 2009).

sustainability, and may have the capability to bring about substantial normative change in the choice architecture.[47]

Will prodding business toward shared value, and promoting social and cultural capital as sustainability drivers in our business schools, end up making workplaces, as well as marketplaces, more productive of well-being than extant arrangements with their allegiance to maximizing profits and egoistic individualism? It is significant to note that a number of countries and organizations (including the Organisation for Economic Co-operation and Development) are taking steps to supplant gross domestic product with a wider lens encompassing the notion of well-being. Listen to David Cameron, prime minister of Britain, in his 2006 speech for the Google Zeitgeist Conference: "Wealth is about so much more than pounds, or euros or dollars can ever measure. It's time we admitted that there's more to life than money, and it's time we focused not just on GDP [gross domestic product], but on GWB—general well-being. Well-being can't be measured by money or traded in markets. It can't be required by law or delivered by government. It's about the beauty of our surroundings, the quality of our culture, and above all the strength of our relationships. Improving our society's sense of well-being is, I believe, the central political challenge of our times."[48]

NURTURING APPROPRIATE CAPABILITIES

Channeling business education to focus on cultivating the sort of talent likely to generate social capital, that will in turn support sustainability, is vital to current and future societies. This suggests taking a critical look at how business school curricula might develop cross-disciplinary understanding of economic, environmental, and social sustainability. It also implies considering alternative approaches to teaching, learning, and assessment so that lifelong learning capabilities are developed. Among such capabilities are creative and critical thinking, oral and written communication, collaboration and cooperation, conflict management, decision making, problem solving and planning, and practical citizenship.[49]

47. Joseph Stiglitz, Amartya Sen, and Jean-Paul Fitoussi, "Report by the Commission on the Measurement of Economic Performance and Social Progress," http://www.stiglitz-sen-fitoussi.fr/documents/rapport_anglais.pdf.

48. David Cameron, http://www.guardian.co.uk/politics/2006/may/22/conservatives.davidcameron.

49. UNESCO, "United Nations Decade of Education for Sustainable Development."

Research shows that we learn over the course of our lifetimes, according to the overall structure of our consciousness.[50] From a pedagogical standpoint, generic enabling skills along with wider sensitizing capacities may be developed, which may be characterized as higher-order dispositions. Ethical awareness and intercultural mindfulness are archetypical higher-order inclinations. Cultivating higher-order dispositions is a crucial task of business education for sustainability.

The very notion of sustainability is grounded in an inclination toward democracy, environmental stewardship, human rights, peace, and socioeconomic justice.[51] So conceived, a person's disposition toward sustainability represents a heightened level of moral awareness and spiritual sensitivity.

Stephen Sterling, an advocate for sustainability education, makes the case for "connective cultural consciousness" shaped by a relational way of thinking, taken to be a necessary condition for cultural and educational transformation.[52] Professor Sterling distinguishes pivotal attributes or virtues linked to such a cultivated moral consciousness.[53] The individualistic and communal transformation Sterling depicts implicates self-awareness and self-critique as drivers of cultural evolution.[54]

An expansive corpus of research details characteristics associated with critical moral consciousness and higher order dispositions.[55] Such qualities involve a widening and deepening of one's boundaries of concern and are taken to be essential in a cultural evolution toward sustainability:

50. Susanne R. Cook-Greuter, "Maps for Living: Ego-Development Stages from Symbiosis to Conscious Universal Embeddedness," in *Adult Development: Models and Methods in the Study of Adolescent and Adult Thought*, ed. Michael Commons (New York: Praeger, 1990), 2; Jenny Wade, *Changes of Mind: A Holonomic Theory of the Evolution of Consciousness* (Albany: State University of New York Press, 1996).

51. Stephen Sterling, *Sustainable Education: Re-visioning Learning and Change* (Dartington, UK: Green Books, 2001).

52. Stephen Sterling, "Riding the Storm: Towards a Connective Cultural Consciousness," in *Social Learning towards a Sustainable World: Principles, Perspectives, and Praxis*, ed. Arjen E. J. Wals (Wageningen, The Netherlands: Wageningen Academic Publishers, 2007), 63–82.

53. Sterling, *Sustainable Education*, 52.

54. Sterling, "Riding the Storm," 63–78.

55. Anna Reid and Peter Petocz, "A Tertiary Curriculum for Future Professionals," in *Understanding Learning-Centred Higher Education*, ed. Claus Nygaard and Clive Holtham (Copenhagen: Copenhagen Business School Press, 2008), 31–49; American Philosophical Association, "Critical Thinking: A Statement of Expert Consensus for Purposes of Educational Assessment and Instruction," in *The Delphi Report: Research Findings and Recommendations Prepared for the Committee on Pre-College Philosophy* (Millbrae: California Academic Press, 1990).

creativity, flexibility, collaborative competence, interpersonal ethics, and sense of responsibility. David Orr posits that because sustainability troubles arise from stresses between contending standpoints they are not resolvable entirely through rational measures, narrowly understood. Such troubles, which are what E. F. Schumacher termed "divergent" problems, are not so much "solved" as transcended. Such an epistemic transcendence happens when we can see differently with spiritual acumen, a higher awareness that reveres life and death, science and mystery, and leads to resolutions by means of higher methods of wisdom, love, compassion, understanding, and empathy.[56]

How do these ideas about sustainability for education, in general, pertain to the context of business education in particular?

LINKING DEEP ECOLOGY TO VIRTUOSITY

Knut Ims and Ove Jakobsen relate the concept of deep ecology to sustainability in business and economics, arguing that higher-order dispositions—depicted as "deep authenticity" rooted in an organic, as opposed to mechanic worldview—are situated within an interpretive framework that has evolved from an ecological, humanistic, and holistic worldview that presupposes, co-creation, interdependence and nonlinear interconnection, and an extended self.[57]

Proceeding from a deep ecological standpoint on sustainability, Fritjof Capra offers this characterization of the consciousness coupled to such a worldview: "Ultimately, deep ecological awareness is spiritual or religious awareness. When the concept of the human spirit is understood as the mode of consciousness in which the individual feels a sense of belonging, of connectedness, to the cosmos as a whole, it becomes clear that ecological awareness is spiritual in its deepest essence."[58] According to another scholar, Harold Glasser, a deep ecology perspective

56. David Orr, "Four Challenges of Sustainability," *Conservation Biology* 16, no. 6 (2002): 1459. See also Bron Taylor, "Deep Ecology and Its Social Philosophy: A Critique," in *Beneath the Surface: Critical Essays on Deep Ecology*, ed. Eric Katz (Cambridge, Mass.: MIT Press, 2000), 269–99, recognizing importance of selflessness for sustainability and as a means for people to advance toward mutual understandings.

57. Knut Ims and Ove Jakobsen, "Deep Authenticity—An Essential Phenomenon in the Web of Life," in *Business Ethics and Corporate Sustainability*, ed. Antonio Tencati and Francesco Perrini, (Northampton: Edward Elgar Publishing, 2011), 213–23.

58. Fritjof Capra, *The Web of Life: A New Synthesis of Mind and Matter* (London: Flamingo, 1997), 7.

indicates the importance of integrating reason and emotion in educa-tion.[59] In this regard, Glasser's discussion is closely related to an assess-ment I give of business school pedagogy, which relates Sartrean existen-tialist concern for reason, emotion, and dispositions specifically to the way business ethics issues are framed[60] and emphasizes the importance of cultivating virtue, a moral sense of community, and sapiential aware-ness in business leaders.[61] Both Glasser, in the general context of higher education, and myself, in reference to the business curriculum in par-ticular, posit that pedagogy for a sustainable world must promote prin-cipled action, through engaging and deepening existential awareness and through helping to bring conduct more in line with that awareness.

In a recent book, I contrast the ancient philosophical tradition of virtue with contemporary expectations for what I term "virtuosity in business"—a disposition for sustainability-directed performance in eco-nomic life and, by extension, business education. Whereas virtue for Aristotle denotes right living within the *polis* or city-state (a community that emerged in turn from the *kome* or village, and the *oikia* or house-hold) virtuosity in the contemporary business context is a broader no-tion, including ethical conduct relating to environmental, ecological, financial, social, and technological spheres and pointing to the universal and therefore beyond any specific community, and not restricted to any given physical and temporal setting.[62]

Heightened moral awareness in the business world is linked to one's attraction to and disposition for truth, goodness, and even beauty. Such a broadened understanding of business motivation, which builds on the writings of Aristotle, Plato, Aquinas, and Sartre, along with worldwide

59. Harold Glasser, "Learning Our Way to a Sustainable and Desirable World: Ideas Inspired by Arne Naess and Deep Ecology," in *Higher Education and the Challenge of Sustainability: Problemat-ics, Promise and Practice*, ed. Peter B. Corcoran and Arjen E. J. Wals (Dordrecht: Kluwer, 2004), 143–46.

60. Kevin Jackson, "Towards Authenticity: A Sartrean Perspective on Business Ethics," *Journal of Business Ethics* 58, no. 4 (2005): 307–25.

61. Kevin Jackson, *Virtuosity in Business* (Philadelphia: University of Pennsylvania Press, 2012), 56–58.

62. Ibid. See also Russell Cropanzano, "Moral Virtues, Fairness Heuristics, Social Entities, and Other Denizens of Organizational Justice," *Journal of Vocational Behavior* 58, no. 2 (2001): 164–209. See also David Orr, *Earth in Mind: On Education, Environment, and the Human Prospect* (Washing-ton, D.C.: Island Press, 2004), characterizing the connection between virtue and sustainability, as well as portraying the primacy of market values, acquisitive culture, and individualism as virtue-deficient phenomena.

TABLE 13-1. Facets of Business Leadership for Sustainability

Creativity	A life force involving both form and expression of productive energy. This creative force is not constrained by outmoded conventions, structures, or norms.
Authenticity and self-knowledge	Sense of who one is; quality or degree of awareness of acceptance of one's freedom, and the responsibility that this freedom entails as one acts.[1]
Authority and moral motivation	Sense of what is right and sufficiently important to motivate one to follow it.
Pursuit of excellence	Disposition to become well trained as a part of self-actualization, "not just technically but in accord with deeper intellectual and professional promptings."[2]
Relatedness	Sense of what it means to be in relationship with the world and others.[3]
Meaning of life	Sense of one's life purpose understood self-referentially and in context of some purpose greater than self.[4]

1. Charles Taylor, *The Ethics of Authenticity* (Cambridge, Mass.: Harvard University Press, 1991).

2. Jackson, *Virtuosity in Business*, 122.

3. Interdependence and interconnectedness, as well as global citizenship, can be taught. Attendant to the dimension of relatedness is a disposition for reverence. The Center for Ecoliteracy stresses building "a sense of wonder, a capacity for reverence, a deep appreciation of place, a feeling of kinship with the natural world, and the ability to invoke that feeling in others." Michael Stone and Center for Ecoliteracy, *Smart by Nature: Schooling for Sustainability* (Healdsburg, Calif.: Watership Media, 2009), 4.

4. Victor E. Frankl, *Man's Search for Meaning* (Boston: Beacon Press, 1962).

wisdom traditions, sees the motives of business leaders to choose and act in harmony with what is understood as true, right, and beautiful as grounded in intrinsic value, and fundamentally divergent from expediency motives—so prominent in mainstream approaches to business education—to choose and act according to what is taken to be instrumentally valuable for advancing short-term and selfish objectives such as hedonism or power.[63]

Correspondingly, a "virtuoso" business leader is characterized as having developed multiple, mutually reinforcing dimensions, linked to the Aristotelian conception of virtue, which ultimately bear fruit in exemplary performance, effective leadership, and overall well-being. These multiple facets include creativity, authenticity and self-knowledge, inner discipline and moral motivation, relatedness, a pursuit of excellence, and an understanding of the meaning of life.[64] As table 13-1 indicates, these

63. Jackson, *Virtuosity in Business*.

64. Ibid.

multiple facets include creativity, authenticity and self-knowledge, inner discipline and moral motivation, relatedness, a pursuit of excellence, and an understanding of the meaning of life.

As one's sense of identity is foundational for what one stands for in one's actions in the world, a *cura personalis* orientation for business education seeks to foster a basic sense of identity as members of a global family that is interdependent and diverse. Educating for this sort of worldview is part of what is required to guide business students to feel a commitment to a common future and to well-being, not only for themselves but also for others. Attention to universal values that unite people across cultures, what has been termed *hypernorms*,[65] will tend to cultivate a globally responsible sense of moral identity.[66] One pedagogical plan that promotes this is the United Nations Educational, Scientific and Cultural Organization Teaching and Learning for a Sustainable Future education program, which contains a module on "Indigenous Knowledge and Sustainability"[67] and another unit titled "Cultures and Religions of the World."[68]

In summary, a *cura personalis* approach to business education is geared toward developing the sort of globally responsible consciousness that inspires sustainable living.

CONCLUSION

The kind of management education needed for sustainability departs from old-school business skills underlying unsustainable expansionist and crisis-perpetuating phases of human culture. For the coming decade and beyond, business students need to be equipped with higher-order dispositions that are more conducive to creating wealth with different sorts of business enterprises than those which now dominate the economic landscape. Sustainable enterprises will be based on more stable, more humanely enlightened foundations than on egoistic individualism, greed, short-termism, and toxic technologies, all of which take more than they give back. Business education for our future world requires

---

65. Thomas Donaldson and Thomas Dunfee, *Ties That Bind: A Social Contracts Approach to Business Ethics* (Cambridge, Mass.: Harvard Business School Press, 1999), 49–81.

66. Anne Colby and William Damon, *Some Do Care* (New York: Macmillan, 1992); Laurent Daloz, *Common Fire: Lives of Commitment in a Complex World* (Boston: Beacon Press, 1996).

67. http://www.unesco.org/education/tlsf/mods/theme_c/mod11.html.

68. http://www.unesco.org/education/tlsf/mods/theme_c/mod10.html.

courage and wisdom to supply leadership for the long run grounded in a clear vision of where we stand relative to larger cycles and trends.

In contrast to traditional orientations in business education, which focus narrowly on an inward look into established disciplines, and on specific techniques, a *cura personalis* orientation will look beyond these disciplines, seeking ways to question, engage, and transform our business students' world—our shared, complex, and deeply imperiled world— into a lasting and better one.

Bibliography

Abrams, Burton, and Mark Schmitz. "The Crowding Out Effect of Government Transfers on Private Charitable Contributions." *Public Choice* 33 (1978): 29–39.

Agle, Bradley R., Thomas Donaldson, R. Edward Freeman, Michael C. Jensen, Ronald K. Mitchell, and Donna J. Wood. "Dialogue: Toward Superior Stakeholder Theory." *Business Ethics Quarterly* 18, no. 2 (2008): 153–90.

Albert, Michel. *Capitalism against Capitalism*. London: Whurr, 1993.

Alibert, Jacques. *Les triangles d'or d'une société catholique: Louis de Bonald théoricien de la Contre-Révolution*. Paris: Pierre Téqui, 2002.

Allen, Tammy D. "Family-Supportive Work Environments: The Role of Organizational Perceptions." *Journal of Vocational Behavior* 58, no. 3 (2001): 414–35.

Amba-Rao, Sita C. "Multinational Corporate Social Responsibility, Ethics, Interactions and Third World Governments: An Agenda for the 1990s." *Journal of Business Ethics* 12, no. 7 (July 1993): 553–72.

Ambrose. *De officiis*. Edited by Ivor J. Davidson. Oxford: Oxford University Press, 2001.

American Philosophical Association. "Critical Thinking: A Statement of Expert Consensus for Purposes of Educational Assessment and Instruction." In *The Delphi Report: Research Findings and Recommendations Prepared for the Committee on Pre-College Philosophy*. Millbrae: California Academic Press, 1990.

Anders, George. "Business Schools Forgetting Missions?" *Wall Street Journal*, September 26, 2007.

Anderson, John R. *Rules of the Mind*. Hillsdale, N.J.: Erlbaum, 1993.

Annas, Julia. *The Morality of Happiness*. Oxford: Oxford University Press, 1995.

Anzenbacher, Arno. *Christliche Sozialethik*. Paderborn: Schöningh, 1997.

Aquinas, Thomas. "De Caritate." In *Quaestiones Disputatae (Disputed Questions on Charity)*, volume II, edited by Pio M. Bazzi, 753–91. Turin: Marietti, 1964–1965.

———. *On Kingship to the King of Cyprus*. Translated by Gerald B. Phelan. Toronto: Pontifical Institute of Mediaeval Studies, 1949. (Original: *De regno ad regem Cypri*. Textum Taurini 1954, edited by R. Busa. Digital rev. ed. by E. Alarcón. Lib. 1, cap. 4, par. 69927. http://www.corpusthomisticum.org/orp.html#69959.

———. *Summa Theologica, 5 Volumes*. Translated by the Fathers of the English Dominican Province. New York: Benzinger Brothers, 1948.

Aranzadi, Javier. *Liberalism against Liberalism*. London: Routledge, 2006.

———. "The Possibilities of the Acting Person within an Institutional Framework: Goods, Norms, and Virtues." *Journal of Business Ethics* 99, no. 1 (2011): 87–100.

———. "The Natural Link between Virtue Ethics and Political Virtue: The Morality of the Market." *Journal of Business Ethics* 118 (2013): 487–96.

Argandoña, Antonio. "Integrating Ethics into Action Theory and Organizational Theory." *Journal of Business Ethics* 78 (2007): 435–46.

———. "Las Virtudes en una Teoría de la Acción Humana." DI-880. IESE Business School, 2010.

Aristotle. "Metaphysics." In *The Complete Works of Aristotle, Volume 2.* The Revised Oxford Translation, edited by Jonathan Barnes. Princeton, N.J.: Princeton University Press, 1984.

———. "Nicomachean Ethics." In *The Complete Works of Aristotle, Volume 2.* The Revised Oxford Translation, edited by Jonathan Barnes. Princeton, N.J.: Princeton University Press, 1984.

———. "Politics." In *The Complete Works of Aristotle, Volume 2.* The Revised Oxford Translation, edited by Jonathan Barnes. Princeton, N.J.: Princeton University Press, 1984.

Aron, Leon. *Roads to the Temple: Truth, Memory, Ideas, and Ideals in the Making of the Russian Revolution 1987–1991.* New Haven, Conn.: Yale University Press, 2012.

Arthur, Michelle M., and Alison Cook. "Taking Stock of Work-Family Initiatives: How Announcements of Family-Friendly Human Resource Decisions Affect Shareholder Value." *Industrial and Labor Relations Review* 57, no. 4 (2004): 599–613.

Artigas, Mariano. *The Mind of the Universe: Understanding Science and Religion.* Philadelphia: Templeton Foundation Press, 2000.

Augustine of Hippo. *The City of God*, Books 8–16. Translated by Gerald G. Walsh and G. Monahan. Washington, D.C.: The Catholic University of America Press, 1952.

Avery, Christopher, Judith A. Chevalier, and Scott Schaefer. "Why Do Managers Undertake Acquisitions? An Analysis of Internal and External Rewards for Acquisitiveness." *Journal of Law, Economics and Organization* 14, no. 1 (1998): 24–43.

Axelrod, Robert. *The Evolution of Cooperation.* New York: Basic Books, 1984.

B Lab. *2014 B Corporation Annual Report.* http://www.bcorporation.net.

———. "Form Follows Function: Benefit Corporation Laws Passed in Seven States." http://www.bcorporation.net.

Bailyn, Lotte. "Involvement and Accommodation in Technical Careers: An Inquiry into the Relation to Work at Mid-Career." In *Organizational Careers*, edited by J. van Maanen, 109–32. London: Wiley International, 1976.

Bailyn, Lotte, and Edgar Scheln. "Life/Career Considerations as Indicators of Quality of Employment." In *Measuring Work Quality for Social Reporting*, edited by Albert D. Biderman and Thomas F. Drury, 151–68. Newbury Park, Calif.: Sage, 1976.

Baker, Bruce. "Human Dignity and the Logic of *Caritas*: The Source and Direction of Economic Justice." *Verbum Incarnatum: An Academic Journal of Social Justice* 5, no. 1 (2012): 1–22.

Barnett, Rosalind C., and Robert T. Brennan. "Change in Job Conditions, Change in Psychological Distress and Gender: A Longitudinal Study of Dual-Earner Couples." *Journal of Organizational Behavior* 18 (1997): 253–74.

Basu, Kaushik. *Beyond the Invisible Hand: Groundwork for a New Economics*. Princeton, N.J.: Princeton University Press, 2011.

Baumol, William J. "Entrepreneurship in Economic Theory." *American Economic Review: Papers and Proceedings* 58 (1968): 64–71.

———. "Formal Entrepreneurship Theory in Economics: Existence and Bounds." *Journal of Business Venturing* 8 (1993): 197–210.

———. *Entrepreneurship, Management, and the Structure of Payoffs*. Cambridge, Mass.: MIT Press, 1996.

Bayertz, Kurt. "Begriff und Problem der Solidarität." In *Solidarität: Begriff und Problem*, edited by Kurt Bayertz, 11–53. Frankfurt am Main: Suhrkamp, 1998.

Bazzichi, Oreste. *Dall'usura al giusto profitto: L'etica economica della Scuola francescana*. Torino: Effatà Editrice, 2008.

Becchetti, Leonardo, Alessandra Pelloni, and Fiammetta Rossetti. "Relational Goods, Sociability, and Happiness." *Kyklos* 61 (2008): 343–63.

Becker, Gary S. *A Treatise on the Family*. Cambridge, Mass.: Harvard University Press, 1991.

Behson, Scott J. "Coping with Family-to-Work Conflict: The Role of Informal Work Accommodations to Family." *Journal of Occupational Health Psychology* 7, no. 4 (2002): 324–41.

———. "Which Dominates? The Relative Importance of Work-Family Organizational Support and General Organizational Context on Employee Outcomes." *Journal of Vocational Behavior* 61, no. 1 (2002): 53–72.

Bellah, Robert N., and Hans Joas, eds. *The Axial Age and Its Consequences*. Cambridge, Mass.: The Belknap Press of Harvard University, 2012.

Benedict XVI. *Address of His Holiness Benedict XVI to the Roman Curia Offering them His Christmas Greetings*. Vatican City, December 22, 2005. http://w2.vatican.va/content/benedict-xvi/en/speeches/2005/december/documents/hf_ben_xvi_spe_20051222_roman-curia.html.

———. Encyclical *Deus Caritas Est*. Vatican City: Libreria Editrice Vaticana, 2005.

———. "Faith, Reason and the University: Memories and Reflections." Lecture addressed to representative of science at the Aula Magna of the University of Regensburg, September 12, 2006. http://www.vatican.va/holy_father/benedict_xvi/speeches/2006/september/documents/hf_ben-xvi_spe_20060912_university-regensburg_en.html.

———. Encyclical *Spe Salvi*. Vatican City: Liberia Editrice Vaticana, 2007.

———. *Address of His Holiness Benedict XVI to the Participants in the 14th Session of the Pontifical Academy of Social Sciences*. Vatican City, May 3, 2008. http://w2.vatican.va/content/benedict-xvi/en/speeches/2008/may/documents/hf_ben-xvi_spe_20080503_social-sciences.html.

———. Encyclical *Caritas in Veritate*. Vatican City: Libreria Editrice Vaticana, 2009.

———. *Angelus message*. November, 14, 2010. http://w2.vatican.va/content/benedict-xvi/en/angelus/2010/documents/hf_ben-xvi_ang_20101114.html.

———. *Address to the German Bundestag*. September 22, 2011. http://w2.vatican.va/content/benedict-xvi/en/speeches/2011/september/documents/hf_ben-xvi_spe_20110922_reichstag-berlin.html.

Bentham, Jeremy. *An Introduction to the Principles of Morals and Legislation*. Oxford: Clarendon Press, 1907 [1789].

Berlin, Isaiah. *Four Essays on Liberty*. Oxford: Oxford University Press, 1969.

Bhagwati, Jagdish. "Markets and Morality." *American Economic Review: Papers and Proceedings* 101, no. 3 (2011): 162–65.

Billis, David, ed. *Hybrid Organizations and the Third Sector*. Basingstoke: Palgrave Macmillan, 2010.

Binmore, Ken. *Natural Justice*. Oxford: Oxford University Press, 2005.

Binswanger, Harry. "Philosophy, the Ultimate CEO." In *Why Businessmen Need Philosophy: The Capitalist's Guide to the Ideas behind Ayn Rand's Atlas Shrugged*. Rev. and expanded ed., edited by Debi Ghate and Richard Ralston, 19–34. New York: New American Library, 2011.

Birch, Charles. "Whitehead and Science Education." In *Process, Epistemology and Education: Recent Work in Educational Process Philosophy*, edited by Garth Benson and Bryant Griffith, 33–41. Toronto: Canadian Scholars' Press, 1998.

Black, Max. "The Gap between 'Is' and 'Should.'" *The Philosophical Review* 73, no. 2 (1964): 165–81.

Blank, Rebecca M., and William McGurn. *Is the Market Moral? A Dialogue on Religion, Economics, and Justice*. Washington, D.C.: Brookings Institution Press, 2004.

Boatright, John. *Ethics in Finance*. Wiley-Blackwell, 1999.

Böckenförde, Ernst-Wolfgang. "Die Entstehung des Staates als Vorgang der Säkularisation." In *Säkularisation und Utopie*, edited by Ernst Forsthoff, 75–94. Stuttgart: Kohlhammer, 1967.

Bollier, David. *The Promise and Peril of Big Data*. Washington, D.C.: Aspen Institute, 2010. http://www.aspeninstitute.org/publications/promise-peril-big-data.

Botsman, Rachel, and Roo Rogers. *What's Mine Is Yours: The Rise of Collaborative Consumption*. New York: HarperBusiness, 2010.

Boulding, Kenneth E. *The Economy of Love and Fear*. Belmont: Wadsworth, 1973.

Bowen, Howard R. *Social Responsibilities of the Businessman*. New York: Harper, 1953.

Braudel, Fernand. *Civilization and Capitalism: 15th–18th Century.* Vol. 2: *The Wheels of Commerce.* New York: Harper and Row, 1982.

Brenkert, George G. "Innovation: Rule Breaking and the Ethics of Entrepreneurship." *Journal of Business Venturing* 24, no. 5 (2009): 448–64.

Brock, H. Woody. *American Gridlock: Why the Right and Left Are Both Wrong.* Hoboken, N.J.: John Wiley and Sons, 2012.

Brooks, Arthur. *Who Really Cares: The Surprising Truth About Compassionate Conservatism.* New York: Basic Books, 2006.

———. *The Road to Freedom: How to Win the Fight for Free Enterprise.* New York: Basic Books, 2012.

Brough, Paula, and Thomas J. Kalliath. "Work-Family Balance: Theoretical and Empirical Advancements." *Journal of Organizational Behavior* 30, no. 5 (2009): 581–85.

Bruehl, Charles P. *The Pope's Plan for Social Reconstruction: A Commentary on the Social Encyclicals of Pius XI.* New York: The Devin-Adair Co., 1939.

Brunkhorst, Hauke. *Solidarity: From Civic Friendship to a Global Legal Community (Studies in Contemporary German Social Thought).* Cambridge, Mass.: MIT Press, 2005.

Bruni, Luigino. *Reciprocity, Altruism and the Civil Society.* Abingdon: Routledge, 2008.

Bruni, Luigino, and Amelia Uelmen. "Religious Values and Corporate Decision Making: The Economy of Communion Project." *Fordham Journal of Corporate and Financial Law* 11 (2006): 645–80.

Bruni, Luigino, and Stefano Zamagni. *Civil Economy: Efficiency, Equity, Public Happiness.* Oxford: Peter Lang, 2007.

———, eds. *Dizionario di economia civile.* Roma: Città Nuova, 2009.

Buttiglione, Rocco. *Karol Wojtyla: The Thought of the Man Who Became Pope John Paul II.* Grand Rapids, Mich.: Eerdmans, 1997.

Calhoun, Cheshire. "Emotion, Feeling, and Knowledge of the World." In *Thinking about Feeling: Contemporary Philosophers on Emotions,* edited by R. C. Solomon, 107–21. New York: Oxford University Press, 2004.

Calhoun, Craig, Mark Juergensmeyer, and Jonathan Van Antwerpen, eds. *Rethinking Secularism.* Oxford: Oxford University Press, 2011.

Cambón, Enrique. *Trinità modello sociale.* Rome: Città Nuova, 1999.

Capaldi, Nicholas. "The Ethical Foundations of Free Market Societies." *The Journal of Private Enterprise* 20, no. 1 (2004): 30–54.

Capra, Fritjof. *The Web of Life: A New Synthesis of Mind and Matter.* London: Flamingo, 1997.

Carlson, Dawn S. "Personality and Role Variables as Predictors of Three Forms of Work-Family Conflict." *Journal of Vocational Behavior* 55 (1999): 236–53.

Carlson, Dawn S., and Pamela L. Perrew. "The Role of Social Support in the Stressor-Strain Relationship: An Examination of Work-Family Conflict." *Journal of Management* 25, no. 4 (1999): 513–40.

Carroll, Archie B. "A Three-Dimensional Conceptual Model of Corporate Performance." *Academy of Management Review* 4 (1979): 497–505.

———. "A History of Corporate Social Responsibility: Concepts and Practices." In *The Oxford Handbook of Corporate Social Responsibility*, edited by Andrew Crane, Abagail McWilliams, Dirk Matten, Jeremy Moon, and Donald S. Siegel, 19–46. New York: Oxford University Press, 2008.

Casanova, José. *Public Religions in the Modern World*. Chicago: University of Chicago Press, 1994.

———. "The Secular, Secularizations, Secularisms." In *Rethinking Secularism*, edited by Craig Calhoun, Mark Juergensmeyer, and Jonathan Van Antwerpen, 54–74. Oxford: Oxford University Press, 2011.

Casson, Mark. *The Entrepreneur*. Totowa, N.J.: Barnes and Noble Books, 1982.

Catechism of the Catholic Church. Vatican City: Libreria Editrice Vaticana, 1992 (English Version: New York: Image Doubleday, 1994).

Chafuen, Alejandro A. "Austrian Economics and the Social Doctrine of the Church: A Reflection Based on the Economic Writings of Mateo Liberatore and Oswald von Nell-Breuning." *Journal des Economistes et des Etudes Humaines* 13, no. 2 (2003): 247–68.

Chinchilla, Nuria, and Elizabeth Torres. "Why Become a Family-Responsible Employer?" In *Occasional Paper No 06/3*. Barcelona: International Center Work Family, IESE Business School, University of Navarra, 2006.

Clark, John, and Aaron Wildavsky. *The Moral Collapse of Communism: Poland as a Cautionary Tale*. San Francisco: Institute for Contemporary Studies, 1990.

Colby, Anne, and William Damon. *Some Do Care*. New York: Macmillan, 1992.

Coleman, James S. "Social Capital in the Creation of Human Capital." *American Journal of Sociology* 94 (1988): 95–120.

Cooke, Jacob E., ed. *The Federalist*. Middletown, Conn.: Wesleyan University Press, 1961.

Cook-Greuter, Susanne R. "Maps for Living: Ego-Development Stages from Symbiosis to Conscious Universal Embeddedness." In *Adult Development*, Vol. 2: *Models and Methods in the Study of Adolescent and Adult Thought*, edited by Michael L. Commons, Cheryl Armon, Lawrence Kohlberg, Francis A. Richards, Tina A. Grotzer, and Jan D. Sinnott, 79–104. New York: Praeger, 1990.

Corning, Peter A. "Spencer and Durkheim." *The British Journal of Sociology* 33 (1982): 359–82.

Cotrugli, Benedetto. *Il libro dell'arte di mercatura*. Venice: Arsenale Editrice, 1990.

Courtois, Stéphane, Nicolas Werth, Jean-Louis Panne, Andrzej Paczkowski, Karel Bartošek, and Jean-Louis Margolin, eds. *The Black Book of Communism*. Cambridge, Mass.: Harvard University Press, 1999.

Cox, Harvey. "Market as God: Living in the New Dispensation." *The Atlantic Monthly* 203, no. 3 (March 1999): 18–23.

Crane, Andrew, and Dirk Matten. *Business Ethics: Managing Corporate Citizenship and Sustainability in the Age of Globalization.* Oxford: Oxford University Press, 2010.

Credit Union National Association. "CUNA Survey: 40k Members, $80m in Savings on BTD." http://www.cuna.org.

Crisp, Roger, and Michael Slote, eds. *Virtue Ethics.* Oxford: Oxford University Press, 1997.

Cropanzano, Russell, Zinta S. Byrne, D. Ramona Bobocel, and Deborah E. Rupp. "Moral Virtues, Fairness Heuristics, Social Entities, and Other Denizens of Organizational Justice." *Journal of Vocational Behavior* 58, no. 2 (2001): 164–209.

Csikszentmihalyi, Mihaly. *Creativity: Flow and the Psychology of Discovery and Invention.* New York: HarperCollins Publishers, 1996.

Daloz Parks, Laurent A., Cheryl H. Keen, James P. Keen, and Sharon Daloz Parks. *Common Fire: Lives of Commitment in a Complex World.* Boston: Beacon Press, 1996.

Dalton, Dan R., and Debra Mesch. "The Impact of Flexible Scheduling on Employee Attendance and Turnover." *Administrative Science Quarterly* 35 (1990): 370–87.

Davis, John B. *The Theory of the Individual in Economics.* London: Routledge, 2003.

Davis, Keith. "Can Business Afford to Ignore Social Responsibilities?" *California Management Review* 2 (1960): 70–76.

Davis, Peter. "Co-operative Management as a Catholic Vocation." In *Business Education and Training: A Value Laden Process.* Vol. 4, edited by S. M. Natale, 157–80. Washington, D.C.: University Press of America, 2000.

DeBerri, Edward, James E. Hug, Peter J. Henriot, and Michael J. Schultheis. *Catholic Social Teaching: Our Best Kept Secret.* Maryknoll, N.Y.: Orbis Books and the Center of Concern, 2003.

Dennett, Daniel. *Darwin's Dangerous Idea.* New York: Simon and Schuster, 1995.

Dew, Nicholas, S. Ramakrishna Velamuri, and Sankaran Venkataraman. "Dispersed Knowledge and an Entrepreneurial Theory of the Firm." *Journal of Business Venturing* 19 (2004): 659–79.

Dickens, Charles. *A Christmas Carol.* London: Chapman and Hall, 1843.

Dirksen, Cletus F. "The Catholic Philosopher and the Catholic Economist." *Review of Social Economy* 4, no. 1 (1946): 14–20.

Dobson, John. "Alasdair Macintyre's Aristotelian Business Ethics: A Critique." *Journal of Business Ethics* 86 (2009): 43–50.

Dodgson, Mark. "An Enterprising Concern." *The Australian,* August 25, 2010.

Donaldson, Thomas, and R. Edward Freeman, eds. *Business As a Humanity.* New York: Oxford University Press, 1994.

Donaldson, Thomas, and Lee E. Preston. "The Stakeholder Theory of the Corporation: Concepts, Evidence and Implications." *Academy of Management Review* 20, no. 1 (1995): 65–91.

Donaldson, Thomas, and Thomas Dunfee. *Ties That Bind: A Social Contracts Approach to Business Ethics.* Cambridge, Mass.: Harvard Business School Press, 1999.

Donati, Pierpaolo. *La matrice teologica della società*. Soveria Mannelli: Rubbettino, 2010.

———. *Relational Sociology: A New Paradigm for the Social Sciences*. London: Routledge, 2010.

Donati, Pierpaolo, and Riccardo Solci. *I beni relazionali*. Turin: Bollati Boringhieri, 2011.

Douthat, Ross. *Bad Religion: How We Became a Nation of Heretics*. New York: Free Press, 2012.

Driver, Julia. "The History of Utilitarianism." In *The Stanford Encyclopedia of Philosophy*, edited by E. N. Zalta, 2009. *http://plato.stanford.edu/archives/sum2009/entries/* utilitarianism-history/.

Drucker, Peter. *El gran poder de las pequeñas ideas*. Buenos Aires: Editorial Sudamericana, 1998.

Duns Scotus, John. *Political and Economic Philosophy*. Translated by Allan B. Wolter. St. Bonaventure, N.Y.: The Franciscan Institute, 2001.

Durkheim, Émile. *De la division du travail sociale*. Paris: Presses Universitaires de France, 1893.

———. *Les formes élémentaires de la vie religieuse*. Paris: F. Alcan, 1912.

Duxbury, Linda E., and Christopher A. Higgins. "Gender Differences in Work-Family Conflict." *Journal of Applied Psychology* 76, no. 1 (1991): 60–74.

Duxbury, Linda E., Christopher A. Higgins, and Catherine Lee. "An Examination of Organizational and Individual Outcomes." *Optimum* 23, no. 2 (1992): 46–59.

Ebert, Thomas. *Soziale Gerechtigkeit: Ideen—Geschichte—Kontroversen*. Bonn: Bundeszentrale für politische Bildung, 2010.

EC. "Commission Recommendation of 6 May 2003 Concerning the Definition of Micro, Small and Medium-Sized Enterprises." *Official Journal of the European Union* L, no. 124 (2003): 36–41.

Edsall, Thomas B. "Separate and Unequal." *New York Times*, August 5, 2012.

Elkington, John. *Cannibals with Forks: The Triple Bottom Line of 21st-Century Business*. Oxford: Capstone Publishing, 1997.

Emirbayer, Mustafa. "Manifesto for a Relational Sociology." *American Journal of Sociology* 103, no. 2 (1997): 281–317.

Engels, Frederick. "Review of Karl Marx's *Contribution to the Critique of Political Economy*." In *Ludwig Feuerbach and the Outcome of Classical German Philosophy*, edited by Frederick Engels, 70–81. New York: International Publishers, 1941.

———. *Socialism: Utopian and Scientific*. New York: International Publishers, 1969 [1892].

———. "Preface." In Karl Marx's *The Poverty of Philosophy*, 9–28. New York: International Publishers, 1992 [1847].

Engels, Frederick, and Karl Marx. *The Holy Family or Critique of Critical Criticism: Against Bruno Bauer and Company*. Moscow: Progress, 1975 [1844].

Escrivá, Josemaría. *Conversations with Monsignor Escrivá de Balaguer*. Dublin: Ecclesia Press 1972 [1968].

Etzioni, Amitai. "Entrepreneurship: Adaptation and Legitimation." *Journal of Economic Behavior and Organization* 8 (1987): 175–89.

———. *The New Golden Rule: Community and Morality in a Democratic Society*. New York: Basic Books, 1996.

European Union. *Council Regulation No. 1435/2003 on the Statute for the European Cooperative Society*. Brussels, July 22, 2003.

———. *Treaty on the Functioning of the European Union*. Brussels, March 30, 2010.

Feigl, Herbert, and May Brodbeck, eds. *Readings in the Philosophy of Science*. New York: Appleton-Century-Crofts, 1953.

Ferree, William. *The Act of Social Justice: An Analysis of the Thomistic Concept of Legal Justice, with Special Reference to the Doctrine of Social Justice Proposed by His Holiness Pope Pius XI in His Encyclicals "Quadragesimo Anno" and "Divini Redemptoris," to Determine the Precise Nature of the Act of This Virtue*. Washington, D.C.: The Catholic University of America Press, 1942.

Feser, Edward. *The Last Superstition: A Refutation of the New Atheism*. South Bend, Ind.: St. Augustine's Press, 2008.

Fisman, Ray, and Adam Galinsky. "Training the Liars and Cheaters of Tomorrow." *Slate Magazine*, September 4, 2012.

Flynn, Patrice. "Global Capitalism: 21st-Century Style." Keynote address at the Praxis Peace Institute's Alchemy of Peacebuilding Conference. Dubrovnik, Croatia, June 10, 2002.

———. "Microfinance: The Newest Financial Technology of the Washington Consensus." *Challenge: The Magazine of Economic Affairs* 50, no. 2 (2007): 1–9.

———. "The Salvadoran Indigo Dye and Sewing Cooperative: A Model of Economic Success and Women's Empowerment." *Salvadoran Enterprises for Women News* 8, no. 1 (April 2011): 2–4.

Frankl, Viktor E. *Man's Search for Meaning*. Boston: Beacon Press, 1962.

Frederick, William C. "The Growing Concern over Business Responsibility." *California Management Review* 2, no. 4 (1960): 54–61.

Freeman, R. Edward. *Strategic Management: A Stakeholder Approach*. Boston: Pitman Publishing, 1984.

———. "The Politics of Stakeholder Theory: Some Future Directions." *Business Ethics Quarterly* 4, no. 4 (1994): 409–21.

———. "Business Ethics at the Millennium." *Business Ethics Quarterly* 10, no. 1 (2000): 169–80.

———. "Managing for Stakeholders: Trade-Offs or Value Creation." *Journal of Business Ethics* 96, no. 1 (2010): 7–9.

Freeman, R. Edward, and David Newkirk. "Business as a Human Enterprise: Implications for Education." In *Rethinking Business Management*, edited by Samuel Gregg and James Stoner, 139–43. Princeton, N.J.: ISI, 2008.

Fremantle, Anne. *The Papal Encyclicals in Their Historical Context*. New York: New American Library, 1956.

Friedman, Milton. *Capitalism and Freedom*. Chicago: University of Chicago Press, 1962.

———. "The Social Responsibility of Business Is to Increase Its Profits." *New York Times Magazine*, September 13, 1970.

Furet, Francois. *The Passing of an Illusion: The Idea of Communism in the 20th Century*. Chicago: University of Chicago Press, 1999.

Gardberg, Naomi A., and Charles J. Fombrun. "Corporate Citizenship: Creating Intangible Assets across Institutional Environments." *Academy of Management Review* 31, no. 2 (2006): 329–46.

Garriga, Elisabet, and Domènec Melé. "Corporate Social Responsibility Theories: Mapping the Territory." *Journal of Business Ethics* 53, no. 1/2 (2004): 51–71.

Geach, Peter T. *The Virtues*. Cambridge: Cambridge University Press, 1977.

Ghoshal, Sumantra. "Bad Management Theories are Destroying Good Management Practices." *Academy of Management Learning and Education* 4, no. 1 (2005): 75–91.

Ghoshal, Sumantra, and Christopher Bartlett. *The Individualized Corporation: A Fundamentally New Approach to Management*. New York: HarperCollins Publishers, 1997.

Ghoshal, Sumantra, Christopher Bartlett, and Peter Moran. "A New Manifesto for Management." *Sloan Management Review* 43, no. 9 (1999): 9–20.

Gilbert, Jay Coen. "On Better Business." Presented at TED X. Philadelphia, December 1, 2010.

Gilkey, Langdon. *Nature, Reality and the Sacred: The Nexus of Science and Religion*. Minneapolis: Fortress Press, 1993.

Glasser, Harold. "Learning Our Way to a Sustainable and Desirable World: Ideas Inspired by Arne Naess and Deep Ecology." In *Higher Education and the Challenge of Sustainability: Problematics, Promise and Practice*, edited by Peter B. Corcoran and Arejen E. J. Wals, 131–48. Dordrecht: Kluwer, 2004.

Gold, Lorna. *New Financial Horizons: The Emergence of an Economy of Communion*. Hyde Park, N.Y.: New City Press, 2010.

Goodstein, Jerry D. "Institutional Pressures and Strategic Responsiveness: Employer Involvement in Work-Family Issues." *Academy of Management Journal* 37, no. 2 (1994): 350–82.

Gouldner, Alvin W. *The Two Marxisms: Contradictions and Anomalies in the Development of Theory*. New York: Seabury Press, 1980.

Grassl, Wolfgang. "Cooperative Marketing: Efficiency Conditions for Alliances." In *Canada/Caribbean Business: Opportunities and Challenges for Management*, edited by

T. Brunton and T. Lituchy, 87–101. Port-of-Spain: University of the West Indies Press, 1998.

———. "L'entreprise européenne—inéxistante, moribonde, ou modèle pour l'exportation?" *Géoéconomie* 28 (2003): 153–80.

———. "Business Models of Social Enterprise: A Design Approach to Hybridity." *ACRN Journal of Entrepreneurship Perspectives* 1, no. 1 (2012): 37–60.

———. "Ekonomia obywatelska: Trynitarny klucz do odczytania ekonomii papieskiej." *Pressje* 29 (2012): 58–82.

———. "Hybrid Forms of Business: The Logic of Gift in the Commercial World." *Journal of Business Ethics* 100 Suppl. 1 (2012): 109–23.

———. "Pluris Valere: Towards Trinitarian Rationality in Social Life." In *The Whole Breadth of Reason: Rethinking Economics and Politics*, edited by Simona Beretta and Mario Maggioni, 313–48. Venice: Marcianum Press, 2012.

———. "Integral Human Development in Analytical Perspective: A Trinitarian Model." *Journal of Markets and Morality* 16, no. 1 (Spring 2013): 135–55.

Grassl, Wolfgang, and André Habisch. "Ethics and Economics: Towards a New Humanistic Synthesis for Business." *Journal of Business Ethics* 99, no. 1 (2011): 37–49.

Greenspan, Alan. "The Crisis." *Brookings Papers on Economic Activity* (Spring 2010): 201–46.

Gregg, Samuel. *The Commercial Society: Foundations and Challenges in a Global Age.* Lanham, Md.: Lexington Books, 2007.

Gregory, Brad S. *The Unintended Reformation: How a Religious Revolution Secularized Society.* Cambridge, Mass.: Harvard University Press, 2012.

Griffiths, Brian, and Kim Tan. *Fighting Poverty through Enterprise: The Case for Social Venture Capital.* Guildford: Transformational Business Network, 2009.

Grover, Steven L., and Karen J. Crooker. "Who Appreciates Family-Responsive Human Resource Policies: The Impact of Family-Friendly Policies on the Organizational Attachment of Parents and Non-Parents." *Personnel Psychology* 48 (1995): 271–87.

Grzywacz, Joseph G., and Nadine F. Marks. "Reconceptualizing the Work-Family Interface: An Ecological Perspective on the Correlates of Positive and Negative Spillover between Work and Family." *Journal of Occupational Health Psychology* 5 (2000): 111–26.

Guerry, Emile. *The Social Doctrine of the Catholic Church.* New York: Society of St. Paul, 1961.

Haakonssen, Knud. "Introduction: The Coherence of Smith's Thought." In *The Cambridge Companion to Adam Smith*, edited by Knud Haakonssen, 1–21. Cambridge: Cambridge University Press, 2006.

Halteman, James, and Edd Noell. *Reckoning with Markets: Moral Reflection in Economics.* New York: Oxford University Press, 2012.

Handy, Charles. "What's a Business For?" *Harvard Business Review* 80 (2002): 49–56.

Hanley, Ryan P. *Adam Smith and the Character of Virtue.* New York: Cambridge University Press, 2009.

Hannafey, Francis T. "Entrepreneurship and Ethics: A Literature Review." *Journal of Business Ethics* 46, no. 2 (2003): 99–110.

Harmeling, Susan S., Saras D. Sarasvathy, and R. Edward Freeman. "Related Debates in Ethics and Entrepreneurship: Values, Opportunities and Contingency." *Journal of Business Ethics* 84 (2009): 341–65.

Hartman, Edwin M. "Virtue, Profit, and the Separation Thesis: An Aristotelian View." *Journal of Business Ethics* 99, no. 1 (2011): 5–17.

Hausman, Daniel M., and Michael S. McPherson. "Taking Ethics Seriously: Economics and Contemporary Moral Philosophy." *Journal of Economic Literature* 31 (1993): 671–731.

Hayek, Friedrich August von. *The Constitution of Liberty: The Definitive Edition.* Chicago: University of Chicago Press, 1960.

———. "The Use of Knowledge in Society." In *Individualism and Economic Order by Friedrich A. Hayek*, 77–91. London: Routledge and Kegan Paul, 1976 [1945].

———. *The Fatal Conceit: The Errors of Socialism.* London: Routledge, 1988.

———. "The Pretense of Knowledge." Nobel lecture. *American Economic Review* (December 1989): 3–7.

———. *The Constitution of Liberty: The Definitive Edition.* Edited by Ronald Hamowy. Chicago: University of Chicago Press, 2011 [1960, 1996].

Hazard, Paul. *European Thought in the Eighteenth Century.* Translated by J. Lewis May. Harmondsworth: Penguin, 1965.

Hechter, Michael. *Principles of Group Solidarity.* Berkeley: University of California Press, 1987.

Heilbroner, Robert. *The Worldly Philosophers.* New York: Simon and Schuster, 1953.

Hewlett, Sylvia A., and Carolyn Buck Luce. "Off-Ramps and On-Ramps: Keeping Talented Women on the Road to Success." *Harvard Business Review* 83, no. 3 (2005): 43–54.

Hittinger, Russell. "Introduction to Modern Catholicism." In *The Teachings of Modern Roman Catholicism on Law, Politics, and Human Nature*, edited by John Witte Jr. and Frank S. Alexander, 1–38. New York: Columbia University Press 2007.

———. "The Coherence of the Four Basic Principles of Catholic Social Doctrine: An Interpretation." Keynote Address Pontifical Academy of Social Sciences, XVIII Plenary Session. In *Pursuing the Common Good*, edited by Margaret S. Archer and Pierpaolo Donati, Pontifical Academy of Social Sciences, *Acta* 14, 75–123. Vatican City, 2008.

Holland, Kelley. "Is It Time to Retrain B-Schools?" *New York Times*, March 15, 2009, BU1.

Hollander, Paul, ed. *From the Gulag to the Killing Fields*. Wilmington, Del.: Intercollegiate Studies Institute, 2006.

Husslein, Joseph. *The Christian Social Manifesto: An Interpretative Study of the Encyclicals "Rerum Novarum" and "Quadragesimo Anno" of Pope Leo XIII and Pope Pius XI*. Milwaukee: The Bruce Publishing Company, 1939.

Ims, Knut, and Ove Jakobsen. "Deep Authenticity—An Essential Phenomenon in the Web of Life." In *Business Ethics and Corporate Sustainability*, edited by Antonio Tencati and Francesco Perrini, 213–24. Northampton: Edward Elgar Publishing, 2011.

International Co-operative Alliance. "What is a Co-op?" http://www.ICA.coop/en.

International Co-operative Alliance and European Research Institute on Cooperative and Social Enterprise. *World Co-operative Monitor: Explorative Report*. Manchester, October 31, 2012.

———. *World Co-operative Monitor: Exploring the Co-operative Economy—Report 2014*. Québec City, October 2014.

Jackson, Kevin. "Towards Authenticity: A Sartrean Perspective on Business Ethics." *Journal of Business Ethics* 58, no. 4 (2005): 307–25.

———. "The Scandal beneath the Financial Crisis." *Harvard Journal of Law and Public Policy* 33, no. 2 (2010): 735–78.

———. *Virtuosity in Business*. Philadelphia: University of Pennsylvania Press, 2012.

Jaki, Stanley. *The Relevance of Physics*. Chicago: University of Chicago Press, 1966.

Jaspers, Karl. *Vom Ursprung und Ziel der Geschichte*. Frankfurt am Main: Fischer, 1957.

John Paul II. Encyclical *Redemptor Hominis*. Vatican City: Libreria Editrice Vaticana, 1979.

———. Encyclical *Laborem Exercens*. Vatican City: Libreria Editrice Vaticana, 1981.

———. Encyclical *Sollicitudo Rei Socialis*. Vatican City: Libreria Editrice Vaticana, 1987.

———. Encyclical *Centesimus Annus*. Vatican City: Libreria Editrice Vaticana, 1991.

———. "A Civilization of Solidarity and Love: An Invitation to *Centesimus Annus*." In *A New Worldly Order: John Paul II and Human Freedom*, edited by George Weigel, 23–28. Washington, D.C.: Ethics and Public Policy Center, 1992.

———. Encyclical *Veritatis Splendor*. Vatican City: Libreria Editrice Vaticana, 1993.

———. *Letter to Families*. Vatican City: Libreria Editrice Vaticana, 1994.

———. Encyclical *Fides et Ratio*. Vatican City: Libreria Editrice Vaticana, 1998.

John XXIII. Encyclical *Mater et Magistra*. Vatican City: Libreria Editrice Vaticana, 1961.

Jonas, Hans. *Il principio di responsabilità: un'etica per la civiltà tecnologica*. Translated by Pier Portinaro. Torino: Einaudi, 1990.

Jüngel, Eberhard. "*Extra Christum nulla salus*—A Principle of Natural Theology? Protestant Reflections on the 'Anonymity' of the Christian." In *Theological Essays*, edited by J. B. Webster, 173–88. Edinburgh: T and T Clark, 1989.

————. *God's Being Is in Becoming: The Trinitarian Being of God in the Theology of Karl Barth*. Edinburgh: T and T Clark, 2001.

Kaletsky, Anatole. *Capitalism 4.0: The Birth of a New Economy in the Aftermath of Crisis*. New York: PublicAffairs, 2010.

Kanter, Rosabeth M. *Work and Family in the United States: A Critical Review and Agenda for Research and Policy*. New York: Russell Sage Foundation, 1977.

————. *On the Frontiers of Management*. Boston: Harvard Business School Press, 1997.

Kerlin, Janelle A. "Social Enterprise in the United States and Europe." *Voluntas: International Journal of Voluntary and Nonprofit Organizations* 17, no. 3 (2006): 247–63.

Kersting, Wolfgang. *Theorien der sozialen Gerechtigkeit*. Stuttgart: Metzler, 2000.

Keynes, John Maynard. *The End of Laissez-Faire*. New York: Prometheus Books, 2004 [1926].

Khurana, Rakesh. *From Higher Aims to Hired Hands*. Princeton, N.J.: Princeton University Press, 2007.

Kingma, Bruce. "An Accurate Measurement of the Crowd-Out Effect, Income Effect and Price Effect for Charitable Contributions." *Journal of Political Economy* 97 (1989): 1197–1207.

Kirzner, Israel. *Competition and Entrepreneurship*. Chicago: University of Chicago Press, 1973.

————. *Perception, Opportunity and Profit*. Chicago: University of Chicago Press, 1979.

————. *The Driving Force of the Market*. London: Routledge, 2000.

Kleymann, Birgit, Hedley Malloch, Tom Redman, and Jacques Angot. "The Dynamics of a Variably Coupled Social System: The Case of Les Compagnons du Devoir." *Journal of Management Inquiry* 17 (2009): 381–96.

Knight, Frank. *Risk: Uncertainty and Profit*. New York: Augustus M. Kelly, 1921.

Kohler, Thomas. "Quadragesimo Anno." In *A Century of Catholic Social Thought: Essays on "Rerum Novarum" and Nine Other Key Documents*, edited by George Weigel and Robert Royal, 29–32. Washington, D.C.: Ethics and Public Policy Center, 1991.

Kohli, Martin. "Private and Public Transfers between Generations: Linking the Family and the State." *European Societies* 1 (1999): 81–104.

Kolakowski, Leszek. *Main Currents of Marxism*. Translated by P. S. Falla. New York: W. W. Norton and Company, 2005.

Kolm, Serge-Christophe. *Reciprocity: An Economics of Social Relations*. Cambridge: Cambridge University Press, 2008.

Konstantinov, Fedor V. *The Fundamentals of Marxist-Leninist Philosophy*. Translated by R. Daglish. Moscow: Progress Publishers, 1974.

Koslowski, Peter. *Ethics of Capitalism and Critique of Sociobiology*. Berlin: Springer Verlag. 1996.

Kossek, Ellen E., Jason A. Colquitt, and Raymond A. Noe. "Caregiving Decisions, Well-Being, and Performance: The Effects of Place and Provider as a Function of Dependent Type and Work-Family Climates." *Academy of Management Journal* 44 (2001): 29–44.

Kossek, Ellen E., and Cynthia Ozeki. "Work-Family Conflict, Policies and the Job-Life Satisfaction Relationship: A Review and Directions for Organizational Behavior–Human Resources Research." *Journal of Applied Psychology* 83, no. 2 (1998): 139–49.

Kossek, Ellen E., and Susan J. Lambert, eds. *Work and Life Integration: Organizational, Cultural, and Individual Perspectives.* Mahwah, N.J.: Lawrence Erlbaum Associates, 2005.

Künemund, Harald, and Martin Rein. "There Is More to Receiving than Needing: Theoretical Arguments and Empirical Explorations of Crowding In and Crowding Out." *Ageing and Society* 19 (1999): 93–121.

Künemund, Harald, and Claudia Vogel. "Öffentliche und private Transfers und Unterstützungsleistungen im Alter—'crowding out' oder 'crowding in'?" *Zeitschrift für Familienforschung* 18 (2006): 269–89.

Lambert, Susan J. "Added Benefits: The Link between Work-Life Benefits and Organizational Citizenship Behavior." *Academy of Management Journal* 43, no. 5 (2000): 801–15.

Langholm, Odd. *The Legacy of Scholasticism in Economic Thought: Antecedents of Choice and Power.* Cambridge: Cambridge University Press, 1998.

Larmore, Charles. *Patterns of Moral Complexity.* Cambridge: Cambridge University Press, 1987.

Leibestein, Harvey. "Entrepreneurship and Development." *American Economic Review* 58 (1968): 72–83.

Leo XIII. Encyclical *Aeterni Patris.* Rome: Acta Sanctae Sedis 12, 1879.

———. Encyclical *Rerum Novarum.* Rome: Acta Sanctae Sedis 23, 1891.

Lewis, Clive S. *Mere Christianity.* New York: Macmillan, 1943.

Lindblom, Charles E. *The Market System.* New Haven, Conn.: Yale University Press, 2001.

Louden, Robert B. "On Some Vices of Virtue Ethics." *American Philosophical Quarterly* 21 (1984): 227–36.

Lubac, Henri de. *The Drama of Atheist Humanism.* San Francisco: Ignatius, 1998 [1949].

Luhmann, Niklas. *Politische Theorie im Wohlfahrtsstaat.* München: Olzog, 1981.

———. *Die Moral der Gesellschaft.* Frankfurt am Main: Suhrkamp, 1988.

Machan, Tibor. "Entrepreneurship and Ethics." *International Journal of Social Economics* 26, no. 5 (1999): 596–606.

MacIntyre, Alasdair. *After Virtue: A Study in Moral Theory.* 2nd ed. Notre Dame, Ind.: University of Notre Dame Press, 1984.

Major, Debra A., Thomas D. Fletcher, Donald D. Davis, and Lisa M. Germano. "The Influence of Work-Family Culture and Workplace Relationships on Work Interference with Family: A Multilevel Model." *Journal of Organizational Behavior* 29, no. 7 (2008): 881–97.

Margalit, Avishai. *The Decent Society*. Cambridge, Mass.: Harvard University Press, 1996.

Marías, Julián. *Persona*. Madrid: Alianza Editorial, 1996.

Maritain, Jacques. *The Person and the Common Good*. Translated by John J. Fitzgerald. New York: Charles Scribner's Sons, 1947.

Marshall, Alfred. *Principles of Economics*. London: Macmillan, 1946 [1890].

Marx, Reinhard. *Das Kapital: Ein Plädoyer für den Menschen*. München: Pattloch, 2008.

Matten, Dirk, and Andrew Crane. "Corporate Citizenship: Toward an Extended Theoretical Conceptualization." *Academy of Management Review* 30, no. 1 (2005): 166–79.

Matten, Dirk, and Jeremy Moon. "'Implicit' and 'Explicit' CSR: A Conceptual Framework for a Comparative Understanding of Corporate Social Responsibility." *Academy of Management Review* 33, no. 2 (2008): 404–24.

Mauno, Saija. "Effects of Work-Family Culture on Employee Well-Being: Exploring Moderator Effects in a Longitudinal Sample." *European Journal of Work and Organizational Psychology* 19, no. 6 (2010): 675–95.

Mbarathi, Nduta. "Kenya: Poverty Eradication Goes Hi Tech with M-PESA." *The Africa Report*. http://www.theafricareport.com/News-Analysis/kenya-poverty -eradication-goes-hi-tech-with-m-pesa.html.

McDaniel, Charles A. Jr. "Theology of the "Real Economy": Christian Economic Ethics in an Age of Financialization." *Journal of Religion and Business Ethics* 2, no. 2 (2011): Article 1.

McWilliams, Abagail, and Donald Siegel. "Corporate Social Responsibility: A Theory of the Firm Perspective." *Academy of Management Review* 26, no. 1 (2001): 117–27.

Meeks, M. Douglas. *God the Economist: The Doctrine of God and Political Economy*. Minneapolis: Fortress Press, 1989.

Melé, Domènec. "The Challenge of Humanistic Management." *Journal of Business Ethics* 44 (2003): 77–88.

———. "Corporate Social Responsibility Theories." In *The Oxford Handbook of Corporate Social Responsibility*, edited by Andrew Crane, Abagail McWilliams, Dirk Matten, Jeremy Moon, and Donald S. Siegel, 47–82. New York: Oxford University Press, 2008.

———. "Editorial Introduction: Towards a More Humanistic Management." *Journal of Business Ethics* 88, no. 3 (2009): 413–16.

———. "Integrating Personalism into Virtue-Based Business Ethics: The Personalist and the Common Good Principles." *Journal of Business Ethics* 88, no. 1 (2009): 227–44.

Messner, Johannes. *Das Naturrecht: Handbuch der Gesellschaftsethik, Staatsethik und Wirtschaftsethik.* 6th ed. Berlin: Duncker and Humblot, 1984.

Michel, Virgil. *Christian Social Reconstruction: Some Fundamentals of the "Quadragesimo Anno."* Milwaukee: The Bruce Publishing Company, 1937.

Milbank, John. "The Real Third Way." In *The Crisis of Global Capitalism*, edited by Adrian Pabst, 27–70. Eugene, OR.: Cascade Books, 2011.

Mill, John Stuart. "Principles of Political Economy with Some of their Applications to Social Philosophy" [1848]. In *Collected Works of John Stuart Mill, Volume II–III*, edited by John M. Robson. Toronto: University of Toronto Press, 1963.

———. *Utilitarianism.* Peterborough, Canada: Broadview Press, 2010 [1861].

Miller, Vincent J. "Saving Subsidiarity." *America: The National Catholic Review*, July 30, 2012.

Mises, Ludwig von. *Human Action: A Treatise on Economics.* 4th rev. ed. Edited by Bettina B. Greaves. San Francisco: Fox and Wilkes, 1996.

Moore, Geoff. "On the Implications of the Practice-Institution Distinction MacIntyre and the Application of Modern Virtue Ethics to Business." *Business Ethics Quarterly* 12, no. 1 (2002): 19–32.

———. "Corporate Character: Modern Virtue Ethics and the Virtuous Corporation." *Business Ethics Quarterly* 15, no. 4 (2005): 659–85.

———. "Humanizing Business: A Modern Virtue Ethics Approach." *Business Ethics Quarterly* 15, no. 2 (2005): 237–55.

———. "Re-imagining the Morality of Management: A Modern Virtue Ethics Approach." *Business Ethics Quarterly* 18, no. 4 (2008): 483–511.

Moran, Peter, and Sumantra Ghoshal. "Markets, Firms and the Process of Economic Development." *Academy of Management Review* 24, no. 3 (1999): 390–412.

Moses Leff, Lisa. "Jewish Solidarity in Nineteenth-Century France: The Evolution of a Concept." *The Journal of Modern History* 74, no. 1 (March 2002): 33–61.

Muirhead, Sophia A., Charles J. Bennett, Ronald E. Berenbeim, Amy Kao, and David J. Vidal. "Corporate Citizenship in the New Century: Accountability, Transparency and Global Stakeholder Engagement." *New York: The Conference Board*, 2002.

Nakamoto, Michiyo, and David Wighton. "Citigroup Chief Stays Bullish on Buy-Outs." *Financial Times*, July 9, 2007.

Nell-Breuning, Oswald von. *Reorganization of Social Economy: The Social Encyclical Developed and Explained.* Translated by Bernard W. Dempsey. New York: The Bruce Publishing Company, 1936.

———. *Kapitalismus—kritisch betrachtet: Zur Auseinandersetzung um das bessere "System."* Freiburg: Herder, 1974.

————. "The Drafting of *Quadragesimo Anno*." In *Readings in Moral Theology, No 5*, edited by Charles Curran and Richard McCormick, 60–68. New York: Paulist Press, 1986.

————. *Baugesetze der Gesellschaft. Solidarität und Subsidiarität*. Freiburg: Herder, 1990.

————. "Die Kirche als Lebensprinzip der Menschlichen Gesellschaft." In *Den Kapitalismus Umbiegen: Schriften zu Kirche, Wirtschaft und Gesellschaft. Ein Lesebuch*, edited by Friedhelm Hengsbach, 405. Düsseldorf: Patmos, 1990.

Nelson, Richard, and Sydney Winter. *An Evolutionary Theory of Economic Change*. Cambridge, Mass.: Harvard University Press, 1982.

Nietzsche, Friedrich. *Twilight of the Idols* in *The Portable Nietzsche*. Translated and edited by Walter Kaufmann. New York: Viking, 1966.

Nisbet, Robert. *The Social Philosophers*. New York: Thomas Crowell, 1973.

Norman, Edward. *The Roman Catholic Church*. Berkeley: University of California Press, 2007.

North, Douglas. "Institutions." *Journal of Economic Perspectives* 5, no. 1 (1991): 97–112.

Nothelle-Wildfeuer, Ursula. "*Caritas in Veritate*: Globalisierung, Wirtschaft und Entwicklung." In *Der Theologenpapst. Eine kritische Würdigung Benedikts XVI*, edited by Jan-Heiner Tück, 83–96. Freiburg/Basel/Wien: Herder, 2013.

Nothelle-Wildfeuer, Ursula. "Die Sozialprinzipien der Katholischen Soziallehre." In *Handbuch der Katholischen Soziallehre*, edited by Anton Rauscher, Jörg Althammer, Wolfgang Bergsdorf, and Otto Depenheuer, 143–63. Berlin: Duncker and Humblot, 2008.

Novak, Michael. *The Spirit of Democratic Capitalism*. New York: Touchstone, 1982.

————. *Free Persons and the Common Good*. Lanham, Md.: Madison Books, 1989.

————. *The Catholic Ethic and the Spirit of Capitalism*. New York: Free Press, 1993.

————. *Business as a Calling: Work and the Examined Life*. New York: Free Press, 1996.

————. *Noi, voi e l'Islam. Lettera aperta all'Europa sulla libertà*. Roma: Liberal, 2005. (English original: *The Universal Hunger for Liberty: Why the Clash of Civilizations Is Not Inevitable*.)

Nussbaum, Martha. *Creating Capabilities: The Human Development Approach*. Cambridge, Mass.: The Belknap Press of Harvard University, 2011.

Nussbaum, Martha, and Amartya Sen, eds. *The Quality of Life*. Oxford: Clarendon Press, 1993.

O'Boyle, Edward J. "Requiem for *Homo Economicus*." *Journal of Markets and Morality* 10, no. 2 (Fall 2007): 321–37.

O'Connor, Daniel A. *Catholic Social Doctrine*. Westminster, Md.: The Newman Press, 1956.

O'Driscoll, Michael P., Steven Poelmans, Paul E. Spector, Thomas Kalliath, Tammy D. Allen, Carly L. Cooper, and Juan I. Sanchez. "Family-Responsive Interventions, Perceived Organizational and Supervisor Support, Work-Family Conflict, and Psychological Strain." *International Journal of Stress Management* 10, no. 4 (2003): 326–44.

O'Neill, John W., Michelle M. Harrison, Jeannette Cleveland, David Almeida, Robert Stawski, and Anne C. Crouter. "Work-Family Climate, Organizational Commitment, and Turnover: Multilevel Contagion Effects of Leaders." *Journal of Vocational Behavior* 74, no. 1 (2009): 18–29.

Orr, David. *Ecological Literacy: Education and the Transition to a Postmodern World*. Albany: State University of New York Press, 1992.

———. "Four Challenges of Sustainability." *Conservation Biology* 16, no. 6 (2002): 1457–60.

———. *Earth in Mind: On Education, Environment, and the Human Prospect*. Washington, D.C.: Island Press, 2004.

Ostrom, Elinor. "Beyond Markets and States: Polycentric Governance of Complex Economic Systems." *American Economic Review* 100, no. 3 (2010): 641–72.

Ostrom, Elinor, Roy Gardner, and James Walker. *Rules, Games and Common-Pool Resources*. Ann Arbor: University of Michigan Press, 1994.

Pabst, Adrian. *Metaphysics: The Creation of Hierarchy*. Grand Rapids, Mich.: Eerdmans, 2012.

Parker, Lauren, and Tammy D. Allen. "Work/Family Benefits: Variables Related to Employees' Fairness Perceptions." *Journal of Vocational Behavior* 58, no. 3 (2001): 453–68.

Paul VI. *Apostolic Letter Octogesima Adveniens*. Vatican City: Libreria Editrice Vaticana, 1971.

Paulhus, Normand J. "The Theological and Political Ideals of the Fribourg Union." PhD dissertation, Boston College, 1983.

Peart, Sandra, and David Levy. *Vanity of the Philosopher: From Equality to Hierarchy in Postclassical Economics*. Ann Arbor: University of Michigan Press, 2005.

Pesch, Heinrich. *Lehrbuch der Nationalökonomie*. Freiburg: Herder, 1905.

Phelan, Anne. "Rationalism, Complexity Science and Curriculum: A Cautionary Tale." *Complicity: An International Journal of Complexity and Education* 1, no. 1 (2004): 9–17.

Piedra, Alberto. *Natural Law: The Foundation of an Orderly Economic System*. Lanham, Md.: Lexington Books, 2004.

Pinckaers, Servais. *Les sources de la morale chrétienne*. Fribourg: University Press, 1985.

———. *The Sources of Christian Ethics*. Washington, D.C.: The Catholic University of America Press, 1995.

Pitman, Lynn. "Understanding the ULCAA: A Report from the University of Wisconsin Center for Cooperatives." *Cooperative Grocer Network* 151 (November–December 2010).

Pitt-Catsouphes, Marcie, and Ellen Bankert. "Conducting a Work/Life Workplace Assessment." *Compensation and Benefits Management* 14, no. 3 (1998): 11–18.

Pitt-Catsouphes, Marcie, and Bradley K. Googins. "Recasting the Work-Family Agenda as a Corporate Social Responsibility." In *Work and Life Integration: Organizational, Cultural and Individual Perspectives*, edited by Ellen E. Kossek and Susan J. Lambert, 469–90. Mahwah, N.J.: Lawrence Erlbaum, 2005.

Pius XI. Encyclical *Non Abbiamo Bisogno*. Vatican City: Libreria Editrice Vaticana, 1931.

———. Encyclical *Quadragesimo Anno*. Vatican City: Libreria Editrice Vaticana, 1931.

———. Encyclical *Divini Redemptoris*. Vatican City: Libreria Editrice Vaticana, 1937.

Plato. "Phaedrus." In *The Collected Dialogues of Plato, including the Letters*, edited by Edith Hamilton and Huntington Cairns, 475–525. Princeton, N.J.: Princeton University Press, 1994.

Polanyi, Karl. *The Great Transformation: The Political and Economic Origins of Our Time*. Boston: Beacon Press, 1944.

———. *The Livelihood of Man*. New York: Academic Press, 1977.

Pontifical Council for Justice and Peace. *Compendium of the Social Doctrine of the Church*. Vatican City: Libreria Editrice Vaticana, 2004.

Pope, Whitney, and Barclay D. Johnson. "Inside Organic Solidarity." *American Sociological Review* 48 (1983): 681–92.

Popper, Karl. *The Open Society and Its Enemies*. London: Routledge, 1966.

Porter, Jean. "The Virtue of Justice (IIa IIae, qq. 58–122)." In *The Ethics of Aquinas*, edited by Stephen J. Pope, 272–86. Washington, D.C.: Georgetown University Press, 2002.

Porter, Michael E. "What Is Strategy?" *Harvard Business Review* 74, no. 6 (1996): 61–78.

Porter, Michael E., and Mark R. Kramer. "Creating Shared Value: How to Reinvent Capitalism—and Unleash a Wave of Innovation and Growth." *Harvard Business Review* 89, no. 1/2 (2011): 62–77.

Posner, George. *Analyzing the Curriculum*. 3rd ed. Boston: McGraw-Hill, 2004.

Post, Stephen, and Jill Neimark. *Why Good Things Happen to Good People*. New York: Broadway Books, 2008.

Prahalad, Coimbatore K. *The Fortune at the Bottom of the Pyramid*. Philadelphia: Wharton School Publishing, 2009.

Pratt, Cornelius B. "Multinational Corporate Social Policy Process for Ethical Responsibility in Sub-Saharan Africa." *Journal of Business Ethics* 10, no. 7 (July 1991): 527–41.

Putnam, Hilary. *The Collapse of the Fact/Value Dichotomy and Other Essays*. Cambridge, Mass.: Harvard University Press, 2002.

———. "For Ethics and Economics without the Dichotomies." *Review of Political Economy* 15, no. 3 (2003): 395–412.

Putnam, Robert D. *Bowling Alone: The Collapse and Revival of American Community*. New York: Simon and Schuster, 2000.

Quine, Willard Van Orman. "Two Dogmas of Empiricism." *The Philosophical Review* 60, no. 1 (1951): 20–43.

Ratzinger, Joseph. "Naturrecht, Evangelium und Ideologie in der katholischen Sozi-allehre: Katholische Erwägungen zum Thema." In *Christlicher Glaube und Ideologie*, edited by Klaus von Bismarck, Walter Dirks, and Hans Götz Oxenius, 24–39. Stuttgart/Berlin/Mainz: Kreuz-Verlag, 1964.

———. "Church and Economy: Responsibility for the Future of the World Economy." *Communio* 13 (1986): 199–204.

———. *Values in a Time of Upheaval*. San Francisco: Ignatius, 2006.

Rauscher, Anton. "Gustav Gundlach, S.J.: One of the Architects of Christian Social Thinking." *Homiletic and Pastoral Review* 103 (October 2002): 29–49.

Rawls, John. *A Theory of Justice*. Cambridge, Mass.: Harvard University Press, 1971.

Reid, Anna, and Peter Petocz. "A Tertiary Curriculum for Future Professionals." In *Understanding Learning-Centred Higher Education*, edited by Claus Nygaard and Clive Holtham, 31–49. Copenhagen: Copenhagen Business School Press, 2008.

Reid, Carolina. "The Community Reinvestment Act and the Authority to Do Good." *Public Administration Review* 72, no. 3 (2012): 439–41.

Rhonheimer, Martin. "Perché una filosofia politica? Elementi storici per una risposta." *Acta Philosophica* 1, no. 2 (1992): 233–63.

Rhonheimer, Martin. *The Perspective of Morality*. Washington, D.C.: The Catholic University of America Press, 2011.

Richardson, Henry. "Some Limitations of Nussbaum's Capabilities." *Quinnipiac Law Review* 19, no. 2 (2000): 309–32.

———. "The Social Background of Capabilities for Freedoms." *Journal of Human Development* 8, no. 3 (2007): 389–414.

Robbins, Lionel. *An Essay on the Nature and Significance of Economic Science*. London: Macmillan, 1935.

Robinson, Marilynne. *When I Was a Child I Read Books*. New York: Farrar, Straus and Giroux, 2012.

Rolfe, John, and Peter Troob. *Monkey Business: Swinging through the Wall Street Jungle*. New York: Warner Books, 2000.

Röpke, Wilhelm. *A Humane Economy*. Chicago: Henry Regnery, 1960.

Rose, David C. *The Moral Foundation of Economic Behavior*. New York: Oxford University Press, 2011.

Rothbard, Murray N. *The Ethics of Liberty*. New York: New York University Press, 1998.

Rothschild, Emma. *Economic Sentiments: Adam Smith, Condorcet, and the Enlightenment*. Cambridge, Mass.: Harvard University Press, 2001.

Samuels, Warren J., Marianne F. Johnson, and William H. Perry. *Erasing the Invisible Hand: Essays on an Elusive and Misused Concept in Economics*. New York: Cambridge University Press, 2011.

Samuelson, Paul. *Foundations of Economic Analysis*. Cambridge, Mass.: Harvard University Press, 1947.

Sandel, Michael J. *What Money Can't Buy: The Moral Limits of Markets*. New York: Farrar, Straus and Giroux, 2012.

Santoro, Michael A., and Ronald J. Strauss. *Wall Street Values: Business Ethics and the Global Financial Crisis*. Cambridge: Cambridge University Press, 2013.

Saul, John. *The Unconscious Civilization*. Ringwood: Penguin Books, 1997.

Saul, Stephanie. "Release of Generic Lipitor is Delayed." *New York Times*, June 19, 2008.

Scandura, Terri A., and Melenie J. Lankau. "Relationships of Gender, Family Responsibility and Flexible Work Hours to Organizational Commitments and Job Satisfaction." *Journal of Organizational Behavior* 18, no. 4 (1997): 377–91.

Schall, James V. *Roman Catholic Political Philosophy*. Lanham, Md.: Lexington Books, 2004.

Schlag, Martin. "The Encyclical Caritas in Veritate, Christian Tradition and the Modern World." In *Free Markets and the Culture of Common Good*, edited by Martin Schlag and Juan Andrés Mercado, 93–109. Berlin: Springer, 2012.

Schneewind, Jerome. "The Misfortunes of Virtue." *Ethics* 101 (1990): 42–63.

Scholes, Myron. "Efficiency and Beyond." *The Economist*, July 18, 2009.

Schubert, William. *Curriculum: Perspective, Paradigm, and Possibility*. New York: Macmillan, 1986.

Schumpeter, Joseph. *Capitalism: Socialism and Democracy*. New York: Harper and Row, 1934.

———. *The Theory of Economic Development*. Cambridge, Mass.: Harvard University Press, 1934.

———. *History of Economic Analysis*. New York: Oxford University Press, 1994 [1954].

Schwartz, Mark S., and Archie B. Carroll. "Corporate Social Responsibility: A Three-Domain Approach." *Business Ethics Quarterly* 13, no. 4 (2003): 503–30.

Searle, John. R. "How to Derive 'Ought' from 'Is.'" *The Philosophical Review* 73, no. 1 (1964): 43–58.

Sedláček, Tomas. *Economics of Good and Evil: The Quest for Economic Meaning from Gilgamesh to Wall Street*. Oxford: Oxford University Press, 2011.

Sen, Amartya. "The Nature and Classes of Prescriptive Judgments." *The Philosophical Quarterly* 17, no. 66 (1967): 46–62.

———. *On Ethics and Economics*. Oxford: Blackwell Publishing, 1987.

———. *Development as Freedom*. New York: Knopf, 1999.

———. *Rationality and Freedom*. Cambridge, Mass.: The Belknap Press of Harvard University, 2002.

———. *The Idea of Justice*. Cambridge, Mass.: Harvard University Press, 2009.

Sennett, Richard. *The Culture of the New Capitalism*. New Haven, Conn.: Yale University Press, 2006.

———. *The Craftsman*. New Haven, Conn.: Yale University Press, 2008.

Sethi, S. Prakash. "Dimensions of Corporate Social Performance: An Analytical Framework." *California Management Review* 17 (1975): 58–64.

Shane, Scott. "Prior Knowledge and the Discovery of Entrepreneurial Opportunities." *Organizational Science* 11, no. 4 (2000): 448–69.

Shane, Scott, and Sankaran Venkataraman. "The Promise of Entrepreneurship as a Field of Research." *Academy of Management Review* 25, no. 1 (2000): 217–26.

Simmel, Georg. *Soziologie: Untersuchungen über die Formen der Vergesellschaftung*. Leipzig: Duncker and Humblot, 1908.

Simon, Herbert A. *The Sciences of the Artificial*. Cambridge, Mass.: MIT Press, 1969.

Singer, Natasha. "A Data Giant is Mapping, and Sharing, the Consumer Genome." *New York Times*, June 17, 2012.

Smith, Adam. *An Inquiry into the Nature and Causes of the Wealth of Nations*. Vol. 2 of *The Glasgow Edition of the Works and Correspondence of Adam Smith*, edited by R. H. Campbell and A. S. Skinner. Indianapolis: Liberty Fund, 1981 [1776].

———. *The Theory of Moral Sentiments*. Vol. 1 of *The Glasgow Edition of the Works and Correspondence of Adam Smith*, edited by D. D. Raphael and A. L. Macfie. Indianapolis: Liberty Fund, 1982 [1759].

Solomon, Charlene M. "Work/Family's Failing Grade: Why Today's Initiatives Aren't Enough." *Personnel Journal* 73, no. 5 (1994): 72–87.

Solomon, Robert C. *Ethics and Excellence: Cooperation and Integrity in Business*. New York: Oxford University Press, 1992.

Solzhenitsyn, Aleksandr. "Templeton Lecture of 1983." In *The Solzhenitsyn Reader: New and Essential Writings, 1947–2005*, edited by Edward Ericson and Daniel Mahoney, 576–84. Wilmington, Del.: Intercollegiate Studies Institute, 2006.

Soros, George. *The Crisis of Global Capitalism: Open Society Endangered*. London: Little, Brown and Company, 1998.

Spitzeck, Heiko, Michael Pirson, Wolfgang Amann, Shiban Khan, and Ernst von Kimakowitz, eds. *Humanism in Business*. Cambridge: Cambridge University Press, 2009.

Statman, Daniel. "Introduction to Virtue Ethics." In *Virtue Ethics*, edited by D. Statman, 1–41. Edinburgh: Edinburgh University Press, 1997.

Sterling, Stephen. *Sustainable Education: Re-visioning Learning and Change*. Dartington: Green Books, 2001.

———. "Riding the Storm: Towards a Connective Cultural Consciousness." In *Social Learning towards a Sustainable World: Principles, Perspectives, and Praxis*, edited by Arjen E. J. Wals, 63–82. Wageningen: Wageningen Academic Publishers, 2007.

Stiglitz, Joseph E. *Freefall: America, Free Markets, and the Sinking of the World Economy*. New York: W. W. Norton, 2010.

————. *The Price of Inequality: How Today's Divided Society Endangers Our Future*. New York: W. W. Norton, 2012.

Stiglitz, Joseph E., Amartya Sen, and Jean-Paul Fitoussi. "Report by the Commission on the Measurement of Economic Performance and Social Progress." http://www.stiglitz-sen-fitoussi.fr/documents/rapport_anglais.pdf.

Stjerno, Steinar. *Solidarity in Europe: The History of an Idea*. Cambridge: Cambridge University Press, 2004.

Stone, Michael, and Center for Ecoliteracy. *Smart by Nature: Schooling for Sustainability*. Healdsburg: Watershed Media, 2009.

Taylor, Barbara L., Robert G. DelCampo, and Donna M. Blancero. "Work-Family Conflict/Facilitation and the Role of Workplace Supports for U.S. Hispanic Professionals." *Journal of Organizational Behavior* 30, no. 5 (2009): 643–64.

Taylor, Bron. "Deep Ecology and Its Social Philosophy: A Critique." In *Beneath the Surface: Critical Essays on Deep Ecology*, edited by Eric Katz, Andrew Light, and David Rothenberg, 269–99. Cambridge, Mass.: MIT Press, 2000.

Taylor, Charles. *The Ethics of Authenticity*. Cambridge, Mass.: Harvard University Press, 1991.

————. *A Secular Age*. Cambridge, Mass.: The Belknap Press of Harvard University, 2007.

————. "Western Secularity." In *Rethinking Secularism*, edited by Craig Calhoun, Mark Juergensmeyer, and Jonathan Van Antwerpen, 31–53. Oxford: Oxford University Press, 2011.

————. "What Was the Axial Revolution?" In *The Axial Age and Its Consequences*, edited by Robert N. Bellah and Hans Joas, 30–46. Cambridge, Mass.: The Belknap Press of Harvard University, 2012.

Thaler, Richard, and Cass Sunstein. *Nudge: Improving Decisions about Health, Wealth, and Happiness*. New York: Penguin, 2009.

Thomas, Linda T., and Daniel C. Ganster. "Impact of Family-Supportive Work Variables on Work-Family Conflict and Strain: A Control Perspective." *Journal of Applied Psychology* 80, no. 1 (1995): 6–15.

Thompson, Cynthia A., Laura L. Beauvais, and Karen S. Lyness. "When Work-Family Benefits Are Not Enough: The Influence of Work-Family Culture on Benefit Utilization, Organizational Attachment, and Work-Family Conflict." *Journal of Vocational Behavior* 54, no. 3 (1999): 392–415.

Thompson, David J. *Weavers of Dreams: Founders of the Modern Co-operative Movement*. 150th anniversary ed. Davis: University of California Press, 1994.

Tocqueville, Alexis de. *The Old Regime and the Revolution*. Translated by Alan S. Kahan. Chicago: University of Chicago Press, 1998.

————. *Democracy in America*. Translated by Harvey C. Mansfield and Delba Winthrop. Chicago: University of Chicago Press, 2000.

Triana, Pablo. "Why Business Schools Are to Blame for the Crisis." *Bloomberg Business*, July 13, 2009.

Uertz, Rudolf. *Vom Gottesrecht zum Menschenrecht: Das katholische Staatsdenken in Deutschland von der Französischen Revolution bis zum II. Vatikanischen Konzil (1789–1965)*. Paderborn: Schöningh, 2005.

UNESCO. "United Nations Decade of Education for Sustainable Development: Reorienting Programmes." http://www.unesdoc.unesco.org/images/154093e.pdf.

United Nations. "United Nations Launches 2012 International Year of Cooperatives." *UN Cooperative News*. http://www.social.un.org/coopsyear.

U.S. SIF Foundation, the Forum for Sustainable and Responsible Investment. *2014 U.S. Report on Sustainable, Responsible and Impact Investing Trends*. Washington, D.C., 2014.

Vatican Council II. Pastoral Constitution *Gaudium et Spes*. Vatican City: Libreria Editrice Vaticana, 1965.

Venkataraman, Sankaran. "The Distinctive Domain of Entrepreneurship Research." *Advances in Entrepreneurship, Firm Emergence and Growth* 3 (1997): 119–38.

Vierkandt, Alfred. *Gesellschaftslehre: Hauptprobleme der philosophischen Soziologie*. 2nd ed. Stuttgart: Enke, 1928.

Wade, Jenny. *Changes of Mind: A Holonomic Theory of the Evolution of Consciousness*. Albany: State University of New York Press, 1996.

Weigel, George, and Robert Royal, eds. *A Century of Catholic Social Thought: Essays on "Rerum Novarum" and Nine Other Key Documents*. Washington, D.C.: Ethics and Public Policy Center, 1991.

Weil, Simone. "Metaxu." In *Gravity and Grace*, translated by Thomas R. Nevin, 200–204. New York: Putnam, 1952.

Wicks, Rick. "A Model of Dynamic Balance among the Three Spheres of Society—Markets, Governments, and Communities—Applied to Understanding the Relative Importance of Social Capital and Social Goods." *International Journal of Social Economics* 36, no. 5 (2009): 535–65.

Wicksteed, Philip H. *The Common Sense of Political Economy*. London: Macmillan, 1933 [1910].

Wojtyla, Karol. *Love and Responsibility*. San Francisco: Harper-Collins, 1981. (First published in Polish as *Miłość i Odpowiedzialnosc: Studium etyczne*. Lublin: KUL, 1960.)

———. "The Person: Subject and Community." *Review of Metaphysics* 33, no. 2 (1979): 273–308.

Williams, Rowan, and Larry Elliott. *Crisis and Recovery: Ethics, Economics and Justice*. Basingstoke: Palgrave Macmillan, 2010.

Williamson, Oliver E. *The Economic Institutions of Capitalism*. New York: Free Press, 1985.

Wilson, Duff. "Facing Generic Lipitor Rivals, Pfizer Battles to Protect Its Cash Cow." *New York Times*, November 29, 2011.

Wood, Donna J. "Corporate Social Performance Revisited." *Academy of Management Review* 16, no. 4 (1991): 691–718.

———. "Social Issues in Management: Theory and Research in Corporate Social Performance." *Journal of Management* 17, no. 2 (1991): 383–406.

Woods, Thomas E. Jr. "Catholic Social Teaching and Economic Law." *Journal des Economistes et des Etudes Humaines* 13, no. 2 (2003): 329–51.

———. *The Church and the Market: A Catholic Defense of the Free Economy*. Lanham, Md.: Lexington Books, 2005.

Yakovlev, Alexander. *The Fate of Marxism in Russia*. New Haven, Conn.: Yale University Press, 1993.

———. *A Century of Violence in Soviet Russia*. New Haven, Conn.: Yale University Press, 2002.

Yang, Nini. "Work-Family Conflict and Supervisor Support." *Eastern Academy of Management Best Paper Proceedings* (1993): 174–77.

Yunus, Muhammad. *Creating a World without Poverty*. New York: PublicAffairs, 2009.

———. *Building Social Business*. New York: PublicAffairs, 2011.

Zaleski, Pawel. "Tocqueville on Civilian Society: A Romantic Vision of the Dichotomic Structure of Social Reality." *Archiv für Begriffsgeschichte* 50 (2008): 260–66.

Zizioulas, John D. *Being as Communion*. London: Darton, Longman and Todd, 1985.

Zubiri, Xavier. *Dynamic Structure of Reality*. Translated by N.R. Orringer. Urbana: University of Illinois Press, 2003.

Contributors

JÖRG ALTHAMMER, born in 1962, is a full professor of economic and business ethics at the Catholic University of Eichstätt-Ingolstadt (Germany). He received his PhD in economics in 1992 and his venia legendi in economics in 1998. He was appointed visiting professor in Passau (1999–2001) and full professor of economics and social policy in Bochum (2002–2007). He is coauthor of one of the leading textbooks on social policy and has authored or edited more than ten books on ethics and social policy. He is a member of the scientific council of the German Bishops Conference and was scientific advisor of the German Ministry of Family Affairs.

JAVIER ARANZADI is a professor of economics at Universidad Autónoma de Madrid, Spain. Dr. Aranzadi has studied at Institut für Wirtschaftspolitik at the University of Cologne and has been visiting scholar at Georgetown University. His main areas of interest are philosophical foundations of economic systems, Austrian School of Economics, and business ethics. His latest book is *Liberalism against Liberalism*.

REVEREND DR. BRUCE BAKER, PHD (theological ethics, University of St. Andrews, Scotland), has a rare combination of academic and professional qualifications in business, science, and theology. As an entrepreneur, he cofounded and managed a high-technology company and earned five patents for his inventions in X-ray vision technology. He then served as a general manager at Microsoft prior to attending Fuller Seminary (MDiv) and being ordained to pastoral ministry in the Presbyterian Church (PC-USA). His academic qualifications include degrees also from Stanford (MBA) and the California Institute of Technology (BS, Applied Physics). Dr. Baker currently teaches ethics, moral leadership, and theological foundations of business and economics at Seattle Pacific University.

FÁTIMA CARIOCA is dean and a professor in the academic area of human factors in the Organisation at AESE Business School, Lisbon, Portugal. She earned her Doctor of Business Administration from Manchester University. She holds an MSc in engineering systems and computers from Instituto Superior Técnico and a master's degree in marriage and family from Navarra University. Formerly an executive, sShe served for more than twenty years in the telecommunications and software industries at PT Telecom and Edisoft. She is a member of the Business Ethics National Technical Committee. Her areas of research and interest are work–life balance, people management, labor relations, and corporate social responsibility.

RICHARD J. DOUGHERTY is the chairman of the Department of Politics at the University of Dallas, in Irving, Texas, and the director of the Center for Christianity and the Common Good. He is a contributor to *St. Augustine through the Ages* and *The Oxford Guide to the Historical Reception of Augustine* and has written and lectured widely on Catholic political thought, Catholic higher education, and American political thought. Dr. Dougherty is completing a manuscript on prerogative power and the American presidency.

PATRICE FLYNN is the Morrison Professor of International Studies with the Bolte School of Business at Mount St. Mary's University, the second oldest Catholic institution of higher education in the United States. She holds an MA (economics) from the University of Chicago and a PhD (economics) from the University of Texas at Austin. Dr. Flynn is a world traveler who has produced an extensive publication record on global capitalism, labor markets, and civil society, including two edited volumes and more than fifty research papers and articles. Previous positions held include labor economist at the Urban Institute, vice president of research at Independent Sector, and senior vice president for administration and finance at Effat University.

WOLFGANG GRASSL holds degrees in philosophy and economics and serves as a professor of business administration at St. Norbert College (De Pere, Wisconsin), where he also holds the Dale and Ruth Michels Endowed Chair in Business. His research focuses on consumer behavior, marketing strategy, business ontology, and Catholic social thought. He has authored or edited six books and more than 120 articles and reviews in the fields of business studies, economics, philosophy, and intellectual history, most recently the monographs *Culture of Place: An Intellectual Profile of the Premonstratensian Order* and *Property*.

RUSSELL HITTINGER is the William K. Warren Chair of Catholic studies at the University of Tulsa, where he is also a research professor in the School of Law. His books have been published by the University of Notre Dame Press, Oxford University Press, Columbia University Press, and Fordham University Press, and his articles have appeared in the *Review of Metaphysics*, the *Review of Politics*, and several law journals (American and European). His current work, *The Popes and the Modern Caesars: Magisterial Teachings on the State, 1789–2005.*, will be published by Yale University Press. He serves on two Pontifical academies. In 1994 he was elected a full member of *Pontificia Academia Sancti Thomae Aquinatis*. On September 8, 2009, Pope Benedict XVI appointed Professor Hittinger as an *ordinarius* in the Pontifical Academy of Social Sciences.

KEVIN JACKSON has published research papers in many top-tier journals, among them *Business Ethics Quarterly*, *Journal of Business Ethics*, *Brooklyn Journal of International Law*, *Harvard Journal of Law and Public Policy*, and *Law and Philosophy*. Currently, Dr. Jackson is a professor of law and ethics at Fordham University in New York City, as well as a senior fellow with the Witherspoon Institute. He also holds the Daniel Janssen Chair of Corporate Social Responsibility at Université libre de Bruxelles in Belgium. Professor Jackson has taught at Georgetown University, Peking University, and Princeton University.

JOHN LARRIVEE is an associate professor of economics at Mount St. Mary's University. Although his background is in labor economics and poverty, in recent years he has begun to focus on Catholic social teaching and questions regarding the morality of markets. This has included reviews of *Caritas in Veritate* and of the labor section of the *Compendium of the Social Doctrine of the Church*. A chapter examining how the Christian criticism of capitalism which misses the materialist basis behind many secular critiques often paradoxically reinforces that materialism and undermines Christian witness and the role of civil society (in *Back on the Road to Serfdom*, Thomas Woods, ed.) provided the starting point for the consideration of how different views of the human person shaped criticisms of the market.

REVEREND DOMÈNEC MELÉ is professor and the holder of the Chair of Business Ethics at IESE Business School, University of Navarra. Over the past twenty-five years, he has researched and written extensively on business ethics, business in society, and Catholic social thought. He has authored and coauthored several books, including *Business Ethics in Action*, *Management Ethics, and Human Foundations of Management* and coedited *Human Development in Business: Values and Humanistic Management in the Encyclical* Caritas in Veritate and *Humanism in Economics and Business: Perspectives of the Catholic Social Tradition*. Professor Melé serves on several editorial boards of peer-reviewed journals and has been guest or co-guest editor of six special issues of the *Journal of Business Ethics*.

JUAN ANDRÉS MERCADO received his PhD in philosophy at the University of Navarre. He has taught ethics and philosophy as an adjunct professor at Universidad Panamericana, worked as an assistant professor of history of modern philosophy at the Pontifical University of the Holy Cross, and is currently an associate professor of the same subject and full professor of applied ethics at the same university. Dr. Mercado is the cofounder (with Martin Schlag) of Markets, Culture, and Ethics, an interdisciplinary research center at the Pontifical University of the Holy Cross. He also serves as a visiting professor at IPADE Business School.

MONSIGNOR MARTIN SCHLAG completed his university studies in jurisprudence at the University of Vienna and in theology at the Pontifical University of the Holy Cross. He began his professional career as an assistant professor for Roman law and Austrian constitutional law at the University of Vienna and the University of Innsbruck. He is currently a professor of social moral theology at the Pontifical University of the Holy Cross, where he cofounded Markets, Culture, and Ethics, an interdisciplinary research center of which he serves as director.

JIM WISHLOFF is an associate professor and an award-winning teacher at the University of Lethbridge in Edmonton, Alberta, Canada. He has a BSc (engineering) and an MBA from the University of Alberta and a PhD from Case Western Reserve University. His publications include articles in the *Journal of Business Ethics*, the *Journal of Religion and Business Ethics*, the *Journal of Business Ethics Education*, *Teaching Business Ethics*, the *Review of Business*, and the *Social Justice Review*.

Index

Sin, 7, 12, 75, 89, 120, 163, 190, 192, 194

Slote, Michael, 54

Smith, Adam, 4, 11, 38, 42, 71–72, 74–81, 85, 91, 94–95, 159, 192–93, 241, 243, 262

Social cohesion, 22, 98, 199, 203n15, 208–9, 212–13

Social institution, 32, 41, 52, 55–57, 59–60, 65, 68–69, 128, 147, 157, 162, 209, 213n27, 222

Socialism, 3, 13, 20, 58n25, 76n10, 87–88, 116–17, 120, 137, 154, 156–57, 162, 200n2, 209; national, 87–88

Social principle, 8, 13, 15

Social question, 21, 162, 187

Solidarism, 13, 211

Solidarity, 1, 4, 11–15, 19–25, 29–32, 49, 54, 93, 96n9, 98, 100, 104, 110, 111n40, 113, 120, 126–27, 150, 155–56, 160, 163, 167–68, 176, 194–95, 199–216, 244, 248–250, 254–55

Solomon, Robert C., 36n17, 53, 57–58, 61, 68

Soros, George, 97

Spencer, Herbert, 203, 205

State, 7, 9, 11, 13, 19n1, 20, 27–30, 54, 88, 99, 116, 118, 136, 143, 144n38, 145–47, 149, 156–64, 166–69, 171, 173–77, 181, 185–86, 188, 191–92, 195, 200, 205–8, 211–16, 221, 234, 240, 247–48, 254, 272, 305

Sterling, Stephen, 270

Stewardship, 240, 254–55, 261, 270

Stiglitz, Joseph E., 95n5, 107n30, 110, 269n47

Subsidiarity, 15, 31, 126–27, 143–50, 153, 156, 161, 163n23, 168, 173, 208, 245, 248–49, 254–55

Sustainability, 1, 19, 92–93, 96, 103, 107, 111, 120, 179, 182n11, 217–18, 233–35, 255–57, 262–65, 268–74

TargusInfo, 108

Taylor, Charles, 7, 9–10, 273

Thatcher, Margaret, 33

Third way, 157, 162, 175, 184, 209

Tocqueville, Alexis de, 4, 144, 165

Trinity, 123n42, 124, 157, 163–65, 167–68, 172, 174

Triple bottom line, 221n14, 233, 239–40, 246, 253

Turner, Adair, 93n1

Unemployment, 94, 118, 152, 214, 243

United States, 3, 28, 41, 45, 157–58, 165, 183, 218n6, 237n49, 240–41, 245–47, 250, 252–54, 265n38, 304

Utilitarianism, 11, 32–34, 39–51

Value-laden, 264

Vienna School, 34

Virtue, 1, 3–4, 9, 12–14, 19–21, 25, 27–28, 39n29, 42n39, 46n46, 47n53, 50–51, 52n1, 53–55, 56n17, 62n37, 64n41, 65n43, 67–69, 74, 76–79, 89, 93, 102, 114, 120, 123, 125, 127, 131, 135–36, 157, 172, 175–76, 180–81, 194, 201, 237–38, 249, 262–64, 268, 270, 272–73

Virtuosity, 271–73

Vogelsang, Karl von, 6

Wage, 119, 129, 139, 148, 152, 188, 211–12, 243–44; living, 129, 139

Wealth, 3–4, 10, 55, 61, 65, 67, 69, 76n7, 77, 93, 101, 116–17, 119, 127, 148, 179–81, 183, 189, 195, 224, 232, 236, 239–40, 241n5, 242, 253–55, 262, 268n46, 269, 274

Welfare, 13, 41, 117, 119, 149, 171, 173, 200, 205–8, 211–16, 220, 240, 254–55, 260, 262n27

Wicksteed, Philip H., 101n19

Williamson, Oliver E., 32

Wisdom, 9, 80, 93–94, 97, 100, 102–4, 112, 115, 129, 143, 151, 155, 176, 190, 194, 264n31, 271, 273, 275

Wojtyła, Karol, 47, 53, 85n32

Woods, Thomas E. Jr., 139n19, 191n31, 305

Work and family life, 217. See also WFL, 217–18, 221–28, 230, 232–33, 236–37

Yunus, Muhammad, 250, 265

Zamagni, Stefano, 95n4, 102–3, 191n34

Zizioulas, John D., 100n17

Free Markets with Solidarity and Sustainability: Facing the Challenge was designed in Bembo with Jenson display type and composed by Kachergis Book Design of Pittsboro, North Carolina. It was printed on 60-pound Natures Book Natural and bound by Thomson-Shore of Dexter, Michigan.

www.ingramcontent.com/pod-product-compliance
Lightning Source LLC
Chambersburg PA
CBHW021850020426

42334CB00013B/273